Marria
The *Da*   Dilemma

In July 1868 the *Daily Telegraph* congratulated itself on providing the arena for a controversy marked by "good sense, liveliness, practical wisdom, and hearty humanity." The controversy was over the choice— "Marriage or Celibacy?"—faced by middle-class youth trying to reconcile economic facts with moral values, social customs—and love. The arena was the correspondence page of a newspaper just establishing itself as the most successful London daily through its appeal to the middle-class reader.

Public attention was first caught by a court report of a failed attempt to entrap a Belgian girl into prostitution. This induced blistering editorial comment and angry letters to the paper deploring ineffectual controls over the "Great Social Evil." The next development was unusual for the Victorian press: readers began to write extensive and richly varied comment on the root of the problem—young people did not have in possession or expectation enough money or the right qualifications for marriage. The *Telegraph* initiated a new form of popular journalism by filling its correspondence columns for almost a month with readers letters under the heading "Marriage or Celibacy?", which they supplemented with lengthy leading articles.

John Robson places in contemporary context the central issues facing Victorian youth: What is a proper marriage? How to balance income and expenditure? What are the ideal qualities of young women and men? "Emigration or starvation?" In examining these debates, he looks closely into methods of argument, connecting rhetorical techniques with public persuasion. The letters being a special kind of discourse, he shows how in the debates rhetorical and logical arguments are specifically designed to persuade the *Telegraph* s readers.

Marriage or Celibacy? contributes to our knowledge of Victorian manners and mores, particularly among the lower middle class, and is a telling episode in the history of popular journalism.

JOHN M. ROBSON is University Professor Emeritus, University of Toronto, and was General and Textual Editor of the Collected Works of John Stuart Mill.

Marriage or Celibacy?
The *Daily Telegraph* on a
Victorian Dilemma

JOHN M. ROBSON

UNIVERSITY OF TORONTO PRESS
Toronto Buffalo London

© University of Toronto Press Incorporated 1995
Toronto Buffalo London
Printed in Canada

ISBN 0-8020-0473-3 (cloth)
ISBN 0-8020-7798-6 (paper)

Printed on acid-free paper

Canadian Cataloguing in Publication Data

Robson, John M., 1927–
    Marriage or celibacy? : the Daily Telegraph
    on a Victorian dilemma

    Includes bibliographical references and index.
    ISBN 0-8020-0473-3 (bound) ISBN 0-8020-7798-6 (pbk.)

    1. Letters to the editor – England.   2. Marriage
    in the press.   3. Prostitution in the press.
    4. Emigration and immigration in the press.
    5. Middle class – England – Attitudes – History –
    19th century.   6. England – Moral conditions.
    I. Title.

    HN385.R6 1995   306.81'0942   C94-932322-5

University of Toronto Press acknowledges the financial assistance to its
publishing program of the Canada Council and the Ontario Arts Council.

For and to

Ann Provost Wilkinson Robson

who made my decision between

Marriage and Celibacy

one not to be delayed and never deplored

Contents

Acknowledgments

Foremost and most indispensable among my institutional debts is that to the British Library and especially its Newspaper Library, whose collection never fails to produce delight as well as instruction. My special thanks also to the Institute for Historical Research, the University of London Library, and the libraries of the University of Toronto. I owe major personal debts for good advice, not always taken, towards improvements in my argument and expression, to the usual suspects, Ann Christine Robson Bacque and James Benson Bacque, William Bertie Provost Robson and Helen Protopapas Robson, and John Sinclair Petifer Robson, and also to those wise and knowledgeable friends, Gillian Fenwick, Leslie Howsam, and Martin L. Friedland. It would be embarrassing to me and perhaps to them were I to mention all the others who made valuable suggestions of various kinds. My gratitude in full measure for needed support and encouragement goes to those at the University of Toronto Press, especially Bill Harnum, Ron Schoeffel, and Suzanne Rancourt, and to Judith Williams for tactful and sensitive editing of the copy.

Marriage or Celibacy?

Introduction

An unprecedented and extensive series of news accounts, leading articles, and letters to the editor, most of the last under the heading "Marriage or Celibacy?", appeared in the London newspaper, the *Daily Telegraph*, in June and July 1868. To most people, old newspapers are mere garbage, but the new archaeology has shown that curious and obsessive diggers are actually rational scholars finding lost social, economic, and cultural gold in the rubbish. Allying myself with them, I present my retrievals from this buried series as important aids to our understanding and assessment of lower-middle-class assumptions, beliefs, and habitual behaviour in the high Victorian period. What particularly caught my attention were the close relations among the issues that concerned the editors and readers of the *Daily Telegraph*, namely, prostitution, its causes and cures; ideal and practical marriage, its joys, duties, and costs; and emigration, its promises and dangers. These themes, it should be emphasized, are connected by the contributors to the series; their interconnections make up the plot, which centres on beliefs about everyday family life and morals.

Material as rich as that on which this book is based is open to many approaches, or, as the modern manner would have it, "methodologies." Not liking either the word or the concept, I should admit to certain biases and limitations. My first admission is related to E.P. Thompson's deservedly famous complaint against the massive condescension of the present towards people of the past. Of course, Thompson was concerned about the voiceless, the inarticulate poor, whose lives and culture were at best ignored by political and (for a time) by social historians. But his successors and epigones have displayed just as massive a condescension towards the middle class, the contemptible bougeoisie, already excoriated and discarded by the *hautes culturistes*. I confess not only to liking but even admiring them, though my aim here is principally better understanding of their mentality and their culture.

Those two words introduce complex considerations: it has been thought by some recent theorists that the "history of ideas" is too limited and "ideational" a term to describe the turbulent flow and interchange of attitudes that characterize group beliefs. Such a history is based on the written record of the articulate and powerful, and "privileges" the intellect over other influences on the beliefs that govern general behaviour. "Mentality" (especially in French and in the plural) has been thought a better guide to description and analysis of the force field of dominant attitudes. Obviously the study of *mentalités* must then attempt to deal with, indeed it largely encompasses, the culture of an area and period, and so opens the study of history and literature ever more to anthropological and sociological considerations—and to their practitioners.

Various problems have consequently arisen in trying to assemble and interpret information. To say that the poor have been ignored is to assume that their culture is different from that of others (usually seen only as the powerful oppressors) which has been recorded. Not one but several cultures (at least two—but what of minorities?) are identified within one area and period, perhaps competing historically for dominance, but certainly competing now for attention and (another pet term) "valorization," as guides and props for modern attitudes to the past—but more significantly to the present and future. (Objectivity is now, to some, less a noble ideal than a tired joke.) But are these various coexistent mentalities and cultures independent of one another? And (as seems obvious) if not, how are they related? Is the culture of "the people" subversive and therefore finally fated to be revolutionary or crushed? Or is there a transitive relation, with influences both ways: in more pretentious words, "a circular relationship composed of reciprocal influences, which traveled from low to high as well as from high to low"?[1] Or indeed is there simply a blend, composed of beliefs sometimes virtually universal, sometimes congruent if varied, and sometimes disparate or even opposed—and not controlled by supposed class discontinuities?

This last view does not appeal to theorists who want vivid and actionable analyses, but its evident (if soft-focused) resemblance to common reality makes it hard to dismiss entirely. It also challenges the rather tenuous processes of inductive generalization that mark even the best of the *annales* accounts, where two suspect logical processes dominate: (1) one or a very few cases (all that apparently have left extant evidence) are perforce taken as illustrative of large populations, when often it seems that it is their very unusual features that have led to their preservation; and/or (2) a mass of material is accumulated but not subjected to discriminate analysis, so that a multitude of inferences is possible. (If there is enough evidence, any hypothesis can find support.)

On the other hand, though the absorption of number-crunching prosopography into history has led to more reliable and sometimes surprising inductions, it can never produce the savour of individually held beliefs, and does not touch the central issue of how mentalities develop and propagate through persuasion as well as compulsion.

I have no delusion that the form or content of my discussion of the marriage or celibacy debate resolves the difficulties or announces a triumphant method. Indeed I believe neither is possible. The main materials, letters to the editor of a best-selling high Victorian newspaper and leading articles in that newspaper, were written by anonymous or pseudonymous middle- and lower-class literate English men and women, mostly Londoners. From internal evidence the marital status of most can be determined, and some data about their families, occupations, and income can be extracted or inferred. The expressed beliefs are clear enough, and can be related to other studies of Victorian attitudes.

That last sentence, perhaps sufficient a generation ago, may now seem naïve in two respects to those deconstructionists who wrongly see traditional critics as gullible: first, nothing expressed in words is clear, let alone clear enough; second, even if the words were clear, the intentions of their authors are not just indeterminate but undeterminable. Both these objections have an epistemological basis, and both are not nearly so novel as postmodernists assume. Their language not being gentle, one might briefly respond: "What's true ain't new, and what's new ain't true." Better, probably, to call attention to the ancient distinction between demonstrable and probable truths, the former the property of abstract sciences, the latter the inescapable limitation on the enduring puzzles of human life, moral and political, individual and social. We have to live with uncertainty, and we try to live more satisfactorily by reducing the amount of unconsidered doubt.

That claim lies behind my assertions about the value of this series. What becomes evident is that while it corroborates much that is generally associated with middle-class mores and manners of the time, it presents significant differences that are instructive not only in understanding the 1860s, but also in seeing the pivotal place of that decade in the development of a broader democracy. To demonstrate the difference and development while giving context to my analysis, I draw on comparable material from *The Times*, from fiction, and from advice books, and discuss briefly the history of the *Daily Telegraph*, which saw itself correctly as giving voice to those who were playing an increasingly important role in political, social, and economic life. This discussion leads to some conclusions about the significance of the series in the subsequent development of popular media.

Considering the material context of my main source, daily journalism in the 1860s, one cannot be quite sanguine about the evidence.[2] There can be no doubt that the proprietors and editors wanted to sell papers, and were tirelessly ingenious in the attempt: consequently, then as now, the editors may well have inspired (or at least solicited) some of the letters, especially early in the series.[3] It is unlikely that a staff member would sign a letter with uninteresting initials, or repeat a pseudonym except in a follow-up letter. It is, however, likely (highly likely?) that they "improved" some of the letters by corrections and deletions, and perhaps additions. Further, they most certainly selected (indeed that is their boast) those published from a larger mass. These legitimate and unremovable doubts make any generalizations from these texts to general behaviour and beliefs among the English (or London) lower middle class uncertain—but the proper question is, can one allow for the uncertainty and make useful if cautious inferences, bolstered by other evidence? My answer is yes, and my attempt to persuade others forms a significant part of the argument of the following chapters.

My other intentions may be inferred. One, not fully realizable in this space or my time, is to add a chapter to the history of the newspaper press, with emphasis on the movement from leaders to readers, that is, editorial authority yielding place to that of the readers (with the caveat that there is no harm and not negligible profit in stimulating the readers to vivid expression of their views). In this movement the newspapers are not on their own, as the recent vogue for political leadership-from-behind feeds on public opinion polls. Robert Browning might be amended to "How they brought the bad news from grunt to aches":

I sprang to the pollsters, and Joris, and he;
We galluped, Dirck galluped, we galluped all three.

That this movement gained its modern momentum in the 1860s gives the story particular importance, and what little I have to say about it may encourage more work on that crucial decade.

Secondly, and even less fully, I have endeavoured to touch on an enduring puzzle about the dispersal and assimilation of information. As will be evident, the literate and informed correspondents of the *Daily Telegraph* felt that their fellow readers were trustees of important facts and opinions that were otherwise difficult to encounter or seize. *Prima facie* they were mistaken, for more reliable information was easily available through official and unofficial studies as well as general works (for example on emigration). But it would appear that they wished to put their trust not in princes but in their own peers. And it would also appear that not much has changed in that respect. Or should I say not changed for the better, given the recent proliferation of interactive "talk media" through which the "people"—or at least the most blatant of them—talk to one another with the encouragement of a highly charged and highly paid medium.[4]

Thirdly, not the least of my intentions is to give voice and some contextual life to the participants in this series, who have given me such pleasure and instruction, and to pay them the tribute of treating seriously (or at least as seriously as they did) their modes of argument and persuasion. The voice heard is not univocal, and to demonstrate the vitality and flexibility of the correspondents and leader writers, I include considerable quotation, though nothing like as much as full justice requires: these letters are extraordinary in their range and command, and the leaders have a force and density equally unusual; further, these voices are little heard elsewhere in the literature of the period.

It is not only their content that should influence our understanding and judgment; their rhetoric[5] quietly shows both how and why the public changes were occurring. In particular, I am concerned to indicate that assumptions about the proper and effective means of persuasion bear upon the fundamental questions of authority: what sort of evidence is best, and from whence does it come? In summary, whom should you believe? and why? To that end I have interwoven rhetorical and content analyses of the letters and leaders, believing that the attitudes of the authors cannot be fully appreciated without consideration of the texture of their exposition and setting.

Were I more ambitious I would ask for honorary membership among the new pop culturists, who carry on their banner the slogan: "Let the people speak!"—though I define "people" in a somewhat different way from many of them. I am closer to the views of Sir Walter Scott, who associates himself with "various great authors" in exploiting the advantage of laying before the reader, in the words of the actors themselves, the adventures which we must otherwise have narrated in our own. . . . Nevertheless, a genuine correspondence of this kind (and Heaven forbid it should be in any respect sophisticated by interpolations of our own!) can seldom be found to contain all in which it is necessary to instruct the reader for his full comprehension of the story. Also it must often happen that various prolixities and redundancies occur in the course of an interchange of letters, which must hang as a dead weight on the progress of the narrative. To avoid this dilemma, some biographers have used the letters of the personages concerned, or liberal extracts from them, to describe particular incidents, or express the sentiments which they entertained; while they connect them occasionally with such portions of the narrative, as may serve to carry on the thread of the story.[6]

It is a pleasure to attach oneself to the car of such a "great author" in this argument, though my characters lack the romantic appeal of his and are nearer actual life. What I should have to add to his defence is a claim for the fascination, much disputed, of the practical and moral views of the Victorian middle class. Their values had a long and thriving history, and have endured into the present if now declining century; no one should ignore their consonance with occurrences and trends that abide in the human condition.

Finally, the "story" of the series itself has its importance and it has seemed useful and instructive to help out of its obscurity what Thomas Hardy so well described, that "dull period in the life of an event . . . when it ceases to be news & has not yet begun to be history."[7]

My hope is that the complexity of the issues will excuse what may seem an unnecessary complexity in my argument. Its order at least is simple: the discussion moves from an account of the inception of the series on marriage or celibacy, and discussion of the initial topic, prostitution, as treated in *The Times* and the *Daily Telegraph* (chapter 1), into a discussion of the way in which the connection was established in the newspapers between prostitution and marriage, and how the *Daily Telegraph* series developed (chapter 2). Then the main themes of the series are explored: marriage and its material costs (chapters 3 and 4), celibacy (chapter 5), the causes and solutions of the dilemma (chapter 6), emigration as the most effective resolution of it (chapter 7), and finally my conclusions (chapter 8). Three appendices give, respectively, a discussion of and information about the correspondents that can be gleaned from internal evidence, detailed budgets from the letters and contemporary sources, and a comparison of the expenditures claimed by the correspondents with those recommended in advice books.

Because confusion may result from the correspondents' use of common phrases as pseudonyms, I have italicized signatures (including those that are apparently actual names) both in my text and in quotations (where they sometimes appear in inverted commas, here deleted). (One signature, ***, is not amenable to this treatment.) In nineteenth-century newspapers, personal names were normally given in small capitals; here the modern upper and lower case are used. The points following the abbreviations for British monetary units have been omitted, and book titles have been given in italic rather than enclosed in inverted commas. To avoid excessive detail, I have not given page references to the letters; their dates can be found in appendix A, where the series is outlined chronologically.

CHAPTER ONE

The Great Social Evil

On 30 July 1868, a rather playful leading article appeared in the London *Daily Telegraph*:

If the public has watched with an amused wonder the flood of letters poured upon our columns by the spinsters, bachelors, wives, husbands, widows, widowers, and old maids of the community, we have ourselves shared the astonishment and interest. We frankly own that we did not know what was coming when we threw open the gates of publicity for the discussion of "Marriage or Celibacy?" We have been like the fisherman in the "Arabian Nights," who caught the simple-looking silver box in his net, and opened it to behold issuing forth a mighty cloud, which rolled right across the sky and filled the blue vault, turning at last into a Djin of tremendous dimensions, who had been locked up ever since the time of Solomon. Or, to choose a still more suitable analogy, it has been with us as with the schoolmaster in the Norse story, to whom the water-elves sent a letter. A damp feeling about the epistle, together with its curious look, made him open it out of doors; whereupon flowed from it, first a stream which filled the yard, then a torrent which inundated the street, then a river which washed the town away, and finally there remained a huge lake which hid the entire country-side. It was a letter that set open the flood-gates of all our amazing correspondence; and the public have seen only so much of the flood as we could turn forth again; the fact being that, for every epistle which has seen the light, twenty at least were of necessity relegated to an oblivion not always deserved. A public discussion more remarkable in many respects has seldom been conducted; and we are glad to have furnished the arena for so much good sense, liveliness, practical wisdom, and hearty humanity as have marked the greater portion of the controversy. . . .

Very different in tone and matter was a leading article that appeared six weeks earlier, on 16 June:

There comes to our knowledge every now and then the evidence of a trade so infamous, horrible, and pitiless, that its prosperity is due to its hateful character. Society will not contemplate the hideous traffic. Justice does not wield against the plague a weapon stern and unsparing enough to use with any effect; the eyes of the kind and good turn from the proof of the evil with a loathing too strong for the sense of duty and action, and after each outburst of irrepressible disclosures, we conspire together to forget the event, lest the open mention of the abomination should make the air of public discussion too foul for Virtue to breathe. It is a trade which survives by its revolting qualities, like those noisome animals whose odour is too insupportable for the hunter to encounter. If there be devils, and they should engage in merchandise and barter, the business is one they would take up with.

The ironic "business" imagery continues into a parallel with the slave trade, which is portrayed, however, as "innocent in comparison with the fiendish buying and selling" of women, because it

only dealt in the bodies of human creatures: this deliberately traffics with their souls, and consigns the womanhood of helpless and friendless creatures to "death in life," as "per invoice," and for "value-received." Sometimes—as with other mercantile transactions—an "article" gets misdelivered in the infernal enterprise, and we are made aware of what goes on between the ports of nations which call themselves "Christian." . . . [T]hese hellish commercial speculations, and the people who are the commis-voyageurs and consignees, murder the spirit, kill with cold, butcherly lust of money, the life of a woman's soul, slay the hope in her, destroy her womanly right to be a happy, honest mother, and to live and die in a home, impair the sweetness and sacredness of her existence, and leave it to rot with guilt, remorse, and self-scorn, into that ghost of God's work and purpose, which we call, to keep ourselves up in the practice of wit and irony, "a daughter of pleasure."

Even this is but "half," though "the direst half" of the murder:

The human or inhuman devils, who feed the maw of a bestial vice with victims, do not stop short at the soul of a woman. Indirectly they finish the job, and murder her body too. Some night—after many dreadful nights and days, it may be more or less—since the Antwerp or Calais boat has delivered the commodity, as per invoice, it goes back to sea—does the "commodity." But it goes upon the tide, a ghastly, festering corpse, with its hair muddy and washing about the face, when the beauty which ruined it is withered. This is their work—these butchers of a sister's soul! Or the policemen for a short time leaves his ordinary "beat," to bring the body of a girl, all but speechless with poison, into the accident-hall of the hospital, and she gasps out a word of a foreign tongue, and dies, while the surgeon seeks to aid her in the misery that is her lot. This is their work—these merchants on the Exchange of Hell; these men who break up souls and bodies to make a harlot, and then a corpse. Or, commoner than either case, the poor victim dies in untold pain, at the workhouse or the asylum, a wretched patient, whose French prayers are taken for raving by the other patients, though God hears every syllable of them, and knows that these monsters murdered that exile and outcast, as much as if they had passed a knife into her unstained bosom.

This leader, unlike most of its kind, does not make a strong demand to finish its complaint, saying only that publicity should make it evident that there is "sufficient social agony" already "in stock," and that "nothing at all" is being done "to lessen it."

The Procuress

Different as these two leaders are, they are part of one story, typical of newspaper practice in its initial form. That is, a news story induced editorial comment in which the story was summarized, and moral judgments, usually accompanied by exhortation, provided an authoritative framework.

The newsworthy event, which occurred on Saturday, 13 June 1868, was reported in the "Police" news of several London papers on 15 June, the fullest account appearing in the *Morning Star*[1] under the heading "Decoying Girls for Immoral Purposes." A "well-dressed" young Belgian woman appeared in the Mansion House police court, where the Lord Mayor was presiding, under what the *Star* called "very peculiar circumstances." She had been brought in Antwerp to the captain of the steamship *Dolphin* by a man who gave him a letter in French, addressed to Miss Page, 22 Somerset Street, indicating that all expenses for her passage would be paid when she arrived in London. However, no one was on the dock to receive her, and consequently the steamship company had brought her to the Lord Mayor's court. Through an interpreter, as she spoke no English (and could not read or write), she told her tale. The letter, translated for the court, said that her clothes would follow in another boat "under the care of a man with a large black beard," and that on receipt of the "commission" "another 'very pretty girl' would be sent over." The Lord Mayor "perceived the 'immoral purpose' behind the transaction," and arranged for the girl, who averred that she had been unaware of the true intent of her adventure, to be sent back to Antwerp.

A report the next day indicated that the "character" of 22 Somerset Street was "precisely what it was suspected to be."[2] However, nothing successful seems to have been done by the authorities about the brothel or about "Miss Page."

These news stories prompted the *Daily Telegraph*'s leading article of 16 June, already quoted in part. In alluding directly to the case of the Belgian girl it continued its commercial analogy, identifying the girl as "an 'article,'" a "commodity," and "It," and portraying her as "poor, fatherless, on bad terms with her mother, and good-looking." The leader crackles with irony as it describes the further events: the "article" having been brought by "the devil's runner" to the Mansion House, where, "strange to say, such is the bewildered mind with which Justice regards this most accursed of crimes, the Lord Mayor, thinking, perhaps, about his next political speech more than the value of a woman's soul, did nothing at first but potter about the payment of the cab."

Then the leader, abandoning narrative summary, moved on to more direct condemnation by way of sarcasm:

Whether the cabman is yet paid we do not know; but we invite the Lord Mayor and others like him in authority to tear themselves from cab fares a little, in order to meditate upon that which is now proved to be a regular and roaring business. If perjury would rouse them, why this is perjury; for the unspeakable villains who entrap, one by one, the hapless women they send over, deceive them with lies before they embark, and here they are welcomed with lies. . . . If felony would excite the Bench to energy, why there is felony here; for the victims are stolen away from friends and native land, and all their little property is shamefully taken from them. If the red word "Murder" must be pronounced to wake English justice to indignation and burning wrath, we say there is murder, too, in the traffic.

And the conclusion involves the common editorial fare of unqualified judgment and appeal:

Let us have the truth out about this respectable No. 22, Somerset-street, Portman-square, and the lady—Miss Page or otherwise—who lives and does business there in foreign arrivals. . . . [L]et the Law do its very utmost to stop the horrible evil; and if the Law can only visit such wickedness with trivial punishment then let some legislator, with a true man's pity and reverence for woman, set it down as a solemn duty to obtain from the new Parliament a statute which shall frighten the murderers of soul and body into some less horrible and damnable vocation.

Law and legislation were not quick to respond, but another typical response was forthcoming: a letter to the editor. On 17 June, the day after its leading article, the *Daily Telegraph* printed, under the heading "The Procuress," a letter signed *John W. Miller, M.R.C.S., and L.B.A.,* dated from 15 Regent Square, W.C. His strong views are expressed in language matching that in the leader:

All honour for the noble article on the infamous procuress of 22, Somerset-street, Portman-square, which must find an echo in every honest and fatherly heart; but shall it rest with mere sentiment? No; let us be up and doing, and root out from amongst us these monsters who fatten on the ruin of the most helpless of our [sic] sex, and by their silent machinery of corruption and collusion, destroy, not only their happiness, but their very lives.

He had attended a twenty-one-year-old girl, "decoyed, ensnared, ruined in health and turned penniless and friendless in the streets, to starve and die," who soon died "of consumption, ... a silent victim to these worse than murderers." Her case is far from singular:

How many a fond parent's hopes have been blasted by such villains, who can tell? How many a lovely girl, just bursting into beauty—aye, perhaps, a mother's delight, a father's pride—has had the bright vision of her youth dispelled, and its imaginative glories changed in them, by such incarnate fiends, to whom the secret poisoner, the midnight assassin, or vile garotter are angels of light?

And while the *Telegraph*'s "denunciation" should ring "Loud and long" in people's ears, it is not enough merely to point "the finger of scorn at ... such wretches, trafficking in this base and vile calling," who care nothing for "scorn."

No, surely as Englishmen, as parents, let us be up and doing, and rout out such dens of infamy at any cost; and I am ready to come forward with my subscription of five guineas. For the good of our name, for the honour of our religion, for the credit of our morality, let them be brought to the bar of criminal justice, and let us ascertain who are the prime movers who gratify their filthy sensuality and lust at the expense of blood.

Surely our laws are sufficient, and, awakened from our apathy, let them be enforced; so that this cancer of our social system may be uprooted—that disgrace to the age which, nevertheless, we glory in as enlightened beyond our ancestors, and purified by our broad and deep reception of humble, benevolent, and chastening Christianity. Let a meeting be called. Let us know who the landlord of 22, Somerset-street, is, and how and why the [Marylebone] vestry hath slumbered.

With this hortatory insistence and promissory note in hand, the *Daily Telegraph* kept the case before the public in a second leading article on 19 June, in which the vigorous fulmination continued. The case of the Belgian girl was but "the sample of scores and hundreds of like nature—a specimen of an infernal trade which flourishes, because the truth is not spoken about, and because the law strikes with feeble hands against this horrible offence; when, indeed, it strikes at all." The journal would, with regret, keep silent on the issue, were it not that such accounts always bring forth immediately earnest responses, "conveyed through that opinion which finds its way to us by letters."

The *Telegraph* was not merely stating a fact, but also praising its readers, and boasting about while boosting its role as mouthpiece for their moral messages. Such letters, the leader continues, provide "an exact echo from the general voice, and an aspiration for some effort at improvement." As instances, it mentions the correspondence "selected yesterday and today from the bulk ... received," specifically citing those printed, from "a surgeon of reputation and a lady," "two specimens of volunteer soldiers for such a crusade." Thus having gently enticed its readers further to indulge their evangelical epistolary urges, the leader writer characterizes the "public's" (i.e., the readers') rectitude concerning prostitution:

The public does not underrate the evils of that ghastly travesty of human passion—that blasphemy of human love—which sets this trade afoot, maintains its consignees and entrepreneurs, makes the evening and the night shameful in our streets, and poisons the moral blood of society. Neither does the public despair of some grand far-reaching cure for the "great sin of great cities," both as regards the sources of supply, and its sad endemic organised phenomena of patient shame and professional infamy and suffering.

And this encomium leads to further praise of the *Telegraph*'s readers: "The two letters which appear in today's issue are samples of the spirit in which we are constantly addressed." But despite "this yearning desire in the public heart to see 'something done,'" the road to reform is not a smooth or direct one:

Everywhere we see shame, compassion, inquiry, irresolute action, and half-and-half plans for dealing with this sorrow and pest of the human race. There is a noble army of kind and high hearts waiting to march against the Devil of Lust, and his hateful works. What it awaits is a leader, a programme, a clear idea of the topic, and the new powers of the people's House of Commons.

Clearly the change in the times demands a timely change, but to emphasize the urgency, the leader writer pulls out resounding stops on the moral organ:

The state of things is like that of a country infested by wild carnivorous animals. . . . Not nearly so many women and children are caught, and killed, and mumbled into festering carcases by tigers and leopards in the worst-haunted districts of the East, as are caught and morally killed in the towns and cities of this Christian land.

Analogy gives way to facts, as typically the strongest fears of physical consequences are stressed:

Look . . . at the statistics of the hospitals in London, where a fourth of the out-patients come to the doors—expiators of the vile wrong—punished for its existence by indelible contaminations. Read the declarations which the Contagious Diseases Association has lately published, declarations which make the Cities of the Plain no longer inconceivably wicked. Glance at the Registrar General's returns, as printed yesterday, or in any week, and note the number of little children written down as dead of a hideous virus, which came to them, in the dreadful irony of outraged nature, from their mother's breast, or as the sole inheritance of the father.

The ethical is not forgotten, but it is not central:

Regard the subject morally or physically, and all others are trifling compared to its immense exigency. On the one hand, the steady, horrible supply of victims; on the other, their sure career of untold misery and mischief—of hard, forlorn life, and ghastly death; while Justice, which avenges Right upon the pickpocket or area-sneak with all the terrors of the statute-book, potters about these murderers of womanhood, and the Legislature redresses anything except the outrageous feebleness of the law upon seduction, prostitution, and procuring.

And so to the conclusion, signalled by that common editorial device, a series of potent questions inexorably demanding not just right but righteous answers, which are supplied in exclamatory form:

Why is it impossible to find a road for the march of the army of public pity and indignation? What is there eternal and necessary in all this perverted instinct, in this horrible self-inflicted human anguish and degradation, to render it hopeless to ameliorate indefinitely the aspect of the public morality, and to rescue, on the one side, and protect on the other, so as to cut off the supplies of the accursed market? Why not cry a new Crusade, a passaggia of bold and wise hearts—a moral Armada of hope and effort, with the new Parliament to help it—which shall refuse to despair of dealing with this vast mass of sin, sorrow, and plague, moral and material, and shall set out forthwith, having facts for weapons, to wrest this city of God—which every single human spirit is—from the Mahounds of profligacy? How long shall we do nought but moralise and air our rhetoric against this wholesale wrong and guilt? Will the industrial class say and do nothing—now that they have a voice and a part in the nation's councils—against this tribute of flesh and blood which is year by year levied upon them by the Dragon of Vice? It is not a necessary thing that so many sad and wretched victims should be offered up yearly for the sake of society! It is not necessary that the life of a peasant's daughter should be lost, that the peer's daughter may be honest; it is not natural, not tolerable, nor Christian, that we should go on face to face with this awful spectacle, and take no great and resolute step against the curse. Let the Crusade be cried! a vast body of public opinion longs to hear the signal—the class which mainly supplies the victims has come to power—now is the time to speak boldly and freely—to tell the truth, and the whole truth, about the wrongs of women; wrongs which the Law does not right, but indirectly sanctions by the force of an indolent contentment and a cynical despondency.

To modern ears this perfervid tone might sound somewhat false, and to some contemporaries such as Matthew Arnold the *Daily Telegraph* epitomized the vulgarity of the immoderate even if the cause was good. It seems probable, however, that the editors knew what their readers wanted—of course no complaints were printed. There was indeed a match as to belief and anger, even if the language and imagery were more the paper's than its audience's. What the editors were seeking, if the obvious implications of their characterization of the times may be taken at face value, was a solidarity deriving from their acting as voice for the newly enfranchised, the lower middle class and the artisans. Unlike those who saw the Reform Act of 1867 as a leap into the dark depths of democracy, the *Telegraph* celebrated the coming to power of "the class which mainly supplies the victims," "the industrial class" that now has "a voice and a part in the nation's councils," and looked forward with hope to "the new powers of the people's House of Commons."

As to its having secured its place, there was in this case more hope than evidence: there is a disconsonance between the force of their moral pump and the head of water (letters received) driving it. One may believe that they used a very fine filter in printing only a few of many offers of action and support, but evidence is lacking. In fact to accompany the leading article they printed only three letters on the 19th, including those from "a lady," signed *Harriet Barnett*, and a second from Dr Miller (this time offering to convene a meeting),[3] and one more on the 20th, all under the heading "The Procuress."[4]

Whatever the long-term effect of the leaders and letters, immediately and practically their result seemed inconsequential, and anyone experienced in such newspaper outbursts in the Victorian period would anticipate that there would be no further ripples, and the matter would be forgotten until another disturbing case was reported.

The Times and the Great Social Evil, 1850s and 1860s

Such indeed was the case in similar episodes dealt with by *The Times* during the period. Many of the elements in the reaction to the story of the Belgian girl are familiar to students of the social history, journalism, and literature of the period. Brief discussion of a few cases in *The Times* will indicate the general pattern and point to differences in the series in the *Daily Telegraph*.

In 1854 *The Times* reported an apparently trivial "action of trover for a riding habit, and for certain linen kept and detained by the defendant, and also for money lent, and money had and received by the defendant for the use of the plaintiff, and for money due on an account stated." What gave the case more interest was that the plaintiff was a prostitute and the defendant a brothel-keeper.[5]

The next day a leading article adopted the journalistic ploy, aptly tagged the "dirty pictures like these" tactic, in which a wicked practice that you assert should receive no publicity is illustrated by an instance of it. The newspaper, it says, generally abstains from comment on cases that must excite "the greatest disgust in every man of ordinary feeling"; otherwise it would give more publicity than necessary to details already too well calculated to excite a prurient imagination, and to stimulate the laggard passions of exhausted debauchers. If for once we break silence, it is because in the present instance vice of the greatest kind is presented before the mind in a manner so strangely prosaic that even profligacy must, we should imagine, shrink back from the *compte rendu*—from the debits and credits—from the journal and ledger of the brothel.

Having, as the *Daily Telegraph* later was to do, ironically introduced the commercial nature of the enterprise, the leader admits that nothing the journal can say or do will prevent "vice of this kind." This note not of condonation but of sad acceptance—far from that of the *Telegraph*—is reflected generally in the rhetoric of *The Times*, even as the analogy with "trade" is developed: "Surely the mind of a man, however profligate, must revolt at the idea of entering a mere warehouse of brutal passion, in which women are bought and sold like cattle in Smithfield-market. The thing has attained the dimensions of a regular trade."
    In treating the international aspects of the wicked trade it falls short of the *Telegraph*'s scornful rage:

Some villain—generally a foreigner—chooses a proper situation for an estab-lishment of this kind: he has his agents and his correspondents abroad; he directs them to look out, generally in France or Belgium, for such young women as are best adapted to his purpose, and that purpose is nothing less than to make his profit out of their prostitution.

    After more details, amounting almost to a handbook for enterprising brothel keepers, *The Times* offers the standard journalistic justification for dirty pictures like these: "If such things exist among us, it is right we should know they are there." But it goes little further: "It is not for us to point out any direct way of meeting the evil." In effect its analysis of the evil remains only an analysis:

There must be something thoroughly wrong in the state of public feeling when the establishments for the gratification of the sheerest bestiality—if the English language contained a more forcible expression we would employ it—can flour-ish and afford a profitable investment of capital; but they have their propri-etors, their foreign correspondents, and are as regularly conducted as any other business establishment in the three kingdoms.

    Certainly the *Daily Telegraph* reached for even "more forcible expressions." And there is another striking contrast. The moral passion of *The Times*'s leader did not result in any published letters to the editor, perhaps because there was no innocent victim. But three years later a series of leaders and letters on the evils of prostitution in the metropolis produced a more marked impression, and achieved historical recognition through its mention by William Acton in his well-publicized *Prostitution.*

In the first letter, a very lengthy one, under the heading, "The Greatest of our Social Evils," I.R.B. called attention to the effort to diminish the evil or at least alleviate the resulant misery "in the chief centre of its activity—the parish of St. James's, Piccadilly," by establishing "'The St. James's Refuge and Home for Penitents,' for the reformation of fallen women of a class superior to those who alone find their way into the refuges and penitentiaries at present in existence."[6] A leader responded on the same day that accepted the good intentions of the founders, but argued strenuously that "Prevention is better than cure," and asserted that proper education in household tasks for the thousands of young women coming into London was the answer. It also argued for emigration of young women (especially if instructed) to Australia, where they might marry.

Here the argument took a turn, as *Theophrastus* on 7 May presented "The Other Side of the Picture," which portrayed young men rather than young women, and revealed the "real cause of our social corruptions" to lie in laws, "in the highest degree unnatural," imposed by society on those in the middle class contemplating marriage. As will be seen, this thematic and argumentative shift from prostitution to middle-class mores adumbrates the series of 1868 in the *Daily Telegraph.*

In a leading article two days later, *The Times*, while pointing out the social joys (innocent of serious sin) available to bachelors but denied to married men on limited incomes, generally sided with *Theophrastus*, though in measured tones.[7] This exchange tended finally not to induce public passion, perhaps because no individual case highlighted the manifest evil. But it has been accepted as important, largely one suspects because Acton refers to "many letters" printed in *The Times*. Perhaps, given the normal practice of the papers (and presumably of their correspondents), the four letters that appeared between 5 and 8 May 1857 almost qualify as "many."[8]

A year later the great social evil again came to occupy the pages of *The Times*, and this time with more attention to social attitudes towards prudent marriage.[9] The discussion began with a report of a meeting on

6 January of the Society for the Suppression of Vice, with reference to
"the flagrant exhibition of street prostitution that nightly disgraces"
especially "the most crowded thoroughfares of the west end."[10] In a
leading article on the 8th, *The Times* with regret ("a very disagreeable
subject which we are compelled to bring, although most reluctantly,
before the . . . public") approved the Society's campaign, but only in so
far as it was confined "to reasonable measures of discouragement and
repression" and did not "nourish any visionary expectations. . . . It is
with moral as with physical disease—there is no use in looking for an
entirely satisfactory result from the treatment of symptoms; there may
be alleviation, there may be diminution of the disorder, but there will
be no perfect cure."

The Times leader almost incidentally brings in an inference similar to
that of *Theophrastus* in 1857, saying: "The preposterous measure which
is taken of the income necessary to support a family, if a young man
would not sink in the social scale, is no doubt a fruitful cause of the
deplorable evil of which we are speaking." This remark was itself a
"fruitful cause" of correspondence, for the hint about social emulation
was picked up by *A Happy Man* in a letter on the next day that effectively broke the series into two parts, reflected in the headings to the
subsequent correspondence, with letters on prostitution appearing
either unheaded or as comment on "The Great Social Evil," while those
dwelling on the theme of *A Happy Man* are headed, like it, "Frugal
Marriages." That is, at least in the judgment of *The Times*, which supplied the headings, the issues had been separated. Following that lead,
I here accept the separation and discuss *A Happy Man* and his cohort in
chapter 2.

Prostitution, the other theme, was continued by *Epsilon*, who
asserted that publicly diplayed, not clandestine, prostitution was the
main problem, to be solved by firmer application of the law.[11] A report
on 15 January of another meeting of the Society for the Suppression of
Vice listed resolutions enjoining the suppression of street prostitution
in the metropolis, "paticularly in the important thoroughfares of the
Haymarket, Coventry-street, Regent-street, Portland-place, and other
adjacent localities." Also the government was called upon to attend to
"the great number of foreign prostitutes systematically imported into
this country." On the same day *The Times* printed a letter from *W.H.T.*,
which recommended—"under restrictions which may well be left to
the discretion of English matrons"—"freer intercourse" than at present
"between young persons of different sexes and of equal position in
society," and earlier closing hours for public houses, to "destroy the

fatal facility which the tavern and the ginpalace and the night-house now afford for fostering the hesitating intent."

On 16 January another meeting of the Society was reported, followed by a leader on the 18th, and on the 19th by a letter on "The Great Social Evil," from *John Edward Kempe*.[12] In the meeting, chaired by Kempe, the attempt was made to ally other parishes with St James's in suppressing the public solicitation that "made this part of London a Sodom and Gomorrah in its moral condition,"[13] even though it was admitted (as by *The Times*) that it was "almost absurd to affirm that it would be possible to suppress prostitution altogether." Telling reference was made to the incidence of venereal diseases among outpatients, ranging from 25 to 50 per cent of treated cases, and the "slop-shop system" was cited as one cause of vice, young women being unable to live on "the pittance they earned from their needle."

The Times's leader of 18 January presented a key precept of the period, asserting without qualification that morality is beyond the scope of legislation, and entreating "the clergymen and gentlemen who are engaged in the conduct of this movement to confine their attention entirely to public, notorious, and insupportable nuisances, and not to hurt their own chances of ultimate success by aiming at what can never be attained by law or police regulation."[14] And it found room for sympathy for the prostitutes: "We have been very busy with our reformatories for criminals, surely it is a pity that there should not be many places to which any woman who is disposed to abandon a shameful career might fly for refuge and protection."

As noted above, this sequence in *The Times* reveals in weaker form the same connection made in the *Daily Telegraph* in 1868 between the great social evil and prudent marriage. For the moment, only one difference need be mentioned: in *The Times* on both topics combined only ten letters were printed,[15] and their range was much more restricted.

For the most part, these flurries of interest in *The Times*, prompted by court cases and public meetings, centred on revulsion against prostitution and consideration of public measures against it, with some passing allusions to discouraging young women from becoming prostitutes and young men from resorting to them. The responses ranged from strong condemnation and calls for immediate police and legislative action to moral exhortation; there is no indication of toleration, although *The Times* itself was sceptical about extirpation of the "trade." In all these respects the series mirror quite accurately the public and official responses to "the Great Social Evil" in Victorian London. The term "Great" denoted not only the moral turpitude and serious physical consequences of prostitution, but also its prevalence, as is evident in the literature of the period, especially that emanating from surgery and pulpit.[16] In the 1850s it was generally held that there were about 5000 brothels in London,[17] but it would appear that the number decreased markedly in the 1860s.[18] As to the number of prostitutes, estimates range widely from a high of 80,000 in the 1830s to a not-so-low 6500 in the 1870s; probably a range from 10,000 to 20,000 is most acceptable as an estimate—nobody in public described it as an acceptable reality.[19]

There is no need here to attempt to summarize the literature on the subject, but a few matters bearing on the "Marriage or Celiacy" series in the *Daily Telegraph* series give some helpful context. Apart from the street-walkers and the "kept women," the brothels attracted many clients and much attention. They were concentrated in the area north of Oxford Street, extending it seems from Soho almost to the Edgeware Road (and including Portman Square).[20] There are several references to the importing of foreign prostitutes, especially from Belgium and France[21]—"Cargoes of them are actually imported from the continent because London represents the best market."[22] The clients are seen principally as married men,[23] and (at least those frequenting "second-class brothels") as men in business, clerks, warehousemen, shopmen, and students.[24] The general belief, probably mistaken,[25] was that the clients were mainly middle-class men. Equally general, and less likely mistaken, was the belief that prostitutes were drawn almost exclusively from the lower classes.[26]

The *Daily Telegraph* Series

Against this background the particular characteristics of the series in the *Daily Telegraph* in 1868 stand out more clearly. The initial incident, the attempted procurement of a Belgian girl by the West End brothel, would fit into any generalized account of prostitution in the period. So too would the reaction of the editors of the *Daily Telegraph*, though the intensity and force of the rhetoric, while not unfaithful to the norms of the medical and clerical reformers, are more illustrative of its own practice than of that of other papers, and their judgment is not as permissive as that of *The Times*. The first letters in response to the news story and leading articles are typical both in tone and purpose: moral outrage and a call for action by individuals and local authorities. What is most significant for the "Marriage or Celibacy?" series are the virtually automatic links seen by commentators of all types between the great social evil and mistaken marriage practices, and between prostitution, prudent marriage, and emigration. As will become clear, there are significant differences between other comments and those in the *Daily Telegraph*, arising principally from the particular readership of that newspaper. In the main, however, it will seem that the series has considerable significance, embodying as it does widespread attitudes towards prostitution.

What will also become evident is that there is very little explictly on prostitution in the series after the first few days. One might, if one ignored the actual evidence from the journalism of the period, attribute this to editorial reticence about a prohibited subject, and it may be that there was censorship by the "gate-keepers" on such grounds. But more likely there were few letters dealing directly with prostitution because there was not much more to be said than the first two leading articles had said, which was in any case almost axiomatic in the debate. Indeed "debate" is not the best term for the central moral issues, because there was no support for "The Great Social Evil." There were those who objected to various ways of trying to reduce or eliminate it, and even those—as became quite evident in the contemporary controversy over the Contagious Diseases Acts—who advanced at least mitigating arguments to the effect that prostitution protected innocent girls by deflecting the irresistible and insatiable sexual demands of men onto professionals. And there can be no doubt that in the privacy of all-male society there was, in spite of the constant near-epidemic status of venereal disease, a good deal of unthinking and vapid jolliness about the "game."

What could be debated, of course, were the causes, and it needed no great subtlety to see that if all sexual behaviour took place within marriage, sex for pay would not be a problem.[27] It may be thought curious—and it may indeed be curious—that this proposition rests on one very shaky premise, that married men did not resort to prostitutes. Given the huge estimates of the number of prostitutes in London in the period, that premise is pitifully weak, because if anything like so many women were on the streets and in brothels, it would take all the men, married and single, all their libido and time to patronize them. But the debate in the *Daily Telegraph* almost sidesteps that issue, concentrating instead on bachelors. The assumptions that propel the central argument are that they can be saved from sin by and only by marriage, and also that so far as fallen women are concerned, the demand side offers the best avenue for attack—remove the buyers from the market and the sellers will disappear. Was the argument propelled in that direction by editorial design or by chance? It seems likely that a letter from one reader prompted responses that the editors decided to foster and that consequently, the immediate result looking promising, they almost by accident started a new chapter in the history of popular journalism—indeed of mass media.

Marriage or Celibacy?
The *Daily Telegraph* Series

Prudent Marriage and *The Times*, 1850s to 1860s

The connection in the public mind between prostitution and the difficulties of early marriage had been raised in *The Times* a decade earlier, it will be recalled (see p. 20–1). In 1857, however, *Theophrastus's* excoriation of "society's laws," set by parents (and custom), that rule out marriage until the young have an income enabling them to begin on the footing already reached by their parents, produced no further comment. But there was more debate in the next year, as indicated in chapter 1 above, when *The Times* printed a series that started, like that of 1857, with discussions of prostitution, but then divided into two parts when *A Happy Man* wrote a letter, headed "Frugal Marriages," that also connected the great social evil with the difficulties of prudent middle-class marriage.

A Happy Man argued that "young Jones" should marry his "fair cousin Jenny" on £300 a year, because the mature and rational joys that come with marriage will more than compensate for the sacrifices. Moreover, he will avoid the miseries "of long delays, hopes deferred, hearts dried up, affections deadened, and, not least important, the children still young when the parents are in the decline of life." He concludes: "There is a wide difference between prudence and pusillanimous caution."[1]

Dissent came from one who chose that last word as his signature above an assertion that on that sum "social position" was unattainable. *St. Boniface* also dissented, pointing out that if his friend Smith, "a fellow and lecturer of St. Boniface," were to marry his "Jane Ann, to whom he has been engaged these three years," he would lose his professional income with his celibacy.[2]

Three days later the heading "Frugal Marriages" reappeared over three letters, one a reply from *A Friend of Jones* to both *A Happy Man* and *Caution*, and two supporting *A Happy Man* from *Another Happy Man* (who provided a budget) and *Jenny's Sister* (the first letter purporting to be from a woman in this exchange). *A Friend of Jones* repudiated "the prevailing spirit of the age, as exemplified in the desire for show and extravagant expenditure," and insisted that society should "relax" its attitudes towards the supposed "degradation" consequent on early marriage on low incomes. *Another Happy Man*, "by birth and education a gentleman," and now evidently a clerk, presents his own exemplary case. To encourage others, he reports his "wife's expenditure for housekeeping during the past year," extracted from their account-books. They (with one child, one female servant and a "nursery-girl") have a regime that allows for some modest entertaining and costs in the year £230 6s, leaving from the £300 proposed in the cases of Jones and Smith a rather handsome balance of £69 14s.

Jenny's Sister is more rambunctious and annoyed than the other correspondents, insisting that only an idiot would marry one "whose preparation for the said state has been made among the loungers of the clubs, operas, and casinos." Jenny should seek a young husband with higher motives, one desiring to be "the best master of the talents committed to him by his God, to whom he must one day render an account, not only of his frivolity, but of the vice consequent upon that frivolity," one who could well live in comfort on £300 a year.

A further letter came on the 19th from *A Married M.A.*, who deliberately took apart the account of *Another Happy Man*, revealing just how meagre the allowances were, and how narrow the margin of safety. His final judgment is close to that proposed by Max Beerbohm, "For people who like that kind of thing, that is the kind of thing they like":[3]

if Jenny . . . is willing to superintend the cooking and washing, besides a very constant and careful supervision of the inexperienced nursery girl; if she is content to dress on £15, and contract her books, newspapers, cabs and excursions into a total of £10; if she is satisfied to entertain no visitors beyond an occasional friend to dinner, and to become a miracle of economy, industry, and self denial, far be it from me to forbid the banns. But if she has been accustomed to a far more liberal scale of expenditure and a better style of dress and living, and does not feel competent to be head nurse, head cook, and head housemaid, or sure of her own powers of self-denial, or—what is quite as important—of those of her husband; or if she hesitates to risk bringing up a large family on such narrow means, let her think twice about £300 a-year matrimony.

This was the theme chosen by *The Times* to close the discussion in a leader employing far less thunderous tones than those in its parallel comment on the great social evil.[4] On the question "What can a man marry upon?" (note "man"), both "facts and judgments differ widely," as its correspondents had indicated. (The amounts cited are an annual £1000, £800, £500, and £300.) "Some people have an itch for spending," the leader points out, and "it is the same with pleasures and with purchases"; such are not good candidates for marriage on £300 a year. The moral judgment implied here is overt in the contrast between, on the one hand, the "claims of society" and their derivative duties, which are good but artificial, and, on the other, marriage, which is "a law of nature" and so has "a plain right to precedence." However, it appears that art has its own imperatives, for the leader continues with qualifications, and the final moral, gently sad, is for delayed gratification:

We are not to expect marriage, under any circumstances, to be quite a paradise in this fallen world; it will have its cares and vexations under the most favourable conditions; still, to give it a fair chance, there ought to be enough to live upon, and if a frugal temper does not secure this sufficiency, then we must suppose a higher income must be the substitute ... A large income is, perhaps, the best substitute which this poor world can afford for a frugal spirit, but it, unhappily, is not always at hand when it is wanted; it is slow in coming, and those who prefer this external source of happiness, if they are saved some sharp trials when they marry, have often to exercise their patience in waiting for that event.[5]

That leader, an essay in itself, ended the discussion in 1858, which included seven letters—an unusually large number—on the theme of frugal marriage. That the series held contemporary interest is shown in a debate in *Blackwood's Magazine* in which Celsus (who is married happily with children and a living) asks his friend Coelebs: "have you not read all the letters in the *Times*, proving how any man can live like a gentleman on three hundred a-year, not to say five?"[6]

One final example from *The Times* again helps in context and comparison. Dealing in somewhat richer and fuller detail with the marriage question, this series in mid-1861 began with a letter headed "A Belgravian Lament" and signed *A Sorrowing Mother for Seven of Them*.[7] The lament of the seven mothers for their twenty-four daughters is that "However unpleasant, indelicate the truth, all dreadful as it is to us to write it, marriage in our set is voted a bore—is repudiated." And why? "Because what our simple-minded daughters call 'the pretty horsebreakers' occupy naughtily and temporarily where we should occupy *en permanence.*"

Here then enters the theme of prostitution in a very different manner; the letter concludes with a plea far removed from those in the *Daily Telegraph*:

Pray help us, Sir. Shall we go to the Bishops who are in town—to Convocation? Is not ours a *gravamen*? What will become of special licences? Who will care for the Sponsor question? Our churches and Prayer-book, they will become mere symbols to us. The whole girl-life of our order is in danger; the pretty confirmations at the Chapel Royal, the prettier ceremonies of St. George's—alas! And then the sin of it all!

It need hardly be said that this has the smell of a hoax, even if one rather likes the odour. Apart from the tone, the references to the "pretty horsebreakers" strongly urge the authorship of Matthew James Higgins, famous for his spoofing letters, often under the alias of *Jacob Omnium*. And there can be no doubt that the editors and readers of *The Times* would be even quicker than we to pick up the clue. Humour of this kind, it should be realized, is as reliable in signalling attitudes and opinions as it is unreliable in presenting facts. The certainty that one Belgravian mother did not write this letter on behalf of herself and six others in no way diminished its appeal for comment on the real issues by others who could read and write in the code of *The Times*: three lengthy letters were published the next day, "A Lament from Belgravia" from *The Very Well-Contented Mother of Four Incipient Old Maids*, "Matrimony" from *A Father of Six*, and "Horsebreakers and Heartbreakers" from *Beau Jolais*.

The first of these simply complains that her daughters—also paragons—cannot find fitting mates among the young men of the present, who desire only "to be esteemed fast, to effect lordly airs and expenses, to rejoice in broad selfishness and sensuality, to boast of atheism," and are indeed "only fit for the company of 'horsebreakers.'"[8]

A Father of Six (sons) takes very different ground, denying the premise of the mothers of twenty-four (daughters) by presenting the difficulties of all his sons but the eldest, Tom, who will "have what his fathers have had before him, and was married long ago." But there matrimony in the family "has stopped ... and seems likely to stop." The parallels with the *Daily Telegraph* material are close enough to justify inclusion of the detailed reasons. The second eldest son is Charley, a city clerk in "his uncle's house."

He works from 10 till 5 as regularly as clockwork, and when there is a press of business till much later. In all probability he will die as rich a man as Tom, and is quite as well off now, but, as he says, when he opens an invitation to Mrs. G.'s ball or Lady C.'s concert, "What's the use of sending these to me? I am in bed when they begin." And that's the truth, and Charley, though he stands 6 feet 2 inches, and is as good-looking a fellow as any in London, does not know half-a-dozen girls by sight.

The next is Henry, a lazy government clerk. A "ladies' man," he is surrounded in the park by a "bevy of girls" and "goes to every ball in London." His father cannot understand how "he always looks fresh; but he says he gets a capital nap every afternoon at his office in Somerset-house. But Harry can't put together £300 a-year, and with all his economy, for he is one of the most economical fellows I know, he can hardly make that do for matrimony." His other sons are still young, and if they do not go "to the colonies" they will probably end up as clerks, in which cases, "matrimony seems equally improbable."[9]

Beau Jolais, adopting a rhetorical framework popular in the period, and which reappears prominently in "Marriage or Celibacy?", admits his rashness, as a "single 'unprotected male' in breaking a lance, even in sport, with the seven redoubtable champions of Belgravia," but still ventures "reverently to pick up the dainty gauntlets they have thrown down," by challenging their analysis of the cause of their failure to find sons-in-law. It is not the "the pretty horsebreakers" who are to blame, but "ye manners and ye customs of ye nineteenth century," "the thorough hollowness, worldliness, and insincerity of the age—in that morbid but almost universal craving on the part of everyone to appear something that he is not."

On the basis of a snatch of autobiography, he presents the moral: "'Respectability' . . . as Diogenes observed with regard to repentance, may be too dearly purchased." The young women of Belgravia must be taught the lessons of economy, and cease to think that "a husband is only a victim created to supply them with the means of prodigality. Thus, and thus only, can Lais and Aspasia, Blondelle and Loribelle, . . . be effectually disarmed."

On the 29th of June *The Times* printed four more letters: two under the heading "The Belgravian Lament" from *Primogenitus* and *N. or M.*, with a third, headed "Hetaerae," from *A London Incumbent*, and a fourth unheaded brief complaint about adultery from *An Old-Fashioned Parson. Primogenitus* had obviously trained in the Higgins epistolary school, the tone, tactics, stance being like those of *A Sorrowing Mother*, though the point of view is quite different. He, unlike Tom, the eldest son of *A Father of Six*, complains that he has, in the face of opportunistic and scheming mothers, for the time renounced marriage and—worse— he says he has "entirely" withdrawn from "unmarried innocence, and now associate[s] only with such agreeable married women as will bear with me, and with 'pretty horsebreakers' who do not expect me to marry them, or even to fall in love with them, if I am not inclined to do so." Perhaps worst of all, he is confident that his present behaviour will not damage his future prospects, for if they but be elder sons, "in this, the year of our Lord 1861, the gambler, the *roué*, the drunkard, the riotous liver, if he calls at the matrimonial mart on business, is as eagerly dealt with as if he had always led a creditable and useful life."[10]

N. or M., like *Beau Jolais* a jouster, wishes "to leave for a while Rotton-row to break, not a horse for, but a lance with," those who uttered the "Belgravian Lament." He, however, expresses bitter distaste for girls who emulate the style of the courtesans.[11] *A London Incumbent* takes a different but equally vigorous line of attack, directed against toleration of the women of the beau monde,[12] and founded on the principle that his cloth would properly exclude him from jolly evenings in their company.[13] *An Old-Fashioned Parson* is unequivocally and briefly of the same party, his letter reading in full:

We seem to be going back to the morality of the last century. Illicit connexion is no longer called adultery, but a "temporary engagement." This is much the same kind of euphemism as I observe in your city articles, where robbery is called "defalcation." I suppose it would be very vulgar to quote the 7th and 8th Commandments in reference to these questions, but a spade is a spade for all that.[14]

On 1 July two more correspondents, once more family members though presumably not related, enlised in the debate: *A Mother* under "Belgravian Laments," and *Grandmamma* under "Horsebreakers and Heartbreakers."[15] *A Mother* asserts the pleasures of parenthood resulting from the proper raising of young girls, not diminished by the realization that marriage will come to them, celebrates what she believes to be an unprecedented increase in happy and early marriages, and denies that the "horsebreakers" "influence, even in the slightest degree, the destinies of our daughters."[16] *Grandmamma*, whose seven children (including five married daughters) have made her a grandmother twenty-four times, had on that day the last word, and it was harsh: "I think the 'Belgravian Lament' exaggerated, *Primogenitus* a

conceited young gentleman, and your *London Incumbent* a prig."
Things "were better managed" in her day, as she indicates in a lengthy
comparison of a past regime with that of the present, but to the discredit of the latter. What is needed is a courageous and principled
stand by mothers, whom *Grandmamma* addresses hortatively as "the
true leaders of society . . . , the class of British matrons—the noblest,
and . . . the purest, that ever distinguished your sex."[17]

At this point *The Times* evidently believed enough space had been
given to the debate, and closed it, as was the practice, with a summary
leading article, dwelling on marriage, though not entirely ignoring the
"social evil."

Matrimony is so popular a subject and appeals to so great a variety of experiences, that such a challenge as the "Belgravian Lament" was sure to elicit
numerous responses, both serious and ironical. At first sight these letters seem
to disclose a state of things that is truly alarming. Mothers scheming to force
their daughters on unwilling heirs; young men of birth and wealth fastidiously
rejecting the homely happiness of marriage, and shamelessly betaking themselves to an alternative as unsatisfying to the heart as it is perilous to the conscience; young ladies tolerating the presence of their "bad rivals" rather than
relinquish their pursuit of titles and fortune,—this view of life and manners, so
worthy of Hogarth's pencil, must surely be an exaggerated picture of our modern Vanity Fair.

Recognizing that the question whether marriages are declining in
number is not a statistical one, because "it is not pretended that the
degeneracy has penetrated below the upper crust of society, or that
marriage is depreciated by any class except that which is or might be
domiciled in Belgravia," *The Times* also allows for "the permanent
causes of celibacy, such as moroseness or restlessness of disposition
and a want of sufficient means to bear the expenses of a household,"
before looking for an answer. And it concludes that the fear of decline
is an unfounded one. The inquiry into causes is not closed, however,
for the leader continues with an allusion to "the vulgar, but almost universal, desire to keep up appearances, which makes newly-married
couples expect to begin where their fathers and mothers ended," and
which unchecked will "mathematically" result in fewer marriages "in
each successive generation." Women are by no means the only or chief
sinners in this respect, although it is true "that marriage is to a woman
far more than it is to a man; it represents success in life, and gratified
female ambition as well as female affection."

On prostitution as not only a succour for but a cause of the supposed decline in marriage *The Times* touches again, as in earlier series, "with reluctance, and only for the purpose of drawing attention to an obvious remedy for an admitted evil." The social influence of the Haeterae can be diminished simply by "not ministering to the vanity" of those who indulge it, and by "giving proper honour" to those who repudiate it. Further, "'Society,' as it calls itself," must become less exclusive, and admit "a large section of the flower of English youth, qualified by education, pinciples, and inclination to make good husbands." On this rather surprising note, the leader concludes:

As it is, numbers of marriageable young men and women, capable of making each other happy, never have the chance of meeting either in town or country, and, for want of opportunities of rational conversation among those who have, marriages are often contracted on a much slighter acquaintance than would be held to justify an ordinary friendship.[18]

So ended another series in *The Times*, consisting of ten letters[19] and one leading article, that combined questions of marriage and sexual sin. Each of the series demonstrates that links were seen between barriers to early marriage and the prevalence of prostitution, and in that respect adumbrates the series in the *Daily Telegraph*. As will become evident, the resemblance is not casual, for the basic beliefs of the period are reflected in both. What will also become evident are the important differences that give special interest to "Marriage or Celibacy?" The most obvious are the different social levels central to the discussions—aristocratic and upper-middle class in *The Times* and middle and lower-middle class in the *Daily Telegraph*—and the much greater scope and bulk of the series in the *Telegraph*. To understand how these came about one must look briefly at the two papers.

The *Daily Telegraph*: From Leaders to Readers

In mid-century *The Times* was approaching, and by the 1860s had achieved, its commanding status as "The Thunderer" and as what is now called the "newspaper of record." While the *London Gazette* was the "official" paper, to which the fashionable world turned for a schedule and summary account of its social and political engines, the same information in fuller form could be found in *The Times*. The *Daily Telegraph* competed with *The Times* on its ground, but not on its terms, especially because the times were changing with telegraphic speed.

The major social and technological readjustments that were being recognized and adopted in the 1860s, when the final burdens of the "taxes
on knowledge" had been removed, resulted in challenges to *The
Times*'s dominance, especially by the *Daily Telegraph*, which played a
somewhat different game on overlapping fields.

The contrasts are somewhat obscured by the physical similarities.
The London (or "national") dailies in the high Victorian period were
large format, running from about eight to sixteen pages. What strikes
the eye first are the advertisements, filling the front and back pages
(with some interspersed).[20] The next dominant feature is the parliamentary report, with what appear to be (but are not) full verbatim texts
of the speeches. Other noteworthy elements (not "sections" in late
twentieth-century terms) are the commercial "intelligence" (especially
the lists of bankruptcies); foreign news, taken from foreign papers or
from "correspondents"—stringers in major centres—or lifted from
competing papers (sometimes with acknowledgment); police and law
court reports; lengthy accounts of public meetings on political, social,
and economic issues; sporting news; "society" notes (there are very
few births and marriage notices, and not many obituaries, though
some deaths are treated as news); and there are occasional reviews of
books, exhibitions, and performances.

Central to the papers (even in the four-page sheets dominant in the
early years of the century) were the leading articles, prompted usually
(as now) by news stories. In them an anonymous guiding voice (in the
authoritative plural) offered informed opinion on the issues of the day,
at considerable length and in detail. Here was determined and displayed the political coloration of the newspapers, most of which were
heavily partisan. Debate on principles was seldom encouraged,
although there was some room for adversarial discussion of details of
public policy, seen in the "expert" opinion offered in letters to the editor or solicited as "from a correspondent." While there were significant
letters to the editor (some from major figures of the day), the quantita-
tive place they played in the normal day's paper was very small,[21] and
letters usually were printed alone or in pairs, placed in the middle or
latter part of the paper with the exigencies of layout rather than sub-
stantive context in mind. And the leader writer had the last word (the
"op-ed page" is a recent invention). One might say, then, that overt
opinion lay in the leaders;[22] the rest of the paper was (to use another
modern and somewhat disgusting term) the "news hole" and advertising. When all is taken into account, there is no better source for examination of the manners and mores of the period, as Thomas Carlyle

indicated in referring to the "forty-eight longitudinal feet of small-printed History in thy Daily Newspaper."[23]

In these respects the *Daily Telegraph*, which began in the mid-1850s as a cheap rag with little claim to public attention, emulated its successful competitors, but began to look for distinctive ways, and very quickly found astonishing success, first through price-cutting, in attaining what was certainly in its time mass circulation.

George Augustus Sala, one of the most active journalists of the period, who was a major contributor to the *Daily Telegraph* from 1858, saw its proprietors as aiming at "a thoroughly comprehensive newspaper" that would also be "a miscellany of humorous and descriptive social essays."[24] He was well aware of the low status of the paper: "There existed, not only among the Conservatives, who thought that the cheap daily press could only be the prelude of sedition and revolution, but also among a large number of journalists, and Liberal journalists too, of high standing, the most violent of prejudices against the new order of journals which were usually contemptuously called the 'penny papers.'" And writers for the more expensive journals—*The Times*, the *Morning Chronicle*, the *Morning Post*, the *Morning Herald*, and the *Morning Advertiser*—"vehemently protested against the [presence in a journalists' informal "club" of] a young man known to be connected with a penny paper."[25]

The *Daily Telegraph* was in fact the leading exemplar: from September 1855 it sold for a penny; by 1861 it was selling almost 150,000 copies daily, and in the next year had a circulation roughly equal to the combined total of all the other London morning papers—including *The Times*. Initially and in the 1860s Liberal and supportive of Gladstone, a broad franchise, and social reforms, it became Conservative only in Disraeli's second administration. As readers of Matthew Arnold will recall,[26] its writers adopted a highly coloured palette and heavy impasto in reaching out to the increasingly significant middle and lower-middle classes, especially those below the professional bar, and became instrumental in the gradual development of the so-called "new journalism" of the last decades of the century.

The nation's addiction to newspapers had long been noted:

...John [Bull] could bear his cloudy days and even the defeat of his party, [because] there still remains a comfort, the want of which even in the happiest circumstances would render him very uncomfortable, and destroy all his good-humour; namely, a newspaper with his breakfast. He would rather do without toast with his tea than be deprived of his gigantic morning paper; for a breakfast without a journal is for him an election without an election dinner, or an Irishman without a bull. . . . [He] reads them with such conscientiousness, that he does not overlook a letter. He not only wishes to see his political opinion reproduced in them every morning, but he reads with so much the more pleasure the "Chronique Scandaleuse" of the town, the less he troubles himself about scandal in society; the more careful and suspicious he is concerning his property, the more he is amused by accounts of robberies, housebreaking, and swindling; though he never risks his money in bets, or gives his wife cause to fear that he should break a leg at a fox-hunt, he never misses reading the interesting sporting intelligence, comprising accounts of hunts, races, cock-fights, &c. Neither does he omit the verses and the fatal accidents, of which regular accounts are sent from the most distant parts of the kingdom, and in which the English take so much interest, that they become as tiresome to the stranger as the importance they attach to the success of a favourite racer on the turf.[27]

What the *Telegraph* had successfully gambled on was the promising growth of a new audience, also adumbrated in the literature of the period. Though the portrait dates from two decades earlier, the proprietors of the *Telegraph* would be aware that even the wretchedly poor Toby Veck, in Dickens's *The Chimes* (1844), was a reader of newspapers—and potentially (once the price had come down) even a buyer of them.

"Why! Lord!" said Toby. "The Papers is full of obserwations as it is; and so's the Parliament. Here's last week's paper, now;" taking a very dirty one from his pocket, and holding it from him at arm's length; "full of obserwations! Full of obserwations! I like to know the news as well as any man," said Toby, slowly; folding it a little smaller, and putting it in his pocket again; "but it almost goes against the grain with me to read a paper now. It frightens me, almost. I don't know what we poor people are coming to."[28]

Both the distaste and fascination of Toby are shared by the newsagent Tetterby (or perhaps the sharer is their creator, an experienced journalist, Dickens):

"You had better read your paper than do nothing at all," said Mrs. Tetterby.
"What's to read in a paper?" returned Mr. Tetterby, with excessive discontent.
"What?" said Mrs. Tetterby. "Police."
"It's nothing to me," said Tetterby. "What do I care what people do, or are done to."

"Suicides," suggested Mrs. Tetterby.

"No business of mine," replied her husband.

"Births, deaths, and marriages, are those nothing to you?" said Mrs. Tetterby.

"If the births were all over for good and all to-day; and the deaths were all to begin to come off to-morrow; I don't see why it should interest me, till I thought it was a-coming to my turn," grumbled Tetterby. "As to marriages, I've done it myself. I know quite enough about them."

Though her opinions seemed to match her husband's, Mrs Tetterby dissented, "for the gratification of quarrelling with him."

"Oh, you're a consistent man, . . . an't you? You, with the screen of your own making there, made of nothing else but bits of newspapers, which you sit and read to the children by the half-hour together!"

"Say used to, if you please," returned her husband. "You won't find me doing so any more. I'm wiser, now."

"Bah! wiser, indeed!" said Mrs. Tetterby. "Are you better?"[29]

As to the popular journalists' intentions, reflected in their "obserwations," Anthony Trollope's *The Three Clerks* gives another insider's view:

"Goodness, Charley—how very moral you are!" said Linda.

"Yes," said he; "that's indispensable. It's the intention of the *Daily Delight* always to hold up a career of virtue to the lower orders as the thing that pays. Honesty, high wages, and hot dinners. Those are our principles."

"You'll have a deal to do before you'll bring the lower orders to agree with you," said Uncle Bat.

"We have a deal to do," said Charley, "and we'll do it. The power of the cheap press is unbounded."[30]

The press wielded and increased that power by expressing the ideals and portraying the lives of the new readers. At first mediated through the pens of the journalists—who were themselves usually from that social stratum—the opinions and facts came to be expressed directly through letters to the editor. Here appears the most startling innovation of the series on marriage and celibacy. Though of course there were letters real—and invented—earlier, there is no previous series matching it in bulk, coherence, and range of interest.[31]

The *Telegraph* was forwarding a revolution by this gradual addition of "opinion" from its readers—gradually, a movement from Leaders to Readers; letters to the editor came to be signals of public attitudes before the invention of the opinion poll.[32] In this respect it gained a march on its competitors on the road to the tabloid (though the *Telegraph* itself soon turned onto another more respectable avenue on which it has remained). Expertise came to be seen as based on experience, not on thought about experience, and "questions" were increasingly left open for the individual to judge. The newspaper (as many of the correspondents in the "Marriage or Celibacy?" series plainly state)[33] came to be seen and valued as a forum, acting in the "public interest."

This was largely an unintended consequence: though the proprietors unquestionably were playing to what they cleverly perceived as the new audience's wishes, they had not a new but a persistent practical problem to solve. There was a yawning gap in the papers and the danger of a yawning audience when the "London Season" ended as parliament and the law courts closed down, and everyone of "consequence" left town. During this period (generally, midsummer until early in the new year,)[34] there was little political, legal, or social news, and the summer months became known as the "Silly Season" because the papers abandoned their habitual earnestness in search of any kind of copy. This was a particularly good time for the "sensational" stories that came to mark the times in fact and fiction.

In his tantalizingly vague history, *Peterborough Court: The Story of the Daily Telegraph*, Edward Lawson, Lord Burnham, comments on the "special and worthwhile silly-season correspondence," saying: "Topics were not unusually silly in the months of August and September, nor for that matter were readers, but it is difficult to-day . . . to realize quite how dead things became at the end of July when the contents of newspapers were mainly political and there was no autumn season and the long vacation of the courts was both long and real." So in the "last twenty years of the century," he says, the *Telegraph* introduced correspondence features, "usually coming in with the grouse and going out with the pheasant," as a "stand-by."[35]

Burnham's narrative suggests that the practice began in the 1880s, and he makes no reference to "Marriage or Celibacy?", though its success should have left lingering traces even in the notoriously short working memories of journalists. It certainly should be seen as having spawned the even larger progeny of the final decades of the century—which have not attracted detailed attention.[36]

The heredity of at least one series cannot be questioned: "Is Marriage a Failure?" in 1888 elicited, according to Burnham, some 27,000 letters, the series running for a month and a half, with about three columns on most days.[37] This series was prompted by a leader commenting on two articles in the *Westminster Review* by the actress Mona Caird, "Marriage" and "Ideal Marriage." Burnham indicates that this series was in some way controlled by Le Sage, then sub-editor, who broadened its scope and interest by sending the paper's Paris correspondent to interview Zola and Dumas fils. It also has the high distinction of mention in that irresistible slice from the period, *The Diary of a Nobody*, in which Charley Pooter, the fine essence of clerkliness, records: "November 2.—I spent the evening quietly with Carrie [my wife], of whose company I never tire. We had a most pleasant chat about the letters on 'Is Marriage a Failure?' It has been no failure in our case."[38]

Was the "correspondence feature," a splendid means of stimulating the readership, the invention of one man? No answer seems forthcoming, and it is unfortunately not easy to decide who was mainly responsible for editing the paper in 1868, let alone responsible for choosing correspondence or planning a series of letters.[39] But the staff's alertness to possibilities was quickly demonstrated, as the readers responded to the issues raised in the letters of *A Barrister* and *R.P.C.*

From "The Procuress" to "Marriage or Celibacy?"

The letter, signed *A Barrister*, that pivoted the discussion in the *Daily Telegraph* appeared on 27 June 1868, still under the heading "The Procuress." While he praises the "able and bold" leader on procuring and applauds the efforts to clean up Marylebone, he insists that the "root of the mischief" lies deeper, "in the exaggerated notions of luxury that pervade our social system, and put an almost impassable bar upon early marriage, in the middle and wealthier classes." The prevalent belief is that young men "when they marry, are expected, if they mean to maintain their social status, to live in almost the same style as their parents and the circle in which their parents move." He continues:

a young man of 24 or 25, the son of parents living at the rate of £1,200 or £1,500 a year, and himself the master of a salary of £250, . . . would find it very difficult to get a wife of his own social position . . . unless his father would settle another £300 a year on him, which the young gentleman's father would probably be unable [and unwilling] to do. . . .

If he did nonetheless marry a girl bringing £100 a year with her, they would soon find that they must drop society of their own class, or that society would drop away from them. What is the result? That very few young men, indeed, can marry under thirty-five, if so soon. But, if young men cannot marry, they will live par amour; and this is the root of the social evil, as it is called, with its aggravations of the shocking trade to which you have alluded.

This theme was picked up by a letter published on 26 June, signed R.P.C., once more under the heading "The Procuress." Accepting *A Barrister*'s account of "the social evil, its cause, and the means of reduction," he had tried to set an example "by marrying at 24 years of age, with an income of £130 per annum." His is a sunny story:

though happy in a little family, [I] can still find an occasional half-crown to go to the Opera, and shall undoubtedly have a vote under the new lodger franchise. Now, if I had listened to the advice of my friends, in all probability I should by this time be equally gay as the friends of my boyhood now are, and in the course of a dozen years have married the lady of calculation, instead of having by my side one whom I know does not wear false hair, and whose bloom of face the baby cannot kiss away. I have another source of pride in my young wife: she believes me to be thoroughly honourable in my detestation of the means by which so many of our sisters are brought to the streets. Do our parents think of these horrible things when they tell us to be worldly, and say that we must not marry till we have earned £500 a-year, and lost all our young feelings of admiration and devotion for the fairest prize of our life?

This concluding *R.P.C.* question produced an answer by the editorial staff in a leader of the same day, typifying their style but more significantly their desire to heighten the readers' involvement. The leader tries to encapsulate the issue, initially pointing out that *A Barrister*'s letter unquestionably "laid bare one main root of the awful evil which we have exposed and denounced in these columns." But the theme called for extensive and decorative embellishment:

The outrageous expectations of parents in behalf of their marriageable daughters, and the inflated sumptuary ideas of the young ladies themselves, are, past all question, a cause—and a cardinal cause—of this cruel traffic in the souls and bodies of foreign women. It sounds like a coarse and ill-bred thing to say—but say it we must, till the ears of the Belgravian mammas and of delicately-reared damsels tingle with shame—that part of the fruit of the selfish and worldly view which they take now-a-days of marriage, is grown upon the bitter and black tree of their sisters' agony. . . .

Relying on "plain words," the writer asserts that "the mercenary pretensions of parents and the positive greed which prevails among middle and upper class maidens for a 'good position'. . . . are directly chargeable with many a sad consignment of trapped women to the London traders in vice, and with much of that marketing of youth and beauty which renders our streets at night so piteous and vile." The connection is provided by "the pertinent modern theory," i.e., "to begin where our grandfathers and grandmothers left off." Rather than asking whether a suitor is "honest, earnest, chaste, industrious, and manly," the questions are, "can he secure his wife 'a position?' Is he 'in society?' Has he 'expectations?' What is his income, and what will his father give him?" Just such a "catechism" is often put also by "the prudent object" of a young man's affections: "she likes her lover to be well gilded, like children's gingerbread; she must be wooed like Danae, with a shower of coins."

Sounding a nostalgic note that was to recur frequently in the series, the writer drew a norm from the past to put beside a sad modern distortion:

Time was when the rule ran, that if two young people loved each other, they went forth into the world hand-in-hand, trusting to God, to their love, and the manliness of the husband; and from such marriages grew up the flower of a beautiful faith, and homes made sweet in the fortunate after days by the recollection of brave past efforts and loving mutual help. Now the Hymenoeus of our nuptial altars is Mammon, the flower of the bride's wreath must be jewelled, her vows must be uttered in silk and brocade, or not at all.

Indeed brides are "bought and sold by a legal process, which thinly disguises the elegant prostitution of the ceremony." Small wonder that "venal damsels pine in 'single blessedness,'" while those who should be young husbands "take their own despair away to resorts not mentioned to ears polite, and there, with their humble means, purchase those 'smiles of silver and kisses of gold' which are far less costly, and scarce less more unlike the true and noble love of natural and honest humanity."

This exculpation of the randy bachelors was not the normal burden of such homilies, and the editorialist entered more common ground by means of an exotic analogy, typifying the comparativist approach of the later century to moral ethnography. The common ground was the search for cures for the evil practices of society, and especially in this case of ambitious parents—mothers being worse than fathers—and vain daughters; the exotic analogy placed them against the "Coles," an aboriginal people from the hills of India.[40] These examples of the "noble savage," a "blackskinned, barbarous race," until recently had, "we regret to state, a weakness for human sacrifice; and if the crops were not good, it was their custom, till we interfered, to cut a little Cole up into small pieces and use him as a kind of super-phosphate." However—the basis of the comparison—as to marriage their notions are "as well-bred and particular as Belgravia itself," for they set a minimum price for "the hand of a Cole 'girl of the period,'" asking fifty bullocks as the equivalent of the West-end's £300 a year. Cole papas match their London equivalents, their first question of any suitor being: "How about the cattle?" There being no abatement of the demand and a shortage of young men with sufficient bullocks, "the result was, there as here, that the Cole young ladies never tied on the bundsari, or marriage dress, while the Cole young gentlemen went to dissolute and disgraceful ways."

Perhaps with an eye to such things as newspaper debates, the writer sketches the next stage for the Coles:

Things came to a frightful pass, and the elders held a Punchayet, or meeting, at which precisely the same evils that we are witnessing were deplored; but the Cole mammas protested that bullocks were better than decency and happiness, and the Cole priests quoted the holy books and immemorial custom; so nothing was done.

Or rather, nothing was done until the British Commissioner, "a man of influence and earnestness"—and a stand-in for the *Daily Telegraph*—"called another Punchayet, and spoke as we have spoken in the ears of the savage Belgravia." As a result of his insistence that their "foolish custom" meant that their children were "debauched instead of married," the Cole papas "put on the puggree of meditation," and

passed a new Act of Fashion, to the effect that five bullocks, instead of fifty, should form the marriage gift, the suitor in other respects being eligible; and ever since "all has gone merry as a marriage-bell" in those hills: morality is restored, weddings are numerous and happy, no worthy lover sighs his soul away for want of cattle, and the number of new Cole babies has made the tribe great in the eyes of neighbouring races; while agriculture is everywhere extended, and there is more wealth than ever, because, on those mountains, instead of cupidity with its ugly consequences of hope outraged and love travestied in profligacy, there is natural affection, with its faithful servant, industry.

The lesson is plain: "the same able and wise Indian Commissioner" should come "to teach the Coles of London, to bid them worship Bhowanee no longer, but prefer the real riches of manliness, honour, and true affection to this miserable question of the fifty bullocks, which, under the form of Three per Cents. and settlements, are exacted as the price of a wife!" With him might well come "a deputation of Cole parents, to talk a little decency and nature in the salons of West London." Those "naked missionaries of humanity" might well consider London the home of savagery were they told "the truth about our vile commerce in foreign women," shown "our streets at night," had translated for them "the horrible truths disclosed by our hospitals and dead-houses," had explained to them "the deadly ruin of honour and youth which comes of Belgravian restrictions," given "some dress-clothes, and [taken] to the balls and kettle-drums where the marriage-market is held," to stare at, "on one side the loveless daughters of the rich, on the other the victimised daughters of the poor—selfish worldliness on the one hand, brutal passion on the other, suppressing wedlock to create sin and shame." And again a leader concludes with a heartfelt if vague interrogative prayer for reform:

Can the sigh of these victims who are shipped for infamy, the drunken oath of the country girl whose purity has paid for Belgravian ideas, the horrible streets, the miserable gaiety, and the wasted youth of our city, arouse no echo of shame and no effort for reformation in the breasts of the cattle-claiming Coles of our own community?

While the rhetoric is different and the analogy novel, this leader can be seen as fellow to those earlier in *The Times*, attacking as it does Belgravian vices and follies. But it came after much stronger and bolder attacks in the preceding leaders, and most significantly, it was presented to another kind of audience. Though it was no more an incitement to epistolary zeal, perhaps to the surprise of the editors, it opened the gate to an unexampled flood of correspondence centring not on the great social evil, prostitution, but on the moot and broad issues relating to marriage, social status, and the cost of living.

Up to this point seven letters had appeared, a number appropriate to the previous history of the genre. But after two more on 27 June (a Saturday) and two more on the 30th, all under the title "Marriage or Celibacy?"—which was certainly an enticement—the crush began. In the twenty-five publishing days in July no fewer than 270 more appeared; and in addition to the three leading articles already mentioned, there was another on 20 July, and then on the 30th the one quoted to open chapter 1 above, which brought the series to an end. Most of the letters (like some of those cited from *The Times*) were far longer than any now printed in newspapers, some running to a full column of tiny type and very few as short as one paragraph: in transcription the series, including the leading articles, runs to almost 600 double-spaced pages, or close to 150,000 words.

What did they say, and what can we learn from them about middle-class beliefs and behaviour in the mid-Victorian era?

CHAPTER THREE

Marriage and Mores: Arguments and Practices

What gave potency to the question "Marriage or Celibacy?" in the *Daily Telegraph* was the widespread anxiety over the belief that young people could not prudently and respectably marry. To understand this anxiety and the discussion it prompted, one must ask what marriage meant to members of the middle class in mid-Victorian England. Their assumptions and ideals were not those of the late twentieth century, and they, of course, were not concerned to explain to an audience some century-and-a-half later what their assumptions and ideals were. Further, they were addressing one another through a new and rather odd medium with its own rhetoric.

Analysis not just of the content but also of the pattern of persuasion in the leading articles and letters in the series reveals a broad and detailed picture of the beliefs of the period. That is, the modes of argument used, the authorities appealed to, the kinds of evidence adduced, the assumptions about audience and about narrative, all are evidence of the writers' basic beliefs; but they also display attitudes towards changing, strengthening, or weakening the beliefs of others, and show the connections they see between beliefs and self-esteem and action.

The essential means of persuasion are common to all forms of communication, and are available to everyone through experience and to many through instruction. Each medium, however, presents special challenges and opportunities, and every speaker and writer meets them in particular ways. The series in the *Daily Telegraph* demonstrates both the common and the special. Letters had a long history, and leading articles, though much newer, amalgamated elements of several traditional genres; however, the situation was novel. A popular newspaper, delighting in an unexampled role, introduced a communication that was not only directed at a wide audience of a socio-economic class with no history of public effectiveness—with, it might be said, little public history of any kind—but also allowed and encouraged interactive communication between the newspaper and that audience and even among its individual members.

Though the focus of the "story" in the "Marriage or Celibacy?" series moves from prostitution, its causes and cures, to prudent marriage, and then to emigration, coherence is maintained through sustained general references to shared issues, concerns, and solutions, and specific references to other correspondents and the leading articles. However, the narrative line is not smooth for several reasons. First, except for the leader writers and the few correspondents who contributed more than one published letter, each performer gave a solo and then bowed out. Second, there is at least one day's gap between a letter and a response to it—and that gap is filled by letters that often respond to letters printed earlier.[1] Sometimes, especially for letters from the provinces, there was a further day's delay. So the published sequence distorts the actual debate; the responses are there, but they are slightly delayed and buffered. (For the contemporary reader some suspense was involved: would someone not refute A's nonsense? can no one answer C's excellent question?) Third, the sequence on each day is evidently random, and some odd juxtapositions lead to unintended effects. Nonetheless, the readers unquestionably saw the letters and leaders as forming a series, encouraged in this judgment by the *Telegraph*'s headings ("The Procuress" and then "Marriage or Celibacy?"), and by the leading articles of 26 June and 16 and 20 July, and especially by that of 30 July, which explicitly ruled closure. And finally, the patterns of request and response, questioning and debate, as well as the consonances of tone and proof, give the series unity. Indeed the assumptions and ideals show through both when correspondents' assertions are unchallenged and when they cause debate.

Full analysis of and comment on the content and rhetoric being impracticable, this discussion of beliefs about marriage begins with an extensive account of the most important early letters, to give a sense of what is settled and what moot, as a foundation for an examination of the images of marriage and celibacy. Then it will become easier to understand the analysis of the problems hindering early marriage and of their proposed solutions.

Five Exemplary Letters

The first letter to appear under the provocative heading "Marriage or Celibacy?" (Saturday, 27 June) is among the most significant in the structure of the series, in argument, and in content. This long and carefully argued letter is signed *Benedick*, the conventional term for a married man, taken from Shakespeare's *Much Ado about Nothing*.[2] His position and status in relation to the discussion being thus quickly fixed, he moves to controvert one of the main contentions in the leading article of 26 June, while further establishing his literary sophistication by a borrowing from *Macbeth*: "Sir—Your very eloquent article denouncing Belgravian ideas of marriage seems to me 'to o'erleap itself and fall on t'other side.'" Emphasis should fall not on the "outrageous expectations of parents" and "the inflated sumptuary ideas" of young ladies, but on an all important determinant of social contentment, the "just expectations" based on "ideas of comfort and refinement perfectly reasonable and perfectly right." *Benedick* wisely chooses not to challenge directly the fine commonplace of the beauty of romantic love, but to qualify it by saying, yes, marriages starting in "humble" homes can be "always beautiful with mutual love and the consciousness of difficulties bravely overcome," on condition that the lovers have courage, coupled "with industry and skill on the part of the man, and prudence and care on the part of the wife."

Benedick introduces direct irony when, having corrected unqualified assertion by citing general experience, he introduces a cultural comparison resting on an explicit scale of judgment:[3] in trying to understand the "superb faith in the future" that establishes minimum material demands for married life, one can compare with the Londoner the "savage" Red Indian and the Irish peasant, both of whom exhibit pure examples of this faith. The Indian needs not the Belgravian £300 a year,[4] or even £40 (on which "Pope's curate passed for rich"), or indeed even £5 which, with a house, "seems wealth enough for an Irish peasant 'establishment.'"

The Indian "marries on nothing a year, lives on herbs and water or on products of the chase, and brings up a large family to run about his wigwam like rabbits." Similarly the Irish peasant: he "marries early; but does he always support the family? No; he very energetically accomplishes the initiatory duties of head of a family, and his children are multiplied with speed." The language indicates clearly enough the judgment: *Benedick* is no advocate of primitive romanticism. But he turns from condemning improvidence (a strong enough basis in the circumstances) to a less common argument: the small comfort and competence found by the savage and the Irishman depend on exploitation of wives. The savage makes "his squaw [the term was strongly loaded] do more than half the work," while the wife of a poor Irishman "not only manages the whole household, but very often" supports her husband, her family, and herself "by her earnings as a wet-nurse." This generalization clinches the argument: the fault lies in early marriage by "men and women who cannot purchase even the meanest food for the children they bring into the world."

If "early marriages" and "courage in facing the world," and "trust in God" and "large families," be signs and symptoms of heroism, then the savages excel the Irish, the Irish the English, and a young man who weighs well his prospects and his means before he gets married is an arrant and contemptible coward in comparison with whom the Irishman is a hero and the savage a saint.

Interestingly, *Benedick* does not let drop what first appears as a contributing element in the argument, the injustice to married women involved in imprudent marriage—"the earlier the marriage the greater the burthen thrown on the wife." Mentioning again the "savage" and Irish demands on the wife, he returns home: "In English life the woman is forced to do all the house and family work—to be, in fact, an unpaid cook, housemaid, and nurse; or sometimes she helps by going out as governess, or by taking pupils at home." In this emphasis one can infer not only his own convictions but probably also, if unconsciously, his awareness that the *Telegraph* numbered among its audience—and hence his—a large number of married women (as the future correspondence on this issue showed).

It is worth noting that *Benedick* does not see any need to argue about the wrongness of these situations: the assertion (with the addition of slight irony) for him is enough for condemnation. Unlike some others, including some people's stereotyped male of the period, he sees nothing "natural" or "right" in any of these practices, all of which result from imprudence.

The lesson is, however, too general, and *Benedick* wishes to bring it home to those who (in the present circumstances) can do most to apply it—young men. Rather than citing the experience of "a friend" or relying on literary illustrations, he advances sympathetically a case he can "fancy," that of "a young man of the professional class." He meets "in society or at her own home a well-bred, cultivated, refined, thoughtful girl, who reads books, sees something of London life, plays and sings, dresses with taste and some pleasant variety, and is in every way a fresh, healthy, honest English girl of his own class." Falling in love, he wishes not occasional but constant companionship for life, consecrated by "honourable and holy union." While all who have "enjoyed the full, noble, perfect happiness of a home" will support such an aspiration, it is "very natural," says *Benedick* (and he might have hesitated over the term and substituted a better), "for the young man to think thoughtfully and tenderly of the future of the girl he loves, and of his possible, not to say probable children." Not a giving in to "luxurious exigence" but a realistic and humane assessment[5] will lead him to desire a neat and decent home in a healthy situation, devoid of squalor. And more, for these are the mere bases of the life he should expect:

desiring that his wife should still be his companion and not merely his cook, he may not unnaturally desire that she should still retain leisure to read books, to practise music, sometimes to accompany him to places of amusement—else their married life will be lower than their celibate condition.

The other entailment of abandoned celibacy should not be ignored by the amorous young professional:

if children come—and we might almost as well omit the "if"—it is not unnatural or disgraceful that he should wish to remove them, say, once a year to the seaside, out of hot, dusty town, that some roses may bloom, even though only for a month, on dear little cheeks, pale and dry in the London air.

The needs and the problem are neatly brought together into assertion: "Now, all these things—a neat house, a healthy suburb, some household service, a holiday trip—are all questions of money."

Benedick's ethical appeal is strengthened by his flexibility (shown by many others in the series) about the actual amount needed for prudent marriage, which, he says, varies "with every class, almost with every home," and by his expressed attachment to "plain living and high thinking." Using the topos of comparison (and citing within it one of its prime nineteenth-century practitioners), *Benedick* lines up on what is clearly the old English side: "a supper of bread and cheese and ale, with wit and good humour and fellowship, is better than rare titbits, unlimited champagne, and a 'cold silly female fool,' as Macaulay says, to sit by your side and to spoil your enjoyment." However, much as the old English folk may put aside such non-essentials as "opera boxes, jewels, a house in the fashionable quarters, new dresses every month, cigars, rich wines, dinner parties, balls, continental trips, etc.," there remain the "habits that civilized men and women cannot lay aside without losing self-respect," many of which may be summed up in one word, "cleanliness": "cleanliness in your house, your servants, your own clothes, yourself." He means not spiritual or moral, but simply physical (he forbears saying that it is next to godliness, but the hint is there); and the point is local and pressing, relevant to the *Telegraph*'s main audience. In "smoky, grimy London" cleanliness is "dearer and more difficult than in any part of the world," what with the high cost of water, soap, and wages for laundry. Mere assertion suffices for the comparison with the relative ease of achieving neatness, sweetness, and cleanliness in a country house, and *Benedick* in another literary allusion moves to refute sentimental nonsense about the town poor: an anonymous writer in Dickens's *All the Year Round* is praised for satirizing "the common cant phrase, 'They were poor, but their house was spotlessly, scrupulously clean.'" Assertion appeals to simple observation: a "really poor person in London finds it next to impossible to be clean."

Benedick's illustration, however, is not that of a truly poor person, for he refers to the enormous cost of laundry of a London family with clean habits: the specific items mentioned are "table-cloths, body linen, sheets, napkins, etc.," which were not the preoccupations or possessions of the poor. Similarly, he refers to cleanliness as a question of "so much wages and so much food, costing so much money, to a servant whose sole mission is to keep it clean, and who works very hard to that end." Here (again preserving the level of discussion) he bolsters his case with a personal anecdote (enriched with yet another literary allusion and with self-denigrating humour apt to the allusion); in this anecdote, appropriately for *Benedick*'s views generally, the obviously rational view is that of a married woman experienced in reality:

In that clear and logical and convincing way with which men discuss home affairs, I recently suggested to my wife that we should keep fewer servants, and she replied that if I did not mind the rooms being rather dusty, and the cook looking a little dark about the nose when she went to open the door, she saw no difficulty in the way. "This," as Artemus Ward said, "was sarcastical," and I immediately discovered something very interesting in the morning paper, and have not since resumed the conversation.[6]

Benedick's penultimate paragraph summarizes so much of the case for others as well as for himself (and wife), and so clearly lays out the lines of rational expectation for the upper income range of middle-class Londoners that it merits full quotation:

If a brave thoughtful girl says to a man—either using English or the language of the eyes, "Rather than live here in Belgravia or Bayswater without you, I would cheerfully dwell with you in Dalston, Peckham, Camberwell, Hackney, or Hammersmith—anywhere, however far from Rottenrow. I could be content with a little room twelve feet square for parlour and drawing room. I would be satisfied with one servant and help myself, and nurse my own baby, and wheel my own perambulator. I would prefer all this with you, dear, to come home to me every evening, and read to me, or talk to me, or walk with me, than all my present surroundings without you;" then, I say, she is a fine honest English girl. Out of such willingness there do grow up happy, beautiful households, though, of course, such risks, deliberately run, sometimes lead to hardships terrible, painful, and severe. A husband sees a wife pining for changes of air; and through poverty cannot afford to give it to her. A wife sees her husband sinking from overwork—an overtaxed brain or body—and he cannot rest for even three months, since rest means loss of salary, perhaps of situation. A man sees a delicate child actually die for want of the purer air he cannot purchase. These things bring throbs of anguish, for which there is almost no consolation; and, when a man and a woman "face the world" with a small income, they run these risks. Income does not always increase as rapidly as children, and a man may be a loving, affectionate husband, and yet not clever enough, or lucky enough, or sufficiently befriended to earn the larger income required for his larger family.

Benedick neatly rounds his argument by asking (on behalf of his audience) what his answer is to the problems so fully described, and rejecting obvious options:

What is the upshot? Do I defend resolute celibacy? No. Do I inveigh against love and early marriage and unlimited increase of babies? No. Do I advocate delayed unions in "society," and the dire prostitution in the streets? No.

His answer, embodying the substance of his narrative, is measured, thoughtful, passionate and compassionate, but above all prudently hopeful—and it is designed to persuade just those who are praised in his account. He holds "that some of the best and brightest men—the most really thoughtful and considerate for women—the men who look on a wife as an elevating companion and not a drudge—do hesitate and pause, and think and calculate, and do ascertain the exact sum with which decency, cleanliness, health, and some security for the future, can be obtained for a married home."

That sentence would do as peroration, but *Benedick* closes with a suc- cinct reference to another weakness in the *Telegraph*'s argument that controverts, without mentioning, *A Barrister*'s view of the uncontrollable sexual urges of young men:

Nor is it necessary that the man who deliberates is lost. You seem to think that there is no alternative between the Haymarket and the conjugal home; but surely chastity and disdain of profligacy are possible virtues to English youth. Surely there are bachelors in London who find in books, or in the companionship of cultivated men, or the society of ladies, resources without sighing for a wife, or, as the French revolutionists say, "descending into the streets."

This adieu, with two wittily turned allusions, is designed to leave the reader admiring *Benedick* and his well-outlined and commonsensical opinions, though perhaps the final joke (the only one concerning prostitution in the whole series) may have detracted slightly from the seriousness of the advice.

The next letters presenting commanding positions in provocative manner appeared on Tuesday, 30 June, and energized the series. The first, signed *Materfamilias*, initiated the accounts by women of their experience and views; the second, signed *Solon Smiff, M.E.*, embeds in the most charming fable of the series one of its hardest lessons.

Materfamilias opens with a comment intriguing in its implications and motive: "Your article on early marriage has aroused considerable interest, if one may judge by the casual conversations one hears on the subject." Did people of her acquaintance generally have "casual conversations" about leading articles in newspapers? When and where would she hear or overhear such remarks? Or is the observation intended to flatter the *Telegraph* into thinking that its readers were typically so engaged—or specially so in this case? Alternatively, is this comment a slight signal that the letter emanated from the ever-ready pens of the staff, so commonly engaged in other literary activities, including fiction? Whatever the case, the views were sufficiently "realistic" to engage the readers either directly in letters referring to and answering *Materfamilias*, or (on the more cynical view) by implication in the canny minds of the editors who used this letter to drive the series.

Materfamilias justifies her intrusion by the popularity of the topic, but more tellingly by asserting that she has "certain facts within her own knowledge" (this may serve as the badge of empiric guarantee) and believes that "a woman's view of the matter may be worth some consideration." Her first argument, which situates her experience at the crucial income level, is a dismissal of ignorant opinion: "It is very easy for those who have not tried, to talk about the pleasures of a marriage on £INNDSWA50 or less per annum."

To heighten her ethical appeal, *Materfamilias* uses easy colloqualisms and domestic dialogue in setting a scene:

When I married on £150 a year I said to myself and husband: "I don't want expensive silk dresses now, and we can't afford them; I shall be content with clean print and muslin." Well, I need not repeat all the pretty things that were then said about my appearance. I did want to be a help meet, economical and yet pleasant-looking.

She cleverly implies the plot by appealing to the good judgment of her readers: "London housekeepers may guess how it turned out." And then she turns to a narrative that, though given in generalized time, embeds telling details:

The first year went on without special troubles. Then came illness, so long and expensive as to throw us back and into debt. During the first year I had managed to carry out my plan of wearing washable light dresses, at what cost may be calculated. I ought to have had two dresses per week regularly; latterly I contrived to make one serve indifferently. The price of washing—I have my laundress's bills near me—was one shilling for a print dress, and one and sixpence for a muslin, fourpence for a white petticoat, and twopence for collar and cuffs. I soon found that the bits of bright ribbon which set off a plain dress had to be dispensed with; they cost money which we could not afford.

A shift into "dark" and necessarily "dowdy" materials was mandated. They sacrificed other goods, including all pleasures "that could not be obtained in each other's society or in walks," such as magazines, theatres, and riding, in order to live in "a decent house (only six rooms)."

Materfamilias then employs a classic device much admired in the nineteenth century, the invented but plausible *refutatio*, with a nicely turned introductory claim to reasonableness: "Now I am prepared to hear some ardent advocate of early marriage say, 'You might have done your washing at home and then it would not be so expensive.'" Her dismissive reply (an emotional appeal on two levels) is immediate: "I had not strength to do it, and one trial of a servant who undertook all the work was sufficient for my husband's peace of mind." This device is then repeated, again with dramatic voices:

"You might have paid less than £33 per year house rent." Yes, and sacrificed our garden and our health by living amongst crowded squalor or in shabby genteel lodgings. "Your husband might see the magazines and papers at his Club or the Institute." True, but it did not enter into his scheme of matrimonial felicity to leave his wife alone in the evenings after an absence the whole day. "Theatres are not good for any one." We differ, and should often have enjoyed a visit if we had felt we could afford the pit even. Before we married we had both gone often—both enjoyed it—but then he had his £150 a year to himself, and I had some £80 also, which I lost on my marriage, as my husband considered it a wife's province to stay at home. To those who say, "You ought to have been able to walk to the parks," I reply, "Yes, I'm very sorry I couldn't, but I did not measure out my own strength, nor did my previous sedentary occupation greatly assist me in forming the good constitutional habits it is so easy to talk of, but so difficult to acquire."

A sad story—but *Materfamilias* is clever enough not to overstate its difficulties: others, she is quite willing to admit, have been much worse off, suffering from "long illnesses, large families, and mutual disagreements." But their history should still be enough to persuade those contemplating marriage to wait for a sufficient income and secure savings of some £200. She offers a rational calculation: if both can live on £150 a year, one can live on £100, and save the sum that would forfend "debt and discomfort."

Her peroration is nicely shaped, moving from summary statement through considered outcomes and logical explanation to reiteration of the moral in colloquial form. Why were they not so wise? Her husband, knowing that she "was never strong," thought she should not give up her salary, but remain "in her office for a year or two after marriage," and so decided they should

"trust to God, our love, and his manliness." Well, we did; and we had our trouble, and trial. Whether it would have stood the test of a lifetime of such straitened means is hard to say: happily it is now a thing of the past. Understand, though, that the change in my circumstances is not the reward of his perseverance, self-denial, and industry. No, he might have had his £150 a year still, and perhaps all his life; but there was not much chance of promotion, or increase of salary, and it is because I know how unhappy the small cares of small means makes one, and how seldom any change for the better takes place, that I counsel people to "bide a wee."

The second letter published on 30 June, from *Solon Smiff, M.E.*, has such charm that it should be a model. His exordium opens with a standard ploy, the pithy statement of a vexing question ("How little can a man venture to marry upon?"), followed by personal validation (he, one who is "anxious to marry," has "carefully considered" the question for "the past ten years"), and a general answer ("in a highly-civilised State"[7] a "happy marriage" is impossible except for the rich). The *topos* of definition controls the argumentative path by restricting "happy marriage" to one "with comfort," "free from the mean dread of absolute want," while *pathos* demands sympathy for those excluded, "the ordinary daily workers—such as the great body of the community consists of." To support this view he cites (appealing to reason) the authority of John Stuart Mill's *Principles of Political Economy*, which condemns early marriages and large families as being as harmful as excessive drunkenness. The reference to Mill is not casual (indeed it recurs in the correspondence), but highly topical. The summer of 1868 saw the run-up to a general election (held in November), in which Mill, who had been elected for Westminster in 1865, was the focus of much attention, which led to increased sales of his works.[8] Those on the Radical side of the Liberal party looked to Mill as an unchallenged authority on matters economic and philosophical; others (including the majority of voters in the borough, who rejected him in the election) were anxious to diminish his authority by calling to public attention controversial passages in his writings.[9] The particular doctrine referred to by *Solon Smiff* (himself a "Smiff," one of the "ordinary daily workers," but also "Solon," wise and potentially a law-giver for the ordinary?) was much cited in political discussions of Mill's views, especially by the Tories, who wished to call attention to his neo-Malthusianism. The specific reference is to a footnote in Mill's *Principles*: "Little improvement can be expected in morality until the producing large families is regarded with the same feelings as drunkenness, or any other physical excess."[10] (It should be noted that, when under the mad spell of love, *Smiff* says he read the *Principles* "like a semi-drunken man.") Such passages abundantly demonstrate Mill's condemnation of improvident marriages (given that he could not openly, even with circumspection, advocate preventive measures of birth control), and *Smiff* is quite right to cite him as a rational advocate of postponed marriage.

In confirming elaboration of Mill's views, *Smiff* like *Materfamilias* employs debate in dialogue. The scene, reminiscent of Scrooge's refusal to give to charities, unashamedly elevates hard-headedness above soft-heartedness; there is more than a hint of irony, but throwing the onus on Mill and displaying the obvious advantage to the prudent prevents a full and easy condemnation of *Smiff*. (There is also an implication that, having heard all that sentimental nonsense before, he and his kind should ignore criticism from the foolish.)

He then moves from explained attitude into supportive personal history, admitting that at age thirty-two his annual earnings are at the "magic sum" for marriage of £300, but noting that he had reached that level only through stinting during his education and apprenticeship, and as a professional having constant calls for "instruments, lectures, professional studies, institute fees, etc., etc., etc.," as well as the need to be respectable, symbolized by him in "a decent coat." No *pathos* here, but it quickly emerges through the adumbrated consideration of marriage. Only men of the "neutral gender," to which he does not belong, could reach his age without longing for a "pleasant or romantic attachment," and "a little home or place of his own." So he is not without normal passion—but (looking to the *topoi* of comparison and cause-and-effect) *Smiff* is "compelled to admit that Mill is right" when he considers his friends Smaff and Smeff, whose imprudent marriages led to suffering and anguish not just for themselves but for their innocent loved ones. (He neatly cites the *Telegraph* as authority here, saying: "Your own columns are daily full of appeals to the benevolent.") The inference is so obvious as to override its unhappy frigidity: "I look around me at thirty-two, and reason coldly approves what I have done."

The apparent coldness, however, hides "an aching heart." *Smiff* is driven into dramatic narrative (the intense emotion leading him into the present tense), centring on his *beau idéal*, whose transcendent holograph image blends with, blurs, and then blots out Mill's stern admonitory visage. Here indeed is the literary zenith of the series.

Sir, it was my misfortune eleven months ago, to meet at the house of a most intimate friend, a lovely girl, and something told me that my fate, either for happiness or bitter disappointment, had come at last. I was a privileged friend, and from time to time was thrown into her society, which I frankly confess I did not avoid as I should have done. I suppose every man has his beau ideal, and here I found mine: a lady born and bred; not rich, but highly cultivated, intelligent, and, to my eyes, the loveliest creature on the earth. John Stuart Mill's philosophy begins to fail me. I make frantic efforts to steady myself by the light of cool dispassionate reason. I never go out without his Principles of Political Economy in my pocket.[11] I cling to them like a drowning man at a straw. His book is always open on my office table; but I read it like a semi-drunken man. I am forced to admit that I am fairly and deeply in love, not with short lived feeling of early youth, but with the deep reverence and strong passion of a fully grown man. I cannot keep away. John Stuart Mill and his philosophy sternly forbid me as a man of honour to propose. Last week I had the supreme happiness of spending a few hours in her society, and the utter misery of seeing an undeniably neat and well dressed fellow paying her too much attention. If I were to propose upon my chances, I venture to hope, though she might not say yes, she would not say no. What shall I do? She and her friends have more confidence in my future than I have myself. Her face and figure haunt me. I see them among drawings of cogwheels, sawframes, and boilers; she is everywhere. I sit down with a dogged determination coolly and dispassionately to think it out, and I take down John Stuart Mill and begin to read. I read on, until I see the well-known features of the honourable member for Westminster before me. I hear his grave voice, addressing me personally. He says, "Solon, Solon, avoid it. Such as she are not for you. Her life should be bright and happy and free from care. You have your own way to make, it is as much as you can do to keep yourself. Leave her in peace, like an honourable fellow, to your well-dressed and well-to-do friend, she is not for you." But gradually the features of the honourable member for Westminster change. His nose shortens until it is a fair delicate Roman nose. His head becomes covered, by a wig that would surprise the House [of Commons]. It is a wig of fair flowing hair, taken off the brows, done up into a "chignon," with a "horse tail" which floats over his shoulders. His eyes change until they become of a dark violet hue. The whiskers disappear and the face fills out until it is a lovely face, blooming and fair, with a delicate colour, which never needs protection from the sun, much less any of Madame Rachel's protection, and the lilies and the roses are ever fighting for the mastery.

The necktie and coat of the honourable member vanish, and a lovely throat and heaving bust, protected by a dainty white dress edged with blue, appear. The voice, so well known in Westminster, changes to a soft and rich contralto, which thrills through one whenever it is heard. Seated in my dingy office, my head sinks upon my hands, and the vision and preaching of the honourable member for Westminster are changed into a glorious day dream, in which every dear look and action and thought, of a lovely girl of twenty-two, are recalled with fond affection. How long it lasts, I do not know. It could not have lasted too long. It is broken at length. A strange step is heard ascending. I awake, and push the hateful Economy away, exclaiming, "O, glorious Lucrece! If this be but a client of the very smallest type; if he brings but the very remotest chance of a job to give me warrant, I will end this wretched struggle between passion and reason as soon as the interview is over; I will hasten to thy feet, oh, darling girl, and learn whether I may venture to hope or must undergo a period of wretched and painful disappointment, which, at any rate, is better than anxious suspense."

The step is, however, that of a creditor's agent, who interjects:

"Mr. Hodl's compliments, Sir, and says your name and assistant's have been wrote up fourteen months, and you have always been away or out of town, and he wants that little account for painting of it up settled to-day particular." I turn around, and from my fast diminishing stock pay the account, and sit me down again to John Stuart Mill and his hateful political economy with a sigh.

This destruction of the dream-state by a representative of real life (a man from Porlock whose only interest in Kubla Khan's pleasure dome lies in the cost of its materials, opium aside), leaves *Smiff* the single option of closing his pathetic appeal in the diminuendo of "a sigh."

The first letter on the next day, 1 July, was another signal performance, both in its great length and its rhetoric. Signed *Erastes* (Greek for Lover), it further formalized the series as debate by fixing the two opposed positions and attacking in detail the argument of *Benedick*.[12] (*Erastes* almost certainly would have made a foray against *Solon Smiff* had *Smiff*'s letter appeared earlier.) The author strains for literary distinction, building his attack on an elaborately burlesqued jousting analogy, and decorating his weapons with as many jewelled allusions as *Benedick* had dropped in his more sober excursion.

The tournament image, with its challenge and weaponry—not rare in the period[13]—opens the letter with an unconventional version of the conventional nod to the *Telegraph*'s role: "I throw a glove down against your thoughtful and able correspondent, *Benedick*, and, with your permission as master of these lists, I mean to splinter an argumentative spear upon his shield." In good debating style, he summarizes *Benedick*'s argument, liberally if tendentiously quoting from it, and attempts to associate himself with the *Telegraph*'s "carefully" expressed protests "against the disastrous matrimonial views that prevail in the upper and middle classes."

Recalling both his controlling image and a piece of advice from Cicero, *Erastes* says he has "challenged this doughty champion of the celibates" because he presents this "huge mischief . . . in the fairest and most plausible manner." Not for him are the unworthy proponents of early marriage, "the sensual, the selfish, the inconsiderate, and the stupid," who, he wishes devoutly, "with the help of Mr. Darwin and a dear loaf," could be rooted "out of the 'struggle for existence' altogether." No, he is considering only "*Benedick*'s own category of worthy swains," in accusing him of disguising "the timid quaver of Cowardice, and the miserable maxims of Fashion" as "the voices of Virtue and

Wisdom." *Benedick*, in setting up a "marriage standard in money," looking for "exact sums," is in fact merely wrapping in the prudential language of "sound sense and social benefit" the false doctrine inveighed against by the *Telegraph*. No exactitude is possible for *Erastes*, an advocate of the circumstantial view. But the beneficial circumstance has a history: he, like others, makes the nostaglic appeal to the wisdom of our ancestors which, despite Benthamite and Dickensian satire, retained its power: "When a man married, as our grandfathers did, upon the plain ground that he loved a lass, and that she loved him, and that he had got a brain and two hands, and all the world to work in, besides such common substance as they could muster, that was ground that could not be mistaken." Now (circumstances and nostalgia once more propel judgmental comparison), "a bride is bought like an odalisque, with an 'establishment;' and wedded life, forsooth, must be guaranteed, like an Indian Irrigation Enterprise, or the lover dares not, and the mistress will not, wed." Sounding like a minor William Blake in his objection to arithmetic and geometric approaches to affection, *Erastes* is enough a man of his pragmatic time to realise the force of a reference to the imaginative but expensive irrigation schemes in India that had for a couple of decades attracted criticism as well as admiration.

But the jesting jousting calls for a more strenuous attack than this "mere caracoling" on the "well mounted" *Benedick*, who "wields a sharp lance when he paints . . . the sad results of passionate and imprudent matches." *Erastes* "must ride straighter and strike fuller to unhorse" him. Away with cowardice: *Erastes*, with Lady Macbeth though in a less sanguinary cause, will "cut the root" of "the 'pale fears and half-nerved manhood' which 'lets the dare not wait upon the would,'"[14] and will enlist "enterprise and courage on the part of a young man, love of worth and virtue before money on the part of parents; and natural affection and brave devotion and simplicity on the part of our English maidens." Such, says he, is the tone of the pageboy in love with "Kate the Queen" in Browning's *Pippa Passes*, who sings (in Pippa's voice):

Why, what costs it to be styled a donor?
Only an earth to cleave, a sea to part.[15]

A "more beautiful and poetic line for a bride than a Broadwood piano can give," says *Erastes*, who strikes the *ad populum* romantic chord in adding:

... I care not if I seem extravagant and transcendental to the "little lovers that whine and cry," when I affirm that the spirit is a more splendid wedding present to lay on the white hand of a lady than all the bracelets of Bond-street, and any amount of the "sweet simplicity of the Three per Cents."

It appears, however, that "Fortune" will surely add true gold to the gingerbread of those whose seemingly fond folly is actually invested with "gallant courage and real manly love." Indeed that is a surer route, for "are securities infallible? do riches never take flight? is cent. per cent. half so safe or good a profit as manhood and brave human love?"

So the wager on love as against prudence is better motivated and a safer bet. And more. *Erastes* uses strong language in direct address to indicate that the results of losing the bet are not so horrible as those like *Benedick* portray them—and indeed more to be cherished than winning the prudent wager: "Great God, Sir! is poverty the worst evil of our life? is the catastrophe of a lady reduced to cold mutton and stocking-darning the one tremendous catastrophe of lady-hood?" Though only "a knave and a fool" would allow a lady to "suffer penury" any longer than necessary, "short commons and a brief slant of ill-luck" are much less to be pitied than "the loveless dames of Westbournia and Tyburnia,"[16] and *a fortiori* "the smug lover, whose Providence is his banker's balance."

Erastes is now ready to assault his adversary's "great argument," but in his own form of battle, as he revives the comparison of the savage and the Irishman with the Belgravian. *Erastes* notes that *Benedick*'s own argument would commit him to say that

the Irishman is wiser than the Belgravian, and the savage wiser than the Irishman. . . . I drive my lance full against his visor, and I say, "No doubt they are!" His Red Indian does exactly what his prudent Briton ought to do. The Red Indian marries upon the capital of his right and left hand, and of the buffaloes upon the prairie; the Briton has his brain and the wide world to encourage him to be even less a sneak and a white-livered lover than the Ojibbeway.

Not content with mere assertion of the (to him) obvious, *Erastes* brings forth a consequentialist argument, which embeds again the negative labelling of his opponents' views as abstract, arithmetical, and geometrical,[17] and calls on his readers (through the mediating editorial "Sir") to consider "what pitiful purblind vices spring out of this youthful avarice, parental sordidness, and feminine falseness to a woman's greatest instinct. Sick with arithmetical love-making, we sicken also with geographical impotency."

Here *Erastes*, recommending emigration, takes a step on the argumentative road that runs though the second half of the series, though he retains his lofty perspective and diction and stays away from vulgar statistics:

We can't see beyond the horizon of our street; we despond because next door, or next door but one, there is no ready-made home for us and the woman we love. The Roman lost the world for love: this miserable breed of British lovers in ring-ties and Bond-street pantaloons can't win a corner of it for the same splendid motive. Is there no other habitable region besides Belgravia? If London is full, are there no more cities in the world? Why, in the same issue of your journal which contained *Benedick*'s mournful conclusions that a London young gentleman must take "to books and cultivated men" in despair of marrying, for fear his wife and children should lack food and fresh air, in the very same issue was a notice from the Toronto Government of land to be given away in hundred-acre lots for nothing. No lack of food upon the free and grand prairies, where the grain grows so thick for year after year without mending the soil that they light the kitchen fires with maize and feed the pigs with russet apples?

Of course the "delicate damsels and hesitating swains" will cry, "Pigs and kitchen-fires, indeed!" and, hearing them, *Benedick* will no longer fear *Erastes*. But this is the essential point and the "ugly secret of this cowardly and demoralising celibacy": unlike his opponents, *Erastes* has goals—spiritual and religious ones—beyond the material limits of "genteel life." The "modern" lovers

look upon marriage as a contract for this world only, and upon children, not as the gift of God—awful and rich, solemn and dear, beyond all other gifts—but as rather undesirable, though not evitable, appanages of the married state, which bring their charm, perhaps, but also their doctor's and butcher's bills. If life and love, I reply, seem not more majestic and eternal than this, then we must go on seeking the "exact sum" at which it is rational to trust in God, in contempt of the beautiful message He has sent us about Belgravia and other human localities in connection with "sparrows." Having so poor a faith, it will have little hope and less charity, and the wretched commodity which it calls "love" will be no more like the glorious nepenthe of life which brave lips drink than doctored drams are like the delicate Nile-water.[18] It will never see why Christ began His work at the Cana marriage-feast, nor what divine spirit it is which ever turns the water of humanity into wine. It will count poverty, ungentility, and plainness of fare the great evils of the earth, when a loveless, an useless, and an unthankful life are the real sorrows.

Continuing this line of argument, *Erastes* is in a strong enough position to admit that nonetheless he, like *Benedick*, values "the graces of human intercourse," and is not advocating the emigration of "damsels of gentle birth into the wilds of the Red River."[19] Indeed he uses as slogans passages from Keats and Tennyson, rejecting "Love in a hut, with water and a crust,"[20] and placing the "grey barbarian lower than the Christian child."[21]

This *concessio* is only a preparation for the concluding blow, however, as *Erastes* quietly smuggles in a moot question that lies behind the debate, the cause-and-effect relation between the insistence on gentility and the great social evil. Admitting the value of civilization, we should still "cry back a little if we can," perhaps not to savageness, but to revered classical standards:

If opera-boxes and ormulu tables make marriage difficult, and the tender touch of children's hands a thing to shun, let us, in God's name, go and hear the birds for nothing, and sit on the ground to dinner as *Benedick*'s happier savages do. But if he is right and I am wrong, then what a fool Augustus was to tax the bachelors,[22] and what a much better thing it is to have sixty thousand women sold to the trade of the pavement, than here and there a lady condemned to starve upon joints of meat and white bread, and perhaps—distressing thought!—to carry the water she washes in, which the Greek princesses of Homer did every day of their lives.

Very different from *Erastes'* convoluted equestrian ride was the direct pedestrian walk of the other letter that appeared with it on 1 July. Signed *An English Girl*, it began with a validating statement (she has read all the letters) and an implied authority. The implication is more subtle and probably not consciously made by her or by the many others who in this series (and indeed throughout the history of communications) assume the same authority: my experience, we commonly say, is important (a) in its typicality; that is, though I am but one, generalization is legitimate because others are like me in this respect.[23] But also it is important (b) because it has certain leading features that bring out its message without distorting its typicality. The pseudonym itself signifies this authority: *An English Girl* can stand for all (True) English Girls while still being singular (if indefinite).

Why would *An English Girl* write to the *Daily Telegraph*, however? Most did (would) not; but this one felt an obligation to counter the potentially harmful doctrine advanced by *Materfamilias*:[24] "I write" in urgency, she says, just having "finished my breakfast" (the traditional time for domestic correspondence). Authenticating personal detail introduces her case, which has to do with the legitimate costs of clothing and washing:

First I will tell you that I am at present unmarried, but for all that, I have been housekeeper to mother and myself for nearly three years, and my salary is £80 a year;[25] not a farthing more from any source. With that we live comfortably, dress respectably (and I am sure I never look dowdy), nor mother either, though, like a dear, sensible old lady, she has always dressed in black since her widowhood, which makes it less expensive for her dress. I wear muslins and prints, though not expensive ones, and I must say that *Materfamilias* had a very expensive laundress. I get my muslin done very nicely for 8d and print dress for 6d. Body and household linen is washed at home, and the folding, etc., of that and washing and ironing my collars I do, and hope to have someone else's to do before very long; that is, if he will only let me do them.

This coy claim to further typicality is not immediately dwelt on, as *An English Girl* wishes to counter the assured statements of *Materfamilias* about the prohibitive cost of the pleasures of town life: she thinks it "ridiculous" to say that the parks are "as good as closed" because they cannot afford to ride; she *walks* in them as a matter of pleasant habit. What of the cost of reading? Each week she pays 6d for the *Daily Telegraph* (of course) and 4d for the *Family Herald*, and each month 4 1/2d for "Scott's novels": a total of £1 14s 10d a year. Though she is often told that this sum is extravagant for one of her "limited means," she (a fine representative of the *Telegraph*'s readership) "would as soon go without [her] breakfast of a morning as without the paper." And she is able to go to the theatre a few times in the year, but she admits, "of course, then I do not pay, but the one who does is going to be my husband."

Can he afford such expenses—and the further ones of marriage? *An English Girl* thinks so. Her fiancé's salary is only £130 a year, but that, in her opinion, will make "us very comfortably off," though "Of course we shall have trouble; who does not, married or single?" Her conclusion is of the cheerful sort that much disturbed those who saw hope as mere wish:[26]

while he has health and strength I shall have only my house to look to, and study him, but if it should happen that he should be ill and not able to work, why, then I would teach again and do my best, and think it greater happiness to share any life with him as his wife than never to have had that joy.

At this early point in the series, the main lines of debate have been set by the four kinds of voice, those of the married woman and man and the single man and woman. The first question—what causes prostitution?—is moving below the level of direct statement, while the continuing issue—at what level of income can English (especially London) couples marry?—is coming into clear focus. Also, the form of debate has been sketched in: a word of gratitude to the convenor (the *Daily Telegraph*), a quick assertion of authority through attention to the topic (correspondents claim to have read all the letters), and an attack on or confirmation of the views of an earlier correspondent or of a leading article. And the principal kinds of admissible evidence have been sketched: types of expenditure and costs, the distinction between the necessaries and the graces of life, group and individual habits, personal experience, authorities (including literary and contemporary),[27] and (as an unstated but an overriding assumption) rational inference.

That summary does no credit to the individual voices, but allows generalizations about those that cannot be given detailed attention in the following analysis, which pauses in its rush only to present moments of special interest.

To most tastes, the liveliest aspects of the correspondence are likely to be the vignettes of married and single life, containing portraits of the ideal and the actual. These often amount to genre paintings, with moral tags attached for the impercipient. Though the subjects are mixed, a convenient division may be made into accounts of married life, comparisons of married and single life, descriptions of single women, and descriptions of single men. Because the debate is between marriage and celibacy, the comments and analysis of each merit treatment in separate sections.

Married Life

Let us begin with a move from shade to sun. *Charlie's Wife* (clearly a relative creature) puts her own case because *Materfamilias* had avowed the value of a woman's view. Tracing her history of fifteen years' marriage in "a large manufacturing town" to "a professor of music," with an income fluctuating around £120 a year, she concedes their three serious mistakes, keeping a servant because she had not been taught to do housework, getting into debt as the babies arrived, and going into business without capital or business habits. Then reform: they sold the business at a loss, paid off the most pressing debts, and let the servants go. Charlie (presumably taking up his profession again) has been earning £250 for three years and, keeping household expenses to half that, they have paid all their debts with the remainder. Their curse was not early marriage, but ignorance and pride in keeping up appearances, causing them great suffering and internal struggle. But "pop in just now," she colloquially invites the reader, and see the reformed home:

My dear husband is lolling in an easy chair, reading The Daily Telegraph—this is his vacation, so he can take all things very easy—my three boys have gone off to their separate cricket-clubs—and fine little fellows they are, too, happy as larks, although they do not live on the fat of the land. One of my little daughters, aged eleven years, is seated at the piano, having finished her share of work for the day; another is playing with some pet white mice in the garden (she washed all the stockings, kerchiefs, and serviettes[28] for me this morning, for this was wash morning); and my baby girl is asleep in her bed. No, I am no slave or drudge. I am the happiest wife and mother in England.

Typical also of those in the sun is *G.L.M.* (a married woman), who celebrates "the pleasure to be found in intellectual, social companion-ship between husband and wife when both are well or even tolerably well educated." (The implicit corollary is not spelled out.) Home evening pleasures are inexpensive and companionable: "new books to read—most women like to be read to while they sew; gardening in summer; chess or draughts, backgammon or cribbage in winter; music, if both or either are musical, at all seasons." Her homily runs in a homely vein that is also typical of such accounts:

Is it not better to wear out than to rust out? Is not one day's hard work begun, continued, and ended for the one dear sake more full of satisfaction, if rightly viewed, than a dozen days spent in luxurious idleness? Once teach our young people that labour is honourable,[29] and you will have done a good work.

Other maxims follow, such as:

A selfish, mean, or inconsiderate man ought not to marry. . . . [It] is every man's duty to tell the woman he is going to marry what his income is, that they may consult together, and see if they can live on it, and, if possible, save . . . towards "a rainy day," for debt must be a heavy burden.

A less sophisticated ally from Brighton is *A Happy Nine Years' Wife*, whose annoyance with *Solon Smiff* erupts in colloquial style and detail: his letter, she says, "put me into such a temper that, if I had not purposed devoting the afternoon to the superintending of my annual stock of preserves, I should certainly have written this letter yesterday.... God bless the man! and give him strength to adhere to his 'Principles of Economy,' and let the 'lovely girl' he mentions escape the misery a marriage with such a man would inevitably result in." And she herself? Married nine years earlier without means, three months before her seventeenth birthday, to an Irishman[30] who was making £100 a year, she now happily has "a darling brood of six—yes, six!—children" around her, with a husband who is not yet in body as old as *Smiff*, and who "in heart, thank God! never will be."

And not only wives were happy. Here is the explanation of domestic delight by *Paterfamilias*, designed explictly to challenge such nay-sayers as *Benedick*, *Materfamilias*, and *Solon Smiff* "to decide whether we have acted wisely or not." Of course the jury, though he does not say so, will be that of the other readers, who will judge his opponents wrong on the evidence he presents. What is their way of life?[31] They live in a rented "snug little house, with a good garden, in a healthy suburb"; from thence he takes an omnibus to work but walks home. Their plain but substantial fare includes "good meat dinners and sometimes meat breakfasts, . . . well dressed and well served," and their amusements are taken at home in one another's company, though they manage a theatre two or three times a year and a visit to the Royal Academy and a few other exhibitions, as well as a family trip out of town every other summer, and they can afford a daily governess for the children. Their reading expenses[32] include the cost every morning, of course, of the *Daily Telegraph*, a denominational paper weekly, a magazine monthly, and "the Charles Dickens edition of his works." A "mite" goes to "one or two benevolent societies"; they have fire and life insurance and a building society account; they hire a piano and pay for "sittings in a place of worship." *Mirabile dictu*, their debts are but £10. The secret is an open one: "rigid economy, industry, and self-denial." In proof of which, *Paterfamilias* opens a window on a Victorian life not often portrayed:

When not employed with extra work from the office, I am cutting my grass, sticking my beans, doing carpenter's work, drilling my children in music, or mending their toys. My wife, also, is never idle. Our washing is not done out, but at home, by a charwoman; and my wife is not too proud to assist in ironing some of the light articles, to lend an eye and hand to the cooking department, to make many of the children's dresses, to trim her own bonnet, and darn her husband's hose. Keeping but one good servant, my wife feels it her duty, and therefore a pleasure to do all she can to preserve the home as one of comfort.[33]

Such comfort and contentment were far from universal. Using the *topos* of comparison so popular in fiction and sermons, *Flo* develops a sententious pair of pictures of married life on £150 per year:

Before me is a fine looking young man, but dingily dressed and with a care-worn expression of face. He is a clerk in a bank, [who] ... a year ago ... at a friend's house in the country ... met an elegant intelligent girl, with whom of course he fell in love, proposed, and was accepted by the young lady, who all her life had been accustomed to her own maid and every indulgence. "We can manage on £150 a year, can't we, Clara?" he asked one morning. They were sitting on a handsome couch, in an elegant drawing-room. "Oh yes, Charley, we'll manage somehow!" was her brave answer. But Clara's papa and mamma did not say, "Oh, yes, Charley." They said, "Oh, no, Charley," in such forcible terms that it was not till Clara said she would either elope with her beloved or have her parents' consent that the wedding-day was fixed.

Soon after marriage a long and dangerous illness of Clara's cost £30, leaving them only £120 for the year, of which £45 went for furnished apartments. Troubled by their poverty,

Clara remained an invalid, became fretful, and scolded Charles because the poor fellow grumbled when he returned home tired from work, and found underdone chops awaiting him (the cooking of course had to be left to their landlady), or because he noticed the holes in his socks growing larger as each week came round; nor is it a wonder that Charley, in his turn, had to dress dingily, and some-times, mind, I only say sometimes, regretted the steps he had taken.

Look on that picture, and then on this:

Here we see a tiny cottage, situated some miles out of London. It has only four rooms, including the kitchen, but it is as charming as it is small. This is where

Tom and Susie live. Tom is an active young fellow, who has just set up in business for himself, and, although his income at this time amounts to only £150, still both he and Susie know that if he remains steady and industrious, it may amount to £200 by next year. Besides this, Susie has always been accustomed to live in a small house, where she used to assist both in baking and ironing, so now there is no need for her to send Tom's shirts to a laundress, and all his collars are pressed by her soft little hand. She is a rosy-cheeked, handy lass, and has hardly known a day's illness in her life, so no serious doctor's bills pull on her little income. She has only one assistant, and everything comes under her own eye, which, if that eye is as saving as it is bright, will make more than half the difference to their expenses. Tom and Susie will have as many joys as Charley and Clara have sorrows; but then look at the difference of their circumstances.

And *Flo* exits from her fiction by reflecting on the determining nature of circumstances, and returning to her main point: "I think I should have as much reason to call Charley selfish for what he did as for your correspondent[34] to say the same of any young man who, while he desires the fate of Tom and Susie, dreads that of Charley and Clara."

With Charley and Clara we are moved to the shady side, whence comes the voice of *One Who Speaks from Experience*, whose non-hypothetical story is a sad one. Ten years previously, with a salary of £150 per annum, savings of about £150, and good prospects, he married one he thought (correctly) would make him a "good wife." They began wisely in rented apartments, but "an increase in family" mandated a rented house and a servant, and unanticipated griefs began: "Illness now occurred, our first baby died, and my wife's health gave way to some extent, causing us to make the first inroad on our savings." The path now being sufficiently marked, further specific detail may be foregone:

from this time our family increased rapidly [seven children who now require education], we had to move to a larger house, expenses continually increased, and at the time I now write, although my salary has been raised to £250 per annum, I have never been able to make up the lost ground, and I regret to say that I cannot assert with one of your correspondents of this morning [*Paterfamilias*] that my debts can be covered by a sum of £10.

The crux in his advice is "to pause awhile and lay by something for contingencies," for he and his wife, "an excellent mother and housekeeper," with no expensive habits—"Wine is a luxury not thought of"—would have "greatly alleviated" their hard struggles had they delayed marriage for a year or two.

Similar is the tale told (of another) by *A Lover of Home*, who, however, dates from the Admiralty, where he is presumably a senior clerk. Using a strong appeal *ad misericordiam*, he describes the sorrows of an industrious and careful friend, married nine years to just such a wife, who started with £100 a year and a yearly increase of £10, and now has nearly £200—and six children. Soon after marriage came "the almost invariable advent of indisposition, weakness, and utter inability to perform anything approaching laborious work; and then the lay-by altogether for a period, and frequently the long after-illness." A servant was found indispensable, and then "the rub—hard, wearisome, up-hill work year by year." Of course there are many moments when the burdens press less heavily, and "the light of [the children's] young eyes" gives joy, and life is not a matter of "no green leaf springing in life's wintry way, no sunbeam flinging light on the darkened day"; but they are circumscribed by cruel hard facts, by "unmet liabilities and a lean purse" that may leave endurance and bravery but destroy "the poetry, the gild." The inference is ineluctable: "to marry on less than £200 a year and an annual increase, would not be safe, and may (should family quickly arrive) be repented of long and bitterly."

The material griefs are woeful, and they are not unaccompanied by cultural ones with even more dire results, as is shown by *Precaution*, whose sketch of married life on an inadequate income begins with a gentle invitation to the viewing:

And now picture a fond husband spending the evening with his wife at the house of some friends, and, "sans doute," if asked to favour them with a little music or song, she replies "en demi voix," she is really very sorry, but since her marriage she has quite forgotten both. How proud her husband must feel to be sure, seeing his wife, perhaps the only one present who cannot add to the enjoyments of her friends! And why? Because since her marriage on £150 a year her music had to be laid aside, as a piano was quite out of the question. What can there be more enjoyable, when all your domestic affairs for the day are over, and your husband returns from his business (children in bed of course)? You dine, and then while he is enjoying his cigar (and if in the winter, in a comfortable arm-chair over a cosy fire) the wife sings or plays an air by Verdi or some other exquisite composer as an inducement for her husband always to spend his evenings at his own fireside; for, depend upon it, if girls are not pleasant and agreeable, men, one and all, will go where they know they will be so; and, recollect, married men are no more proof against temptations than bachelors.

That observation will serve as introduction to the blackest pictures, drawn by women in the true-confession mode. *Jane,* for example, "has tried the experiment, and . . . exactly knows 'how the shoe pinches.'" The suffering and sacrifice in "these 'love-in-a-cottage' marriages" fall to the wife's lot; a husband, if the home "lacks excitement," can easily escape to "temptations abroad." If he is possessed of "a 'tolerable appearance,'" able "to say 'pretty things' in an earnest, tender tone, woe to the wife who has married 'for love' and a 'companion!'" The implied personal plaint continues with a sad recognition that the "'girls of the period' bow down and worship" such husbands, "'married though they be'—if they will only minister to their vanity." The tone becomes more bitter even as the account moves to the general and the circumstances are less *Jane*'s own:

No; rely on it matrimony will become every season more and more a thing to avoid. The English "home" that poets have raved about no longer exists. The "girls of the period" only care to disport themselves in Rottenrow, there to meet their pet cavaliers, and to hope to meet them again either at the opera or the ball-room in the evening. Here and there a man becomes entangled in one of these flirtations, and is bound to marry the girl; but before another season comes round both have repented, and each rush their own way after fashion and excitement—that is, if there be money—but if the "means" are wanting, the wife remains in her lonely home, whilst "Benedick"[35] finds for himself "another dear girl," "whom he could have loved, had he only waited," far better than that "grumbling, stupid wife he has left at home," with only her own regrets for happiness gone out for ever, to bear her company in her many, constant, evenings alone.

Jane's peroration leaves her and the romantic no room for hope: "Who is it that has said, 'Possession is the grave of love!'[36] I forget; but who will dare to say it is not?"

Comparable is the account by *Beta,* in loose and rapid style, of a trusting girl who thinks she has "a protector and a loving husband—but has she?"

Oh, no, he must keep up appearances amongst his friends; he must dine at the most fashionable place, and ask one or two friends, and of course after that they must go to the opera. Where is his wife? sitting at home, waiting, hour after hour; and when he does come in, and is kindly asked where he has been staying so long, the answer comes, "Oh, Mr. So-and-So and I were talking over business matters;" and that is quite sufficient—we, poor wives, must not say any more.

This plaint ends in unexceptional advice freighted with traditional wisdom:

My advice to girls is, don't marry, unless you are sure of what the man you are going to have for a husband is, and even then don't be in a hurry. Remember, there are just as good fish in the sea as ever were caught, and be careful and do not marry in haste and repent at your leisure.

The most bitter account is from a woman who signed herself with three asterisks, whose experience of marriage, sufficient for the plot of a sensation novel, has moved her into what has recently been called the femisphere. Knowing that much marital unhappiness is caused by lack of candour about income—husbands make wives suppose that "it is less than it really is, for some selfish or suspicious reason"—she asserts that "once a wife discovers she has been deceived, in this or in any other way, she loses confidence, and with it heart, to work with a will, as she did before." This judgment serves to introduce an attack on men deriving from moral rather than purely monetary grounds. They have "called into existence" the girl of the period, and they have much more irredeemable faults than that "deformity and . . . libel upon her sex":

the follies and vices of fast life are too deep-rooted; they are a part of the very nature of man, and, unless early training be such as to correct the evil in him, he most undoubtedly grows up vain, self-indulgent, and autocratic; so, when he does marry, he seeks rather to exercise dominion over others than to bring his own passions and predilections under prescribed control. Men of this description often marry from motives of public policy, for the sake of appearances only; it "looks" respectable to be a husband and family man; the wife's robe of purity is made a cloak for the husband's immoralities; the sanctity which attaches to the idea of "home" screens many an impure deed.

The letter signed *** comes closer than any other in the series to indicting married men for perpetuating the great social evil:

it cannot be doubted that many a husband leads a bachelor life, to all intents and purposes the same; and, after a brief lull, when the novelty of his new position has passed away, all the old habits are resumed, and the wife feels neglected and is often left alone. What can bring a more deadly chill to a young wife's heart than the feeling that, without any fault or change in her, the husband begins to regard her with indifference, which is the precursor of coldness?—her charms, which are the same to other eyes, are losing their attraction to him, whose looks of love she seeks, and seeks in vain.

Her feeling is so strong that she alters her audience to the sinners and her mode to the vocative:

Oh, husbands, if you knew the bitterness of these thoughts to those tender hearts which beat so true to you, long, long after you have ceased to return the affection which they give, you would perhaps pause in your callous conduct. How many a wife pines alone, not daring to speak her sorrows to another! And at length her health gives way, her spirits sink, and she departs to a happier world. None guess the cause of such fading away, save One who knows all things, and will reward the evil and the good hereafter.

And even that, as the writers of sensational fiction asserted (and profited from their audiences' agreement), was not the worst:

there are other wives not so true; they, perhaps, hold on to duty for many a day, not willing to hasten after sin, although the example is so strong; for women are not so rash as men, and pause to weigh the consequences of an ill deed; but then a thought will come—the devil suggests these things—the tempting, wicked thought comes whispering, "Why should not I have my pleasures as well as he have his? Why should I sacrifice all for him who cares no more for me?" and then she plunges into pleasure—it may be into sin.

The fallen wife has her excuser if not her defender, for the cause is the wickedness of husbands, however female weakness accedes to it. The appropriate forensic technique (the heavenly judge being ensured, the earthly jury may be impanelled) is the accusatory question:

Whose fault is it? Who is to blame for this? Oh, lay not all the charge upon her: he has perjured himself before God, and broken his marriage vow, though the world—false world!—may think lightly of his sin, or call it not sin at all; but has he not released her from her vow? If there be justice for woman on earth, as there assuredly will be in heaven, I believe it must be even so ere long!

Such despairing and accusatory voices are not typical, however, even among those most concerned about the married state. The majority turn to particular difficulties that have general applicability. Some instance, for example, the education of children in shabby genteel families, the theme of *M.B.E.* The sanguine ladies advocating marriage surely admit that families will grow over time, and when the time for education comes,

what sad hearts those mothers will have to see them go to cheap schools, where the mistress herself knows nothing of real education, to see the children acquire habits and sayings which annoy their mother, and yet she has no time to correct them; for work, household work, all day must be her portion, with an income of only £150 a year—unless, indeed, this lady and her husband are contented to live as artisans of a similar income do—namely in the kitchen on week days, and in the parlour Sunday afternoons. When the husband comes home in the evening, where is the pleasant, cheerful companion he had hoped to find? Surely not this prematurely old-looking woman, fagged and weary with her day's work and worry. She cannot talk of the leading topics of the day, or enter into the spirit of the Laureate's last new poem. No; she cannot help dwelling on the incorrect manner in which Nellie, the eldest girl, begins to speak, and which grates upon her own refined and cultured mind; or she begins to tell her husband of her little servant's delinquencies, or of the hole Bobby has made in his knickerbockers, and wonder how they can be made to last till the money can be spared for new ones.

As though on oath, *M.B.E.* says that this "dark" but "true" picture is "but a true one" that she has "witnessed . . . in so many instances."

An alternative is presented by *An English Wife,* who obviously has more material resources. She, as part of her plaint about improper education by others, presents her precepts as based on "the actual experience of everyday life":

I have my children nearly always with myself when they are in the house, instead of consigning them to the constant care of a maid. . . . Little girls will get tired of their toys; and I often give them a little thimble, with needle and thread, and teach them to work, partly as an amusement, and with a view to future usefulness. I have girls of various ages, and I have found by the time they are nine or ten years old, they can make some part of their own underclothing very nicely; and, a few years older than that, dust drawing-rooms and bed-rooms; and if servants are unwell, or having a holiday, see them make their own beds.

More formal learning is not ignored—the girls are meanwhile making "gradual progress" with "books, writing, &c."—but then to school they needs must go.

And what is the consequence? The young lady may have her "crochet," tatting, and wool work, but plain needle-work is out of the question. If she goes to boarding-school she comes home at the end of the term with the contents of her trunks in sad disorder for want of a stitch in time; and if she goes to a good day school her spare time is so completely taken up with exercises—oftentimes very useless ones for young ladies—that she has little time and less inclination to do the most trifling thing for herself, and when she leaves school, instead of being an assistance to the mother who has done so much for her, she adds very considerably to her cares, her indolent habits acquired at school have become so confirmed, and the young lady thinks herself so very important a person that she is quite beyond being spoken to or taught. She may have received a good education and be able to dress herself and fritter away her time at the piano, but if she expects to be happy and enjoy a happy home she must understand all the wants and requirements of home life.

So, she concludes, show and tell at home, remembering "that a very great deal of harm is done by the system of school teaching of the present day."

Two other kinds of comparison will serve to close this survey of the gallery of married life. *A Woman* offers a social contrast between "true gentlefolks" and a special group of workers, ironstone miners, many of which earn from £300 to £500 yearly. Saving a fuller discussion of the comparative expenditures, I cite only one instance, where class distinctions emerge in typifying names: "Why, Polly's mother spends as many pence during the year in trash and sweetmeats for her as in the hands of Edith's mother would have furnished two or three interesting and useful magazines weekly throughout that time."[37]

The other comparison is made by *Giglio*, who has "French provincial connections of small fortune, though good position in the world."[38] He offers a general picture of a French couple, beginning life on a limited income, say the equivalent of £100 to £150 annually.

They keep one servant, who frequently is theirs only for a portion of the day. The mistress, often of high descent and proud demeanour, does not think herself lowered by attention to domestic duties, the getting up of fine linen, dusting and arranging her rooms, and the keeping of strict accounts. She is usually an admirable needlewoman. She goes to market herself, and makes successful bargains with the fierce ladies in white caps, who are more than a match for us foreigners. She is, her morning duties over, elegantly though most inexpensively attired.

Comparison between "the slatternly English wife and the neat, active Frenchwoman of a lower grade" is enlightening. The latter, a genuine helpmeet, "notwithstanding the French love of pleasure, always contrives to lay by une peu pour la soif."

Married vs. Single Life

Lying closer to the basic issue in the series are comparisons between celibate and married life. These, however, are not frequently drawn, probably because the general assumption ran in favour of marriage as the normal state. One frank account by *A Welsh Bachelor Pro-Tem* that wounded and invited annoyed responses presents a telling comparison between a married clerk with a large family, unable to take a seaside holiday, and himself, who returns refreshed from such a vacation.

Unit, whose signature like that of *A Welsh Bachelor Pro-Tem* signals a desire to marry, points out that it is unreasonable if not virtually impossible

for a man suddenly to change his whole manner of living, relinquish his position, give up the society of his friends, and settle down quietly with his wife, uncared for by the world. His isolation must become irksome at times, and his mind will carry him back to those days of mirth and enjoyment when his heart was light and he had nought but himself to provide for—no cares, no troubles —whilst now his sole thought is how to eke out his money to the utmost, as he sighs in vain for the companionship of those whom he cannot now afford to entertain, and who in consequence seldom offer to entertain him. Is this man happy? Will all the smiles, &c., of his wife rouse him from his melancholy?

Such reluctance may be attributed solely to selfishness, as other correspondents noted, but there are also moral issues, as *Benedick* argued in a second letter. He begins with a constrast between the provident married man who can "give more time, and thought, and money" to his children's education and future prospects and the "man with the same income who becomes, with great rapidity, the father of thirteen." The latter, a "'chartered libertine' of home," may lead "a very jolly life," with a house "brimful of young joyous humanity," a "wife and daughters to soothe illness, and to be his companions and friends; and, like Mr. Dickens's old lady who never went to sea, he 'dies triumphantly in bed.'" But in truth this is a direly selfish delight: because his income dies with him, "his old widow is left to starve, his daughters become governesses, or ladies' maids, or worse; his sons vegetate as clerks at

£60 a year; and in the next generation his grandchildren are day labourers or kitchen wenches." Here a married man is portrayed as selfish,
and the comparison is made, not as one might expect with the earned
and responsible happiness of prudent married folk, but with the virtue
shown in "the self-denial, the noble self-sacrifice, that very often distin-
guish bachelor life." He appeals to the readers' experience to confirm
his affirmation that commonly young men devote their earnings to
support mothers, sisters, or younger brothers, "putting marriage by for
years as a forbidden fruit." Now "*Erastes* and his school" are placed in
a bad light, as saying, "Oh! no matter! leave your old mother to Providence, let your sisters work, send your younger brothers to sea or the
devil; trust in God, and marry the girl of your heart." No response is
needed; *Benedick* rather asserts that such "tender, thoughtful self-sacrifice" by a son shows "tenfold the nobility there is about any sexual
love." To this point *Benedick* has been dwelling on the middle class:
when one looks to the poorer people, the supposed superiority of family life is revealed as a wicked sham. Poverty often means "the abnegation of decency, of all intellectual pursuits, of all refined habits, of all
thoughts above the hard necessity of material life." The children who
ought to come into a home "like smiles of God" are regarded "not in
words only, as 'greedy little devils.'" Though the poor are "wonder-
fully, almost miraculously, fond of children, considering the burthen
they bring," it is obvious to all that the arrival of baby does not bring
"pure joy," and its death is "not an unmingled grief." This, says *Benedick*, "loving children as I do," is the worst realization:

And yet men who have loved children and held them in their arms say to the
poor, "Marry, multiply your babies, and bring them up to the misery and squalor, and wretchedness and want we see swarming in our towns."

The contrast is then between foolish and rational expectations and
behaviour, and this is indeed a major theme. For example, placing the
blame on girls as much as on young men, *A Real Help-Meet* deploys
personal anecdotes to depict the two states. She first reports an
exchange just before her marriage (at nineteen), when a young friend
aged seventeen asked:

"What income will you have when you settle down?" I said, "None."[39]
"None!" she exclaimed, "well, how do you mean to live?" "By working
together," was my reply. "Oh," said she, "I do not mean to marry unless my
husband can keep a carriage for me; I should expect that at least."

On the day of their marriage they "possessed £20 (voila tout)," but soon her husband (a professional man) found "something to do." Both were economical by experience and design.

I never got anyone to do a thing that I could do myself. I have taken a door off its hinges, painted my stairs when they were dirty, and a thousand other things that many people would turn up their noses at.

Her young friend came to visit about two years after their marriage, and informed *A Real Help-Meet* that she would now accept a man with £500 a year.

"Oh," said I, "you are coming down in your terms." "Yes," she replied, "it is no use sticking out for my carriage." A couple of years ago she again came to stay with me, and, to my amusement, informed me that she would now accept a man (otherwise approved) with £200 a year if he offered. What a calculating way of setting to work! My friend is still unmarried.

Implications and Assumptions

It would appear that these letters speak for themselves—whatever that cant phrase may be taken to mean—but some speaking about them seems necessary to assess their importance. In sum, the participants in the series are typical of their age and kind not only in describing the problems of marriage but also in identifying causes and villains and in proposing solutions. Consequently their attitudes are in substance or comprehensiveness not those that late twentieth-century worriers and carers might wish, because the grounds of debate are different. What did the correspondents of 1868 think so obvious as not to need overt explanation?

Supporting and propelling their arguments are several nearly tacit and almost unchallenged beliefs, the most important of which are that marriage is the proper (natural, moral) state for mature men and women, and that children are a proper (natural, moral) result of marriage.[40] Other significant assumptions bear on the meanings of "prudent," "genteel," and "respectable," with particular reference to the appropriate expectations and expenditures of different classes. The implications are evident in the letters themselves, but a few comments on the basic beliefs may help their interpretation.

Though the series in the *Daily Telegraph* is dominated by secular concerns and language, there is no doubt that Christian, indeed English Christian, notions of marriage are assumed.[41] The basic text is therefore that of the wedding service in the *Book of Common Prayer*: God instituted wedlock for "the procreation of children," to provide a "remedy against sin and to avoid fornication, that such persons as have not the gift of continency might marry," and to contract men and women to live together in "mutual society, help, and comfort." The importance of this belief is seen in comments such as that by Frances Power Cobbe in an article entitled "Celibacy *v.* Marriage," in which she shares the dominant fear that marriage was becoming less common: "But the tide must turn at last. Marriage was manifestly the Creator's plan for humanity, and therefore we cannot doubt that it will eventually become the rule of all men and women's lives."[42]

The moral framework supporting this religious structure was the classical notion of "office" as defined by status. Deriving from the natural-law tradition, office entailed duties through tacit contracts that had no clauses granting subjective rights. Such terms as "estates" ("states") and "orders" should be seen as circumscribing objective conditions and ruling out individual natural rights; consequently there is no justification for complaints about the ultimate cause of one's condition (plaints about specific circumstances are allowed). As has been seen, Victorians complained a good deal about the attitudes of certain people, but in this context these people were seen not as devils causing evil but as misguided exacerbators of it.

Politically, such quasi-contracts entailed by office implied mutuality between governors and governed. A similar mutuality was seen as existing ideally between husband and wife; though their duties were different, they were jointly supportive. The details are seen most clearly in eighteenth-century "conduct" books for women, but the nineteenth-century exemplars of the genre continued the tradition of basing household governance and behaviour on office.

While both husbands and wives were seen as "relative creatures," there can be no doubt that the term was accepted in a stronger sense for women,[43] on whom the main onus fell, and who were seen as incomplete outside marriage in a way men were not. An earlier expert witness is Jane Austen:

Without thinking either of men or of matrimony, marriage had always been her [Charlotte Lucas's] object; it was the only honourable provision for well-educated young women of small fortune, and however uncertain of giving happiness, must be their pleasantest preservative from want.[44]

And a contemporary one, George Eliot, spoke volumes in a few words:

The market's pulse makes index high or low,
By rule sublime. Our daughters must be wives,
And to be wives must be what men will choose.[45]

Other witnesses are not far to seek. In Elizabeth Gaskell's *Cranford* Miss Matty refers to "the old story, you know, of ladies always saying, '*When* I marry,' and gentlemen, '*If* I marry.'"[46] Madeline Vesey Neroni (whose views are cynical, not to say corrupt) speaks for many in Trollope's *Barchester Towers*: "I say that a man is a fool to sacrifice his interests for such a bargain [as marriage]. A woman, too generally, has no other way of living."[47] And in his *The Vicar of Bullhampton* the narrator glosses the comment that "Marriage is the most proper and happiest thing for the young woman," by saying "Nature prompts the desire, the world acknowledges its ubiquity, circumstances show that it is reasonable, the whole theory of creation requires it."[48]

It is, however, crucial in understanding these attitudes to accept that middle-class women in particular were seen as charged with an essential role, that of household management, "economics" in its original sense. One of the strongest concise statements forms the hortatory peroration of Mrs Eliza Warren's preface to her best-seller, *How I Managed My House on £200 a Year*:

Daughters! diligently and zealously learn and practise every domestic duty and every feminine accomplishment; so will lovers eagerly seek you without fortune or other adventitious circumstances, and no longer will they say, "We cannot marry; our income will not suffice."

Wives! if you would retain your husband's love with a deeper affection than when in its youthful freshness, cultivate every winning charm of mind and manner—every grace of proper attire, but let your household management be such as shall ensure comfort, pleasure, and recreation, and your own knowledge of simple cookery that which shall not only tempt the appetite, but as much as possible ensure health, by banishing indigestion and all the evils which arise from it.[49]

These exhortations follow more specific advice, based on the premise (shared by most of the correspondents of the *Daily Telegraph*) that many "light-hearted happy young wives" are devastated within a year of "wifehood" because they do not know the value of money. As others

than Mrs Warren witness fictionally (and realistically), some thought
they were calculating properly:

There are plenty of women who have enjoyed all the luxuries and pleasures
of wealth, still ready to sacrifice grandeur to affection. Who would sink from
their former sphere without a murmur, content to live a homely life for the
sake of the sympathy of a true man, and the blessed prattle of children.[50]

But their sums were based on ignorance of the facts and of arithmetic:

Young ladies . . . are apt to have very obscure notions about money matters,
and their ideas of poverty are generally rather poetical. They think that being
poor means only not having *a great deal* of money—the being unable to afford
many luxuries and conveniences to which they themselves have always been
accustomed, and which it seems odd that people should be obliged to do without. Having *no* money is a thing they have no conception of.[51]

The "inexperienced," Mrs Warren affirms, thinking £200 a year ample
to commence housekeeping, allow small expenditures to run away
with the income. But if

a young wife of the middle class be handy with her needle, and has experience
under her parents' roof, she will find two hundred pounds per annum a sum
all-sufficient to steer her matrimonial craft safely over shoals and breakers,
provided always that love sits at the helm. Not passion, not caprice, least of all
indifference, for the rose of summer could as soon bloom in the Arctic zone, as
love dwell where the cold heart is reflected in the chilling aspect or careless
action.

While such accomplishments as singing, playing, dancing, and painting make a home "more charming, and more variedly interesting, than
where a woman is a mere household drudge" (a common term, paired
frequently with "slave" in the *Daily Telegraph*), they are not required
"to live comfortably"; what must be avoided if a girl is "to become a
happy wife and mother" is ignorance "of any household duty—any
domestic art," including the abilities to make and mend clothes, wash,
bake, cook ("economically and well"), and to clean and scour.[52] Mrs
Warren notes that "in the present day" she may not have to do all of
these herself, but in that case—a constantly reiterated message in these
guides—she must teach her servant properly. And she must avoid the
view, which she attributes to "Mrs. Grundy," that such work is "low

and vulgar": to illustrate the folly she reports the response of a servant who, when asked "to clean knives or boots, or to wash, very compacently replies, 'I've allays been 'spectable, and had no call to do sich things.'" (Pp. iii–iv.)

The sorry result of lack of frugality demonstrated in the sad fictional tale of married life that makes up the body of Mrs Warren's book is paralleled in the much better known events of David Copperfield's homes. First his mother, Clara, reveals her hopelessness at housekeeping, especially after his father, who tried to instruct her, died.

"I kept my housekeeping-book regularly, and balanced it with Mr Copperfield every night," cried my mother in another burst of distress, and breaking down again.

"Well, well," said Miss Betsey, "Don't cry any more."

—"And I am sure we never had a word of difference respecting it, except when Mr Copperfield objected to my threes and fives being too much like each other, or to my putting curly tails to my sevens and nines," resumed my mother in another burst, and breaking down again.[53]

And then David's child-wife is even more incapable of her office:

"If you will sometimes think [that you are engaged to a poor man], and look about now and then at your papa's housekeeping, and endeavour to acquire a little habit—of accounts, for instance—"

Poor little Dora received this suggestion with something that was half a sob and half a scream.

"—It would be so useful to us afterwards," I went on. "And if you would promise me to read a little—a little Cookery Book that I would send you, it would be so excellent for both of us."

... I had done it again. Oh, she was so frightened![54]

The road to the abyss is much more vividly drawn in a trans-atlantic guide book strongly resembling in its imagery the *Telegraph*'s account of the wages of the great social evil:

Extravagance should rather appear as a corrupting corpse, a hangman's rope clutched in its discolored hand; a ghastly wound across the throat; a gibbet behind it, and a pit of perdition yawning in front; for this extravagance, equally common to men and women, equally criminal to both, stands at the back of ninety-nine one-hundredths of the suicides, defaulters, murderers, forgers, delinquent guardians and trustees, plunderers of widows and

orphans. This extravagance leers at us over the wrecks of homes and reputa-
tions and brains; it gibbers at us from the mad-house; creeps to the peniten-
tiary cell; sweeps slowly by in the dishonored bier; lies ghastly in the morgue;
goes down darkly and rises festering from the waters in the "unknown
drowned."[55]

There was, indeed, near unanimity about women's proper office. For
instance, in its scathing account of the causes of distress in mining, the
report leading to the Act of 1842 recommended that each woman
should "attend to a mother's and housewife's duties."[56] The advice
offered by Gilbert Markham's mother to Helen Graham in Anne
Brontë's *The Tenant of Wildfell Hall* (1848) is completely consonant:

> "On household matters, and all the little niceties of cookery, and such things,
> that every lady ought to be familiar with, whether she be required to make a
> practical use of her knowledge or not. I gave her some useful pieces of infor-
> mation, . . . and several excellent receipts. . . . [W]hat every respectable female
> ought to know. . . ."[57]

Even when a hint of satire is inescapable, the message is dominant. For
example, because Dr. Robarts in *Framley Parsonage* (1861) is wealthy
enough to have competent servants, the narrator is able to say that
Lucy's elder sister had "managed the house; that is, she had made the
tea and talked to the housekeeper about the dinners"; the fun is
directed at some ladies' pretences about their fulfilment of duties, not
at the duties themselves.[58] Similarly this fuller description allows us to
look down on the speaker, an elderly female relative, but not on the
office:

> if you can get some simple, proper, house-keeping girl to think you the greatest
> man in all creation—the most worthy to be attended, cooked for, and listened
> to—you will ensure a happy home in the ordinary sense of that word. Never
> mind intellect and education; they are not wanted for getting ready a good din-
> ner, or warming one's slippers. The nursery can be kept clean and noisy [sic]
> without them; the shirt-buttons can be put on, the holes in the stockings
> darned, the children taught their catechism, the maids scolded into good
> behaviour, the back-parlour kept in good order, and the tea-parties properly
> managed. These are the tangible things which make life run smoothly on in the
> domestic groove.[59]

What of the husband's office? Apart from helping (or, like David, trying to help) his wife, his duty was similarly to economize, but also to ensure that there was wherewithal to economize.

Now among all its other havings, the Home must have a money basis. Money must build its shelter; feed, and clothe, and school its inmates; provide for their old age; and as new members are added to the family, parental foresight discerns their coming needs, and reaches out for means to supply them. To provide this money basis of the Home, Providence has bestowed upon us humans, acquisitiveness, or an ability for getting. The bestowal of this impulse is beneficent; for, setting aside a deal of absurd declaiming on the incompatibility of wealth and virtue, we face the facts that pauperism prevents a man fulfilling his duty as a man and a citizen, and in nine cases out of ten is the child of laziness and twin-brother of crime; while though wealth does not create virtue, it is obviously not inimical to it, and dwells with it very peaceably in the same nest; and between these two is that safe middle-ground, affording living room, scope for useful labor, where, as on a plain removed alike from burning heats and biting cold, the Home may be happily established.[60]

Such careful industry marks the good mate, as Darwin noted:

With mankind, especially with savages, many causes interfere with the action of sexual selection as far as the bodily frame is concerned. Civilised men are largely attracted by the mental charms of women, by their wealth, and especially by their social position; for men rarely marry into a much lower rank. The men who succeed in obtaining the more beautiful women will not have a better chance of leaving a long line of descendants than other men with plainer wives, save the few who bequeath their fortunes according to primogeniture. With respect to the opposite form of selection, namely, of the more attractive men by the women, although in civilised nations women have free or almost free choice, which is not the case with barbarous races, yet their choice is largely influenced by the social position and wealth of the men; and the success of the latter in life depends much on their intellectual powers and energy, or on the fruits of these same powers in the forefathers.[61]

The definitive male qualities are not hard to outline, though the performance of the office depends on resolution and habit. To forestall the direful contingent as well as to establish a reputation for respectability, a man should cultivate dependability, regularity, and punctuality in his vocation and avocations. Such behaviour is, of course, a darling target for the satirist, and Dickens's aim is deadly as he turns to Mr Podsnap (whose business is, aptly, insurance):

Mr Podsnap's notions of the Arts in their integrity might have been stated thus. Literature; large print, respectfully descriptive of getting up at eight, shaving close at a quarter past, breakfasting at nine, going to the City at ten, coming home at half-past five, and dining at seven. Painting and Sculpture; models and portraits representing Professors of getting up at eight, shaving close at a quarter past, breakfasting at nine, going to the City at ten, coming home at half-past five, and dining at seven. Music; a respectable performance (without variations) on stringed and wind instruments, sedately expressive of getting up at eight, shaving close at a quarter past, breakfasting at nine, going to the City at ten, coming home at half-past five, and dining at seven.[62]

More generalized is another satire:

They eat, and drink, and scheme, and plod,
And go to church on Sunday—
And many are afraid of God—
And more of *Mrs. Grundy*.[63]

So runs the mid-Victorian tale, and not without justice. As Shaw's Doolittle complained, after his unwilled transformation from a care-free loosely attached dustman to a gentleman, a respectable lecturer for the Wannafeller Moral Reform World League, middle-class moral-ity had ruined him, not least by insisting that he marry Eliza's mother. And "respectability has broke all the spirit out of her."[64] A much more violent reaction to this kind of model behaviour is seen in D.H. Lawrence's *Studies in Classic American Literature*, in which sputter stands in for argument against the thoroughly bourgeois code in Ben-jamin Franklin's *Autobiography*, where the major virtues are Temper-ance, Order, Frugality, Moderation, and (most of all) Chastity.[65] But whatever scorn the *fin-de-siècle* decadents and their more recent allies might delight in splashing about, the majority of Victorians had no rea-son to be ashamed of or even regretful about the proclaimed moral standards for daily life.[66] The abyss of unrecoverable degradation was too easy a forecast for those who were unwise, and the degradation was not merely metaphoric or social.

Rather than seeing the dominant secular morality as a debased utili-tarianism, one can view it as embodying the three classical virtues relating to duties to the self, which once again are not narrowly cul-ture-bound: prudence, temperance, and fortitude have practitioners as well as advocates in all places and all times. These are abundantly evi-dent in the precepts concerning proper marriage goals in the nineteenth century (the classical moralists were bourgeois before their time). The nature of the debate about marriage, especially in the forum of the *Daily Telegraph*, made reference to justice, the fourth cardinal virtue, not specially relevant.[67] In the debate, there was little disagreement about the need for temperance and fortitude; the main contention in the *Daily Telegraph* was over prudence. (It may be noted that the pseudonyms include *Prudence*, *Prudens*, and *Prudentia*.)

Though there is a great deal of assurance in Victorian literature, much of it is designed to face down insecurity. Life, especially mutual life, was surrounded by threats to its happy continuance. Generally, the realization that difficulties will come often without signal made preparation for the contingent a moral if not a religious duty, as people more and more assumed responsibility for their own lives.[68] Against the combination of the foreseeable and the unforeseeable prudence had a constant battle: avoidance of what could be prevented and a margin for the unexpected were the weapons of the wise and the injunctions of the instructors. The keynote of liberal political thought, security for person and property, became the wedding music of the middle classes. That the march might be accommodated to an unconscionable length of aisle was explained by such cautions as this:

Each of you may manage so as to live under a perpetual fear of being pushed into ruin by the first touch on you of sickness, loss, a death in the family, or by sudden hard times; or you may walk confidently inside of a safe, strong margin wherewith you have hemmed your affairs.[69]

Once again, this assumption seemed the merest common sense; the only effective arguments against it, emotional and satirical, were successful because, and to the extent that, the pursuit of security became mixed with envious and vain emulation of the economically secure— or at least of those whose consumption and demeanour let the world judge them affluent. So in the controversy in the *Daily Telegraph*, while prudence is adjudged a perfectly admirable quality, when not tinged with over-caution and lack of affection, warm-hearted critics of the hard-headed dwelt on their inflated notions of what prudence demands. Its denigrators presented it not as virtue, but merely as a character trait developed by the fearful and selfish; against it the optimists placed trust (which trait they sometimes valued as a virtue), whether in the character and powers of another person, in providence, or in chance. For most of the debaters, however, there were limited disagreements about prudence. In general, there was unanimity that a certain condition was essential for marriage: the fair assurance of

"respectability" and "decency." One other associated term, "gentility,"
is apparently less the goal for this part of the middle class; a glance at it
aids focus on the other desiderata.

The "paraphernalia of gentility,"[70] such as male servants, carriages,
horses, extensive holidays, and a wide range of dress, were the property (secured or sought) of the upper middle class, gentry, and aristocracy. These play little part in the budgets of the main body of *Daily
Telegraph* readers, who do not so much hope to be considered "genteel"
as to avoid falling into shabby gentility. *An Old Married Man*, in referring to the possiblity of mechanics marrying properly on £150 a year,
sets the standard fairly when saying that the case is very different "in a
grade where gentility (I can use no other word) is aimed at." That it
was not seen as an acceptable goal by the labouring classes is crudely
shown in that block-buster of the period, *Lady Audley's Secret*, in which
Luke Marks, a labourer (to become an innkeeper through blackmail), is
to marry his cousin, Phoebe Marks, maid to Lady Audley. Phoebe has
returned from a continental honeymoon tour with Lady Audley and
her husband, Sir Michael Audley.

"But they say travelling makes people genteel, Luke. I've been on the Continent with my lady, through all manner of curious places; and you know when I
was a child, Squire Horton's daughters taught me to speak a little French, and I
found it so nice to be able to talk to the people abroad."

"Genteel!" cried Luke Marks, with a hoarse laugh; "who wants you to be
genteel, I wonder? Not me for one. When you're my wife you won't have
much time for gentility, my girl. French, too! Dang me, Phoebe, I suppose when
we've saved money enough between us to buy a bit of a farm, you'll be *parly-
vooing* to the cows?"[71]

In the *Daily Telegraph* the references to "gentlemen and ladies,"
sharper socially than they would become in later decades, seem to
associate the standard of gentility with the upper middle classes, as
when *Plain Truth* refers to "genteel habits" or a leader writer to "genteel existence," but some correspondents democratically lower the
stakes in mentioning clerks as being in one of the "genteel professions." The dominant use of the term, however, is economic, in the
terms "genteel poverty" (five occurrences) and "genteel beggary."
Gentility had grades, and even those who had no expectations of possessing its paraphernalia felt the charm of its label. So they were not
willing to lose the status, even when falling below the middle-class
income level. As *Erastes* sarcastically said, the less worthy of the class

counted "poverty, ungentility, and plainness of fare the great evils of the earth." Even shabby gentility is still gentility and so self-bolstering; it is of a good kind, though not good of its kind.

The related term, "respectability," seems to be one of those that everybody understands but no one can define adequately. The *OED* slightly fudges the issue by saying only "The state, quality, or condition of being respectable in point of character or social standing," which forces one to consult "Respectable," to find "Of persons: Of good or fair social standing, and having the moral qualities naturally appropriate to this. Hence, in later use, honest and decent in character or conduct, without reference to social position, or in spite of being in humble circumstances." There is much here relevant to high Victorian attitudes, but it needs some sorting out.

Humans, as social animals, desire group status (not necessarily top ranking, but necessarily ranking), which is by definition socially determined. "Respectable" therefore properly suggests "being seen" (making a spectacle of oneself), trying to place oneself in the estimation of others, and to retain or improve that place. In stable societies, changes of status are difficult, and attempts to change are attacked as unnatural. While in the mid-Victorian period there was increasing opportunity for at least minor social movement, the desire was seen as (in the original meaning of the word) "snobbery," motivated mainly by desire of pretentious emulation. The normal process of linguistic comparison led to a contrast of "respectable" appearances with unseen "realities," and consequently the term was open to interpretation as merely an artificial surface, and hence to exposure through irony and satire.[72] It is always risible and usually derisible to see people trying to keep up with the Joneses, whosoever they may be. Softer criticism is found in Dickens's *David Copperfield* when for his wedding Barkis dresses out of his carter's role, blooming

in a new blue coat, of which the tailor had given him such good measure, that the cuffs would have rendered gloves unnecessary in the coldest weather, while the collar was so high that it pushed his hair up on end on the top of his head. His bright buttons, too, were of the largest size. Rendered complete by drab pantaloons and a buff waistcoat, I thought Mr Barkis a phenomenon of respectability.[73]

That instance is innocent of fraud, but not so the comparable one in *Martin Chuzzlewit*. When the porter of the Anglo-Bengalese Disinterested Loan and Life Assurance Company sat upon a seat erected for him in a corner of the office, with his glazed hat hanging on a peg over his head, it was impossible to doubt the respectability of the concern. . . . The whole charm was in his waistcoat. Respectability, competence, property in Bengal or anywhere else, responsibility to any amount on the part of the company that employed him, were all expressed in that one garment.[74]

Not many Victorians failed to take the point of Thomas Carlyle's assaults on "gigmanity," one of the more opulent manifestations of the desire for false respectability. And of course the respectable may just be a covering for the vile: this meaning appears in the leading article of 16 June in the *Daily Telegraph* series with reference—a commonplace in social criticism—to the area north of Oxford Street where the procuress had her den:

Viler by far than the assassin with the knife hidden in his hand are the "men with the black beard" and "ladies" dating from private residences in respectable streets. . . . Let us have the truth out about this respectable No. 22, Somerset-street, Portman-square, and the lady—Miss Page or otherwise—who lives and does business there in foreign arrivals.

In human character too the hidden may be sinister, if the strong examples provided by Dickens are convincing. In *David Copperfield*, for example, Steerforth's servant, Littimer, who is a most consummate villain, was "in appearance" to David (and presumably others)

a pattern of respectability. I believe there never existed in his station a more respectable-looking man. He was taciturn, soft-footed, very quiet in his manner, deferential, observant, always at hand when wanted, and never near when not wanted; but his great claim to consideration was his respectability. . . . [E]very peculiarity that he had he made respectable. . . . He surrounded himself with an atmosphere of respectability, and walked secure in it. It would have been next to impossible to suspect him of anything wrong, he was so thoroughly respectable. Nobody could have thought of putting him in a livery, he was so highly respectable. To have imposed any derogatory work upon him, would have been to inflict a wanton insult on the feelings of a most respectable man. . . . Even the fact that no one knew his Christian name, seemed to form a part of his respectability. Nothing could be objected against his surname, Littimer, by which he was known. Peter might have been hanged, or Tom transported; but Littimer was perfectly respectable.[75]

And in *Our Mutual Friend* Charley Hexam, pupil of Bradley Headstone, determined to rise to respectability through association with
him, thinks that his effort to get his sister Lizzie to marry Headstone
has everything on its side, "Respectability, an excellent connexion for
me, common sense, everything!" He tries vainly to persuade Lizzie by
saying, "As Mr Headstone's wife you would be occupying a most
respectable station, and you would be holding a far better place in society than you hold now, and you would at length get rid of the river-
side and the old disagreeables belonging to it, ... and the like of
that."[76]

Even in the *Daily Telegraph* correspondence there is one powerful
example of this negative use. Men given to "the follies and vices of fast
life ... often marry from motives of public policy, for the sake of
appearances only; it 'looks' respectable to be a husband and family
man; the wife's robe of purity is made a cloak for the husband's immoralities; the sanctity which attaches to the idea of 'home' screens many
an impure deed" (signed ***).

Nonetheless, and for very good reason, the search for respectability
was seen by many of the lower middle class and artisans as morally
and practically justified. And why not, when it is seen how closely
"self-respect" is related to "respectability"? Usually the expressed
"need" is only for the security resulting from acceptance or, at most, a
gradual material improvement earned by demonstrated reliability. The
attacks on "respectability" assume that it is wholly other-determined,
but in truth its concomitant "dignity" is self-determined. The connotations are most important: the term suggests a standard of manners and
mores apt to an "order," and while *pretension*[77] to a higher status was
seen as obnoxious, there was a range within which differences were
accepted and evaluated positively. This evaluation is dominant in the
letters to the editor of the *Daily Telegraph*.[78]

First, as to admirable people, the term has the force of a "character
reference." For example, *A Barrister* affirms that the law is deficient in
punishing seducers because its remedies are limited to "damages in an
action that no respectable father will bring—a remedy, therefore, which
is a mere mockery." Quite commonly, it applies to families: "highly
respectable middle-class people" (*Home Made Bread*); "A.B. was one of
three sons of poor but respectable parents" (*Preceptor*); "our respectable
and educated middle classes" (*Ring*).

A second common application is to a mode of life. For instance, it is
said that *R.C.P.* is unrepresentative in asserting that on a limited
income it is possible to "'keep house,' live respectably, and still have

money to spare for an occasional visit to the opera" (*G.J.L.*). In past days, such a standard was seen as sufficient: "Years ago, a clerk on £150 to £200 per annum did not look upon himself as a 'gentleman,' or his respectably homely wife consider herself a 'lady.' Their incomes, therefore, went much further than do those of young people of the present day, and they brought up, respectably and comfortably, large families of children." (*Plain Truth.*) In this in as other uses the term becomes a code for responsible behaviour: "to keep a wife and several children in any degree of respectability" (*A Bachelor*)—even across the Channel: "I have French provincial connections of small fortune, though good position in the world. They are as happy and respectable in their marriages as any English couples I know of." (*Giglio*)

Similarly, types of employment are so tagged. In British Columbia a man "may pursue any occupation without, as long as it is an honest and respectable one, losing caste" (*Colonista*); many steady artisans wish to apprentice their sons "to some respectable business of trade, but no opening is anywhere seen, and for years they are obliged to remain idle, or seek a lower sphere of labour" (*A London Mechanic*).

Applied to an urban area, the term need not, as in the leader cited above, have any but favourable connotations: "My income is less than £150 a year, yet it furnishes us with every necessity of life, and . . . enables me to occupy a comfortable house in a respectable locality" (*J.W.J.*).

A common association is with dress. For young women, the option is not attractive: "[On] my salary [of] £80 a year . . . [my mother and I] live comfortably, dress respectably (and I am sure I never look dowdy)" (*An English Girl*). For young men, and in particular, for clerks, it is a requirement of office: There "are thousands of well-educated, intelligent young men employed in the City counting-houses who get scarcely £50 or £60 a year salary. They have to appear respectably attired, or they discredit their employers." (*S.A.L.T.*) Again: often a "husband's position—and I mean his official position—obliges him to keep up a respectable appearance" (*A Plain Man*).[79]

A term closely related to "respectable" should make even clearer its generally positive associations—for whatever the case now, "decent" then was decent, even in Dickens's satire:

Bradley Headstone, in his decent black coat and waistcoat, and decent white shirt, and decent formal black tie, and decent pantaloons of pepper and salt, with his decent silver watch in his pocket and its decent hair-guard round his neck, looked a thoroughly decent young man of six-and-twenty.

The problem is not with the decent clothing, but with its wearer:

He was never seen in any other dress, and yet there was a certain stiffness in his manner of wearing this, as if there were a want of adaptation between him and it, recalling some mechanics in their holiday clothes.[80]

The term or its cognates appear thirty-one times in the series, with overlapping significations.[81] Among these, six pertain to appearance, including clothing: "A professional man wants but a decent coat" (*Solon Smiff*); children need to be "decently clothed" (*One Who Married on £120 A Year*); "external decency" is a necessity (*S.A.L.T.*); it costs a great deal "to present a decent appearance to the world" (*M.T.M.*); only with strict economy and without a family can "a man and his wife . . . keep up a decent appearance on an income of £130 to £140 per annum" (*A Prudent Bachelor*); and, for young married men, "the struggle to maintain a decent appearance too often ends in debt and difficulties," while "a single young man in London on the same salary . . . can live well and dress decently" (*F.M.*). It would appear that in these cases the appropriate antonym is not normally "indecent"[82] but at its weakest perhaps "unpleasing" or "inappropriate," and at its strongest "shameful" or "squalid." That is, "decent" is closely related to "respectable." A parallel case that many will recall is portrayed by P.D. James:

[Adam Dalgleish] remembered from childhood the voice of an old aunt exhorting him to change his vest. "Suppose you got run over, Adam. What would people think?" The question was less absurd than it seemed to a ten-year-old. Time had taught him that it expressed one of the major preoccupations of mankind, the dread of losing face.[83]

The most common uses of "decent" (eleven in all) pertain to a standard of living. Really "thoughtful and considerate" men before marriage try to "ascertain the exact sum with which decency, cleanliness, health, and some security for the future, can be obtained for a married home" (*Benedick*; quoted by *Erastes*); poverty must be avoided if one wishes to enter "any decent society" (*Solon Smiff*); one must live "in a decent and comfortable manner" (*C.S.C.*), "decently and happily" (*Prudens*); "amongst the poorer classes family life often means the abnegation of decency, of all intellectual pursuits, of all refined habits, of all thoughts above the hard necessity of material life" (*Benedick*); plain living is compatible with "common decency and strict economy" (*Plain Fact*); £150 a year allows a couple only "the common necessaries and decencies of life" (*Independence*); someone should outline "the most economical way of securing a decent maintenance for a family" (*Life Assurance*); what is sought is "a decent income" (*A Prudent Bachelor*), "a decent living for [oneself] and family" (*Scotch Civil Engineer*), or "a decent competence" (*O.E.S.*).

Closely related are the eight descriptions of houses and their localities as decent. The first gives the proper context:

Without being open to the charge of luxurious exigence, [a man] may wish that his home should be neat and in a healthy situation, that his own or her eyes, accustomed habitually to some decencies of life, should not be forced into contact with squalor—in other words, that, however small and unpretentious his house, and however remote from the fashionable world in situation, it should not be foul within or miserably dirty outside, and that the situation should be healthy (*Benedick*).

Other comparable accounts mention sacrifice "to live in a decent house (only six rooms)" (*Materfamilias*), "a home of comparative comfort and decency" (*W.J.W.*), "decent lodgings" (*Vieux Moustache*, 7 July), "apartments of any pretensions to decency and cleanliness" (*Plain Fact*), "a decent dwelling" (this, for an artisan, "consisting in many instances of only one room") (*M.B.*), and the struggle "to keep a home in something like decency and comfort on £150 a year" (*J.A.B.*).

An Anxious Father, who is contemplating emigration, reveals the basic assumptions most compactly:

Given, educated parents, wishing to keep a decent house, with one servant to save the wife from the more menial offices; to feed, clothe, and educate their children in a plain and not extravagant way; and to compass, without running into debt, the ordinary and inevitable expenses which are daily to be borne, and to which, if you add any extras, many of which are not only legitimate, but very desirable to all thoughtful and well-regulated minds; for instance, subscribing to a newpaper, to a book-club, and holding sittings in a place of worship—I say, given these necessary expenses to the maintenance of every decent home, and a very limited income will not suffice.

One anomalous case, where the word relates to moral conduct as opposed to ostentation, is found in the leading article of 26 June, in the midst of the parable about the savage Coles: "the Cole mammas" protest that the traditional wedding gift of bullocks is "better than decency and happiness"—but they are eventually defeated, and the leader writer closes with a plea that "a deputation of Cole parents" be brought "to talk a little decency and nature in the salons of West London."

Once again it is abundantly evident that the *Daily Telegraph* appealed—and intentionally—to the middle class, especially in its lower ranges, and no surprise should be elicited by the concentration in this correspondence on middle-class problems. It should not be assumed, however, that the beliefs about class differences expressed by members of that socio-economic grouping are unique to it. First, as has already been shown, its members varied greatly in income and ways of life. Second, it was not merely self-gratifying propaganda that portrayed the middle as increasingly showing the way for the lower—and even the upper-classes. Third, much of the motivational base for behaviour and belief was common to most of the English.[84]

Another implication of the letter writers needs reinforcement because of the negative view so often taken of bourgeois Victorian mores. Commonly, adverse description and analysis are taken as universally applicable when the basis is limited and individual. It should now be evident that much of the discussion in the *Daily Telegraph* demonstrates that the giving and taking in marriage (and after it) was not without much joy and wide contentment; the period was marked by earnestness, but the high Victorians took pleasure—not perversely—in being earnest as well as in being, as so many of them were, jocund. Consider Pooter's explanation to his wife Carrie:

> I could not help thinking . . . that half the pleasures of life were derived from the little struggles and small privations that one had to endure at the beginning of one's married life. Such struggles were generally occasioned by want of means, and often helped to make loving couples stand together all the firmer.
>
> Carrie said I had expressed myself wonderfully well, and that I was quite a philosopher.[85]

For the late twentieth-century reader, much of this complex of assumptions and beliefs is both irritating and amusing. But in assessing it, one difficulty should be acknowledged: many of our attitudes are received wisdom from the accepted "sages" of the period, all of whom fit somewhere in the "middle class," and almost all of whom were mightily critical of the middle class as it moved towards ascendancy. Matthew Arnold's heavy sarcasm in 1864 about the material complacency of such as Adderley and Roebuck is perhaps the best-known example,[86] but readers of Carlyle, Mill, and Ruskin will easily think of telling examples. And not only the sages were self-critical: if there has been a culture more given to deploring its own moral short-fall, at a minimum the Victorian middle class set a new mark in making it a game for everyone.[87] As will be already evident and will become more so in the following chapters, the correspondents of the *Daily Telegraph* are in this as in other respects typical.

CHAPTER FOUR

"The Equation of Income and Expenditure"[1]

Whatever interpretation one wishes to put on the fact, a fact it is that the Victorians, and particularly those who were middle class, were greatly concerned about money. In assessing the attitudes towards it in the "Marriage or Celibacy?" series, a useful way of testing perceptions against realities is to ask a series of questions: How much money was needed? How much was there? How was it spent? In attempting to answer these, it is instructive to compare once again the advice in the *Daily Telegraph* with that offered in fiction and advice manuals.

In sum (though the specific sum is rather low) one of George Eliot's narrators poses the question that faced the kind of people who comprised the main readership of the *Daily Telegraph*:

And now, pray, can you solve me the following problem? Given a man with a wife and six children: let him be obliged always to exhibit himself when outside his own door in a suit of black broadcloth, such as will not undermine the foundations of the Establishment by a paltry plebeian glossiness or an unseemly whiteness at the edges; in a snowy cravat, which is a serious investment of labour in the hemming, starching, and ironing departments; and in a hat which shows no symptom of taking to the hideous doctrine of expediency, and shaping itself according to circumstances; let him have a parish large enough to create an external necessity for abundant shoe-leather, and an internal necessity for abundant beef and mutton, as well as poor enough to require frequent priestly consolation in the shape of shillings and sixpences; and, lastly, let him be compelled, by his own pride and other people's to dress his wife and children with gentility from bonnet-strings to shoe-strings. By what process of division can the sum of eighty pounds per annum be made to yield a quotient which will cover that man's weekly expenses?[2]

Dividing the issue into component questions helps understanding, if it does not solve the problems.

How Much Money Was Needed?

There is no one satisfactory answer to the question—less frequently
asked now than in the 1860s—What annual income is necessary for a
couple to enter on marriage with the intention of having a family and
living comfortably and respectably?[3] One of the best known mid-
Victorian answers—not the only one, and not necessarily the right
one—appears in the title and text of Mrs Eliza Warren's *How I Managed
My House on £200 a Year*, an advice book presented through first-person
fiction with a strongly exhortative preface.[4] She sets £200 as likely for
the lower professional class, commenting in her preface that it is "large
by comparison with thousands of incomes" (pp. v–vi).

It certainly is not too much for the family in her sad narrative. Both
Milly, the protagonist, an inexperienced young woman, and her husband, starting a career as a solicitor, begin with misapprehensions. He
infers from her background that she knows housekeeping; actually she
is innocent of money managing, and thinks his meagre income "a mine
of gold." Her initial reaction to the reality of her responsibility for
household management is strongly reminiscent of Dora's in *David Copperfield*—but Frederick is more stern, though no more immediately
effective, than David is.[5] His drawing up a budget provides initial
improvement, but they are plagued by incompetent, flighty, dishonest
servants, the death of a child, and finally the death of Frederick, after
mental and physical decay. Impoverished, but aided by older women
friends, she becomes "famous as a household manager" (p. 30), being
upheld by "a *higher* Power." However, she is forced to become a housekeeper for a philanthropic lady—and here the tale ends with what
seems a postmodernist fictional twist: "how to manage with [£200 a
year] was all I was requested to write about." The overall effect is less
tragic (except for poor Frederick, who is little lamented) than didactic,
embodying moral "truth" in "realistic" fiction.

Comparing such third-rate fictions with better-known first- and sec-
ond-rate works to test the "realities" and expectations of the period,
one immediately sees that the remembered works normally portray a
higher economic standard. That is, even realist novels embody dreams:
"Great Expectations" is a better fictional title than a sociological one, in
spite of the constant insistence in the period that the fledglings were
unrealistically and dangerously demanding to start flying from too
great a height. The revolution of rising expectations had begun, but it
was far from triumph. In the standard novels the portrayal is most
commonly of the upper middle class, minor gentry, and aristocracy,

and their notions of a competence are based not merely on what everyone would agree to be necessities but also on what most would consider luxuries—not seldom, of course, they are consequently subjected
to satire.

In using Victorian fiction to aid understanding of the *Daily Telegraph*'s readers, then, one can safely ignore the odd symbolic silver fork
remaindered from the society fiction of the earlier part of the century,
such as the dismay portrayed by a man with an income of £2000 who
discovers that a girl "has a right to expect half that sum nearly, to be
settled upon her as pin-money."[6] It is not so easy to ignore the more
determinedly social fiction of mid-century, however, as it has been
taken (on its own implied or explicit claims) to deal with what may be
called the "middle middle" (or typifying) class. Whatever that slippery
term may mean, when income, expenditure, and expectations are considered, there is no doubt that those most engaged and described in the
Daily Telegraph debate are and *expect to remain* on a lower rung, even if
they perceive the possibility of climbing. Indeed it is more apt to think
of a series of ladders, each leading to a different economic storey of
contentment; clerks need sure footing, determination, and prudence to
gain a rung, and they do not anticipate opportunities to start climbing
a higher ladder reserved for others—unless they kick over the ladder
altogether and move to what seems a new and socially level world
overseas.

The fictional evidence, however, should not be ignored, especially
that found in Anthony Trollope. Much of his acute description dwells
on professional and commercial groups, the country gentry and aristocracy, but he also portrays with quiet but telling detail various mid-
dling folk. At the higher end of this scale one finds one of his
characters in *Framley Parsonage* referring to top flight clerks and mod-
erately successful business men as "us second-class gentry with our
eight hundred a year—there or thereabouts."[7] In context, this statement suggests exaggeration, as does the tone in his *Miss Mackenzie*:
"The ordinary Englishman, of whom we are now speaking, has eight
hundred a year; he lives in London; and he has a wife and three or four
children."[8] This level is presented without irony by W.M. Thackeray,
who indicates that in the country a modestly successful professional
man, an apothecary practising medicine like Pen's father John Pendennis on £800 a year, with "the best economy and management," could
not live "with the great folks of the county; but he had a decent comfortable society of the second sort. . . . They had out their plate, and
dined each other round in the moonlight nights twice a year, coming a

dozen miles to these festivals; and besides the county, the Pendennis's had the society of the town of Clavering, as much as, nay, more than they liked."[9]

On the basis of his unrivalled reading of less-enduring Victorian fiction, Myron Brightfield identifies about £800 as representing, "between 1840 and 1870, a respectable and comfortable income, though it certainly could not encompass luxuries"; he does not, however, point out that the class described in his testimony is not lower middle or even middle middle, members of which would not be apt to comment: "Out of seven or eight hundred a year, it is just possible to job a small carriage, to rent a small house, and to keep a couple of livery servants on board wages, if the proprietor of this surface splendour be content to feed upon air."[10] When in George Eliot's *Middlemarch* Dorothea brings an annual income of £700 to her second marriage, it is more than adequate, but in her uncle's upper-middle-class provincial circles it was thought a small amount.[11]

For one of Trollope's young women—and here we move a bit closer to the *Daily Telegraph* discussion, for her intended is a clerk, albeit of superior qualities—£600 was moot: "like most English girls of her age," she was "at first so ignorant about money that she hardly knew whether £600 was or was not a sufficient income to justify their present mode of living; but she soon found reason to suspect that her husband at any rate endeavoured to increase it by other means," i.e., through dealing in stocks.[12]

Brightfield is nearer the mark though still above it when he says: "The decisive line of separation—parting ladies and gentlemen from those who were neither—bisected the middle class at a certain rather undetermined point—perhaps at five hundred pounds or thereabouts." Part of the reason for the high estimation is indicated in his further comment—once more, in spite of the reputed prevalence of "snobs," applicable in a stronger sense to fiction than fact: "It was natural for families living somewhat near this level to fortify their gentility by seeking the society of those who were at a much greater interval above the line."[13] Certainly that is the practice, not always unsuccessful, of Thackeray's never reliable Irish Captain Costigan in *Pendennis*, who is of opinion that "'with aconomy,'" £500 a year is "'a handsome sum of money'": "'Faith, I've known a man drink his clar't, and drive his coach-and-four on five hundred a-year and strict aconomy, in Ireland, sir. We'll manage on it, sir—trust Jack Costigan for that.'"[14]

The great majority, of course, had (like Costigan) to make do on less in England as well as in cheaper Ireland, though fictional folk, like one

of Thackeray's narrators, purported to puzzlement: "You ask, my genteel friend, is it possible that people can live on four hundred a year?
How do they manage, *ces pauvres gens*?"[15] Brightfield agrees that it is—
in fiction—a problem; "the estimates of the 'thirties seemed pathetically inadequate in the 'fifties and 'sixties," he says, and quotes a novel
of 1869: "The failure of the 'three-hundred-a-year marriages,' so much
talked of once, has no doubt been demonstrated long ago."[16] Joseph
Ambrose Banks, whose *Prosperity and Parenthood: A Study of Family
Planning among the Victorian Middle Classes* broadly covers the question,
asserts that in these years £300 was perceived as the lowest limit for
safe marriage. This being not easily attained by a young man, Banks
rather overstates a good case:

A "proper" time to marry!—more and more as the century wore on, this
became the theme of the middle classes, until the words "prudence" and
"postponement" became the two most hackneyed in their vocabulary. . . . Hes-
itation, and a weighing-up of the consequences were the true virtues; to plunge
into an ill-considered early marriage was the height of folly.[17]

In *The Adventures of Philip* Thackeray dances towards the £300 figure,
illustrating its attraction because it is possible (though far from certain)
and its danger because it is inadequate: "Poverty, debt, protested bills,
duns, crime, fall assuredly on the wretch who has not fifteen [hun-
dred]—say at once two thousand a year; for you can't live decently in
London for less."[18] Even a less exalted and just attainable standard,
£450 a year, is then presented as "preposterous and absurd": "People
do live on less, I believe," says the narrator, "But a life without a
brougham, without a decent house, without claret for dinner, and a
footman to wait, can hardly be called existence." (Pp. 576–7)

But Thackeray portrays the marriage, based initially on less, as rap-
turously successful (Trollope's characters' meditations, one judges,
would be less rosy).[19] Philip sums up the case playfully:

"What idiots we were, my love, to be happy at all! . . . with a purse which
didn't contain three months' consumption, would we dare to marry now? . . .
We were paupers, Mrs. Char, and you know that very well!"

"Oh, yes. We were very wrong: very!" says Mrs. Charlotte. . . . And herewith
she will begin to kiss and fondle two or more babies that disport in her room—
as if two or more babies had anything to do with Philip's argument, that a man
has no right to marry who has no pretty well-assured means of keeping a
wife.[20]

Thackeray, in spite of his enthusiasm, admits that there is a practical as well as a theoretical problem in hewing to the regime, and when figures in the £300 range are mentioned in fiction, there typically are cautions, such as the need for "a bright household fairy" as wife.[21] And Mrs Craik is really warning against the wrong assumption when she has a narrator set a lower limit—for single men only: "the sum of one hundred and fifty pounds a year seems to me sufficient to maintain in as much comfort as is good for him, and in all the necessary outward decencies of middle-class life, a man without any expensive habits or relations dependent on him, and who has neither wife nor child."[22] And that would not do for all, not only the young and adventurous but the old and spoiled being too constrained by such incomes. For example, in Trollope's *Marion Fay*, Mr Greenwood, the lazy and long-serving chaplain to the Marquis, has become odious, and is to be turned out, with £200 a year, which (though he is totally unencumbered) will not enable him to live as he has been accustomed.[23]

Nonetheless, when a step down to the lower middle class is taken, incomes below £300 are presented as possible for marriage, assuming continued prudence. Such prudence is associated with serious self-denial only when young bachelors are talking. The usual interpretation is that they are less liable to foolish sentimentality than are young girls, but there are deeper roots to the distinction, the female marriage "offices" still being more obviously accepted than the male ones;[24] that is, the "double standard" had wider ramifications than a narrow focus on sexual behaviour reveals.

So it is after Bella Wilfer's abandonment of selfishness that she is able to say in *Our Mutual Friend*:

"Listen, sir," said Bella. "Your lovely woman was told her fortune tonight on her way home. It won't be a large fortune, because if the lovely woman's Intended gets a certain appointment that he hopes to get soon, she will marry on a hundred and fifty pounds a year. But that's at first, and even if it should never be more, the lovely woman will make it quite enough."[25]

A little later in life, presumably, she would expect to be a near neighbour of those visited by a Trollope character, who took a cab to Islington, where "he knocked at a decent, modest door—at such a house as men live in with two or three hundred a year."[26] These are married men, one must assume, perhaps like Tommy Traddles in *David Copperfield*, who cannot wed until he has reached the level set by his fiancée's father, £250 a year. Noting this matter, Jo McMurtry comments: "Two hundred fifty pounds is pretty much the bottom line, if not below the bottom line, and Dickens's picture was understood by the original readers to be something of a caricature."[27] Perhaps—but many readers of the *Daily Telegraph*, who doubled as readers of Dickens, would have called it realism. And well within that group falls Harry Clavering, one of Trollope's headstrong suitors, who is quite willing to contemplate such a life. When his prospective father-in-law indicates that he will provide £100 a year on marriage, but adds, "'a hundred a year will be nothing to you,'" Harry responds: "'Won't it sir? I think a very great deal of a hundred a year. I'm to have a hundred and fifty from the office; and I should be ready to marry on that to-morrow.'" And the experienced reply moves him not at all: "'You couldn't live on such an income, unless you were to alter your habits very much.'"[28] Less confident was someone else who probably read the *Daily Telegraph* at least from time to time; on leaving school Havelock Ellis confided in a private note: "I know . . . that I should have too great an affection for the object of my love than to marry her on £120 a year."[29]

The mental, moral, and behavioural implications of such an attitude cannot be fully appreciated without recognizing that those in other "stations" were not similarly liable to threats to their security. Those who did not share middle-class notions of financial competence and "necessaries"—artisans, for instance—were not, and according to several commentators, need not be, deterred from marriage. For example, "Espoir" entitles her fictionalized advice book *How to Live on a Hundred a Year, Make a Good Appearance, and Save Money*, insisting that one can cope on £100, though many with £300 will be

sitting in constant dread and anxiety, lest the ring at the hall door should be followed by the announcement of Mr. So-and-So, the grocer, or the tax-gatherer, or some such odious person, who has the "impudence" to inquire (of course, bowing most politely) if it would be convenient to settle the small account, due in 1870.

Paraphrasing Mr Micawber (see p. 116 below), she points out that one must be able to say "No," "to live just a little bit 'under your income,' and 'not a little bit beyond it.'"[30] And so she has done for at least ten years—but she is single, well educated, brought up from childhood as a lady, the "daughter of ["wealthy"] parents occupying a good social position in the middle class of life."[31] Further, she lives in the country with only one female servant, and so is not like the main body of correspondents of the *Daily Telegraph*.

From all the admissions that judgments about a reasonable competence will vary, two assumptions clearly emerge that are not fully compatible with late twentieth-century assumptions: first, there are class
differences in expectations, and these differences are legitimate; and second, prudent good management is essential and learnable. Consequently context is needed when interpreting the estimates, as is evident
in the judgment of a fictitious "cautious dowager of wealth" in the 1860s
about the sum sufficient to stay above poverty: "I should say three or
four thousand—that is, for comfort; Dr. Rowley would say eleven or
twelve hundred. Poor Mr. Willmott the curate would say one, two, or
three. It is not a question that can be answered by generalities."[32]

Turning to the advice manuals, one finds them attempting, *inter alia*,
to deal with these variations. It should be borne in mind that such
guides had two goals, often within the same covers: one to show how
to do things properly, and so to establish the etiquette for respectability, the other straightforwardly to instruct in economical housekeeping.
How to climb up and how to get on. The contrast is evident in manuals
that deal with different levels of income, such as the anonymous *Economy for the Single and Married; or, The Young Wife and Bachelor's Guide to
Income and Expenditure on £50 per Annum, £100 per Annum, £150 per
Annum, £200 per Annum; with Estimates up to £500 per Annum. Comprising also a Variety of Useful and Original Information for the Single, As Well
as All Subjects Relating to Domestic Comfort and Happiness, by One Who
"Makes Ends Meet."*[33] The author does not pretend that all is possible
through love and care, indicating that on £100 a young man should not
marry; regret is expressed that of the thousands who "are compelled
by their position to keep up a respectable appearance on the very moderate income of £50 a year," some "are married, and have young families!" (pp. 24, 9). It seems unlikely that many young people at that level
would be concerned with respectability as understood by the majority
of the middle classes.

John Henry Walsh, in his *A Manual of Domestic Economy; Suited to
Families Spending from £100 to £1000 a Year. Including Directions for the
Management of the Nursery and Sick Room, and the Preparation and Administration of Domestic Remedies,*[34] has in mind an ideal audience of young
married couples who value prudence but need and seek advice, as his
table of contents indicates:

On the Practice of Economy; The House and Accessories; Furniture and Furnishing; Domestic Servants and Their Duties; The Supplies of the House; The
Natural Economy of Man as Affected by his Artificial Habits; On the Mainte-

nance of Health by Proper Cookery; On the General Management of the Skin, Teeth, &c.; the Domestic Management of the Lying-in Room, and Nursery; Horses and Carriages; Social Duties of Heads of Families; The Domestic Treatment of Disease.

Getting all this down in clear expository form takes well over six hundred pages. In spite of the gloomy forecasts there is some fair light, for Walsh does not rule out entertaining, giving bills of fare for all levels (pp. 607–14, 626–35). Once more, class assumptions about proper management and different expectations are evident.

Still and seemingly forever "How Much Is Needed?" keeps getting asked, even though almost every attempt to answer it involves the admission that there is no one answer. Nonetheless—or perhaps consequently—the estimates of the mainly lower-middle-class readers of the *Daily Telegraph* become themselves instructive as revealing group and individual attitudes related to but not identical with those found in fiction and advice books.

A quick survey of their responses gives an initial sense of the views of these correspondents. Because so many qualifications are made, the best initial focus is on the figures that mark the break point. In many cases, a range is given by a correspondent (e.g., £150 to £300); I have taken the lower numbers in these ranges as suggesting the minimum at which debate is engaged. Further, it should be noted that mere mention of a figure does not indicate acceptance of that amount as sufficient. Indeed many assert its inadequacy, taking it only as a starting point for discussion. First the general picture, and then the qualifications.

Perhaps the strongest single indicator of the economic status and expectations of the correspondents of the *Daily Telegraph* is the rarity of larger amounts being accepted as the basis of discussion. Only two go as high as £500,[35] an amount that seems quite beyond the dreams of most in this group. Many mention £300, the "magic sum" according to *Solon Smiff*, but they appear merely to follow the general tune of the times.[36] But only six fix on it, five of whom, in a class perhaps not their own, see it as a minimum, the sole dissenter being in any case in favour of emigration. Once more it is evident that the assumed standard of contentment was higher in earlier and fictional accounts. A reasonable inference is that while the cost of living had not much altered, the actual and anticipated levels of income for a majority of these correspondents were lower than for the group in the 1840s and 1850s corresponding with, and being written about in, *The Times* and other periodicals, and imagined in the fiction.[37]

Two hundred pounds is the minimum for twenty-two writers (24 per cent of those who cite annual incomes);[38] at this level, as one would expect, more view such an income as adequate, though certainly there are still objectors—especially among those in professions and those advocating emigration. Forty-five (nearly 50 per cent), much the largest group, take £150 as the debating point; with them may fairly be included the three correspondents who respectively assume £160, £170, and £180: as illustrated below, actual budgets support the argument for some of these figures. Significantly, then, nearly 75 per cent of the relevant letters think £150–£200 the proper annual income for genuine debate about prudent marriage.

A few—very few—correspondents in the *Telegraph* mention an annual income of £80, but only one (*Preceptor*) suggests it as reasonable; the others treat it as ridiculous—for those thinking of themselves as middle class.[39] Twenty-four writers mention £100, though few think it acceptable; one, *Hammer and Nails*, thinks it enough for a workman like himself, and indeed there is no dispute that such a level is adequate for artisans, who have less costly social demands in attaining respectability—as they define it. With the £100 group may be included the two correspondents who cite £120, and the ten who mention £130, a favourite target early in the series. These more specific sums suggest actual experience, but probably have no more validity than the fully rounded numbers.

The levels of debate in the *Daily Telegraph* can usefully be isolated according to the minimal incomes. Ignoring the untypical citations of £300 and up, and using the interrogative appropriate to the debate, one can begin with

Should One Marry on £200 per annum?

Given the popularity of Mrs. Warren's book, it might be assumed that this would be the crucial figure in the debate, and indeed, as noted, it features significantly in some twenty-two letters, but more than twice that many cite lower sums. Because the higher range is more prominent early on, before the correspondence settles on the lower middle class as its main concern, there is a "Belgravian" note about some of the first letters, reflected not only in higher figures, but also in references to "society" standards (whether they are accepted or condemned). He who writes as *B.——* best illustrates. A couple accustomed to "the best society" would, on £200, be entirely separated from their friends and "accustomed pursuits," deprived of luxuries they had thought necessaries. In this "abnormal position, it is ten to one that the 'happy couple' would allow discontent to make, unopposed, his first insidious advances, and eventually, aided by poverty, to drive love out of the window." In these circumstances, "the daughter of a 'Belgravian mamma'" could not "reasonably expect a happy married existence."

Although in each of the salary ranges there is some difficulty in deciding exactly who are pro and who con, at this level there is more fence-sitting, with several indicating that married life may be practicable on £200, but not without genuine problems, so perhaps is unwise. They include those with experience of marriage on that scale and those without. *Espero* may speak for both: "We may on this [evidence] safely say that £200 per annum, with care and economy, is barely sufficient for married life of even an ordinary kind. What it may be for anything extra is impossible for me to say."

While *A British Matron* is resolute in dismissing the "absurd . . . farrago of nonsense about the impossibility of living in comfort on £200 per annum," only four correspondents agree with her, while twelve strongly dissent, arguing severally that this amount is not sufficient even for a bachelor,[40] that the coming tide of babies will make for constant anguish, and that whatever may be the case for others, it will not do for "ladies" (says *A Young Englishman* who is "a gentleman"). The clergymen who contributed to the series congregate in this group, all of them oppressed by the near certainty that they are unlikely to get better livings, and consequently believe their financial rewards will never much exceed £200; one with experience demonstrates through budgetary detail that he could keep the household functioning only by doing other work for fees and gifts—which in fact made up an important part of the actual income of many such.

Traveller speaks succinctly for the emigration lobby: "We cannot marry on £200 a year, and we can scarcely hope to make that in the land of our birth." The case that best illustrates the tone and concern of the series as a whole is that of *C.S.C.*, who, with wife, two children, and a servant, spends £200 with great care, and much desires advice on how to reduce expenditures.

Should One Marry on £150 to £180 per annum?

The argument and evidence in the range £150 to £180 are of course similar to those found in nearby ranges. It might well be anticipated that those who have as much as a quarter less than those at £200 would have less confidence in marriage, yet more than those with 50 per cent less at £100. But that anticipation is not fully realized: the sides are almost even, some twenty thinking that £150 to £180 is adequate, some twenty-five dissenting. Early in the series, there is a preponderance of the hopeful; this is offset later by the fearful, especially when emigration becomes an important theme. The connection is not surprising, for those who favour emigration are likely to dwell specifically on the economic motivation: they are planning to leave England because an income permitting marriage (say £150) is neither in hand nor prospect.

There are of course many qualifications, mentioned by people on both sides of the issue, including the proviso that circumstances alter cases, that the place of residence must be considered,[41] and the all-important caveat that proper attitudes, including unstinting love and fortitude, can make endurable all but the worst sufferings. An important point made by one or two of the hopeful is that an income in the £150 range justifies marriage only if there is a comparatively secure provision for increases, for nothing can be saved at that level. *Foreigner* insists that on such an income a husband should immediately take out a large life insurance policy (say for £500).

Special points made by the cautious include the fact that in London £150 is barely enough for a bachelor, the observation that improvident marriage is not just male folly[42] but wickedness,[43] the warning that, no matter how incautious the young lovers, no responsible parent or guardian would give assent (not unhappily argued by *One Who Is Content to Wait*), and the all important issue of issue—what may be enough for two will prove quickly and woefully inadequate for three . . . and four . . . and. . . .

Should One Marry on £100 to £130 per annum?

Very few thought so, but, remembering the beatitudes, it seems wise to cite one, the least demanding, who did. Early in the series, *Preceptor* rebutted *Solon Smiff*, who strongly argued that £300 is not sufficient, by citing cases in his own experience that give the lie to those who counsel long delay in marrying:

A.B. was one of three sons of poor but respectable parents, and having a turn for study was educated for a school-master. At the age of twenty-two he married, and has since that time, on an average of £80 per annum, purchased his house, studied and passed B.A. at London University, and is now a clergyman. He has not been childless, having three still living, and I believe four buried, one having lived to the age of sixteen. I need not add anything further. I at present know two clerks in a City office, one in receipt of £4 10s weekly and the other of £1. The junior one had the audacity to marry to the disgust of the senior, who, I may add, spent more than the £1 on billiards.

The advice is minimal: "both parties" must "make up their minds to live comfortably, but not sumptuously, on a small income of, say, £80 to £100"; the source of error is quickly identified: "while parents ask the fifty bullocks as the smallest fortune the husband is to possess,[44] marriages will be few, while crime and misery will increase."

Such advice was to many, such as the aptly named *Prudens*, sheer folly: "A may be content with £80 a year—so much the better for A; but the habits and education of B may perfectly justify him in declining to start under £400 annually." The optimists, however, were not to be silenced. *A Happy Nine Years' Wife* (also in a rage about *Solon Smiff*) married on £100 a year and has seen both family and fortune grow in joy. So she is

an advocate for early marriages. Let youths and young maidens marry while the freshness of heart and sweetness of the present is on them, and not wait till years sully the mind, break down the spirits, bring on lethargy. . . . Happiness and love give confidence, expand the energies, and stimulate a man to ultimate success, while coldness and selfishness deaden the heart and warp the intellect, and at last bring blank despair.

The most enthusiastic of all in this group is *A Happy Married Man*, "of seven years' experience." With only £100 per annum, he is buying through a building society a six-roomed house (letting two rooms), which will be his own by the time his three children will need "a little more schooling or apprenticing." He has insured the house for £200, and the furniture for £100, and is in a benefit society. Without any luxuries, they are happy and contented.

The secret is this. I am blessed with a really good and industrious, cheerful, and affectionate wife, who knows how to economise and do anything and everything that is useful. She is one of the homely jewels that, though scarce, are to be found, and which young men should look after, instead of the dressy, useless dolls that are too much in demand.

Still caution is necessary, say those like *A Would-Be Reformer*, who, though highly censorious about "the extravagant style of living and habits of luxury which prevail to so great an extent amongst the middle and upper-middle class; the class above all others which is likely to be most affected when the question of marriage comes before it," emphasizes that circumstances alter cases, and thinks there is no doubt that a "man with an income of £100 a year is just as rich and happy as if he had a thousand, provided only he has been brought up accordingly, and has never known anything different, nor been taught to estimate everything by a money standard."[45] Of those who believe that respectability and happiness are possible below £150, *A Draper* introduces specially interesting points: first, most who have attained say £130 will have spent many years doing so, and so been able to save enough to make the marital venture practicable; and second, the question is really not "whether a couple can provide for themselves and children on £120 or £130 per annum," but "whether they will"—and he gives figures showing how he and his wife did so.

But the negative side dominates in numbers, as one would expect. For instance, *A Bachelor* (mentioning the £100–200 range) justifies his own prudence by "inquiring why he should give up his present state of comparative independence and comfort for one which may, and in all probability will, involve him in unknown cares, troubles, and anxieties (which he would never have known if he had remained single), however good a partner in life he may secure." With him is *Joseph*, who would never "lower" a suitable mate by impoverishing her, and *A Lover of Home*, who describes a friend of his who married ideally but on £100, to be faced almost immediately with a serious illness of his wife's, which made for unavoidable anguish and deprivation. Among several who dwell on personal history are *Bread-Winner's Wife* and *Charlie's Wife*, who married unwisely on £100 and £120, and *One Who Speaks from Experience*, who, while admitting that a couple might initially scrape by on £100 to £200, points out that without "a decided chance of an advance in the annual income, the home comforts must decrease as the little ones increase."[46] *An Eldest Daughter* (aged nineteen) is more scornful, saying that only "genteel beggary" is possible for people in their "station" on £100, and to think that country life on that income can be comfortable is "simply madness." And *Three "Girls of the Period"* are equally frank: "In our estimation [£100] is little enough for one,[47] and to have such an encumbrance as a husband attached to it (although, poor creature, he may have to earn it) is enough to deter a girl with any common sense from running her head into the matrimonial noose."

M.T.M., who judges (as do some others) that the difference of opinion is sex-based, ignores cautious and scornful girls[48] as well as enthusiastic male youths[49] when he asserts that young girls claim that a small income will do, while young men are more cautious. His explanation is not *a priori*: girls of the upper and middle classes are not accustomed to buying things for themselves, while men "have to provide for themselves, and know—alas! too well—how much money it costs to present a decent appearance to the world."

It may be said in summary that there is general acceptance of actual economic circumstances as limiting and enduring. The difficulty is plain enough to the cautious and the sadly experienced: the social (and to a serious extent also the physical) demands of life in London are such that the married lower middle class are at least pinched and at worst crushed. Those optimistic as a whole do not deny the difficulties; what they assert is that, all taken into account, good management and constant love leave a balance of happiness sufficient to those who recognize the imperative (divine or personal) to marry and breed.

Just how the trick was or was not done will be dealt with below, but first it is appropriate to hear at length from *A Woman*, who raises in a representative manner many of the central issues and reveals many of the major assumptions that summary distorts.[50] She begs leave to "have [her] say amongst the rest of the good people," on the two main questions being discussed: first whether "whether it is possible for a man and woman to marry upon from £80 to £300 yearly," and second, whether they ought to do so, considering both "duty and expediency."

As to the first question, she notes that the evidence of many of the correspondents and of general experience shows that in fact many married couples do live on such amounts; however, it is still necessary "to glance at the various classes of people who do so, with a view of understanding how far justice has been rendered to our wives and daughters." She would include "many professional men, clerks, small shopkeepers, mechanics, and a great number of labourers." Within this grouping there are most marked differences, including at the top "the most carefully-managed households, the best-regulated and most comfortable homes." The reason is that they are made up of some of "the socially highest, the most truly educated and refined both of men and women." They are "true gentlefolks who can, and what is more, who do, turn their hands to anything that circumstances require of them." In contrast she places (claiming personal observation) miserably regulated households of the ironstone miners, among whome there are "many families earning from £300 to £500 yearly." "The way in which many a small shopkeeper and well-to-do mechanic live would astonish many a lady and gentleman living on their £600 a year." Consider the provision of food: "Why, Polly's mother spends as many pence

during the year in trash and sweetmeats for her as in the hands of
Edith's mother would have furnished two or three interesting and useful magazines weekly throughout that time." Commonly the ironstone
miners' fare will include "salmon, fowls, and every delicacy during the
fore part of the week, and dry bread upon Friday and Saturday."

On the other hand, there are many "refined and gentle ladies"
reduced "to comparative want" who willingly and effectively "turn up
their sleeves and cook, bake, sew carpets, and wash and dress their
children, teach them, work for them if need be, and so, almost unaided,
keep a comfortable and happy home over their heads for their young
children to grow up and thank them for." Those who think "a general
servant" would make an ideal wife should be told that "there is no
more recklessly-wasteful class of people than these same general servants—partly, I suppose, from a low state of morals, and partly
because they never know what it is to have to put their hands in their
own pockets."

A Woman continues with an even more loaded class assertion in high
rhetoric that it would be shameful to summarize:

but a few short years ago [during the Crimean War], [did we not find] that
from the ranks of what were to outward show our most curled and faultlessly-
attired fops and dandies came forth in the hour of danger and terror our bravest and most noble examples of heroism and unselfishness? Well, men of
England, look up your memories; you turned heroes then—aye, many of you,
from whom your own mothers would hardly have looked for it; did we do
less? Who worked for you then? Did not thousands of jewelled fingers throw
down the cambric and embroidery, and work—yes, hard—upon the roughest
of flannels and thickest of serges? Was it our fault that you did not reap the full
benefit of our labour? Have you forgotten the women who left home and comfort for the privations of a Russian hospital? Have you forgotten that it was
white hands that nursed you then—hands that you little thought skilled in
ought but the last fashionable fantasia? It is not usual for a nation to require the
chignons of its women; I only know of one such case, when Carthage was
besieged desperately, and rigging could not be procured for the ships. Raven,
golden, and chestnut locks were then shorn off, and unhesitatingly twined into
rope and cord. Doubt not but that there is stuff in us for this also. Character
comes out as there is occasion for it.

Her passions move her to misreading when she asks what the correspondence proves and answers her own question. It proves only that
the untried bachelors are the ones who think the English girl "unfit for

her duties as a wife." Those with experience have without qualification asserted that "they both can and do live in happiness and comfort upon that very sum which the unmarried men declare it to be folly to take a girl upon."

Getting at length to her second question, ought young folk to marry on from £80 to £300 yearly, she affirms that it is "the duty of every man . . . to keep himself a respectable member of society." And each man is "bound to answer to his own conscience" whether he has "a right to marry and bring children into the world without a reasonable and fair prospect of being able to keep them in the common necessaries of life." As to the expediency of the question, she insists that no line can be drawn, for it is simply a matter of comparison:

It is more expedient for John, a talented fellow who can turn his hand to most things, to marry upon £80, than it is for Thomas, a dull ne'er-do-well, upon £150, without any further prospects for the next twenty years. A quick, clever, healthy woman can marry upon £100, where a weakly, ailing one could not physically attempt it upon £200.

At this point she moves into peroration in a fashion that so well illustrates one of the rhetorical modes in the series that again it deserves attention:

Do not be too worldly-wise, nor calculate overmuch; but still Providence does help those who help themselves, and surely it is expedient to allow a little margin for sickness, or loss of employment even, which happens to many or all at some time or other. Then, having found yourselves to possess all those requisites which you think make it either advisable, expedient, or desirable that you should marry upon such sum, lastly, have you a brave heart? If not, look before you leap.

How Much Money Was There?

This second essential question may be answered more quickly and assuredly. There can be little doubt that the figures given by the *Daily Telegraph*'s readers represent reality. One exactly contemporary estimate of national incomes, which placed 2,759,000 people in the upper and middle classes (as against 10,961,000 in the "manual labour class"), found the great majority of them receiving "small incomes," with 1,026,000 in the £100 to £300 range and 1,497,000 under £100.[51]

In that "small income" group fall most of the correspondents of the

Daily Telegraph, though they should be seen as falling into a sub-group that might have the greater expectations entailed by the high level of literacy they demonstrate. Taking from the series the statements of the two most representative groups of the wage earners, clerks and clergymen, and using for comparison evidence about two other groups with similar economic status, journalists and young professionals and intellectuals, one can accumulate evidence from fact and fiction sufficient for generalization.

First the clerks. In 1866 figures were given to a Commons Select Committee on the salaries of clerks and others employed by the Metropolitan Board of Works:

there is a clerk to the Board [of Works] with a salary of £300 a year, an assistant clerk, £130; a medical officer of health, £150; sub-inspector of nuisances and messenger, £70; surveyor and chief inspector of nuisances, £275; clerk of paving works, £98; clerk of sewer works, £78; two inspectors, £78; all these officers are appointed for that small district [Strand].[52]

In the mid-1830s Anthony Trollope began his career as a clerk in the Post Office at £90 per annum, and by 1841 had reached £140 (with an almost assured rise soon to £180). However, he accepted a transfer to Ireland, where travel allowances made up his basic salary of £100 to £300.[53] He knew the civil service thoroughly, and consequently his fictional comments on the income and habits of the government clerks are unrivalled. A few extracts from *The Three Clerks* will confirm some of the norms and expectations: in the "more respectable branch" of the "Department of Weights and Measures," "the establishment called the Secretary's Department," young men enter at £100 a year, while at no other public office do they "commence with more than £90—except, of course, at those in which political confidence is required."[54] Henry Norman, therefore, was well placed with £10 more than most others, but whether he could have lived up "to that tone of society to which he had been accustomed cannot now be surmised"; however, he soon inherited some £150 or £200 a year, and consequently was "placed above all want" (p. 16). The salary of Charley Tudor, after three years as a government clerk in his office, had risen to £110 per annum and a little later to £150 (pp. 28, 189). The third clerk, the high-flyer Alaric, succeeds in competition for a senior clerk's position which raises him from £200 to £600— and consequently really up to another social level (pp. 65, 70).

The other novel by Trollope that most dwells on clerks is *Marion Fay*,[55] which equally contains confirming details. George Roden, who in five years had risen in "the official elysium of St. Martin's-le-Grand," the Post Office headquarters, to £170 a year, lived in comfort with his mother because she had "means of her own amounting to about double as much," and economical habits (p. 32). However, when it becomes known that he is an Italian aristocrat by birth (the Duca di Crinola [horsehair]), although he refuses to be known by his title, he is made Registrar of State Records in the Foreign Office at £1500 a year (pp. 448–9).[56] Other clerks in the novel include Zachary Fay, Marion's father, who as a senior clerk in a commercial house had a salary of £400 (pp. 109–10). At lower levels one finds Tribbledale, also a commercial clerk, who had fallen back to £120 a year and had no prospect of an increase—though when he marries, his employers raise his salary to £160 (pp. 396, 425).

The expectations, Trollope fairly indicates, were usually limited, and only occasionally, as with Alaric Tudor and George Roden—and himself—were large leaps possible. What most could hope for was the success of Guppy in Dickens's *Bleak House*: when proposing to Esther Summerson, he proudly says his salary as a solicitor's clerk has just been raised from £1/15 to £2 per week, and in one more year at the utmost it will increase a further 5s. to £2/5 (i.e., from £91 to £104 to £117).[57] Compare the later raise that came suddenly to Charley Pooter (whose actual salary is never revealed): after twenty-one years as a clerk with the same firm, getting an annual rise of £10, he is elevated to the status of senior clerk (one of two), and then, instead of the expected increase of perhaps £15 or £20, he is given a £100 rise![58]

Leonard O'Lavish, an Irishman with a public appointment in Manchester at £500 per year, appears in an intentionally broad satire, *How They Mismanaged Their House on £500 a Year. A Narrative, in One Volume*,[59] where the main point is that only the very prudent (and non-Irish) could possibly cope on Mrs Warren's budget of £200.

As to clergymen, figures from a little earlier in the century giving the incomes of clerical incumbents and curates of the Church of England reveal the potential for despair and misery. In the 1830s, 297 had under £50 a year, 1629 and 1602 had respectively from £50 to £99 and from £100 to £149; at the other end, fewer than 1500 received over £500 (and of these, eighteen were over £2000).[60] As with clerks, there is a bulge just below the middle, with nearly one-half the clergy receiving between £100 and £300 per year. Just here fall many of the fictional clergymen of the period, for in this respect novelists were seemingly committed to real realism, as in the cases of Mr Greenwood in *Marion Fay* and Mr Willmott in *Mary Lyndsay*. In another novel, Jane, "of an economical turn of mind," marries "a good little ugly parson on £300 per annum, and kept him very trim and tidy on that minute sum."[61] Trollope once more is nearer the gnawed bone, with one of his best-known exemplars, Crawley in *Framley Parsonage*, suffering miserably until a preferment occurs: "Poor Mrs. Crawley, when she heard of it, thought that their struggles of poverty were now well nigh over. What might not be done with a hundred and thirty pounds by people who had lived for years on seventy?"[62]

A third group, not represented directly in the letters to the editor, but comprising their recipients, are journalists, some of whom dragged out a miserable existence, while others aspired to and some achieved the status of gentlemen, often by turning their pens to less ephemeral literature. One who typifies the early struggles, bohemian and varied, but who emerged triumphant, was George Augustus Sala, an important member of the *Daily Telegraph*'s staff. As a youth, he worked first as a theatrical scene-painter and general dog's-body, earning 15s a week.[63] Then at nineteen, as an illustrator, he earned on an average about 35s a week, but some weeks he got only 10s–12s, and he always lived in a garret, dining when necessary (to save for a purchase) on bread and cheese for a week. He began to contribute to *Household Words*, receiving five guineas for each article, often writing two a week, and reached a "tolerably certain income" of £300–400 a year, moving up to and beyond the mean for journalists.[64]

Though mediated fictionally, the first-hand evidence of many novelists who had written for newspapers rings authentic. For example, Thackeray gives details in *Pendennis* that establish the social level and possibilities of young men in the trade. Jack Finucane is appointed sub-editor of the newly founded *Pall Mall Gazette* at four guineas a week. Pen gets the same amount for his contributions, and by further "furnish[ing] Magazines and Reviews with articles of his composition," and being London correspondent of the *Chatteris Correspondent*, a country paper, he is enabled to earn "a sum very nearly equal to four hundred pounds a year,"[65] thus, incidentally, answering the question of a similarly situated young man wanting marriage in another of Thackeray's novels. Philip asks his friends: "How could he be put in the way to earn three or four hundred a year?"[66]

Less, it seems, is dangerous even if inviting, as Trollope indicates, when he has Charley Tudor remark enthusiastically:

"The editor says that [my story] "Crinoline and Macassar" will come to £4, 10s."

[Alaric] "And when will you get it?"

"The editor says that the rule is to pay six months after the date of publication. The Daily Delight is only a new thing, you know. The editor says that, if the sale comes up to his expectations, he will increase the scale of pay."

"A prospect of £4, 10s for a fortnight's hard work! That's a bad look-out, my boy; you had better take the heiress."[67]

A fourth group, not integral to the *Daily Telegraph* series but often thought of as typical, has been identified above as professionals and intellectuals. Its composition is very difficult to define, not least because it overlaps with journalism in its "higher" manifestations; Stefan Collini looks to its members' chosen and perceived role as reaching for and sometimes achieving the status of "public moralists." Generalizing from his extensive evidence, Collini gives the "absolute minimum on which a single young man could live and still maintain appearances" as about £250 a year in the mid-Victorian period.[68] He indicates that the average student at the bar spent about £200 a year; prize fellowships paid £250 on average.[69] But such positions were seen as take-off points for high flights; most of those who are remembered as public moralists[70] moved into positions in the civil service, the higher journalism, the universities, and the law that were well beyond the aspirations of those who were and expected to remain in the lower middle class. In short, it is not such as they who are in focus here; they serve only as a contrast.

In the fiction and social commentary of the period there is of course much description and analysis of the lower wage levels, and increasingly in the latter half of the century, when national and political solutions to social distress were sought, there is complaint. Much of the anger was expressed by the middle-class social agitators, the incipient "social workers" of later days, the focus of whose rage was those like themselves who made up the "establishment." From that perspective, what is instructive about the correspondence of 1868 in the *Daily Telegraph* is the virtual absence of complaint against any institution, vague group, or divinity for their suffering from they what clearly perceive as realities of life. Some correspondents criticize groups (including useful collective fictions such as the "Girl of the Period" and the "Young Man of the Period") whose attitudes place sensibility above sense and make good housekeeping impossible, while others abuse those whose hard hearts and heads deny life its excitement and romance; but these are objections to behaviour, not even hinting at the kind of wicked abuse or neglect of others involved in a socialist theodicy. It simply did not occur to them that the "state" was responsible for personal or class poverty: there are no assumptions about the value of state intervention, and adherence to self-help is implied as the only practical and moral recourse.[71]

How Was the Money Spent?

Practical moralists of the mid-nineteenth century, especially those writing advice books, were intensely concerned to impress on a changing society the need to control expenditures, measuring them always against income, and to leave a bit over for emergencies unforeseeable but almost certain.[72] Wilkins Micawber spoke for a host when he enunciated his bitter experience:

"My other piece of advice, Copperfield," said Mr Micawber, "you know. Annual income twenty pounds, annual expenditure nineteen nineteen and six, result happiness. Annual income twenty pounds, annual expenditure twenty pounds ought and six, result misery. The blossom is blighted, the leaf is withered, the god of day goes down upon the dreary scene, and—and in short you are for ever floored. As I am!"[73]

But exhortation was not enough; specific instructions were needed, and they were amply provided. A few instances will serve to illustrate.

The first lesson needed by the young housekeepers—and especially the young brides—was how to keep records properly. The anonymous *Domestic Economy* of 1856 (which sold for 1s) gave a model:

Money Spent		£	s	d		Money Received			
Jan.	Coal bill	1	7	0		Jan 31	£	s	d
1–31	Bread	1	0	0		Money received	15	10	0
	Meat	2	3	0					
	Washing	0	12	0					
	Grocer, etc.	1	15	0					
Feb.	Taxes	1	14	0		Feb 28			
1–28	Servant's Wages	2	10	0		Money received	10	14	0
	Bread	2	2	0					
	Butcher	1	19	0					
	Washing	0	12	8					
	Grocery, etc.	2	0	0					

Mar.	Bread	1	0	0				
1–31	Butcher	1	14	0		March 31		
	Grocer, etc.	1	5	0	Money received	15	10	0
	Washing	0	12	4				
	Quarter's rent	6	10	0				
	Pd. into Saving's							
	Bank	3	15	0				
		£32	11	2				
	Balance	9	2	10		£41	14	0
		£41	14	0	(Next entry,) Apr 1			
					Balance in hand	£9	2	10[74]

It may be noted that nothing is listed for clothing or charity; the text mentions such expenses, but without giving amounts.

Having mastered the form (and seen some figures), the newly wedded couple (or those contemplating marriage or even contemplating disaster in marriage) would be ready for two of the more comprehensive comparative guides already cited, the anonymous *Economy for the Single and Married* and Walsh's *A Manual of Domestic Economy*.

The first provides tables of expenditure for categories of annual income and marital state, beginning at £50 and continuing at fifty-pound increments. The single categories are implicitly for men only, living away from home; no mention is made of single women. At £50 a single man would pay £12 for a bedroom; at £100 he could have "Chambers with extras" at £35. On food the comparable amounts are £20 14s and just under £40;[75] on clothing £5 and £10. The better-off man could add £2 for "linen" to the £5 for washing; and to "church" might be added "charity" with "extra" to the extent of £6 12s 6d (rather than the £2 16s of his £50 counterpart)—but he would not have on such expenses the surplus £4 10s (p. 23).

As for the married at these levels, the 100-pounder would somehow rent off two furnished apartments rather than the one of his £50 counterpart, and so, though paying £6 more in rent and taxes, have only a £5 cost for housing. However, he would also have to add the costs of servant's wages (£4); coals, etc., would increase by £1; and food and drink (fish at £2 2s is added) would jump from £28 to more than £55 (including, perhaps because of the servant, beer at £4). The sum for dress, "extras," and washing at home could now be £22 8s rather than a very stinted £8; "church" now supplemented by "charity" could rise from £1 to £3; and "doctor" appears as £2 (p. 25).

In summary the recommendations of *Economy for the Single and Married* at the levels crucial in the "Marriage or Celibacy?" debate are: the single man at £150 might spend on chambers £38, on food (excursions now more than occasional) £59 10s, on clothes (with "boots, etc.") £12, on washing and linen £11 10s, and on church, charity, and extras £25—again with no margin (p. 34). His married counterpart, now no longer letting off apartments, would have a total of £31 in rent and taxes with £6 10s for servant's wages; coals (£7), wood (10s), candles (£1) could total £8 10s; washing at home (with more detail, comprising soap, wages of a woman three-quarters of a day per week and her meals, soda, ironing, and mangling) is up a full pound to £6; the expenses for dress rise potentially to £22 because "say two children" are added; and church, charity, and doctor's bills comprise £10 13s. The oddity (partly explaining a potential surplus of £14) is that food and beer are calculated at a total of £51 7s, down from over £55 (p. 35).

At £200 the single man disappears from the calculations, probably because there are fewer problems and not because all such should be married. The married 200-pounder could expend £35 on rent and taxes with a servant at £10; coals and candles (minus wood for no assigned reason, but now plus soap) could increase by £4 10s to £13; washing "and sundries" might add up to £10; dress, now broken down into £10 for the "gentleman," £12 for the "lady," £12 for the unspecified number of children, and £5 for shoes, "etc.," now totals as much as £34; church and charity (the doctor seemingly will not be called on) could be £5. An allowance of £78 16s is now made for food and drink (sadly, vegetables are down, and beer has disappeared to be replaced by "porter and occasional spirits" at £10), and excursions, "etc." are permitted just over £9 (p. 41).

For married folk with higher incomes the author gives only estimates of additional costs (pp. 42-3):

£250: + wine £5, clothing £15, servant's wages £5, rent & taxes £12, coals £5 = £42, leaving £8 more surplus

£300: + wine £12, clothing £20, servant's wages £9, rent & taxes £30, coals £8 = £79, leaving £21 more surplus

£350: + wine £20, spirits £7/10, clothing £25, butcher & poulterer £20, greengrocer £7/10, baker £7/10, beer £5 = £92/10, leaving £57/10 more surplus

£400: + wine £30, spirits £10, clothing £30, butcher, poulterer, fishmonger

£30, greengrocer £10, baker £10, beer £7/10 = £127/10, leaving £72 [sic for £72 10] more surplus

£450: + keep of a horse £30, tax on Stanhope &c. £5, wages & keep of manservant £30, surplus reduced by £15, amounts to £57 [sic for £57 10s]

£500: + proportionally nothing beyond £450, so the surplus amounts to £107.

Walsh's *A Manual of Domestic Economy* (1857, revised ed. 1873) gives a comparable estimate to those in *Economy for the Single and Married* in rather different form.[76] In his households, made up basically of the married couple, two children, and servants, he allows for housekeeping in the 1857 version £150 at the £250 level, £65 at £100; for rent and taxes respectively £31 5s and £12 10s, and the same amounts for clothing; for wages and incidental expenses £18 15s and £5; and for illness and amusements (an odd couple) £18 15s and £5. These certainly suggest the need for pinching at the lower level, especially in the vital housekeeping category, which includes food and heat. In 1873, at the lowest levels he gives, now £350 and £150, housekeeping is listed, respectively, at £220 and £95; rent and taxes at £45 and £17 10s, as is clothing; wages and incidentals £20 and £10; and illness and amusements £20 and £10.

The budget in Eliza Warren's *How I Managed My House on £200 a Year* (1864) allows £25 for rent and taxes, £80 for various household expenses, £10 for a servant, £35 for clothes, £20 for doctor's bills, unforeseen sundries, or exigencies, and rather surprisingly—but in the event wisely, given the husband's illness and death—£25 for insurance (a policy, presumably on his life, for £1000).

The interest in the subject and the popularity of Mrs Warren's work is demonstrated by its calling forth a spoofing indignant answer to the parent's stern voice by one purporting to be her daughter. In the *Girl of the Period Miscellany* in 1869 she quotes her mother's budget, commenting, as a true "Girl of the Period" should, that the details are ridiculous. Where in London is there a house renting for £25 that one could live in? The estimates for running expenses, servants, and dress are equally absurdly low, and there is no need for insurance. Her own experience is a better guide: five years ago she married Tom—of course there is "no baby" or "such nonsense"—and their annual expenditure has been £800, income only £200; so they have resorted to staying with friends. On this system they have spent in ten months only £166 13s, and actually saved 4d on their allotted outlay.[77]

The flippant narrative voice of *How They Mismanaged Their House on £500 a Year*, another much less interesting sequel by yet another member of the family, "Mr. Warren," does not dwell on enough specific costs to allow budget details to be inferred, but his household in Manchester (consisting originally of his wife, two domestics, a duck, and a tomcat, soon enlarged by the birth of twin humans) managed to cost a total of £600, of which nearly £250 went for "Casual house expenses"—rent, taxes, painting, papering, "and such-like items," "so there was not much left for meats and drinks, and bodily requisites, and nothing to deposit in the bank." Faced with disaster, the family moved to a less expensive house (renting for £40 a year), where, with other lower costs and a change of heart and habit, they were able to bank £100 a year (pp. 252–3).

An interesting comparison is afforded by an exchange in the *English-woman's Domestic Magazine* in 1871, which makes abundantly clear the centrality of women not just in the details but the planning and management of home economy. The series was initiated by a letter from *Housekeeper*,[78] who, married for four months, is overspending her weekly allowance for food and servants' beer of £4 10s by about a pound, and has to make up the difference from her dress allowance. Her obvious recourse for advice, her mother, is useless, because the mother's task is only to draw up a list of the month's bills, which her husband pays by cheque. Copious advice came in the next issue from *Mrs. S.*, married seven years, who now, with three young children and two grown-up daughters, plus three servants, has a monthly allowance of £26 to cover wages, food, beer, washing for all ten people, clothes for the children, and occasional in-house assistance from a dressmaker and a washerwoman. Her record-keeping is meticulous: in addition to her memorandum-book (an "inseparable companion"), she has two account-books, one for housekeeping proper and the other for dress, children's clothes, wages, and sundries. In yet a third book she keeps a summary of the month's expenses. All the detail indicates that her expenses are in the neighbourhood of £340, obviously appropriate only to the upper middle class.

In December *Silkworm* (probably a staff member) asked for letters giving budgets.[79] The exchange continued in the next month with answers, requests for even more precise information, and further questions about the relation of expenditure to incomes, and provision for contingencies. In February (p. 126) *Mrs. F.* (presumably a widow) supplied a detailed food budget for her father, herself, and a servant that totalled just under £1 12s per week, and a quarterly budget for all other costs that amounted to just over £53, adding up, with an allowance for contingencies, to £220; because she comes closer to the *Daily Telegraph* figures, it is useful to give some of the expenses, such as rent and taxes at £40, food at £82 4s 6d, heating and light at £11 10s, washing and related cleaning expenses at £7 10s, doctor and chemist at £5, clothes (the lady's costing £2 less than the gentleman's) and charity[80] at £38, servants' wages at £10, and newspapers and books at £4.

One further response, which again is upscale, came in May (p. 318) from *Roberta*, who had been married twelve years, and now has a household of thirteen people (seven children, a nephew, a governess, and two servants); she supplies a quarterly record that amounts to an unstated annual outlay of just over £260 for food plus the cost of household help.

A little later, in 1874, "Espoir," in *How to Live on a Hundred a Year*, offered advice to a group generally ignored in the other sources, prudent single ladies of restricted means. For rent and taxes they could expend £13 16s; for wages, £9; for food (including brandy!—probably medicinal), £39; 17 12s; other expenses, including gardening, clothing, charity (£2), and sundries, brought the annual total to £73 10s 6d—and left enough for a new silk dress every three years out of savings.[81]

The exchange in *The Times* in 1858 mentioned above adds two more opinions on the issue.[82] *Another Happy Man* (15 Jan.) answered a correspondent's question by detailing his full outlay for 1857, his household including himself, wife, one child, one woman-servant, and one nursery-girl. His rent was £25, taxes £3 12s 7d, wages £12 6s, clothes £40, insurance £12, medical expenses £12, travelling, railway ticket, books, and newspapers £18, church and charity £20, and food and other household expenses just under £100 (tallowchandler £6 3s 7d!) for a total of £230 6s.

These figures were subjected to searching criticism by *A Married M.A.* (19 Jan.), who inferred that *Another Happy Man* must be "a clerk in a most respectable London office, with a salary of £250 a-year," living in a suburb about six miles from his office. All the expenses are so contracted, and so liable to inescapable demands with increase of family, that any young woman who does not wish to be "head nurse, head cook, and head housemaid" should be warned off marriage on £300 a year, or forestalled by papa.

All these accounts from varied sources give context to the figures provided by the correspondents in the *Daily Telegraph* in 1868, many of whom supply incidental information about the scale and kind of expenditures, while some offer full accounts. They have special value in portraying a social level below and more densely populated than that assumed in most of the advice books and in *The Times*. At that level the economic pressures were greater, while the demand for respectability was at least as onerous if slightly different in kind.

One of the first correspondents in the *Telegraph* to give some figures is *An English Girl*, who acts as housekeeper for her mother and herself on £80 annually. She takes exception to the excessive expenditure on washing of *Materfamilias*, an earlier correspondent who had married on £150 annually. She herself manages to have a muslin and a print dress washed for 1s 2d, and does her "body and household linen" as well as collars at home. While *Materfamilias* has had to give up her periodicals, *An English Girl* is able to find £1 14s 10d per year for the *Daily Telegraph* (6d per week), the *Family Herald* (1d per week), and Scott's novels (4 1/2d per month), and unlike *Materfamilias* gets to the theatre a few times during the year—as noted above, that cost is borne by her intended, who earns what she sees as an adequate £130 a year.

E.F.H. has a fuller tale to tell. His old and valued friend ("O.A.V.F.") proposed to a young lady, mentioning that his income was nearly £200 per annum. Her reply, enclosing a budget, suggested without subtlety that delay was necessary, as her estimate was that at least £217 16s would be needed. For example, house rent would require £30, a servant £10, "living for three people" (presumably the servant lived in) £72 16s, and a laundress £15. Dismayed but resolute, O.A.V.F. "untiringly" sought evening employment, and like many a fictional character looked afield, offering "to conduct a newspaper, edit a satirical review, manage a bank, and sing comic songs at a music-hall." Still sanguine ("youth is sanguine"), O.A.V.F. believes that his "fair young lady" will willingly wait until he achieves "the magic height at which wedlock is possible."

Paterfamilias, married for ten years, who wed at age twenty-seven on an income of £120, now has six children and a salary just short of £300 a year, on which they manage very happily.[83] He mentions a wide range of expenses, including those for an omnibus to work (he walks home in the evening to their "snug house in a suburb"), a daily governess for the children, and good meat dinners always and meat breakfasts sometimes. They enjoy a theatre two or three times in a year, though generally they take their amusements at home, and they indulge in a family excursion out of town every other summer, as well as a few exhibitions including that at the Royal Academy. Reading costs include that for the *Daily Telegraph* every morning, one denominational paper weekly, a magazine monthly, and the Charles Dickens edition of his works. Add to these a "mite" subscribed to one or two benevolent societies, and fire and life insurance premiums. The only specified amounts are for rent, £45 per annum, building society, 15s per month, piano hire (on "the three years' system"),[84] 21s per month, and sittings in a place of worship, £3 per annum. The sum total of their present debts, including the doctor's bill, is only £10.

A *Bachelor* would find *Paterfamilias*'s marrying on £120 a very hazardous move, for he is astonished at the suggestion that a couple could live on £100. Assuming that one took a small house on one of the lines of railway leading out of London, he lists the minimal expenses as rent £25, taxes £5, railway tickets £7 16s, dinner (in town) £15 12s, clothing, self and wife £20, for a total of £73 8s, leaving for all home expenses an obviously inadequate £26 12s. A *Bachelor* concludes that in such a state the married man "will evade the income tax, for which [he] freely forgive[s] him."

An *English Wife*, husband's salary £350, offers only three specific annual figures, rent £35, wages £24, and insurances £26. Their circumstances include putting out most of the washing, educating three children, having a comfortable table every day for eight people,[85] supporting the church, responding to many charitable "calls made in a manner apt to [her] husband's position," and attending no theatres but occasionally enjoying a concert. They enter a little into society at dinner parties, for instance, a pleasure she can reciprocate, and she dresses well at a moderate expense by making her own gowns.

An interesting minor argument was advanced by *A Few True Girls of the Period*. Young men, they point out, claim they cannot afford marriage, but in fact, if they "cannot make it convenient to live with their friends, [they] must live somewhere, most likely a furnished apartment, with partial board and attendance." Such arrangements will cost them £1 per week; this, added to their City dinners at 10s per week and other necessary expenses, must come to about £2 a week, an amount that would let them live comfortably "with a good, sound, practical, domesticated wife."

A rigorous and conveniently rounded account of how £200 is expended is given by C.S.C. for himself, his wife, two children, and a servant. They find it very difficult to keep within such costs as rent at £30, housekeeping at £98 16s, servants' wages at £8, and clothes at £30.

Distressed that people might be misled by *Paterfamilias*'s over-optimistic judgment, *Vieux Moustache* supplied the figures for the outlays that *Paterfamilias* had admitted to; these come to £112 7s 4d. He then adds figures for the necessary costs ignored by *Paterfamilias*, including the obvious outlays for household expenses, taxes, and dress, as well as one category ignored by almost all of the other budgeteers: "sweep, clearing bin, breakage, materials for cleaning house, table linen, and carpets, brooms, &c." amounting to £10. All this comes to a sum, £258 10s, that added to the other reaches a total, £370 7s 4d, sure to dismay all but the economically secure. His cautionary tale includes also a rebuke to *A Happy Nine Years' Wife*, joyful on the £100 a year that allows them "parties and picnics"; *Vieux Moustache* is of opinion that that sum "would be absorbed in decent lodgings and in food, and leave nothing for washing, clothing, books, and stationery, amusements, or church."

As seen in chapter 3 above, *Flo* takes a more narrative approach in drawing two contrasting pictures of married life on £150 a year, in one of which Susie and Tom are cheerfully confident about the future. *A Match-maker (Matrimonial, not Lucifer)*, though a professional who not infrequently entertains friends, "including clergymen and men of that stamp," is not unlike Susie and Tom in his management and like them and *Paterfamilias* in his sanguinity. With a wife, one servant, and an eight-room house with garden, his actual expenses total only £186 15s, including housekeeping at £84, rent and taxes at £43, and dress at £25. Their economies include his taking sandwiches for lunch and always dining at home. However, the servant gets a good meat dinner, with vegetables and beer every day, and sometimes pastry. He admits that he has not included costs of such variables as pleasure trips and books that depend on individual means. But had he only £150 a year he could cut back further—indeed to £138 15s—by entertaining less, taking a smaller house and walking to the office, reducing the dress bill, drinking less wine, and doing his own gardening.

This and the other cheerful accounts induced *Vieux Moustache* to a second attack directed at the great underestimation of housekeeping costs. He has to hand records for some years, itemizing daily, weekly, monthly, and quarterly expenses under the necessary categories:

1. Rent, taxes, gardeners, pew rents, and Easter offerings;
2. Food and drink;
3. Coals, wood, gas, and lights (candles);
4. Wages and occasional assistance in house;
5. Washing, soap, soda, &c.;
6. Stamps, books, stationers, newspapers, and subscription to libraries;
7. Breakage, renewing furniture or repairing it, tables and bed linen, sweep, bin-clearing, &c.;[86]
8. Medicine and medical attendance;
9. Charity, gratuities, and amusements;

10. Cab-hire and travelling;
11. Insurance (burial, subscription, or benefit societies can be substituted, and then all items of expenditure form charges even in the humblest households);
12. Dress for myself and wife.

Were people to list actual figures under these heads, they would not be misled by such as the early correspondent *R.P.C.*, who married at twenty-three, had three children, and, though his father had kept carriages, claimed he felt most comfortable on £130 a year. *Vieux Moustache* infers from *R.P.C.*'s comments that he "lived in a healthy position, and kept a servant," but even if he failed in his duty to subscribe "to a burial society, or insure his life for a small sum, say at £100," the sum of expenses must be more than £130, indeed amounting, as figures he supplies show, to just over £164. And this leaves no margin for confinements and the consequent cost of paid attendance, or for children's dresses, which alone would swell the amount to £170. Even with economies such as doing without beer and allowing a mere 2s rather than 3s for food, only £28 1s 8d would be saved. "Where," asks *Vieux Moustache* triumphantly, "is the margin for the occasional opera ticket" that *R.P.C.* laid claim to?

One Who Would Be a Good Deal Happier If He Had It, married four years, presented a similar challenge to young ladies: how could his expenses, totalling £180 10s, be reduced to £150, let alone £100? The major items were rent and taxes, £40, housekeeping, £78, clothes, £20, and "sundries (no myth)," £10. He too, he points out, had allowed nothing for confinements, and omitted holidays and amusements, all "very expensive items."

In more detail, a somewhat higher expenditure (£232 2s 9d) for himself, wife, and one servant was reported by *Plain Fact*, whose rent and taxes came to £43 and clothes to £25; housekeeping (carefully broken down into such items as "butcher, 14s per week, £36 10s per year") amounted to some £80. This account, he adds, leaves nothing to meet those "great bugbears," petty cash disbursements, but it is "based on the plain living expenses of persons used to common decency and strict economy." He comments, however, that, though to think of having a house on less than £300 a year is "simple folly," apartments with some "pretensions to decency and cleanliness" can be managed comfortably on £130 to £150, and that with economy in "sundries," about £20 a year could be put in the savings bank "to form a nucleus against a rainy day or the arrival of any young branches."

R.F.H. was of similar mind: twenty-five years of age, living in "not over-aristocratic" Islington with an "exemplary" wife and four young children, he finds his income of £200 per annum totally inadequate, though he is not extravagant in what some would call personal luxuries, such as cigars. He gives details for only one basic category: "Rent £40, Taxes £8, Let off the parlour floor furnished £ – 22: Total for rent and taxes, £26." Of like opinion, as his pseudonym indicates, was *An Anxious Father*, who supplied figures in the range proposed by *Vieux Moustache*, covering the expenses for himself, his wife, and three small children that come to little more, £223 17s in total. Their rent and taxes amount to £37, clothing to £30, and housekeeping to £84; of special note are the cost of his dinners in the City, £15 12, and wear and tear to the furniture, £10.

The most comprehensive account is that of *A Clergyman, Aetat 47*, who reports that he has kept a daily record for thirty years (twenty of them single; ten married). When he married his "loving and thrifty wife," his income was £200 a year (at which level it has remained) and he had £50 in hand. After the first five years of marriage, they had four children, and so, with two servants, a household of eight: the resultant increased expenses absorbed, he emphasizes, nearly £400 in that fifth year. As a guide to others, he extracts from his records the expenses during the last five years of his single life and the first five of marriage. As the best record of a cleric's progress—with implications for others in his income level—it is here given in full.

	Before Marriage					After Marriage				
	1855	1856	1857	1858	1859	1860	1861	1862	1863	1864
	£	£	£	£	£	£	£	£	£	£
Household and living expenses	54	54	68	43	48	97	119	160	113	180
Clothes	8	17	9	15	15	37	20	18	14	38
Washing	5	5	5	5	5	9	9	4	3	3
Gifts—Charities and donations	13	10	11	14	20	13	10	8	12	21
Household furniture	–	–	–	–	–	40	9	47	16	64
Sundries, i.e. Travelling, postages, stationery, medicine, and every disbursement not included in above heads										
	25	31	24	24	31	66	37	40	28	82
	105	117	117	101	119	262	204	277	186	388

Some of his explanations and comments deserve mention: he notes that in every year since marriage expenditure has exceeded income; the excess has been met by extra employment (presumably fees for priestly services) or, occasionally, by sums borrowed (though he has now no debts), and by money given, "not an unusual practice from kind-hearted relatives who are better off to poor clergy." He calls attention to the fact that furniture became a regular expense only on marriage—but it should not be assumed that such costs are other than current, for there was "very little to show" for the nearly £200 spent in the first five years of marriage at the end of that period. As to washing, that frequent concern in these budgets,[87] he explains that the diminution in its cost after the second year of marriage resulted not from any "abatement of cleanliness," but from having it "done at home" instead of "giving it out."

Yet a third letter appeared signed *Vieux Moustache*,[88] this time in reply to *Cassio*, who laid claim to £350 a year, but did not indicate whether it came from property of his own, or whether it all depended on his life or health. Assuming the former to be the case, *Vieux Moustache* says *Cassio* ought not to marry a young lady without means of her own until he has saved enough to furnish a house and to add some £150 more to his permanent income. At 4 per cent, in ten years £150 laid by yearly will amount to £1800. Applying £300 of this for furnishing, etc., *Cassio* would have an increase of £60 to his income by investing the residue (£1500) at 4 per cent. "Having then an income of £410 a year, and, humanly speaking, not so likely to have as many children as if he married forthwith, surely he could meet some suitable lady, by whose means he would have the minimum income on which I think it would be prudent for a man in the position of *Cassio* to marry."

After this careful advice, *Vieux Moustache* presents the actual expenditure for 1867 "of one pretty much on the same social level" as *Cassio*; he does not specify his profession (he is probably a military man), but says that its members, like the clergy, "can live on a smaller income—holding a certain position—than those of any other": the costs cover those of himself and his wife,[89] and servants—at least two, judging by the bills for wages (£22 14s 8d) and food and drink (£136 18s 2d). Their housekeeping costs include £17 4s 3d for "breakage, repairing furniture, and renewing table and bed linen, and sweep, brooms, and materials," and "washing, soda, soap, etc." at £15 19s 2d. In all, these accounts totalled £336 16s 6d in 1867.

For unassigned reasons he does not list the income tax, and says he has no need for life insurance because he paid "a few hundreds" some years ago to an office to secure his wife a small income if she survives him. They live in a provincial town; he estimates if they were in the suburbs of London an additional £50 per year would go on rent, cab or 'bus hire, and wages and washing, making a total of at least £386 per annum. Concerned to prove that his prudent advice is based on prudent practice, he itemizes their controls:

1. We never give dinners, or go out to them.
2. We never take trips, except occasional visits to friends.
3. We drink cheap wine, and little of it.
4. Our expenditure in amusements is only a few shillings a year.
5. My wife and myself, being well connected, never attempt to vie with the more wealthy residents in our neighbourhood, who, being of an inferior extraction, seem to be obliged by entertaining and keeping carriages to hold on to society.

From outside London came another country voice of a different kind. *T.Z.*, a "simple-minded Norfolk farmer who, thinking that free-trade and open markets" would ruin the agricultural interests, had (about 1850) disposed of his farm and retired, investing his money partly in land and partly in house property, thus realizing an annual income of £150–£200. The outbreak of war with Russia increased prices, and he had to economize, with his wife's great aid. Announcing that he has their accounts from 1851 to the present, *T.Z.* gives the annual cost of their establishment, which includes one servant. The total of £168 10s 1d includes rent and taxes of £26, housekeeping and drinks of some £80, and "the various little foxes which are constantly plucking at your purse-strings" at £10 6s 3d.

An Old Married Man, hypothesizing for a younger person, say a clerk in respectable position in a banking house or merchant's office who is "respectably connected," sets a lower standard and target, £198. This includes rent, rates and taxes, water, and gas at £38, clothes at £30, and food at just over £85.

But *A Draper* thinks even that level need not be seen as minimal. For him, it is not so much a question whether a couple with children *can* live on £120 or £130 but whether they *will* do so; certainly £150 is enough for a newly married couple, if proper attitudes govern. For instance, if the husband cannot afford daily travelling expenses (on which *An Old Married Man* spent £7 10s) he had better live within walking distance, and common sense indicates the avoidance of mistaken economies such as buying cheap dresses of cambric or muslin, which require weekly payments of as much as 1s 6d for washing. Rent and taxes need not be more than £25, provisions for two only £40, and clothing £30; indeed all predictable costs come only to £117, leaving £30 for the unforeseen. Not so, replies *George*, who points to omissions such as the cost of books, newspapers, doctor's bills, etc., and to under-estimates for coals, washing, soap, &c. He concludes that anyone with less than £300 annually should stay single.

In close agreement was *A Young Man of the Period*: the keeping up of appearances entirely precludes the idea of marriage on anything like £200; indeed it is impossible for a bachelor such as himself with more than that sum, even when "vegetating" one-quarter of the year at his father's country house. His account justifies his adopting that presum-ably intentionally provocative pseudonym. "Certain—or perhaps I ought to say uncertain—expenses which your calculating correspon-dents, I presume, include under the item 'sundries,' are always the most formidable part of my expenses," he says, and then lists the costs of an unusually expensive—but occasionally unavoidable—evening's amusement at an opera followed by a ball, whence he walked home to save money: lavender gloves, 3s; white tie, 1s; flower for button-hole, 1s; cab to opera, 1s; seat at opera, 10s 6d; to attendant for taking care of coat, 6d; and cab from opera to ball, 1s 6d. These total 18s 6d, obviously too much were he married on his income, but they provide too great a pleasure for him to forego.

These accounts are full of individual and collective interest, but they are not numerous or commensurate enough for statistically reliable inferences. How much easier would analysis be had the budgeteers followed the advice of the guides in drawing up their account books! As it is, the categories overlap, and almost always some likely expenses are not listed (as some of the critical letters pointed out). Especially difficult to compare are the household expenses, where often the determining factor seems to be what falls within the wife's responsibilities. Also, the expenditures are sometimes presented as actual and sometimes as ideal, and in both cases are occasionally but not always tailored to income and to the size of the family.

Some observations that go beyond impressionism are nonetheless of value. For instance, what was spent on servants by these correspon-dents?[90] First, the majority of those who give information on this sub-ject are drawn from the upper level of this income group; it may be assumed that those on the lower levels (most of them single, of course, and the males among them living in lodgings) had no live-in servants, but only daily or weekly help. That is, while those who do comment are comparable with at least the less affluent of those who appear in the series in *The Times*, in fiction, and books of household management, the servant problems of the more affluent had not arisen (and perhaps never would arise) for most of the correspondents in the *Daily Telegraph*.

To the situations of those who had faced the problems, the summary given by Jo McMurtry is a good guide, though of course most of her account deals with high income levels.[91] She indicates that an annual wage of £15 to £20 (plus board and room), "allowing for a rise in prices from the beginning to the end of the century," marks "the boundary between an upper and a lower servant's wages." She mentions, for instance, that a footman in a less sumptuous household (without wig, and obliged to spend more time carrying buckets of coal up back stairs and less time standing elegantly in the entrance hall) could be had for £20 or less. The cost of a coachman would be about £30, a butler or valet £40–50, a "good plain female cook" £25, a male cook (especially if French) £50. At the lower level, but still implying living-in, McMurtry says that a girl going "into service" aged ten or twelve (or a page-boy) would begin at £6 a year, and an under-housemaid, who cleaned fireplaces and emptied chamber pots, or a scullery maid, who washed pots and pans, would receive £10 or less.[92]

What becomes evident once again is that the correspondents of the *Daily Telegraph* were not at the level covered by such statistics: they did not employ male servants, had no carriages, and if asked to define a servant for themselves, would have thought first of a young girl of all work, being paid £10 or less a year. They were, of course, aware of the habits of others, especially when in a sarcastic moral mood: when *A Would-Be Reformer* argues against ostentation he refers to "poor Mrs. Tom Doodle, who only keeps five maid-servants, [and] is ready to go into fits if she hears that her neighbour, Mrs. Charles Wankleback, has just added a sixth to her establishment, and will worry her husband's life out of him and spend his last shilling rather than be outdone." And the few like *Bunny*, opulent on £500 a year (or perhaps just dreaming of it), are easy with references to two "respectable servants," who are paid "as such ought to be paid." Even more persuasive is *Vieux Moustache*, who, on an income of £370, lists wages for a servant at £14, and expenses for a charwoman, who with her food and materials costs £12 a year. Later *Vieux Moustache* mentions having "excellent servants"; he then warns those who assume that *R.P.C.*, who says he enjoys a comfortable married life on £130, can live in a healthy situation and keep a servant that such is impossible. Later still he (or perhaps now another correspondent using the same signature) mentions that his outlay of £336 (in a provincial town) includes for "wages and occasional assistance" £22 14s 8d. The only other correspondent at this level of income who mentions servants, *An English Wife* (who has £350 a year), lists wages of £24, implying that she has at least two.[93]

Hiring more than one servant indeed marks a social distinction closely related to income.[94] On this as well as other evidence, it would appear that the break-point was between £150 and £200. Instances include *A Clergyman* with four children who employed two servants at a time when his stipend was about £200 and their expenditure about £388. *Paterfamilias* on under £300 wisely makes do with just one regular servant plus a daily governess for children and that ubiquitous character, the charwoman who comes in to do the washing. *Plain Fact* includes in their expenditure of £232 a servant's wages of £10, while *An Anxious Father* on £223 has a servant at £10, an expenditure he deems necessary to avoid his wife's doing "menial" work. A different attitude is reflected in the tale of *A Real Help-Meet*, who reports that her husband determined to marry her when he saw her washing up the breakfast things at her home, "when we were a servant short." On marriage he had £200 per annum, but he subsequently "lost" it, and she has had to do without a servant, even when a baby arrived. Others in the same area of income include *E.F.H.*, who tells us that the fiancée of his "old and valued friend" in drawing up a budget that totals £217 16s includes a servant at £10, and *C.S.C.*, who spends £200 annually and gives £8 of that to a servant.[95] The lower one-servant range, about £150, is supported by the evidence of nine correspondents,[96] their position being summed up by *M.B.E.*, who implies that £150, which in his view is not enough for marriage, is about the limit at which one might keep one servant. People forget "the responsibilities and anxieties there are, even where servants can be kept—how much more when the means do not permit of one, or only a little drudge, who is more trouble than good." (The echo of David Copperfield's woes is pervasive.) Other warnings include that of *A Lover of Home*, who points out that those who propose to do without a servant forget that illness makes one necessary.

Below £150 the difficulties became immediately evident. *Charlie's Wife*, for example, says it was a mistake for them to keep one servant on £120. After their first baby was born, they had a nursemaid and another maid in the house, and put clothes out to wash. They went into business and soon accumulated debts of £500; they had to sit up doing their accounts while the servants were in bed. Subsequently they dismissed their servants and moved towards prosperity. And *Bread-Winner's Wife*, who married a clerk on under £100, mentions that after two children were born they had to keep a servant. When one of the children needed to go out of town for its health, she could not afford to take a servant along with them, although then their income was rising towards its present £220.

Nonetheless, there are the optimists, some of whom are prepared to trim the cost by part-time or less qualified servants: *A Draper* for instance includes, in a hypothetical expenditure of £150, a servant one-half day at £7 per annum, while *George's* outlay of £7 on a servant, out of a total of £117, suggests a limit on time or experience. Z.Y.X. apparently assumes that an income even as low as £100 will allow for "a servant girl." An interesting point is made by *A London Girl*, who, advancing the romantic view that marriage on £100 is practicable, asks why people should choose to live in a house when apartments, in which a servant is unnecessary, can be rented. And the enticing French comparison is offered by *Giglio*, who comments that in France couples beginning married life on the equivalent of £100–£150 keep one servant.[97]

The almost complete disappearance of the servant question from the correspondence once the emphasis shifts to emigration is not coincidental, although the reason is dwelt upon only by *Colonista*. While it is true that in a colony (she has experience in British Columbia) it is hard to find servants, and indeed difficult at least initially to afford them, she implies that one can have better than just "a common servant." However, this possibility is not significant: *Colonista* closes by mentioning the more important fact that in colonies one can escape the heavy costs of servants incurred in England.

What lies behind these figures and comments is a notion of the wife's duties and responsibilities, which are further suggested by the kind and range of household expenditures. As indicated above, the basis of comparison is anything but solid, for the budgets and isolated remarks are not in this respect commensurate. But they are not without interest. In the following account of housekeeping, the amounts generally may be assumed to include the cost of food, even when it is not mentioned, if it does not appear elsewhere in the accounts. The individual ranges run from the estimate of *A Bachelor*, who gives what he calls an inadequate £26 12s for "all home expenses," to the £136 18s 2d *Vieux Moustache* (on a much higher income) lists as the cost of "food and drink" alone in his limited household. It should be noted, of course, that a larger absolute expenditure on food as income increases generally means a lower percentage expended on such costs.

The ten-year account of *A Clergyman, Aetat 47*, which begins with five years of bachelorhood and concludes with five of marriage, runs from £54 to £180 per annum, the latter a higher sum than that of *Vieux Moustache*, but covering a larger household and a wider range of "household and living expenses." Otherwise the lowest and highest estimates are those of *A Draper*, who suggests £40 as an initial cost for "provisions" only, and of *Vieux Moustache*, who insists on £120, not for himself but as "living" costs for *Paterfamilias*, covering three adults and three children. Disregarding these extremes, the range is more confined and probably more reliable, running only from £69 13s 3d for *Plain Fact* (including food and £3s 10 for "sundries about house") to *C.S.C.*'s £98 16s (which includes her husband's luncheon in the City, probably costing about £15 per annum). The other accounts are these:

R.P.C. (as estimated by *Vieux Moustache*): about £70, covering meals, breakage, bed linen, furniture, cleaning materials, soap, sweep, and bin-clearing
E.F.H.: £72 16s, covering "living for three people"
Flo: £75 (an inadequate amount), including clothing
One Who Would Be A Good Deal Happier If He Had It: £78, including his lunch in the City
T.Z.: £78 15s 9, including washing
A Match-maker: £84, including servants' wages and washerwoman
An Anxious Father: £84, "all inclusive"
An Old Married Man: £92 10s, food only

Many of these must include the cost of beer[98] and (when indulged in) wine and spirits. A few list them separately:

£7 10s: *An Old Married Man* (estimating for a younger one) for beer
£10: *Vieux Moustache* for *Paterfamilias*, and *A Match-maker*, who includes medicine with wines and spirits
£10 1s 8d: *Vieux Moustache* for *R.P.C.*
£25 12s: *Plain Fact*, who breaks the total down into £9 2s for beer, £6 10s for spirits, and £10 for wine

Obviously some of these household lists quietly encompass what are otherwise described as "sundries" or are not named. The kind as well as extent of the costs point to typical cares and concerns:

£3 10s is spent by *Plain Fact* for "sundries about house"

£5 is given by E.F.H., and by *An Old Married Man* (per a younger one) for "replacing furniture, &c."

£6 is *Vieux Moustache*'s estimate on behalf of R.P.C. for breakage, table, bed linen, and furniture, cleaning materials, soap for family, sweep, and bin-clearing

£10 is *Vieux Moustache*'s estimate on behalf of *Paterfamilias*, who has a larger establishment, for sweep, clearing bin, breakage, materials for cleaning, table linen, carpets, brooms, &c., and also that of *One Who Would Be A Great Deal Happier If He Had It* (he notes that such expenses are "no myth"), and of *An Anxious Father*, who instances "wear and tear to household furniture"

£10 6s 3d is mentioned by *T.Z.* as the cost of "various little foxes which are constantly plucking at your purse-strings"

£17 4s 3d, the greatest cost, is as usual that for *Vieux Moustache*'s own household, encompassing breakage, repairing furniture, renewing table and bed linen, sweep, brooms, and cleaning materials

The separate accounts of the cost of washing should be considered in this context. Once again they are not strictly compatible, especially in their reflecting often unstated differences in the size of families and income. The range given by *A Clergyman, Aetat 47* over ten years is instructive: from £5 when single up to £9 when married, and then down to £4 and to £3; he explains the reductions as resulting from the washing being done at home in the later years. Otherwise the lowest account is that of *Plain Fact*, who gives £3 19s 6d as the cost of not only a washerwoman and her materials, but also of her food. The highest is again that of *Vieux Moustache*, whose bill for his own household comes to £15 19s 2d, including materials. In between come those *Vieux Moustache* estimates for R.P.C. (£5 for materials and a charwoman to do large articles once a month) and for *Paterfamilias* (£12 for materials and a charwoman once a week), and that of E.F.H. (£15 to a laundress).

What of clothing? Here the main variations arise apparently not from ostentation but simply from the size of the family. The range given by *A Clergyman, Aetat 47* over ten years shows a practical irregularity from year to year: his lowest cost was £8 when single, their highest in marriage with children, £38. The expenses given by others explictly for two people run from £12 10s to £37 10s (*Vieux Moustache* for himself and wife being as usual the highest), others being £20, £25, £28, and £30.[99] Only two give figures for larger families, both mentioning three children, one estimating £30, the other £45.

Another category dependent directly on the arrival and survival of children is medical expense, mentioned by all the canny and ignored by the innocent young and healthy. Noting that both *R.P.C.* and *Paterfamilias* omit this contingency, *Vieux Moustache* suggests that a doctor would cost the former £3 and the latter £8 (in this case including medicine); he lists £8 15s 10d as his own payments for a doctor and medicine. Three mention £5 for doctoring, while two cite £10—but these figures include in one instance sundry expenses, and in the other what one hopes was unrelated to doctoring, tradesmen's bills for repairs of house property.

House rental runs from under £18 to nearly £50 (in both cases including taxes); these figures come from *Vieux Moustache*, the first being his inference about *R.P.C.'s* costs, and the second his own, in which he subsumes not only taxes but gardening, pew rents, &c.[100] In looking at the middle range, one must recall that letting-off rooms was much recommended and practised as a way of recovering part of the cost, and that the location stated or implied is normally suburban London.[101] The rental figures include

£20 for *T.Z.*
£25 for *A Bachelor* and *A Draper* (as always, he is drawing a design for beginners)
£30 for *E.F.H.* and *C.S.C.*
£35 for *An English Wife*, *A Match-maker* (who says it could be reduced to £24 if need be), and *Plain Fact*
£37 for *An Anxious Father* (including taxes)
£38 for *An Old Married Man* (who is estimating for a young married clerk; he includes rates and taxes, water, and gas)
£40 for *One Who Would Be A Good Deal Happier If He Had It* (including taxes, water rate, and income tax) and *R.F.H.*
£45 for *Paterfamilias* (he does not mention taxes and so calls forth *Vieux Moustache's* corrections) and *Flo* (she has furnished apartments and so no direct taxes)

It would appear that most of those who do not actually mention house taxes in rental are in fact including them, for only a few mention them separately: £5 is cited by *E.F.H.* and *A Bachelor*, £6 by *T.Z.*, and £8—seemingly the normal charge—by *C.S.C.* (who includes water rate and income tax), *Match-maker* (who could reduce the cost to £6 if need be), *Plain Fact*, and *R.F.H. Vieux Moustache* in correcting the account of *Paterfamilias* places his charge at £12 (including water and the poor rate).

An actual water rate is mentioned specifically only by *E.F.H.*, who gives it as £5. Fuel and lighting costs are again difficult to extract confidently, because the categories are confused. However, the general range of expenditure seems fairly firmly established. Under the main heading "gas" one finds:

£4: *One Who Would Be A Good Deal Happier If He Had It*
£5: *E.F.H.*
£8: *Plain Fact* (including coals)
£9: *C.S.C.* (including coals)
£10: *An Anxious Father* and *T.Z.* (including coals and newspapers [one hopes not incendiary])
£12: *Vieux Moustache* for *Paterfamilias* (including coals and wood)
£20 10s: *Vieux Moustache* for himself (including coal, wood, and candles)

Sometimes the main heading is "coals":

£5: *E.F.H.* and *A Draper* (again for young beginners, including candles, washing, "&c."—*George* says this estimate is inadequate)
£5 10s: *One Who Would Be A Good Deal Happier If He Had It*
£5 15s: *A Match-maker* (including coke)
£6 10s: *Vieux Moustache*'s estimate for *R.P.C.* (including wood, gas, or candles)
£7 10s: *An Old Married Man* (including wood)

The suburban location of most of the homes is reflected in two not infrequently mentioned items, the husband's dinners in town and his daily travel expenses.[102] The former are given as £7 10s by *An Old Married Man* (for someone younger), as £15 12s by *A Bachelor, Vieux Moustache* (for *R.P.C.*), and *An Anxious Father*, and by the more gourmandizing *E.F.H.* as £25. The latter (varying according to distance) are given as

£3 18s by *Vieux Moustache* for *Paterfamilias* and for *R.P.C.*, and by *An Anxious Father*
£6 11s 2d by *Vieux Moustache* for himself
£7 10s by *An Old Married Man* (for someone younger)
£7 16s by *A Bachelor*
£10 by *E.F.H.* and *Plain Fact*
£15 by *A Match-maker* (but this includes "sundries about house")

A category now likely to be forgotten is found in several of the budgets: pew rental. *Paterfamilias* gives £3, *An Anxious Father* £4, *One Who*

Would Be A Good Deal Happier If He Had It £5 (but he includes charities, "&c."). Higher rates include those of *A Draper*, who mentions £10 for beginners, but his category included such anomalous items as "occasional trips, and petty expenses," and of *T.Z.* at £10 16s 9d, who also includes charities. Charitable donations are (surprisingly?) given as a main heading by only two correspondents, *Vieux Moustache*, who includes gratuities and amusements (!) in a total of £11 7s 7d, and *A Clergyman, Aetat 47*, who averaged £13 2s over ten years—interestingly, the average dropped from £13 6s when he was single to £12 8s when married.

To moderns, the meagre sums devoted to what may be summarized as recreation, amusement, leisure, and culture imply a degree of self-denial not compatible with full humanity; however, for these correspondents it may more justly be ascribed to habitual and realistic expectations—for married people, that is; as has been seen, single folk, women as well as men, *ought* to be prepared to give up inessentials in a normal, moral marriage. What remained is suggested (but surely not circumscribed) by the piano rental of £12 12s mentioned by *Paterfamilias*,[103] who is also the only one to specify theatre costs, at £1 4s annually (he includes admission to the Royal Academy)—he can hardly have been a frequenter.

Similarly, he is the only one to mention holiday travel, giving the cost as £10 10s annually. But his surely was not the only family even in this group to budget for a holiday; otherwise they are certainly not typical of the salaried white-collar workers, who were different from others in having fixed annual holidays of at least one week (some senior clerks had three to four weeks or even more) with pay and sometimes additional gratuities. The professionals with sufficient funds as well as the employers could take their holidays at their will, and the working classes did not enjoy paid holidays until after the turn of the century.[104] Perhaps for the *Daily Telegraph* group of clerks, the holiday was spent at home.[105] While there, some at least of them were reading the newspaper as well as writing letters to its editor. Although only four correspondents mention in their budgets the annual cost of the *Telegraph*—£1 6s—almost all if not all were regular readers of the newspaper. And the other specific expenses are again suggestive rather than definitive: 12s for a subscription to Charles Dickens's works, 4s 6d for a subscription to Scott's, 8s 4d for a denominational paper and 12s for a magazine, and 21s for a library membership. Their literacy also could not be confined to the few who mention expenses for paper, postage, etc.: £2 suggested by *Vieux Moustache* for *Pater-*

familias and for *R.P.C.* (encompassing postage, papers, library), and by *An Anxious Father* (for "correspondence with friends"); and—a figure more attractive to stationers—£9 18s 11d by *Vieux Moustache* for himself (stamps, books, stationery, and papers).

After all these expenses, one cannot be surprised that so few of the correspondents bother to mention even trivial savings of any kind after marriage, though a few point out how important it is to begin wedded life with a reserve. *Paterfamilias* is able to put £9 into a building society, and *Vieux Moustache* suggests that he also should add £1 10s for a benefit society; and *A Draper* insists that beginners in marriage should put aside £33 a year as savings "or to meet unforeseen expenses." That note indicates that in fact one should properly include another kind of saving, insurance, an increasingly popular means of dealing with the very real insecurity of the period.[106] The comprehensiveness as well as the prudence of the correspondents is shown by those who mention this as a regular expense. Those who list it give as little as £1 7s for fire insurance, from £1 18s 4 to £5 (which bought £200 coverage) for life, and 3s 6d to 7s for furniture. Unspecified coverage amounted to £6 4s for *C.S.C.*, £10 for *Plain Fact* and *An Anxious Father* (which includes life insurance and income tax), and the more comprehensive coverage given by £26 to *An English Wife*, who is comparatively wealthy.

Are the budgets typical of the *Daily Telegraph*'s correspondents as a whole?[107] Probably not, for two reasons. First, those who keep budgets are generally from the higher range of income and, second, almost all the details are given in the first part of the series, in which the proportion of married people is much higher than in the second part, where the main impulse towards emigration is the relative poverty of the single young men.

But what individual is typical? These voices have great value, impressionistic or not, in telling us in detail about their individual homes in ways that allow for comparison and generalization. And collectively they certainly demonstrate that the balance of expenditure and income was central in their definition of prudent marriage—and imprudent marriage for the Victorians was marriage only in a legal sense.

CHAPTER FIVE

Celibates and Celibacy

As the preceding discussion bears full witness, the title of the series in the *Daily Telegraph* was not fully appropriate: for the married folk, the choice between marriage and celibacy had been made. There was no dilemma, and their options were determined by the need to live decently on a small income.

But the series had of course another set of questions, for those unmarried truly faced the dilemma, Marriage or Celibacy? This did not present, culturally or morally, an even choice, as has been seen, for the overwhelming weight of opinion was that marriage, with children, is the "natural" state. As a necessary corollary, the celibate state is incomplete. Ideally, marriage is not an "if" but a "when" question, and *caeteris paribus* (which things never are) the earlier the better.

The dominant view is generally supported in fiction, even that dwelling on difficulties. For instance (and here the case is posited on an annual income of £500): "It might be very foolish for a man (who had his own way to make in the world) to marry at five-and-twenty; but still, perhaps it was rather more foolish when a man did not marry at all, and was left in his old age all alone in a great vacant house."[1] To postpone was often seen as finally to elect celibacy:

How many of the best years of a man's life are to be spent in waiting? that is, in gaining selfish habits and modes of thought that unfit him at length for the duties as well as for the happiness of married life! . . . The woman he loved in his youth sees him becoming day by day less worthy of her love, and less able to contend with the sacrifices a home of poverty must entail upon him. She waits for him—she would sacrifice every luxury for him—but he has learnt to think cautiously; the maxims so sedulously taught him in his fresh, joyous youth are learnt too well, and he ceases even to wish to give up his habitual luxuries for the sake of affection which he has outlived.[2]

The male viewpoint being dominant, most attention is paid to the single men's losses through marriage. Considering them was judged legitimate, but they could dominate only at a moral cost. That is, bachelor "pleasures" were viewed first as "despite" (*faute de mieux*), and second as selfish, no matter how some young men tried to defend them as necessary to a decent life.

The general state of belief is sarcastically laid out by Anne Gilchrist in 1865. The opinion of "prudent, experienced persons," she says, is that a young man should marry only if he can "begin the world where his father left off as to income." There being no honest way to "grow rich in a hurry, we must accustom ourselves to look upon the Temple of Hymen as a sort of Asylum for the aged, whither venerable bride-rooms will lead young brides," who will soon be left alone to cope with "nurseries full of babies." The alternative is celibacy, with "marriage and babies go[ing] out of fashion altogether, except in those uppermost and lowermost strata of society where there is nothing to fear and nothing to hope pecuniarily."[3]

Needless to say, even in the face of experienced and rational accounts of the dangerous outcomes, people continued to marry, and most of those people were young. As background to an analysis of common views of the solutions to the evident problems, the portraits in the *Daily Telegraph* instructively indicate how the unmarried young saw themselves and one another. First, the young women.[4]

The Single Girl

Several of the correspondents were not reluctant to sketch a fond self-portrait:

Well, I am nineteen, and can only play the piano, and make a pudding, illuminate cards and dust a room, waltz and mend my stockings, and should not hesitate a minute to marry a man I loved (he would be a man, though; not a "puppy") with £150 a year; and there are many others the same as I am, *An Ordinary-looking English Girl.*[5]

A London Girl offers what seems even more obviously a "character," a self-advertisement, suitable for the classified section of a newspaper. The twenty-two-year old unmarried daughter of a professional earning £150 to £200, living in a "healthy suburb," she is "proud" to list her qualifications:

I can make a pudding, darn my father's hose, and look after his house with quite as much ease and pleasure as I can go into the drawing-room and play a piece of music or sing a song. I very seldom go to theatres or operas. My amusements I find principally in reading good sensible books, with a novel occasionally, or in music. I am also rather fond of languages.

As they keep only one servant, her mornings are spent in superintending or doing household work. Indeed she is "not ashamed to own" that when her servant had a fortnight's holiday, she did all the household work with two days' help from a charwoman who scrubbed. All this without "the advantage of good useful training," because when she was two her mother died, and she continued her education at "a first-rate boarding-school, or rather college" until nineteen, when she "had to begin housekeeping directly."

Others present similar portraits from slightly different perspectives. For example, the second who signed herself *A London Girl*, nineteen years old, is unique in this series in describing herself as one who, having had "a good plain education," is "now in business"—annoyingly she does not specify further. She feels it necessary to explain that this choice was not forced on her by her father's penury, but willingly elected because there was not sufficient to keep her fully occupied at home, and because she could not see "the least reason" why she should not keep herself "in dress and pocket-money for the next few years." The explanation is necessary because such behaviour was still viewed as *déclassé*; in her words, "many men have the greatest horror of girls in business," considering them "fast, frivolous, extravagant flirts" who, "living away from home" are entirely unfit "to become the wives of comparatively poor men." *A London Girl* may be the sole woman in the series admitting to a "business" occupation, but she is not unique in life: she has known "dozens."[6]

Another perspective, well known from other literature but little revealed in this series, is that of *A Young English Governess*.[7] Her account accords with those in fiction that have aroused admiration and anger in ardent sorrowful readers. She briefly sketches her condition:

I was brought up in absolute luxury, until eighteen years of age; when loss of relatives and property made me resolve on becoming one of the numerous class of governesses; and though until then I scarcely even knew the frightful hardship of dressing my own hair, I can now teach from morning until night (which is real hard work) amongst strangers, with no friend near to enliven, when the weary task is done, and yet not think myself very hardly used.

Not surprisingly, she believes that marriage on love and £100 to £150 is practicable, for she will not see it as hard drudgery "to try and make the home which my husband may provide me bright and happy"; rather, she will not be "too proud . . . to 'assist in ironing,' but [will be] ready to scrub the floor, should necessity require it," if so doing will "preserve a home of happiness and love, and save [her] husband from feeling the miseries which marrying with a small income had brought upon him."

Here experience may insist that in shedding worse, better need not wait on best, but some single women also counselled wise foresight. For example, *Precaution*, living solo in Brussels, energizes her argument with a touch of drama:

It is all very well when Tom proposes, and says he has only £200 or £150 a year, for the object of his affections to exclaim, after a little conversation on the subject, "Rather than to be separated from you, darling, I'll sacrifice anything, do all the work myself; in fact, I would live in a room, such is my love for you. As you know, dear, I've always done so and so at home, and I think, Tom, with a little economy (which turns out a great deal) we shall get on very comfortably;" quite forgetting the so and so's she had to do at home would be a mere speck on a wall compared to what they would have to do under the above circumstances.

The inference, though obvious, calls for exclamation: "Oh, no!" Otherwise, the "miserable" result is that "Husbands become dissatisfied with their wives, and wives with their homes."

Thinking of cynical readers, *Precaution* turns to ethical proof as *refutatio*:

I'm young (twenty-one), highly accomplished [as her French tags demonstrate], and thoroughly domesticated; and as to personal appearance, I'll remain silent, as "chacun à son goût;" but excuse me in sounding my own trumpet by saying that I could make a husband's home as comfortable and as happy as he could possibly wish it to be on not much short of £300 a year; and a girl of the class I allude to cannot do "grande chose," or have a "menage comme il faut" under [that amount].

Two other correspondents adopt the convention of the outside observer to show the position of a single woman, the one in pathetic, the other in satiric mode. *Hannah*, a young Scotch girl on her first visit to London, denigrates romanticism about marriage, but her claim seems moot when she chances her hand by denying the force of the *ad populum* proof, indulging in the grand Scots tradition of dialect drama:

An old friend of mine who married late in the day, and had no very exalted ideas of the happy state, said, in advising my brother to get married, "'Od, man, it's a gran' thing to hae a wife if ye got siller wi' her. Nae doot, they're a bother, but then there's aye buttons on my sark, and my stockings are aye darned;" and honest "Daavid's" opinion, with higher flights of ambition, is very generally held, till we reach Mr. Fitzgerald, who carefully calculates the probable fortune of his intended, Dora, when her governor or uncle dies, if he don't marry, &c.

And then, pathetically, she reports her own heart-rending state:

It is now nearly two years since I was engaged to a big-hearted laddie. His salary was scarcely £100; to-day it would have been £300. But my noble boy was struck down with sickness. Oh, that he had been mine oh! mine; and then sickness, anything, would have been welcome. Never did he so much want kindness and attention; and to me it would have been a labour of love to minister to his every want. My love has never wavered, and I shall love him till he dies; and, after that, God help me!

The other outsider sheds no tears. *A Country Girl* (perhaps avoiding Strephon in rus while observing for a few weeks Phillis in urbs)[8] diffidently and apologetically[9] treats her readers to proof that one solid block to marriage for young women is "the great want of rational topics of conversation," which she illustrates anecdotally:

Take a sample of the conversation I have heard among the ladies at an ordinary friendly call, or an evening party, as the case may be: Mrs. E.'s dress, how elegant it looks! Miss C.'s ornaments, what are they worth? the cut of a Marie Antoinette, the length of a skirt, the exquisite style of Mr. A.'s moustache, the bad taste young Wilson always shows in his neckties, the last new thing in trimmings, the lovely complexion of Miss D.,—the last remark followed up by the whisper, "Ah, but do you know she uses rouge and pearl powder?" the size of Miss K.'s chignon, and the false curls Mrs. L. delights to wear.

She was but an observer to all this, feeling "out of [her] depth—overwhelmed, as it were, beneath flounces and trimmings, muslins and laces." Wishing and willing (again making an ethical appeal) to engage in "sensible general conversation" about "the great events of the time; the arts, literature, and politics," she ("poor little me") was met with disdain, "obliged to admit that the colour and texture of a butterfly's wing, or the discovery of a new fern in some cool, shaded glen, afforded [her] more pleasure to talk of than the latest mode of dressing the hair, or Mrs. Johnstone's last new bonnet."

Rebuffed, she sat in her "quiet corner, listening to the wavelets of small talk which flowed hither and thither," and considered in revery the plight of "a sensible young fellow [with an annual income of say £200] entering that same society in search of a wife" who would be "a helpmate, not a hindrance in life." In despair, he would "hold aloof from such silly, idle chatter," or join only from courtesy, thinking the while, "Well, this is a sort of thing I should soon tire of if this is all I am to hear after the business of the day is over." And gone is his dream— one fully approved by *A Country Girl*—"of a cheerful, cosy room, a dear little wife by the fireside, an orderly, neatly-served dinner, a store of books and papers to talk over, and a simple ballad or plaintive air to soothe and cheer him after his labour."

Many of these accounts, as will have been noted, cast blame—and a few stones—on behaviour and attitudes standing in the way of rational and happy marriage. Two examples relevant to the problems of young women are seen in the letters of *A Wife and Mother* and *Philos*. The former is one of those employing nostalgia, as she recalls better days. When seventeen years ago she left school, "a dark merino dress ... or a dark, useful silk" was "quite sufficient" for evening parties in the country. "Then there was an influx of girls who wore white dresses, low in the neck and short sleeves, quite as much in the fashion as if they had £200 a year pin-money, and who hated to talk about servants or housekeeping, it was so vulgar." Now, if married to men with under £300 a year, they are "uncomfortable as can be."

Blame falls on the parents, who, knowing that a good income with a large family is a matter of subtraction not addition, should have continued their daughters' education beyond school leaving: "they should have taught them every housekeeping duty, so that they might be able to do with more or less servants as they could afford," as well as "now and then instructing an ignorant servant," who, *A Wife and Mother* asserts, "I can assure you," will be grateful for such instruction. Even in the country, everyone "is now determined to be as fine or higher than their neighbours, and those with £200 will vie with those who have £600 a year."

And *Philos.*, writing from Norwood, turns to the lower income level, discoursing regretfully on the training and behaviour of servant girls, the proper wives for "hard-working, respectable mechanic[s]":

It is with mingled feelings of pity, grief, regret that I observe them on the Sunday, dressed to ape, as nearly as possible, their mistresses, in long, muslin skirts, chignons real or false, small blond bonnets and flowers, light kid gloves, and black silk mantles of fashionable cut! This is no exaggeration of the style of dress they adopt, and is it a becoming and proper one for the future wives of the hard-working classes? If servants' wages admit of so much expenditure, how much better and wiser it would be to lay out less on such unnecessary and unbecoming finery, and to save a portion to become a little store for future contingencies.

In this folly they are—the criticism was sure to come—but copying a wealthier class, the ladies of which might well adopt for their own sakes as well as that of their imitators "greater simplicity and moderation."

In the fiction of the period many of these attitudes, favourable and unfavourable, are amply portrayed, and the stereotypes moulded. A few examples will suffice. Frances Browne presents the positive image of a wife, on a low clerkly income, who could not be "a lady," but would be a helpmate:

Rosy, cheerful, and bustling about with her smooth fair hair, clean print gown, large apron with pockets, and the perpetual jingle of keys; looking after the linens, looking after the lodgers; waiting on her aunt, making ready for her uncle—that gentleman was now in a warehouse in Holborn, and his home-comings demanded serious attention; up early and down late, boiling and baking, scrubbing and scouring, she had little time for folly or fretting, for albums, valentines, or any sort of young ladyism.[10]

But just this sort of view was strongly denied in fiction as fiction:

"One reads of that sort of wife in a novel. But can you find me such a one nowadays, Sigismund? The women of the present day live only to look beautiful and to be admired. They are pitiless goddesses, at whose shrines men sacrifice the best gifts of their souls. When I look at the splendour of these carriages, the glory of the butterfly creatures who ride in them, I think how many plodding wretches are toiling in Temple-chambers, or lecturing in the theatres of hospitals, or pacing to and fro on the dusty floor of the Stock Exchange, racked by the thought of hazardous time-bargains, in order that these frivolous divinities may have gorgeous raiment and high-stepping horses, and plant the arrows of envious rage in one another's tender bosoms.... [When] some fine day a poor man falls in love with one of them, [he] finds that it would have been infinitely wiser to have dashed out his brains against a stone wall than to have been beguiled by the mad hope that a penniless lover's devotion could have any value in their sight."[11]

Not a stone wall but celibacy seems the option for one struggling young professional, who would "as soon think of taking the largest mansion in Belgravia as taking a wife." To the girls he meets at parties, "life would be a blank without a large allowance for millinery, and a grand piano by Broadwood, price one hundred and thirty guineas. Ladies change their condition, as servants places—to better themselves."[12]

And as usual, Anthony Trollope manages to convey realism in a clerk's view, resolving accusation into explanation:

"False!" said Charley; "and how is a girl to get along if she be not false? What girl could live for a moment before the world if she were to tell the whole truth about the get-up of her wardrobe—the patchings and make-believes, the chipped ribbons and turned silks, the little bills here, and the little bills there? How else is an allowance of £20 a-year to be made compatible with an appearance of unlimited income? How else are young men to be taught to think that in an affair of dress money is a matter of no moment whatsoever?"[13]

The Single Young Man

The period's portrayal of bachelors is equally mixed, but different in character. In the *Daily Telegraph* there is whimsy and savage attack, but also realism, as in the unpleasant tale told pleasantly by E.F.H. of his "old and valued friend" (henceforth referred to as "O.A.V.F.").[14]

E.F.H.'s O.A.V. (and also "confiding and ingenuous") F. fell in love with just such a paragon as *Smiff's*, "a fair young lady, whose accomplishments were only eclipsed by her radiant beauty and her mental acumen." His proposal being accepted, they ran "a brief course of theatres, Saturdays at the Crystal Palace, etc.," until his O.A.V.F. thought the time had come for setting a date, at which time he gave "a kind of Claude Melnotte description of their future home by mentioning, apropos, that his income was nearly £200 per annum."[15] The immediate outcome is not described by E.F.H., who, denying himself the novelist's omniscience, was "not in a position to narrate the particulars of the next half-hour's conversation," though the tenor was clear from some words his O.A.V.F. "moodily let fall during the same evening." More confidingly, if no more joyfully, next day he gave *E.F.H.* a letter "in the characteristic hand of the fair young lady": "'Read that,' he cried, with a hollow laugh, 'and ——.' Here followed sundry alliterative mutterings about 'money,' 'misery,' and 'mercenary.'" The "billet" included a budget totalling £217 16s,[16] and the comment: "I enclose you the account I said I would, and must leave it to you to suggest how it can be reduced. But I think my dear Freddy will agree with me that it will be wiser to bide a wee than to rush into matrimony and inevitable debt."

The subsequent events are sufficiently *Smiff*-like in description to merit full quotation:

Some months have elapsed since these unrelenting figures made my O.A.V.F. temporarily insane, and now, his former habits being again restored to him, he is striving might and main to raise his earnings to a trifle above the total of that dismal "account." But at present in vain! To ingratiate himself with the head clerk, with whom is vested the patronage of the firm, he gave that potentate a gold snuff-box—an heir-loom—and a pound of rare rappee. As these proved of no avail, he resolved upon an appeal to his feelings, but never got further than "If a fellow ——" Evening employment he has sought untiringly; and as a further proof of his determination to achieve wealth I may mention that he recently offered to conduct a newspaper, edit a satirical review, manage a bank, and sing comic songs at a music-hall. But my O.A.V.F. is still sanguine— youth is sanguine—and he assures me that the fair young lady will wait, if it be a hundred years, until his income has reached the magic height at which wedlock is possible.

What will others make of this tale? *E.F.H.*'s moral is somewhat disconcerting:

If others would but emulate her example, and, in place of poetry, cultivate mathematics and "the sweet simplicity of the Three per Cents.,"[17] I would venture to predict a considerable diminution in the next census, and, as a corollary, a rapid increase of buoyant bachelors and "spirited proprietors" of places for recreation.

But caution was not the property of young women alone. *A Prudent Bachelor*, typical of many, justifies his state through personal detail:

I am now a Government clerk, but have been in the City a clerk also, and dur-

ing the five years I was there I became acquainted with several distressing
cases of middle-aged clerks of good character, broken down and unable to procure situations, and plenty of young men in the same predicament, and judging from the little I have seen of life, being still young, I would rather be a
hermit for life, than marry and bring up a family to such a future as must be
before them some thirty years hence, if they are unprovided for; and though I
might keep a wife and rear a family respectably, the doing so would take all my
income and deprive me of making provision, in part at least, for them after my
decease.

A valuable distinction, instructive especially for the desperate clerks,
is made by *W.E.W.W.*, who divides bachelors into two classes, "those
who live at home, and those who do not." The former, who (more logical bifurcation) either make a living by themselves or are have an
allowance from their fathers, will not marry[18] because

they are very comfortable at home, and can see much more society than they
could if they were married; they have plenty of money to spend on their individual pleasures; they can wear not only a good coat but they can also afford to
wear gloves; a decent cigar is not beyond their means, not even an occasional
dinner at Richmond or a stall in a theatre; finally, they always have a sovereign
or two in their pockets.[19]

The other class, those "unfortunates whose lot is cast in furnished
lodgings" and who (he "safely" says from personal experience) can
barely live on £150 a year, do not have the problem of renouncing pleasures, for "rarely accessible" to them are good cigars, little dinners at
Richmond, or theatres, and in their pockets "no spare sovs. can jingle."
The strong inference that neither class (and there are no others!) will
marry wisely suffices to clinch the argument.[20]

A Young Englishman, also arguing the question from a male upper-
middle-class position,[21] agrees in the main. He sees, not surprisingly,
the calculation for bachelors who live at home as an easy one, and not
conducive to early marriage; the second class, living in furnished lodgings, will find the calculation less obvious, and so are more likely to
wed.

It seems that *A Young Bachelor* (writing from Regent's Park) is in the
first class. He forthrightly objects to the "twaddle that has been written
upon the subject of 'Marriage or Celibacy,'" but promises that it will
not disrupt "the even tenor" of his daily life, or tempt him "to enter the

bonds of, so called, connubial bliss" upon his moderate income. He likes his cigar, and is "fond of a row on the river, but can do without 'patent leather boots,'" and so (seemingly on that firm base alone) denies being in the numerous "class of young 'men of the period.'"

Not at home and certainly from a different social level is *A London Mechanic*, who portrays the great danger surrounding single men in lodgings in London—"not confined to the mechanic alone"—arising from the want of good "home" society. While some frequent lecture rooms in working-men's institutes, and "places of worship in the great city," of necessity a majority

walk in our parks and squares, they visit the music halls, theatres, casinos, and public houses during their leisure evening hours, and what estimate do they, what estimate can they form of the acquaintances they must and do make? Why, Sir, they lose all faith—if they ever had any—in female virtue, and then look upon the social evil as a necessity.

His closing advice to young men is authenticated, as anticipated, by his personal experience:

Do nothing rashly; well weigh the subject in your mind; make up your mind to assist by all means in your power, in all the duties of life, her whom you intend to take to your bosom for better or worse, and, with a unity of purpose, a firm resolve not to incur debt, and a strong trust in God.

Using like so many others the empirical appeal, he concludes: "I know from experience that, although trials and troubles will assuredly be yours, you will experience a large share of joy and happiness."

L.C.J. is less grim but also perhaps less consoling in an embroidered vignette designed to expose an earlier correspondent, *A Pilgrim of Love*:

Were the Israelites of old the last of their kind that shall bend the knee to the golden calf? Nay, the Patriarch did but break the huge thing into a thousand pieces, which, subdivided into countless idols, have entered into the hearts of the young men of our time, and dwell there.[22] Go with me into one of the pleasant salons of modern times, we shall meet our friend the *Pilgrim*, aforesaid—(I am sure he goes to evening parties)—we will remember that he is professedly a man of moderate income; we will introduce him, if you please, to a young lady, in whose sweet face the lily and the rose contend for mastery. She is well born and accomplished, but the plain grey silk and neatly braided hair seem sadly out of place among the elaborate toilettes of most of our party; he bows with an easy unconstrained grace, as a gentleman should, follows up the introduction by a few listless remarks, and, hey presto, he is by the side of that superb creature in blue, whose fair shoulders gleam like ivory under the masses of gracefully disordered hair. She is a banker's daughter, and will most likely "come into some money;" she may or may not marry our friend, according to papa's requirements, but she is open to sing or waltz with him; and do you think—while he can as a single man enjoy the society (with, perhaps, the chance of marrying one) of ladies in a circle in which as a married man he could not hope to move on a small income—that he will devote that which provides him handsomely with dress coats and other requisites, to the formation of a home in what he would call a poor neighbourhood, with the possibility of a dowdy wife and four small children?

This view from the other side is confirmed by *An English Girl*, who explictly wishes to let other "English girls know it is not their fault there are not more marriages than at present." How to prove the case? Another vignette:

Last Saturday evening a "Man of the Period" crossed my path: amongst other subjects we discussed "Marriage or Celibacy." His income is £180; he says he cannot marry on that sum, as cigars cost 3s per week, he must go to the theatre or some place of amusement once or twice a week, and cannot do without patent-leather shoes and silk stockings; he likes to take a trip to Richmond or Kew; and these things he cannot do without. If he marries, his wife must never look dowdy, but have things for light or cloudy weather, and not wear a dress longer than a twelvemonth; when he takes her out she must look and dress like a "Woman of the Period."

Rising from these last two letters is more than a whiff of gunpowder from the war of the sexes. In the letters from married people, allowing for the bitter complaints about deceit from three angry wives (and there are only three in the series), blame for distress was not directed against sexual stereotypes. Not so in many of the celibates' letters, which demonstrate the danger Gilchrist had commented on three years earlier:

the singular and unhappy phenomenon of a sort of snarling antagonism between those who were created for mutual help and comfort, the one sex tacitly saying, "A wife is too costly an incumbrance; I can get on better without her:" the other, bridling up in pardonable pride and resentment, and rejoining,

"Marriage is not the sole, or necessarily the highest lot for a woman; we have faculties like yours, and can provide for ourselves, and live a life worth living alone, if you do not unjustly shut us out from the business of the world." True it is, this independence on the one side, this resentment on the other, quickly vanish under the beams of Love. But then, too often, the sequel is such as almost justifies the croakers and sneerers, and the pair have to wade for long years through the mire of pecuniary difficulties.[23]

Girls of the Period

In 1868 a term, the "Girl of the Period," seen in letters already quoted but not available to Gilchrist, had come into extensive use. In the *Daily Telegraph* series, *A Young Briton*, who like others disapproves the easy categorization of attitudes by sex and marital status, being "quite refresh[ed]" by the views of *An English Girl*, introduces to the series her antitype, that "ugly phantom known as 'The Girl of the Period,'" who he trusts is the exception, "if not altogether the creation of a diseased imagination."[24]

The supposed "diseased imagination" was that of Eliza Lynn Linton, who had published anonymously in March 1868 an article entitled "The Girl of the Period" in the *Saturday Review*. Later in the year it was reprinted as a pamphlet, with her name, under the same title.[25] This had a remarkably wide circulation, up to 40,000 copies being issued by a single publisher, and there was more than one publisher.[26] And the article appeared also (still in 1868) in *Modern Women and What Is Said of Them*, a volume of thirty-seven essays from the *Saturday Review*.

Linton begins with an account of "a fair young English girl" as formerly implying "the ideal of womanhood." In relation to marriage, the entailment was that the girl "would be her husband's friend and companion, but never his rival; one who would consider their interests identical, and not hold him as just so much fair game for spoil; who would make his house his true home and place of rest, not a mere passage-place for vanity and ostentation to go through; a tender mother, an industrious housekeeper, a judicious mistress," "content to be what God and nature had made" her. The modern Girl of the Period, in contrast, hungers only for the "demi-monde"—and here Linton parallels the discussion in *The Times* described above—and so takes the route to moral depravity, urged on by fashionable young men. These impressionable young women never stop

to reflect at what a price they have bought their gains, and what fearful moral

penalties they pay for their sensuous pleasures. She sees only the coarse gild-
ing on the base token, and shuts her eyes to the hideous figure in the midst,
and the foul legend written round the edge. It is this envy of the pleasures, and
indifference to the sins, of these women of the demi-monde which is doing
such infinite mischief to the modern girl.

In Linton's uncompromising and encompassing indictment the
modern English girl is not "tender, loving, retiring, or domestic," having no desire for "Love in a cottage, that seductive dream which used
to vex the heart and disturb the calculations of prudent mothers." Her
idea of marriage involves no sense of attendant duties or consequences, for she sees it as merely a "legal barter of herself for so much
money, representing so much dash, so much luxury and pleasure." But
she seldom marries: "Men are afraid of her; and with reason," for she is
unreal, only a poor copy of the "one kind of thing," which, if we must
have, "let us have it genuine; and the queens of St. John's Wood in their
unblushing honesty, rather than their imitators and make-believes in
Bayswater and Belgravia."

That is, of course not Linton's true moral, which is stated crisply:
"All men whose opinion is worth having prefer the simple and genuine girl of the past, with her tender little ways and pretty bashful mod-
esties, to this loud and rampant modernization, with her false red hair
and painted skin, talking slang as glibly as a man, and by preference
leading the conversation to doubtful subjects."

This cutting indictment, which Bevington calls "perhaps the most
sensational middle article" ever published in the *Saturday Review*,[27]
was an irresistible incitement to entrepreneurs and their willing cus-
tomers. Not only did the term become a catch-phrase, but "Girl of the
Period" parasols and articles of clothing appeared, and dramatists
were not slow to pick up the theme:

[*Wyatt.*] Ah, pretty enough, but prim. Nature in stays and high heel'd boots.
Nature with a Grecian bend. Mother Nature made a girl of the period, nothing
but the old *trees* left as Adam saw them.[28]

Eager publishers exploited the opportunity with such magazines as
The Girl of the Period Almanack and *The Girl of the Period Miscellany*, both
published out of the "Echoes" Office in the Strand, and edited by
"Miss Echo." The former featured each month a cartoon with letter-
press commentary and illustrative captions such as "The Pallas Billiard
Club," "Amazon Athletic Club," "The "New Law Courts—at last!,"

"The Sisters' University," and "The Very Latest Bathing"—not, perhaps surprisingly, nude. The fare offered by *The Girl of the Period Miscellany* was similar, its cartoons featuring sequentially Girls of the
Period of various types such as Scottish, Irish, Abyssinian,[29] Evangelical, and French, and articles such as "Women's Spelling," "Education
of Women," "Girls of Past Periods," "Governess of the Period," and
"Society for the Prevention of Cruelty to Men."

It will be evident that these materials, while not ignoring Linton's
themes, had another satirical centre, that of sexual equality,[30] which is
not important in the *Daily Telegraph* series—a fact interesting in itself.
Also significant is that not only comic serials picked up the theme: a
pamphlet entitled *The Sequel of the "Girl of the Period"* is a religious exor-
tation, devoted to the vanities encouraged by Ritualism, with no reference to Linton's work or ideas.[31] It is small wonder that *Punch*, just as
the *Daily Telegraph* series was getting into full flow, had vainly
enjoined: "Where a Full Stop is Wanted.— To the Girl of the Period."[32]

That the unmarried correspondents in the *Daily Telegraph* would
exploit the term, debating its justness, was surely inevitable. The
young women for the most part adopted the view of *A Plain Girl*. She
objects to the stereotyping of the "girl of the period," who is "carica-
tured in the comic papers, sneered at by single men, [and] spoken
lightly of by married men . . ., pictured as extravagant, idle, and fond
of dress." Like others, she asserts that there are fortunately "many very
happy exceptions—women who are like beams of sunshine, brighten-
ing, purifying, and blessing wherever they go," those who lead a husband to say: "Some call her angel, but I call her wife."

But there were more spirited female responses, typified by that of *A
Few True Girls of the Period*, who, begging "Dear Mr. Editor" kindly to
"insert a few lines" in his "valuable paper," admitted that their attention had been snagged by the letter of *Solon Smiff*. They quickly draw
the contrast between the genuine character of girls of the period and
that presented by the *Saturday Review*: "those who are not above assist-
ing in the house when required; those who have a clear idea of domestic economy," as against "those who, like wax dolls, only dress for
admiration, whose only pleasure it is to attend and give balls and parties, to make and receive calls, and take an after-dinner walk in the
Park." They fall into angry abuse of the "writer of the critique" in the
Saturday Review, who, with twenty different possibilities, has chosen to
illustrate the Girl of the Period out of "the one class in whose sphere
she [the author] moves." Indeed their rage moves them to the lowest of
ad feminam thrusts in saying they "are thankful we are girls of the

present (and not of her) period," if one is to take of it "for specimens
the two old women who have cut such a sorry figure in the eyes of the
public lately, who shall here be nameless."[33]

One of the "Girls of the Period" acts as prosecuting and defence council. In the former role, her premise is that "one sex naturally seeks to
attract and please the other." Consequently, if girls "seem" to become
"heedless, worldly creatures," it is because just such behaviour ensures
"greater attention, . . . entrance to fashionable society, often through it
to comfortable homes." "Do we not," she asks, "see such girls sought
after to their heart's content at ball rooms, flower shows, &c., while
others of the simpler kind remain wall flowers?" Moving into defence,
she explains the earlier "seem" by asserting that this "outer nature" is
assumed "contrary to the inner workings of the heart," the girls not
being "so bad as depicted" in their "frivolous talk, . . . minute attention
paid to dress, . . . habit of judging people and things by a golden standard, [and] . . . continual and sometimes undignified striving for fashion's honours." Indeed the "seeming heartlessness" conceals the
qualities that "in the hour of trial" women reveal as "unselfish, for-
bearing, and devoted wives." And thence back to prosecution: if men,
who "generally consider themselves superior beings," show themselves "desirous and worthy of such helpmates . . . they will find them
awaiting on every side." The irony becomes slightly more evident as
the argument concludes: "As superior beings they form the heads of
society and of homes: it is only fair that they should strike out the path
for inferior beings to follow. A reform headed by the male sex would
be the appropriate and truest remedy to apply to the evils of the time
concerning marriage and celibacy."

The Young Man of the Period

As that letter suggests, almost inevitably the antitype, the Young Man
of the Period, was being conjured. Not so identifying himself (but
rather presenting himself as a "rational bachelor") was *A Welsh Bachelor Pro-Tem*, who intentionally or not stirred the pot of sexual controversy. He sets up a comparison, based he says on personal experience,
intended to leave no question as to the easy rational choice for bachelors who are practical men and not "philosophers."[34] On the one side,
a married clerk with family (say, as his acquaintance suggests, including from three to six children), and £200 a year, who cannot spend his
holiday (about which everyone is thinking at this time of year) at the
seaside; on the other, a bachelor with £100, who "is able to do his

annual tour at the sea-side, and returns to his desk refreshed in mind and body." These are often found in the same office, where their feelings are easily imagined: the junior clerk will say, "Thank God, I am not as other men are," while his senior will be full of "discontent, ay, and very often of regret—discontent at seeing young men able to go and breathe the fresh air, while he has to remain at home, regret at his foolishness in getting married."

Among those responding were *Two Plain English Girls*, who profess playful amusement as a cover for annoyance at his views. Admitting that no one can "live upon love," they insist that a salary of £200 will give more. He admits that half that sum allows a bachelor to have a seaside holiday, so (by parity if not subtlety of reason) £200 would cover an annual holiday week or fortnight with wife and one or two children. As to his question—"whether the sacrifice a man makes on getting married is ever repaid to him in domestic comfort?"—the answer depends on the definition of "sacrifice." If the billiard table, the gambling house, the theatre supply his happiness, "home joys" will not seriously rival them. So much the worse for him: "the true man, by his very instincts, seeks a home, seeks some one to love; some darling to pet and fondle, some creature on whom he can pour out the first fruits of the wealth of affection that friendship, even in its best form, only partially employs, far less exhausts." And against such "sacrifices" as he might make, what of those (forgotten by him) that women accept "cheerfully and willingly" when they marry out of true love: "the happy home, kind parents, cheerful society, and loving companions." Their parting hope—it is no more—is "that our 'rational bachelor' will return from Wales a wiser and a happier man,[35] fully convinced that a bachelor's life is not the most desirable."

Stung by what he calls this "stern rebuke" and by another from *A British Matron* who expressed "thorough disgust" at his (imputed) selfishness, *A Welsh Bachelor Pro-Tem* wrote again in vigorous protest. While *A British Matron* simply misunderstood him, *Two Plain English Girls* share with many other correspondents in erroneous generalization, putting down all young men as "rakes," caring only for the billiard-table, the gambling-house, and the theatre; he (presumably a type for many others) is a rational bachelor who has never gambled and but seldom attended theatres. Further, in contrasting the meagre sacrifice young men make in relinquishing such pleasures, they exaggerate the costs to young women, who they say give up a "happy home, kind parents, cheerful society, and loving companions"—but *A Welsh Bachelor Pro-Tem* looks in vain for the sacrifice, because on marriage they move into homes to which they can invite all their "dear ones," making even happier the loving relationships. On the other hand (and argumentatively it seems a rather distant one), a rational bachelor indeed must give up parents, relations, and friends, "sometimes a few of the necessaries of life, and most certainly all its luxuries"—and he himself is not yet ready to sacrifice his "little comforts," his boat club, cricket club, and tour at the seaside, "which *British Matron* thinks so little of, and [he] so much." His conclusion cannot have pleased his opponents: "when sitting on the Castle-hill, admiring the beautiful sea, listening to the band of music in this town of Tenby [South Wales], I feel with St. Paul, that he who marries may do well, but he who does not marry most certainly doeth better."

This moral most certainly did not please or silence *Three "Girls of the Period."* Knowing that attack is an excellent defence, they dismiss the abuse of the "girl of the period" in the *Saturday Review* as resulting from the writer's[36] "total inability to find words to describe the folly, vanity, and selfishness of the 'young men of the period'"; however, they continue, the letters from *A Welsh Bachelor Pro-Tem* make further demonstration unnecessary. Their arch scorn continues to the end, as happy holidays lead to homely maxim:

Having just returned from a charming trip to the sea-side, we can deeply sympathise with those unfortunate wives, who, if blest with husbands after the pattern of *W.B. Pro Tem*, have probably had the supreme felicity of seeing them start off to the Welsh mountains, or some equally delightful locality; whilst they themselves remain at home to darn socks, iron shirts, and nurse babies. Not wishing further to encroach on your valuable space, we will conclude by advising young ladies wishing to change their position not "to jump out of the frying-pan into the fire."[37]

This excursion aside, the *gravamen* of the charge remained dominant in young women's letters. *A Plain Girl*, who had objected to the caricature of the Girl of the Period, insists that more peccant were the "young men of the period." Their "least questionable recreations" involve the billiard table, and more expensive ones, gambling. They cause the mischief by favouring those girls "whose chief attention is given to outward show, and whose conversation is vapid and silly." More strikingly detailed is the indictment by *A Simple Country Girl* who, admitting by *concessio* that some young ladies and their mammas are mercenary, attacks young men on the same grounds, *a fortiori* and in dialogue: "This is the general tone of their conversation: One says to another, 'That is a jolly girl.' 'Yes,' says number two: 'Has she got any money?'" The indictment continues through judgment embedded in comparison; they search for mates "at balls, parties, concerts," rather than "by the domestic hearth":

They infinitely prefer young ladies who can sing and play, and paint and sketch, wear chignons and trailing dresses, to those who can make puddings and jams and jellies, iron a shirt, and, on a push, dig up a few potatoes or gather a peck of pease for their dinner. They look down in the most disdainful manner on a girl who answers her own door, does her own clear starching, and wears a cotton apron; and I can assure you, Sir, would go three miles out of their way to avoid walking up the street with a girl who was going marketing with her little basket on her arm.

Significantly, even in their strong condemnations of young men's attitudes and behaviour, the young women are aiming not to condemn the villains to celibacy, but to reform them into suitable suitors. For instance, *A Few True Girls of the Period*, having defended their own corps, offer advice that is less than kindly in its form to the young men who, not finding it "convenient to live with their friends," find they must have a furnished apartment with "partial board and attendance" at a cost of at least £1 per week, with a City dinner adding another 10s, so that all in all their weekly expenditure must average about £2: on that, they speak with assurance, having "a good, sound, practical, domesticated wife," they could live, "not extravagantly or expensively, but certainly comfortably," enjoying "all the advantages and privileges of home comforts." Q.E.D.? "Our advice to all single young men is to get married as soon as they can for the sake of society in general, and themselves in particular." And *A London Girl* reveals similar goals. The problem, she thinks, lies in the desire of false young men for "'Girls of the Period' of the Saturday Review style." Those who fit that role suffer from a lack of "healthy mental and physical employment," which leaves their heads empty for nonsense and the behaviour "either absurdly romantic or fast." In spite of her comparative independence, that is, *A London Girl* leaves the determining (if epithetically loaded) choice of women's character to men: "which is the greater treasure—a pretty senseless golden toy whose heart has been frittered away season after season in endless flirtations, or a girl who, without money, in knocking about the world has learnt to sympathise and love truly, to economise, and work?"

There were, of course, young women who purported to sympathize with the celibate young men, though fewer of them took up pen. One who did was *Flo*, writing from Birkenhead and admitting to being "scarcely eighteen years of age," who objects to *A Plain Girl*'s attack on the billiard-playing young men of the period. It is unfair to think of such as her intended (referred to in the language of the day as "a certain individual") as selfish because he will not "leave his father's house or his snug rooms, perhaps give up his share in a friend's yacht, and indeed relinquish altogether his happy independence," to assume married responsibilities. But then he is her "intended."

Clerks

And he was also not typical of those in the minds of most of the correspondents, being one of the comfortable middle class whose worst fear in marriage was shabby gentility. The problem for most of the celibate men who wrote to the *Daily Telegraph* was that even that state seemed beyond their reach. While these included (as the correspondence demonstrates) a few from the professions and business, the numerically dominant group among them was drawn from the rapidly expanding army of clerks, both in private and governmental employ, with whom may be allied in financial matters and mores the poorer clerics, the lesser retail merchants, and others from what is now called the "service sector."

Fictionally, no one comes close to Trollope in portraying vividly and sympathetically the lives of clerks, his most detailed accounts coming in *The Three Clerks* (1858) and *Marion Fay* (1882). In the former, the initial stages of the clerkly careers in London of three related young men are traced and compared. One, a high flyer, rises after a good marriage to a well-paid higher level of the civil service; a second takes the middle road with some difficulties; the third, Charley Tudor, best illustrates the themes of "Marriage or Celibacy?" He is charming but feckless; well intentioned but open to temptation.[38]

Charley is, like many another, in lodgings, where problems of morals and morale are legion. "The first great question to be settled, and it is a very great question with a young man, was that of latch key or no latch key." His landlady would, as the custom was, have given him one, but his mother objected; however, his disturbance of the household when arriving after midnight soon led the landlady, finding it "useless to attempt to keep a grown gentleman in leading-strings," to leave it available on the toilet table.[39]

His work in the "Navigation Office" was not conducive to instruction in "the pleasures of decent society," for he rushed "headlong among the infernal navvies too quickly to allow of that slow and gradual formation of decent alliances which is all in all to a young man entering life." Nothing else is to be expected, for while it is possible for him to "eschew the bad, . . . as to the good, he must wait till he be chosen" (p. 30.)[40] Of mixed nature, he leads a mixed life:

One week he would consort mainly with the houri of Norfolk Street beer-shop, and the next he would be on his good behaviour, and live as respectably as circumstances permitted him to do. His scope in this respect was not large. The greatest respectability which his unassisted efforts could possibly achieve was to dine at a cheap eating-house, and spend his evenings at a cigar divan. He belonged to no club, and his circle of friends, except in the houri and navvy line, was very limited. Who could expect that a young man from the Internal Navigation would sit for hours and hours alone in a dull London lodging, over his book and tea-cup? (Pp. 112-13)

He cannot, as Trollope insists, "live without society, and so he falls"; in the end, not irredeemably, but in progress distressingly for his family. In fact better society had been available (as the two others clerks demonstrate) at a suburban home well supplied with suitable daughters. Trollope's advice is clear: "Society, an ample allowance of society, this is the first requisite which a mother should seek in sending her son to live alone in London" (p. 30).

In the words of Mrs Henry Wood, what such lonely young men needed was "a bright, pleasant evening home, where [they] will find amusement, merry society, and loving faces."[41] And such was hard to find.

In *Marion Fay* a rather different set of clerkly themes is examined by Trollope, with some pungent accounts of snobbishness and of comparative advantage in public and private employ.[42] Snobbishness is presented mainly in relation to George Roden, a post-office clerk (like the young Trollope) who is loved by a woman of higher birth, and who is accepted (and promoted) when it becomes known that he is by right of descent an Italian count (a distinction he refuses to recognize); this matter is not relevant to the themes of "Marriage or Celibacy?"[43] Public *vs* private employment is only tangentially relevant, but the detail is indicative of general attitudes, as when the attractions of two clerks, Crocker of the post office and Tribbledale of a commercial house, are compared by a young woman courted by both:

Crocker's salary was £150; and, balancing the two young men together as she [Clara] had often done, though she liked the poetry of Tribbledale, she did on the whole prefer the swagger and audacity of Crocker. Her Majesty's Civil Service too had its charms for her. The Post Office was altogether superior to Pogson and Littlebird's. Pogson and Littlebird's hours were 9 to 5. Those of Her Majesty's Civil Service were much more genteel;—10 namely to 4.[44]

If young men were anxious for advice they need not look to fiction. The anonymous *Economy for the Single and Married*, referred to in chapter 4 above, spread its net (supportive, not entwining) for both sexes, as part of its subtitle indicates: *Comprising also a Variety of Useful and Original Information for the Single*.[45] It compares life in nasty lodgings (12s per week, plus 3s for an extra bed-sitting room) with chambers (£25 a year, plus £5 for attendance), recommending the latter for those who have, in addition to £100 a year, £50 for furniture. Other details suggest a pattern of life: the young man should eat out, and incidentally save by reading magazines where he dines; he can attend galleries and museums (a list of those that do not charge admission is given), as well as free "Places which form an agreeable morning lounge";[46] and he should cultivate culture at the theatre, musical and balletic performances, scientific displays (including Mme Tussaud's), print shops, excursions, and (last at any rate) churches. Certain dangers are signalled: do not frequent "singing rendezvous in certain localities" or public houses where acting is permitted. And the guide might well, in some respects, have been written for or by some of the correspondents of the *Daily Telegraph*: "Let no foolish pride, no ridiculous example, no superficial advice, make you incur expenses in furnishing" beyond your needs, and avoid credit (p. 24); dress "respectably" but at "the cheapest rate" (p. 32); and above, all, do not marry on £100 a year, because children will come (p. 24). Indeed: "Steel yourself against the tender passion—for marry you cannot, with any propriety, or hope of providing for a family" (p. 26).

The views of the correspondents in "Marriage or Celibacy" accord well with the accounts above, though a few are sanguine. *R.O.* is the first to portray the clerk's progress, concern about which underlies so much of the series. After countering *A Would-Be Reformer*'s slander on parents, he mounts an attack in telling detail on sons:

I speak, Sir, of young men entering banks, counting-houses, &c., and contracting fast habits, and thus wasting the money which, if laid by, would enable them at a proper age to marry. Take, as an instance, a young man entering a banking-house. He will receive for his first year's service £80, with an annual increase of £10, and supposing at the time he entered he was eighteen years of age (the usual age), he can, by being careful, live comfortably upon the amount of his first year's salary; and if he continues to do this until he is 26 years of age, his salary will have reached £160 per annum, and he will, in the meantime, have saved £350, without taking into consideration the interest, which will have amounted to something considerable.

The tale ends (in terms of the writer's world) happily and compellingly: "With the £350 in hand and £160 a year salary, you will agree with me that he could afford to marry comfortably, and that the causes of celibacy rest as a rule with the young men, and not with their parents, as *A Would-Be Reformer* thinks."

The message here is that while early marriage for clerks is foolish, delay and prudence promise some hope of wedded happiness. The first part of this proposition was contested by only two, the most optimistic being *Preceptor,* who, against *Solon Smiff,* presents counterinstances (non-fictional?) to support early marriage. He begins with that other penurious group, clerics:

A.B. was one of three sons of poor but respectable parents, and having a turn for study was educated for a school-master. At the age of twenty-two he married, and has since that time, on an average of £80 per annum, purchased his house, studied and passed B.A. at London University, and is now a clergyman. He has not been childless, having three still living, and I believe four buried, one having lived to the age of sixteen. . . . I at present know two clerks in a City office, one in receipt of £4 10s weekly and the other of £1. The junior one had the audacity to marry to the disgust of the senior, who, I may add, spent more than the £1 on billiards.

The only other hopeful note is that sounded by *B*—, who is clearly viewing the problem from a distance, taking "no small amusement" at "the paper warfare."[47] He is quite prepared to defend the Belgravian mammas' "sober judgment and . . . common sense" in preventing their daughters from marrying young men with inadequate incomes, such as £200. In noting that the discussion has turned away from that topic to another, "On what may clerks and tradesmen marry?" and having no "wish to offend a most respectable and well-educated body of men," he will observe dispassionately that

the clerks in a commercial house [the "generality of them are the sons of tradesmen"] do not enjoy a social position entailing on them any but the most moderate expenditure—nothing, in fact, being expected of them than that they should appear respectably dressed in their principal's establishment, and if they concede thus much to society it demands no more, and leaves them to model their domestic economy and arrangement on a scale to be determined by their individual receipts and requirements.

B—'s advice is not merely abstract: "Let each, then, marry in the position in which he and (not 'or') she have been accustomed to move," and even then waiting until there are savings adequate to "the contingencies of a rainy day."

So even he, whose attitudes towards the cost of clerks' respectability are untypical, would postpone marriage. Others drew different lines and conclusions, one being *Another Mechanic*, who uses his position to develop a *topos* of class comparison, employing folk myth embellished with wit:

Were even that ancient fairy who presides at the metamorphosing department in nursery tales to offer me, in place of my present celibate and pecuniary condition, a city clerkship at £100 a year, with, of course, a loving and intelligent helpmate, in a suburban villa, enlivened by a small assortment of ourselves in miniature, but with all the risks of ordinary mortality remaining, I am afraid I should deem the proffer a rather equivocal instance of her favour; for I think a working man on £70 is not so ill off as a gentlemanly City scribe on £100.

Certainly in agreement is *S.A.L.T.* (of the earth or the saving pinch of?), who locates the source of the correspondent's "diverse and conflicting opinions" in "the impossibility of drawing a 'hard and fast line' that shall be universally applicable." He gives the fullest account in the series of the growing army of the shabby genteel, the "thousands of young men, clerks in the city of London [counting-houses], whose miserable pittance is hardly sufficient for their own maintenance, much less for the support of a wife and family." From "personal knowledge" he informs the editor (as mediator for the readers) that these thousands, well-educated and intelligent, get scarcely £50 to £60 annually, on which they have "to appear respectably attired" to avoid discrediting their employers. "Painfully conscious of the necessity of external decency, they have to sacrifice comforts, and often necessaries, in order to be able to wear the garb of gentlemen." Although there are so many in this class, and their remuneration and prospects so paltry,[48] there is a crush at the door: "hundreds are continually soliciting situations of the same character—their only resource, indeed, to prevent absolute want." For them to marry is "not only an act of folly, but positive sin" except in the very rare cases when they wed a woman with some independent means.

And that, with variations on the dangers, was the dominant view from both sides of the marriage lines. Three examples will illustrate. First, an unmarried man who offers as validation of his own scepticism a glimpse of his condition as a bachelor who is neither "crusty" nor "old":

After ten years of service as chief clerk in a City house, I find myself, through changes caused by the long prevailing stagnation of business, without employment, and my heart aches for numbers I meet at newsrooms every day, who, like myself, vainly scan the advertising columns of your paper and others, in the hope that something suitable may appear; and if, after months of waiting, I succeed in getting something to do, probably it will bear a salary of less than half of that to which I have been accustomed. My case is only one of many. Among them, I fear, are a large proportion who tenderly love both wives and children, but who, in presence of absent means, would wish in their hearts that they had never been possessed of either, and could be, as I am, *A Bachelor*.[49]

Confirmation comes from *An Old Married Man* whose experience demonstrates that £150 would not provide in London a "respectable" life for a clerk such as himself[50] who has "more than once . . . been out of employment," no matter what the economies,[51] especially in the face of the "extraordinary expense" of such inescapable woes as family illnesses and deaths. Therefore, while believing that marriage is "a natural obligation," and holding out to hopeful young girls the rather surprising possibility—the only such suggestion in the whole series—that while incomes may increase family size may not, his main recommendation is caution in the face of the fact that in ninety-nine out of a hundred marriages insufficient means lead to unhappiness, so often increased by the dissatisfaction of the children who seek society elsewhere.

And finally on this theme *F.M.*, who typically urges thought and restraint on lovers who tend to act without calculating consequences. He too cites his own married experience: while £150 annually with rigid economy will permit a comfortable house, good substantial fare, and respectable dress, the income may not be progressive while the outlay certainly is, and no savings can be made for "the winter of life," when "labour is either painful or impossible." He sounds a note of proud resentment not found explictly elsewhere in the series:

When a man marries and is dependent on a small salary, let him bid farewell to independence. If, unfortunately, he has bad tempered and ungenerous employers, he is fair game for them; they know he is morally bound to submit to much that a single man would resent.

So he can close with advice to bachelors that summarizes the views of his kind: better to be wise and remain "in single blessedness than run the risk of joint misery."

Giving him the last voice on his side of the debate does not imply its victory. Judgment awaits a more impartial jury.

CHAPTER SIX

Problems and Solutions: The Ways In and the Way Out

Can "The Marriage Question" be summarized? The *Daily Telegraph*'s concluding leading article in the series made a comprehensive attempt, based on the early battle between *Benedick* and *Erastes*, under whose banners they enlisted other correspondents. And indeed the contrast between the realists and the romantics is important, not least because their differences were not, and could not be, resolved. Not only did the seemingly irreducible distance between pessimists and optimists separate them, but also the pragmatic force of belief and physical desire that propelled the young into marriage meant that unhappy and happy outcomes both provided evidence. Nonetheless, on the question as to whether prudent marriage was possible on about £200 a year, a majority came down on the negative side, and that majority had the better empirical evidence.

There was a tendency in the correspondence, supported by the leading articles, to say that romantic views were the property only of inexperienced young girls, while experienced married men had the franchise on realism. This judgment is but a rough induction: after all, the redoubtable champion *Erastes* led the idealists' charge and the qualified *Paterfamilias* was in his cohort, while the bitterest condemnations of rose-coloured views of rose-covered cottages were women. And the strength and subtlety of the presentations do not allow for such rigid categorization. Still, the contrast at the extremes is worth a brief sketch.

Lucy presents the most uncomplicated instance in the series of a would-be angel on the hearth,[1] saying:

True love is strengthened in trial; and to a woman there can be no experience more pleasing than the feeling that she is a help to her husband, that her smiles, her kind words, and her tenderness are aiding him in a worldly point of view, and, far sweeter thought! increasing his happiness. This is my ideal of matrimony, one which my mother, to whose pure influence I owe anything good in my nature, has ever inculcated.

Also of the romantic self-sacrificing school is *One of England's Daughters*, "a true-born English [engaged] girl," who is convinced that "even poverty, shared with one's dear husband, is preferable to luxury and comfort in one's maiden home parted from him." Her account of unrequited love could be drawn from many a contemporary novel or poem: "Why is it so many girls grow pale and thin and anxious when engaged? Because there is a secret pining and longing and anxious care—a seeming gnawing of the very heart, which none know but themselves."

Though not alone, and not deprived of male company in their beliefs, these idealists faced formidable opposition. These warriors include, of course, *Benedick*, who wrote two long and powerful screeds giving no quarter to the sentimentalists, and *Vieux Moustache*, the practised campaigner signalled by his signature, who had but one purpose in his three letters (assuming they all came from the same pen), to deflate any expectations resulting from the "captivating" accounts presented by such as *Paterfamilias* and *A Happy Nine Years' Wife* of "what a married man with six children can do on less than £300 a year." For the hard-headed, the monetary is mandatory, and the danger in the correspondence arises from the gross underrating of housekeeping costs. The realists won praise from other correspondents, including *A Lover of Home*, who condemned the "vast amount of sentiment" in the discussion.

Also recommending common sense over sentimental "silly trash" is *One Who Would Be a Good Deal Happier If He Had It* (i.e., £200 a year), who broadens his gaze from the editor to an ideal audience: "I say to all whom it may concern, if you would save yourselves and your wife what is to be many a bitter hour (and God knows how bitter it is to see your wife and children wanting the sea breeze and other things which you cannot afford to give them), don't marry on less than £200 a year." And *W.H.S.* even dares avow Scrooge's credo: it is not his fault if six children of an improvident father are near the workhouse wall. "The fault rests with their fathers, who rushed into matrimony with no other prospect than to bring up their progeny to pauperism and want. . . . If society had fulfilled nature's laws, there would have been no need for the cry, 'Oh, don't marry, but think of me, benefit me.'"

The women who defend the cause of realism are only slightly less censorious, but their messages are more friendly to marriage, if postponed until competence is within reach, than to celibacy. One such is *An Eldest Daughter*—though eldest, at nineteen not old. She denies and defies the typing of young girls as foolish dreamers, being herself of the "life is real, life is earnest" school,[2] and knowing from her own family's "station" that nothing but "genteel beggary" or "genteel poverty" is possible on £100, which is less than the wages of a "respectable mechanic." She also refutes, from her "certain knowledge," rural romanticism; to think of married bliss on that sum in the country, where everything but house rent is at least a third dearer, is "simply madness, . . . unless the couple mean to keep pigs and take in washing, or something equally remunerative." She is an outspoken advocate of marriage between social equals, in the same "station" and even "circumstances"; but in saying that girls should be "domesticated and true helpmeets to their husbands," she is tactically giving only to take away: Would any true and affectionate "gentleman" wish to see his wife, "a refined, well-educated, intellectual girl . . . scrub, wash, cook, &c., in fact be jack-of-all-trades in their home?" The answer is obvious but needs exposure: "No, those who expect such should marry what they want—a servant!"[3] After that attack, it is meet that the conclusion should be not quite bleak but certainly stern:

Marriage is, after all, not merely a commercial speculation—I would prove that not all "girls of the period" are waxen dolls—but a sacred responsibility. Let young men and maidens undertake it as such with all due regard to each other's welfare, and that of their "probable children," and God would make marriage to be to us more of a blessing than it usually proves itself to be.

Close to her view but perhaps more inclined to celibacy are *Three "Girls of the Period,"* writing out of the experience of large families with small incomes. They dissent, as was seen in chapter 4 above, from those who think happiness lies in having a husband and £100 a year. And one final female witness, *Enemoplem*, closes her letter in a flurry of dubious inverted commas that demonstrate her adherence to the common sense deposited in maxims—at least those that enshrine prudence:

Yet, when everything has been said, a "fair start" may equally be desired for matrimony as for the "Established Church;" for we know that when "poverty comes in at the door love flies out of the window." When I was "sweet eighteen"—that romantic age when everything appears couleur de rose—in common, I presume, with others of my sex, I was given to building Chateaux d'Espagne; and my idea of perfect Elysium was "love in a cottage adorned with woodbines and roses;" but, since I have reached woman's estate, I have learned to look with a more practical eye on life and its realities. And the "bacon and greens" which we are assured are the natural accompaniments to "love in a cottage" do not appear to me very attractive or romantic now.

With her is a male from Derby who is *Pegging at It*. He is almost equally addicted to proverbial wisdom, and has a most unusual turn of metaphor, encased in a dialectic of qualification. For instance, after citing "who marries in haste repents at leisure," he develops the notion further in his own style:

he who marries indiscreetly, depending on self and the future, should lead his wife home, cut the roots of his ambition, pluck out his heart's sensibilities, look cheerful in all things, and dream no more. Nay, he should strip face to face with fate, and, with his foot, his best foot, upon the poetry and dead things of the past, abjure superfluities to a shave, and put his head in the collar of everlasting prose before him.

Admitting that the urge which led him to these rhetorical heights is vain, he acknowledges that "the sanguine aspirants to the mythical matrimonial bliss of £130 a year will not be proselytised by these observations"; nonetheless he wastes a word on *Erastes* and those of his acolytes "who 'go in' for marriage on the cheap": "the imaginative lure of love in a cottage and perpetual smiles turns stale and stinks in the nostrils when 'the wolf's at the door.'" And his peroration is, if convoluted in form, unequivocal in exhortation:

Though temperate in all things, to the exclusion of physic bottles and doctor's bills; though versed in the ways of the world, "up" in human nature, and adepts at marketing, in the language of your facetious contemporary, to all those who are bent upon marrying for a "long life and happiness" upon small means, I would say "Don't!"[4]

That final word might well be taken as the final word in summation of the debate. However, another way of capturing the direction and tone of the series is more subtle and revealing. The correspondents were all reformers, and like all reformers, were faced by a series of questions: What is right and good? What is wrong and evil? What are the sources of wrong and evil? How can we get from wrong to right?

And like almost all reformers, the correspondents severally concentrated on some but not all of these questions.

What Is Right and Good?

Answers to this question are the easiest to summarize and have been fully illustrated: almost without exception, Victorians—and most strongly the middle classes—believed that to marry early was proper. "Early" needed no exact definition, but the range was from about nineteen to twenty-five for women and from about twenty-four to thirty for men. And there was unanimity about the attributes necessary to make marriage a success: love and devotion were so obvious as to need little emphasis (and were usually emphasized only when they were lacking or weak); always demanding attention were the qualities entailed by a true appreciation of the "offices," namely prudence, moderation, and fortitude. These were not in competition any more than they were in question, and sufficient evidence has already been given to demonstrate the ubiquity and strength of the demands for them.

What Is Wrong and Evil?

Here, though the general assumptions are not much in question, the opportunity to lay blame invited some variation in specific indictments. The Great Social Evil was, as its euphemistic name self-evidently shows, evil; what was moot was the reason for its "greatness" in the sense of prevalence. For most contributors to the series—and in this respect they reflect at least publicly expressed Victorian views— the lust of men, and specially of young men, is necessary cause, and also sufficient cause in the absence of moral control. More narrowly, then, that absence is seen as a remediable evil; however, Biblical injunction as well as common belief supported the view that marriage was a practical aid to lessen the "burning." For that reason, and because the moral control was assumed to work more effectively after marriage, the resort of married men to prostitutes is not emphasized in the series, though, as has been shown, some bitter comments were elicited.

The general theme about impoverished marriages, however, included the implication that, in addition to other vile results, such difficulties might drive husbands towards sexual sin. The evils—and they are the dominant ones in the *Daily Telegraph* series—leading to such failure are easily identified as the opposites of the virtues seen in good marriages: that is, imprudence, immoderation, and lack of fortitude.

Ruled out of court are other weaknesses of character, as not material to this case: what are needed are not the pleasant virtues that make family life happy, but those stern ones that make it endurable in the face of material deprivation. This limitation also helps explain the relative absence of Christian exhortation: it is not that the Christian virtues are unimportant; it is simply that the pagan ones are those needed to deal with the obstacles in the way of early marriage.

It is important also to emphasize that the correspondents concentrate on remediable evils. Consequently, while there is regret about the operation of impersonal forces, including material conditions, they are not cursed and reviled. Just here appears a marked difference from analysis a century and more later: the definition of "impersonal" has changed, most significantly with reference to governments, who are now generally thought responsible for causing economic and social evils, or at least for mitigating them. In the "Marriage or Celibacy?" series, the onus is on individuals, on their attitudes and habits. They are portrayed as personally responsible, particularly when the person making the criticism is not the person criticized, although there are some admissions of failure—which is usually said to have been rectified.

How Did Things Go Wrong? And How Can They Be Put Right?

The described deterrents to prudent and respectable marriage may be summarized in bare outline: first, there is too much demand for luxuries that are seen as necessities, because notions about marriage have changed for the worse and selfishness, vanity, and folly have been encouraged. Second, young women (and to a lesser extent young men) are inadequately trained for household management. Third, there are too many children and a surplus of young women.[5] Fourth, social practices, especially in the city, prevent suitable mates from meeting. Fifth and finally, given the facts of existence and the desire for human dignity, there is just not enough money. Each of these peceived causes leads to a single question: What can be done about it? And the practically minded middle class was anxious to find solutions.

Because exposition of dangers and difficulties is intertwined closely with proposed solutions, they can be treated together under the heads outlined above. Because each has been at least adumbrated in the preceding three chapters, only relatively brief treatment is needed to focus attention on the difficulty of the dilemma, "marriage or celibacy?"

1 *Improper Notions of Marriage*

This criticism, applied to parents as well as to young women and young men, is most evident early in the series, when the discussion, in dwelling on upper-middle-class homes and ideals, resembles more closely that in the manuals and novels as well as in *The Times*. In the *Daily Telegraph* there is some self- and class-satisfaction, but very little; the dominant tone (though the specific targets vary slightly) is that of *A Would-Be Reformer*, who early in the series made a comprehensive indictment that will serve as a representative sample. He finds the central issue in

the extravagant style of living and habits of luxury which prevail to so great an extent amongst the middle and upper-middle class; the class above all others which is likely to be most affected when the question of marriage comes before it. A man in this class, as a rule, from small beginnings, finds himself getting on in the world, and begins to keep a large establishment, and his wife adopts all the luxurious and expensive habits of a lady of fortune. They bring up their children in the same expensive style, and spend every shilling of the husband's income. There is no thought of saving money for the children, though they worship it themselves; but, in lieu of that, the children are made to understand their first care must be to marry well. They are brought up to regard money as the one thing needful; and, as they will have none of their own, must turn fortune-hunters, and estimate every man and every woman they meet in society by their weight in gold. Character, conduct, principles, every worthy attribute in man or woman, is made of the least possible importance. The father dies, leaving his family comparatively penniless, but full of pride and pretension as ever.

What is the result?

In their fallen condition, it is hardly possible for them to marry up to the exalted notions which have been instilled into them; and other families brought up in the same way, and with the same money principles, would scorn to look at them for the same reasons. . . . The marriage question is certainly getting to be serious for all young women who have not their wings tipped with gold dust. In a few years marriage will become a sealed book to many of them, unless a change in the dynasty of the God of Marriage should work them a revolution, by effecting a change in the views and habits of parents themselves, who are more to blame than their children for the dead-lock in which they are now cast by their own extravagant and selfish example and precept.

He has lots of support concerning the gravamen of his charge, which is the first of the answers mentioned above to the question of why prudent marriage is so difficult, i.e., the "extravagant style of living and habits of luxury which prevail to so great an extent amongst the middle and upper-middle class," and which, because of parents' folly, were deemed necessary by their children as a condition of marriage. (One of the most perceptive remarks in his letter is that the middle class is "above all others" that "which is likely to be most affected when the question of marriage comes before it.")

One who agrees with him is *An English Girl*, who directs her defence of her cohort somewhat differently from those others who appear to be writing either directly to the men (irredeemable and redeemable alike) or to the general readership of the *Telegraph*. She explictly wishes to let other "English girls know it is not their fault there are not more marriages than at present." Asking "where the evil lies?" *An English Girl* stays for a partial answer: "Certainly not in 'Girls of the Period,' for all men admire a well-dressed, jolly girl." She then elaborates, regrettably weakening her case by shilly-shally; she prefaces her identification of the evil as caused by "everyone trying to outdo their neighbours in dress and everything," with "I think," and continues:

I do not mean to say the girls are free from blame, but the men make them what they are; they snub the plain-dressed girls, and flirt only with those dressed in the height of fashion; therefore, what can men expect but expensive wives? Until they alter things will remain as they are.

Implied is a regret over lost ideals. *A Dutchman* (seemingly in the sense of cautionary) delivers a strong sentence on modern mores:

Dress and the study of appearances in general, worthless novels, parties, operas, and the desire to outshine others—habits not solely confined to the fair sex—have of late years become an intolerable nuisance and curse to society, and have caused wretchedness, misery, and poverty in many married homes where happiness and plenty could have existed in their stead.

Indeed he is able, recalling his bachelor days, to conclude by affirming the report given by *A Simple Country Girl*, quoted above, of "general conversation and 'small talk' at friendly gatherings or parties." (Perhaps in comradely spirit, he omits *Simple* from her pseudonym.)

Part of the problem, as is evident in those quotations, was the increasing visibility of material goods and of their enjoyment: not only was there an increase in the standard of living throughout society,[6] but the increasing ease of communication spread the news more quickly. The pace of change made for difficulties of understanding between the generations, with older folk steadily less sympathetic with what they saw as the young's unrealistically enhanced views of what was due them. Though he should not have identified only young women of the upper middle class and aristocracy as the culprits, Myron Brightfield describes the main tendency: "Truly, the older generation of the 'sixties could scarcely be made to realize the great elevation of the level of upper middle class and aristocratic living since the 'thirties—brought on by the huge increase in industrial wealth. But the expectations of the young women of these classes had kept pace with the change."[7]

The growth of class consciousness in Britain in this period is well—perhaps too well—documented, but less has been said about the concomitant breakdown of barriers of expectation as the older notion of "orders" disappeared. One effect was a broadening of social emulation when the revolution of rising expectations began to turn the social world. Illustrative is the view of *Philos.*, who, considering the vanity of "unnecessary and unbecoming finery" in young servant girls, traces the folly—once again the criticism was sure to come—to their copying a wealthier class, the ladies of which might well adopt for their own sakes as well as that of their imitators "greater simplicity and moderation."

So, while *A Would-Be Reformer* is correct in seeing upper-middle-class notions of marriage as central, he also could have presented them as normative. And marriage was much more than one event in a life (or lives)—it in concept and fact influenced the whole pattern of middle-class expectation and realization. An article entitled "Marriage" in the *Englishwoman's Domestic Magazine* in 1865 claims the wider range: "it is not true to say that this system of beginning the world with a more ostentatious and expensive outlay than people considered necessary in former times is confined altogether, or even chiefly, to domestic matters. On the contrary, it pervades every condition, every object around us."[8]

In 1865, Anne Gilchrist, in the course of arguing that women's domestic management is essential to resolving the problem, makes clear what the problem is:

A hundred years ago the income we now regard as constituting genteel poverty [say £150 per annum],—that income which during the first ten or fifteen years of a man's career is all he can hope to realize in England, whether by the professions, the civil service, or literature, and which the majority never get beyond,—was no poverty at all, genteel or ungenteel, but a competence; and what is now mere competence was wealth. If the material progress of the time has enlarged the circle of men's wants it has also abundantly cheapened the supply of them: therefore on this score a balance with the past may be pretty evenly struck. The breaking down of class distinctions, and growing infatuation of each grade in vying with the grade immediately above it, is a more active cause of the embarrassment.[9]

The embarrassment, not to say shame, is strongly evoked by George Fordham in his pamphlet, *The Age We Live in; or, a Glimpse at Men and Manners*. With everyone "going at a railroad pace to tread on the heels of those before him," greengrocers' daughters, envious of the cheese-monger's piano, insist successfully on one, and young gentlemen demand stick-up collars because Jimmy Jones had them last midsummer. "The dust-contractor's family make an annual tour on the continent—round Calais one year, through Boulogne the next—just to let the coal-meter's wife see that 'other people have got money as well as Mr. Brown.'" Two other fads equally demonstrate that "This is indeed a march of intellect": "What an amount of physical endurance must be displayed in the efforts of the rising generation to smoke 'the fragrant weed,' but what a *status* is gained if they can but conquer the rebellious stomach! What joy fills the youthful breast as the first symptoms of coming crop appear, to reward the lad's continued labours with his father's razors!"

Small means generally co-exist with high aspirations. Persons of low degree, like the frog in the fable, emulating the dimensions of the ox, make it their highest ambition to be thought temporal peers: the result is inevitably the same—the bubble bursts, and rank and character are gone together.... The very names of our indispensable requisites are so many temptations. Boots and shoes become heroic, and are dubbed "Wellingtons" and "Bluchers;" necks are encircled with "the Albert tie;" stays are intolerable, but obtain a new lease as "the Corsaletto di Medici;" new mantles are dreamt of at sight of "the Queen's own."[10]

The bad effects of foolish class pride are rather differently seen by *S.A.L.T.*, who instances "the false and pernicious idea" held by "parents of easy means that tradespeople is another name for vulgar people, and that to apprentice their sons to any branch of trade is to degrade and denigrate their families." In consequence they "drift" their educated sons into the "mercantile world." Being "comfortably housed and fed at the parental domicile," they need care little about their earnings, "but—and here lies the evil—they exclude others who, not having had opportunities of entering into business on their own account, are compelled to resort to this, their only means of gaining a livelihood." Only the extinction of "this social disarrangement" and the resultant direction into independent business of those with sufficient means will reduce the number of "dependent clerks" and increase their pay sufficiently to justify their marrying.

An authority external to the series, Thomas Hughes, an advocate of "the people's culture" before his time, detected a different bad consequence of class, deploring the "further separation of classes consequent on twenty years of buying cheap and selling dear, and its accompanying overwork." He echoes others more closely in regretting that "our sons and daughters have their hearts in London Club life, or so-called Society, instead of in the old English home duties; [and that] farmer's sons are apeing fine gentlemen, and farmer's daughters caring more to make bad foreign music than good English cheeses."[11]

The ethic of self-help was active, however, as Samuel Smiles's popular *Lives of the Engineers*, for instance, amply demonstrated. So the danger of emulating the accidental and vicious was overbalanced for many by the genuine promise of betterment. John Hill Burton (earlier an editor of Jeremy Bentham) made the points clearly:

If [the working classes] desire an example of an order of men raising their position in the social scale, let them look at the progress of the middle-class for the past century, and the changes that have taken place in their position towards the high aristocracy. The moderate capitalist, the clergyman, the lawyer, the physician, the professional author, the artist, stand respectively higher than they could have stood a century ago, when between them and the hereditary aristocracy there was a great gulf fixed.[12]

Perhaps so, but correspondents in the *Telegraph* tended to see this broadened horizon as making successful early marriage less likely by encouraging vain emulation. Perhaps not very helpfully but still understandably, the correspondent signing himself as 3 best captures this aspect of the problem by blaming, in addition to mothers, "our moralists and philosophers," who fail to "impress upon the minds of the people that society is at fault," and that there must be alteration in "the laws by which it is guided."

While awaiting that improbable and distant consummation, however, it was imperative for most that targets be more specifically identified. And one group that attracted much attention, as has been seen, were parents, particularly mothers. Not all the *Telegraph*'s correspondents were as forthright as the transAtlantic Sophronia, who traced the sin back to indulgent parents: "Girls thus recklessly given dress and spending money are really driven into extravagance, and are at last the women whose husbands become bankrupts, defaulters, suicides."[13] But *A Wife and Mother* in the *Telegraph*, as noted in chapter 5, fixed the blame for incompetent wives on parents who fail to see that a good income with a large family is a matter of subtraction not addition, and so, forgetting that they cannot provide for all, fail to provide practical domestic education.

Here, as almost always (and in the advice books), it is the mothers who are at grievous fault. For instance, *Charlie's Wife* blames her and Charlie's initial sufferings not on early marriage, but on her lack of training:

The fault lay in my not being taught as a girl that the wife of a tradesman or professional man must not think a husband can afford to keep her for show alone. She ought to be something more than his pet and plaything, and if mothers would only take as much pains to teach their daughters to be sensible and useful as they to to make them accomplished, they would make better wives, and young men like Mr. *Solon Smiff* would have no excuse for keeping single.

The false treatment comes from false goals, as *3* points out. Mothers educate daughters so that they may "marry them quickly and to the best advantage," dwelling on "a smattering of what are called accomplishments," and omitting anything producing "useful housewives and good mothers." Of course men of limited means will not marry such girls.

The faulty seeds when sown tend to mature in unattractive ways: daughters are too often the obvious children of their parents, as Mrs Warren had said: "while girls are so thriftless and manifestly so unfitted for managing a house young men cannot marry; it must not be said, 'will not;' it is impossible with the luxurious and idle habits which have been cherished by both sexes of the middle class that they can do so."[14] In the *Telegraph* an important, if not fully representative view is that of one who identifies himself as a member of the "upper middle" class and signs himself *Comfortably Single*. He is certainly the latter, but dubiously the former, for his explanation of young men's reluctance to marry reveals him as an advocate of early marriage. He portrays himself as unable to act because of a dilemma that he poses (a rational procedure), which puts the onus on women: "Either young marriageable ladies must lower the standard by which they measure a husband, or must be content to remain in their present position."[15]

One of the comprehensive indictments is that of *Spes*, a civil servant from Burton-on-Trent, who naughtily perverts a biblical injunction, saying, "Man cannot live by bread and cheese alone." He insists that different antecedents and expectations make for greatly different views of necessities, but is also willing to throw blame on young girls, outlining three (not unconnected) causes for their failing to take "a sufficiently serious view" of the duties of marriage. First come the "perverse ideas entertained of . . . amusement, dress, and social intercourse." Consequently "an unhealthy amount of rivalry . . . plays the bear with moderate incomes" and leads to "jealousy and estrangement."

Second is the male fault, learned from recent literature, of transforming "the woman into a toy, [and] ceasing to remind her of the sterner facts of existence," with the result that there is "a scarcity of women able and willing to be of assistance to us in the ordinary trials that we have to contend with." From thence derive "the peculiar ideas of beauty entertained by the sex, and the pictures of *Punch*, &c., are a sufficiently uncomplimentary reflex of the 'girls of the period'—mere dolls, not lacking beauty, but [lacking] that which gives beauty its lasting charm, expression, which is merely proper education."

Third is the valuing of the pleasures over the responsibilities of marriage, so that in the event "dissatisfaction and complaint" result. What a pity, for

a starting income of £100 to £130, if rightly managed, holds out a promise of a life of much joy and happiness. With it the wife is not condemned to the rougher domestic duties, but only to such an amount of work as is wholesome for us all; but, on the other hand, she cannot be "clothed in purple and fine linen, and go somewhere" every day.[16]

The second fault identified by *Spes* is male, not female, and though the young women, as we have seen, were much attacked, their male contemporaries were not without critics in fiction and fact. Brightfield summarizes the attack in fiction thus: "the broadest and most often urged allegation [was] that eligible bachelors, through vanity and selfishness, diffidence, or laziness, refused to interest themselves in the business of selecting, loving, and courting a suitable partner in matrimony."[17] In the *Telegraph*, the point was made by *A Would-Be Reformer* (quoted earlier on social causes): "Numbers of young men in the present day, with no pretensions whatever to birth, fortune or position, spend half their income in the merest luxuries of fashion and folly, and then declare they cannot afford to marry. Of course they cannot; and woe betides the woman who gets tied to one of this class." And even if such go a-courting, their view of women is sadly distorted, claims *L.C.J.* (also already cited), who stood out in the chorus of complaint from unmarried girls because of her grace of manner and controlled irony. She notes the grave and tender tones of those who see each girl "as a costly piece of Sevres, or a rare exotic, something to be brought out for the possessor's delectation, when the cares and trials of the day are folded up and laid aside," and calls on her cohort to lay down their embroidery and quit their music stools, for "the altar cloth and the last new song can wait while we investigate the charges against us, and enter upon our defence." She finds herself faced with such insulting views as those of *One Who Looks before He Leaps* and *A Pilgrim of Love*, the former deploring "the shocking waste of time accompanying the study of languages and music," the latter bemoaning the necessity that forces a man with moderate means, "perhaps conversant with three or four languages," to marry an inferior. She is obliged to plead sarcastically: "In the name of all that is fair and manly, will some one tell us what we are to do?"

Abundantly evident is the belief that the sins of the parents were passed on to the children, who enjoyed them only too much. A comprehensive brush is the weapon of *Enemoplem*, who in signature reverses the name of the Greek muse of tragedy, Melpomene, but certainly does not in content repudiate her cast of mind. She infers three causes for the widespread prevalence of celibacy, the third of which has just been discussed, the "false pride" seen in those of both sexes who are "equally inclined to call 'necessaries' what were heretofore deemed 'luxuries.'" But the first two are the "incompetency" found in many ill-educated girls and the "selfishness" of the bachelor "lords of creation," with their self-indulgent clubs, operas, rides in "the Row," daily newspapers, and cigars.

The indictments, probing the wells of evil-doing, almost always point to methods of purification, either by looking to ends and strategy, or to means and tactics. As to the former, practical and ideal morality is served when both parents and children abjure the meretricious lures of money and social position, and adhere to traditional satisfactions, including contentment with one's received place in the world. It should be noted that the shaping of ideal models and practices was part of the war of the sexes—who should be in moral charge was a crucial if seldom articulated question.

In the spirit of the age, well displayed in the series, self-cure was obviously the main specific for these ills. A few correspondents, however, made what seem rather unlikely appeals—however pleasing to the vanity of the *Daily Telegraph*. Pointing to the educated young men in London, who are not wise enough to refuse to wed on a salary insufficient for a married artisan and are in danger from "these self-confident young ladies," *A Philanthropist* (not feeling able to man the oars himself?) surprises with his final exhortation: "Stretch forth your strong right arm, Mr. Editor, and in common mercy and humanity save them from shipwreck." Similarly, *M.T.M.* expands into the plural for an appeal to the editor:

We want you, Sir, to lecture the parents, and to tell them that they ought not to object to their children marrying on moderate incomes, considering that they themselves most probably did so, and have had no occasion to repent it. If we could only get the parents to moderate their views, I think we should in a great measure get over the evil.

Equally desperate seems the plaint of *A Simple Country Girl*. Decrying the double standard, which encourages the young men to break as many hearts as possible, she looks for a cure (somewhat surprisingly and vaguely) to the law and the government:

the race of good husbands in England is fast becoming extinct; we shall have to import a new stock, Sir; cannot you induce some courageous M.P. to put his shoulder to the wheel and help us; or while waiting for womanhood suffrage are we to pine away in single desolation? If so, where is the future generation to come from? Ought not the Queen to see about a new method of rearing soldiers and sailors to defend the will-be future defenceless country her descendants will reign over?

The practical focus, however, was sharply on tactics. A realistic view, even when elevated by hope, incorporated the household virtues: the ability and will to economize and to eschew luxuries, to make and to follow a plan, and to perform one's "offices." In Mrs Warren's words: "Each household, with its more or less and very opposite requirements, needs a different ordering, but the great principle for ruling, directly, and acting must ever remain fixed."[18] And here the second spawning ground of evil spread itself.

2 Lack of Useful Education

Deeply embedded in the criticisms of vain and selfish parents and children is the distress over inadequate education for prudent married life. Once again the main emphasis is on girls' education, demonstrating the universality of the axiom that household management was their office. It is also assumed (in consonance with the facts) that their training would be domestic in both senses, taking place in the home as well as dealing with its daily demands.

Food management was the most cited issue. The version of *Modern Domestic Cookery: Founded on the Principles of Economy and Practical Knowledge, and Adapted for Private Families* that appeared in 1865,[19] observes in opening:

If our ancestors made domestic occupations too exclusively the aim of female education, it may truly be said that the present generation has fallen as unwisely into the contrary extreme. It is indeed a very common, but a very erroneous supposition, that attention to culinary affairs is unnecessary in a gentlewoman; yet there can be no question that elegance, comfort, social enjoyment, and, it may be added, health, materially depend upon attention to the table; and the prudent management of her family ought to be considered an important object amongst the duties of every lady when she marries.

In the *Telegraph*, similar complaints are common, as for example by Z.Y.X., a London bachelor, that London girls are not trained to be fit wives. His plaint is echoed by *An English Wife*, who insists that she is neither slave nor dowdy, not surprisingly, as her husband brings in £350 a year. She ends her account: "It is a matter of deep regret that the good old custom of making girls and young ladies good housewives has, in a great measure, fallen away. I intend to teach mine to do as I do; they will be none the less refined by understanding the requirements of the kitchen as well as the drawing room."

In these sentiments they were echoing the advice in chapter 6 of *Economy for the Single and Married*, entitled "The Working Economy of a House":

[too] frequently, in the middle classes, have we instances of young women whose education has completely unfitted them for their sphere of life: by a pro-

cess simply *ornamental* they have been rendered indolent, useless, and a disgrace to their connexions.

That man is, indeed, sincerely to be pitied who takes such an one as his wife. . . . With boys, extremes on this point [encouragement of ambitious hopes that are never likely to be realized] seldom do harm: they fight their way onward to success: but with girls, it may be prejudicial in the highest degree, and even ruinous. The great aim in *their* rearing should be to instil a fondness for home and domestic associations. (P. 44.)

While many found their models in "good old customs," a few looked abroad. For example *Nachod* advises English mothers—the fathers make only a brief appearance in one sentence—to imitate "the so oft despised 'foreigners,'" and "inculcate their [daughters'] minds with a taste for the cookery book as well as for a necessary smattering of Italian, German, Latin, drawing, music, &c., and the countless accomplishments they are so desirous of procuring from the poor governesses at the rate of £20 a year."

As so often, this attack is on the substituting of graces for necessities, a complaint picked up by *Another English Girl*,[20] who gives one of the most concise accounts of the "immense deal of misery endured" in "many an unhappy home." The typical young girl is quite untrained for management:

There is the cause of debts, duns, and difficulties innumerable, and I fear ultimately of the flight of affection that (had the husband found the assistance he was right in expecting, instead of a girl with a great deal of music and very little else) might have endured for years. I would not complain of a girl's devoting hours each day to acquiring an accomplishment that in itself is very delightful, but I would argue the necessity of learning how to become somewhat more than a pretty musical doll. That, when all the new dresses had been worn, and all the pretty and difficult pieces played, there might be found by the husband a promise of a companion for his years of toil, instead of the expensive addition to his establishment that, without doubt, a wife is now.

Class awareness marks the comments of *One Who Looks before He Leaps*. Admitting that early marriage will seem charming for a while, he proverbially insists that "when the gilt is taken off the gingerbread" the true and low quality of imprudent wedlock is revealed, as in the "old adage" (much cited by other correspondents of similar mind): "When poverty comes in at the door, love flies out of the window." His cure, well suited to his diagnosis, is bluntly stated: "I say, let girls be brought up according to their respective stations in life, and not above them."

And *Home-Made Bread*, though like *A London Girl* in status, age (she is twenty), intention, and exordium ("I beg to offer you my humble opinions"), advances a point about social class that is all her own, and perhaps as bold as biased. She defends "the girls of the middle class whose ancestors have always been highly respectable middle-class people" from the censures that "more properly apply to those whose parents have been servants." Not that the latter are innately deficient, but they have been raised to think that using low tools such as dusters is "the height of vulgarity because forsooth their parents have been obliged to do it before them as a living." It is actually creditable to have raised oneself by industry, but the daughters, in false pride through vain emulation, are likely to dress extravagantly and refuse to marry anyone who cannot give them at least as good a home as the family one.

Once again the solutions are embedded in the complaints, and need but brief treatment. The overall maxim is enunciated by one of the girls in Wright's *The Complete Home*: "*how* are we to economize? where shall we make our savings, small and great?" And the answer is pat: "Here . . . is field for self-denial. We must not expect to set out in life as lavishly as we should like to end." (P. 395.) But this kind of generality never guides without training in its details. Once again Mrs Warren is ready for the willing:

to make the most of any working man's or clerk's income, a girl, if she be the wife of either, must be educated to cook, wash, make, and mend, if she would have peace, comfort, and respectability; also, she must have other and more refined accomplishments if she would make her home socially pleasant, or educate her children; which she must do, or let them run wild into every sin to which a vacant mind can tempt them. . . . (Pp. v–vi)

Most comments concerning the lower middle class either take for granted that the "more refined accomplishments" will take care of themselves or can be accepted in moderation. The emphasis is on training to "cook, wash, make, and mend," with heavy insistence on the first. Anne Gilchrist, who is partly with Mrs Warren as to accomplishments, thinks them compatible with,[21] if subordinate to, the main need, which is to educate the present generation of prospective wives out of their "complacent and entire ignorance" of household duties.

There was not complete unanimity on the question of blending talents, the *Englishwoman's Domestic Magazine* asserting, as though prompted by the experience of Caddy Jellyby in Dickens's *Bleak House*, "it is proverbial that the partner in a dance and the partner for life require very different qualifications."[22]

Joseph in the *Daily Telegraph* would not be very pleased with this contrast, for he would want a dancing partner. He animadverts on the wicked abrogation of "the laws and general impulses of society" by those who recommend early marriage and the consequent lowering of ladies to the level of servants. Some even openly "force upon [the] attention" of a bachelor "their potato-peeling or washing-tub woman as a suitable partner for him, and assert that with his £100 or £150 per annum they might live most happily together," and if he rejects their advice "he is at once assailed as a selfish and unreasonable man." The effects of this single cause are multiple: when either party is lowered by marriage, there is some truth "in the adage, that 'when poverty comes in at the door, love flies out at the window'"; the cost of their imprudence is passed on to their offspring; and even society suffers "by the gradual degeneration of the middle class." He is taking his own advice (or, some might say, justifying his decision by *post-hoc* rationalization): "Therefore, until my income is sufficient to enable me to marry one who is my equal, and to maintain for her that position which her education and social standing require, I will, with your permission, enter my protest against the levelling arguments of so many of your correspondents on this subject."

The main channel of belief in the correspondence is, however, that charted in "A Neglected Art (Cooking by Ladies to Save the Expense of a Cook)," in *Macmillan's Magazine* (1865), where the verdict is clearly in favour of the traditional office, and on its central task. While "a thorough insight into *every* branch of household work" is important, it is in the "culinary department that the worst and most uncontrollable leakage in the expenditure takes place." Gilchrist expects "a storm of indignation" from those appalled at the requirement that they spend half their time "in the kitchen getting red faces, coarse hands and sour tempers ... like an old-fashioned farmer's wife" only "to screw down expenditure a hundred or two a year." For them, "Existence itself, much less marriage, were it with an archangel, is not worth having on such terms!" She can assure them, however, that her twelve years' experience shows that the price of the necessary practical knowledge is much less than they think, and that, as to "the sacrifice of time and complexion, ... the part of cookery which chiefly demands skill and gives scope to clever management is not the tedious and fatiguing one of actually dressing the viands upon the fire, but the preparation of them for this final process." And she cleverly constrasts an alternate activity with which her audience would be familiar, needlework, which "consumes an enormous amount of time in proportion to the result, and demands as good as no brains." Constrast "culinary achievements" which "take only a moderate portion of time"—say a couple of hours a day—"but *do* require head."[23]

As will be seen, correspondents in the *Telegraph* emphasized culinary achievements as an essential part of education. And other aspects of practical education attracted strong comment. One specially concerned is *A Prudent Bachelor*. Like others, he expects much useful education to take place in the home—in his case, supervised by the father. Eventually the children need "more time and closer attention than a man who is engaged in winning their bread and cheese could possibly allow them himself." His views are perhaps coloured by his being one of the clerkly horde who "live by educated labour, with their brains and pen alone to depend upon for a living," whose financial condition he knows well.[24] His is the fullest sketch in the series of the potential future of the children of this class, the cargo of the emigration movement:

Their parents may have reared them, but can give no further help, and each one must struggle on as best he or she can, content if they can exist, and having far worse prospects in view than ever their parents had, on account of the greater competition to live, and the increase of a population already too numerous, gradually having the tone of mind and spirits lowered by the inevitable struggle against privation, until at last borne down by poverty perhaps they sink into crime and dishonour.

Another issue occupies two correspondents, *An English Wife* and *M.B.E.*, both of whom find disconsonance between good home education and bad "school education." The former indignantly notes "how often a mother finds her teaching and toil completely scattered to the winds by the system carried on in the generality of young ladies' schools!", while the latter describes how improvident wives will, when the time to educate children comes, have "sad hearts . . . to see them go to cheap schools, where the mistress herself knows nothing of real education, to see the children acquire habits and sayings which annoy their mother, and yet she has no time to correct them; for work, household work, all day must be her portion, with an income of only £150 a year."

A higher income is implied though denied in the complaint, unique in this series, of *Foreigner*, who condemns English boarding schools. Against that practice he sets the Continental norm, illustrated by his own experience:

I am not ashamed of saying that I had my father's clothes altered to fit me, and so on; but I went to one of the large day schools for 200 to 400 boys, which you find everywhere on the Continent, not representing a certain class of society, but being composed of all classes from the nobleman's son down to the labourer's; and as respects the girls the same is the case on their part, although to a less extent.

Equality is fostered by such day schools, where the cost is minimal, and which allow parents to continue daily home education. Young people are thus enabled to "judge and esteem each other's good and bad qualities; they are not so easily be led away by impulses," and are helped to bear "hard trials and misfortunes" with "resignation." ("Fortitude" would seem a happier choice of term.)

3 Surplus Children and Surplus Women

The memorable if shaky reliance of *Solon Smiff* on J.S. Mill's views of early marriage and the size of families is found in others, whether or not they mention the economist. *Precaution*, for example, sees it "as a sin to bring children into the world, scarcely knowing how they will be fed and clothed," while *A Woman* puts a rhetorical question and gives it a rather unexpected reply, unless the irony is stronger than might be guessed: "Has any man a right to marry and bring children into the world without a reasonable and fair prospect of being able to keep them in the common necessaries of life? Such a question a man is bound to answer to his own conscience."

The sobriquet chosen by *Moderation* has a rather special sense: his necessary condition for comfort on small means is "a small family." Those "dear people" who contemplate "the arrival of 'baby after baby,' as if the circumstances were matter for pride," and "insist upon increasing, and multiplying, and replenishing 'the earth' with families of a dozen, or more," should look for dictionary aid in interpreting Scripture. Why does he place "the earth" in quotation marks? Because dictionaries will show that it signifies not "only a semi-detached villa in a London suburb, but a set of continents (I apologise for the word)"—a rather surprising pun in this setting—"which still wait to be populated." In short, he is another Millian, arguing that it is "brutal selfishness to fill a house with children" who cannot be fed, clothed, or educated properly. And the peroration is *de haut en bas*, typical of debate but not markedly effective in an *ad populum* forum: "I write for the rational only, and it is therefore unnecessary to follow up the subject, or to deprecate the inevitable gush which will follow discovery, by sundry, of the end of the argument."

T.T. offers advice for young ladies: "better become old maids than poor neglected wives." And as for young men, who see husbands who have "drudged all day in the City" for a "miserable pittance which barely provides their daily bread,"[25] while their poor wives have "drudged all day at home," all income pledged in advance, babies rapidly arriving, and unemployment threatening, they had better remain bachelors. The strong Malthusian element emerges in a single proposition: "If for one year only no child was born throughout our land it would be an inconceivable blessing to the present and rising generation."[26]

The main message, of course, is to delay marriage until means can match progenitiveness, as in the coda of a second *One Who Speaks from Experience*, humble in form but firm in belief: "I will leave others more able than myself to write more on the subject; but I do hope it may be the means of making young people wait a little longer, until they have a little put by for a rainy day, before they bring a family in the world to swell our now over-populated country."

The other reason for delay, obvious but not quite proper to explain, is brought forward by the intrepid *Vieux Moustache* in the third letter with that signature. He advises *Cassio* to postpone marriage (unless his bride has means of her own) until he has saved enough "to furnish a suitable house and to add some £150 more to his permanent income." But he then remarks that delay will have another financial benefit, for later he will "humanly speaking, [be] not so likely to have as many children as if he married forthwith."

Because there was no discussion of contraception in any form, married continence being at best a stay, delayed marriage was the only efficient and moral means of limiting the onrush of babies, one of the constant themes of the correspondence. But that, we have seen, no one recommended as ideal but only as sad necessity, running as it did counter both to the commanding belief that marriage with children is not only the proper state but the most fulfilling one, and to the strong if not universal imperatives of romantic love. So this sensible solution was, in effect, not an effective solution.

A similar though less commented on difficulty was that for one-on-one marriage women were in surplus supply, an increasing concern as statistics continued to bear out the trend.[27] Though this conundrum may well have been in the correspondents' minds, it found its way into the correspondence only in the letter signed B—. The factor making that aspect of the marriage question prominent, it is averred, has been mistakenly identified as young men's not marrying as freely as formerly; the true determiner is "the preponderance in number of women over men," made worse each year as "a swarm of marriageable men leave our shores," making "the competition . . . all the higher" for those who remain.

4 Obstacles to Sane Courting

As urbanization and industrialization fundamentally altered social life, not least in loosening parental control and guidance, there were fewer traditional opportunities for courtship through communal institutions such as church and marketplace. And mixed schooling and employment in large firms, those powerful engines of modern times, did not exist.

In the country, the scope of choice was narrow (see Jane Austen *passim*), and the bonding only too quick, a prevailing condition David Hume had noted a century earlier:

there is no kind of report which rises so easily, and spreads so quickly, especially in country places and provincial towns, as those concerning marriages; insomuch that two young persons of equal condition never see each other twice, but the whole neighbourhood immediately join them together. The pleasure of telling a piece of news so interesting, of propagating it, and of being the first reporters of it, spreads the intelligence.[28]

The correspondents in the *Daily Telegraph* were aware of the difference between town and country in this respect, and were willing to accept the older rural practices as better. C.A.J. argues that the difficulty young people have in assessing the characters of their prospective mates is less troubling in the exurbs:

Young men usually do not go about seeking a wife. The most ordinary way amongst country young men is accidentally to meet at some friend's house with a nice girl, probably from some other town. The two are pleased with each other's society, and find that their tastes and inclinations are similar, and a friendship springs up—purely Platonic as they imagine—but which, carried on more earnestly than friends and guardians think wise, ends, as might be expected, in mutual love, and a determination to share life's joys and troubles together.

In the cities there were problems for parents, captured neatly in a vignette given by the prolific Eliza Warren in yet another of her fictionalized guidebooks, *How I Managed My Children from Infancy to Marriage* (1865), the preface of which opens typically: "Matrimony to a young girl often presents the fairest prospects of earthly happiness: 'it is the desired haven where she would be.'"[29] In chapter 9, which includes in its title "the Duty of Parents to Give their Daughters an Opportunity of Marrying," the wife asks her husband, having asserted that "there is no real happiness but between husband and wife," "how is a girl to find a husband if she have no opportunity of mixing with the opposite sex?" They have been negligent in not fostering relations with other families: "What youth have we ever invited here to make acquaintance with our daughters—to see them as they are, with loving natures, with simple manners, and truthful bearing? And how are we to repair this thoughtlessness?"

Accusing her of telling sad spinster tales, he responds sarcastically: "What am I to do? I cannot go and invite a lot of young men in to marry my daughters." This retort is not well received: "In an instant my face became scarlet, and I am afraid my tone was rather sharp as I said—'That is an unmanly way of treating the subject.'" Still he thinks her proposal "rather indelicate." Not at all, she replies; it is merely "common sense, when wanting in parents is just what leads many girls to be restless, unhappy, and frequently to forsake their homes. We have a duty ... to put before them, *as far as able, the opportunity to choose between a single or married life.* And it is this opportunity which we must make." And in the event they invite selected young folk in to a party, with dancing, and then another party—and love blossoms (pp. 61–4).

While the girls not so sensibly displayed pined at home, worse dangers faced the young men on the town. The best fictional witness is again Anthony Trollope, as already indicated in Charley's tale in *The Three Clerks*, but incidentally elsewhere, as in *The Small House at Allington* (1864):

so little is done for the amusement of lads who are turned loose into London at nineteen or twenty. Can it be that any mother really expects her son to sit alone evening after evening in a dingy room drinking bad tea and reading good books? . . . [D]oes it never occur to you that provision should be made for amusement, for dancing, for parties, for the excitement and comfort of women's society? . . . If I were a mother sending lads out into the world, the matter most in my mind would be this—to what houses full of nicest girls could I get them admission, so that they might do their flirting in good company. (Pp. 230–1)

Here, as in education, it seemed that roads to happier lands were open, if only people could be induced to follow them. The first way was rather cynically signposted. For some, including the better-off, Belgravians or not, the problem was seen (not always ironically) as one of marketing: the supply (mainly of daughters) being in excess of demand, and the markets not well established, display advertising was cultivated. The *Englishwoman's Domestic Magazine*, in "Getting Our Daughters off Our Hands," thought an opportunity was being missed:

if we consider the opportunities men have of inviting the more eligible of their acquaintance to come home to a quiet dinner, or, perhaps, to take a bed, and return with them to business next morning, after seeing the young ladies in all the charms of the family circle, the very pictures of neatness and all the domestic virtues, the wonder were that with such dextrous opportunities any single ladies should remain in the land. (P. 215)[30]

But such opportunities were all too rare, in the eyes of bachelors. For instance, one contributor to "Marriage or Celibacy?", *A Plain Man*, regrets his lack of opportunity (it is not clear that *Solon Smiff* would concur in the regret), noting the social circumstance that meeting lovable girls—of whom there are no doubt many—is adventitious; he even (perhaps chancing his arm and fortune) suggests that under proper social arrangements, the *Two Plain English Girls*, whose letter may have prompted his, "could soon be made happy"—at least one of them, we may infer, in the company of *A Plain Man*.[31]

When meetings occur, the circumstances are wrong, say others. H.B. rates "the difficulty young men have to get a real knowledge of a young lady before marriage" as "the greatest bar" to wedded bliss. Acceptance of the *Saturday Review*'s picture of the "girl of the period" is so widespread because potential suitors see girls only "at balls, theatres, and evening entertainments," and indeed it is there that "the bulk of marriages are made up." The difficulty and the needed reform are social:

I say that young men have not access to the homes of the girls until they have
made a formal proposal and have been accepted. . . . Now, if young men were
permitted to appear at home, instead of all the twaddle we have lately heard of
the worthlessness of women of the present age, we should find young men settling down with happy young wives, and women would be seen in their true
light, instead of being wronged by the estimate formed of the few who try to
shine in society.

In close agreement is *T.T.*, who—although evidently married—
regrets the incomplete knowledge lovers have of one another before
wedding, showing "only the sunny side of their dispositions," and aiding the "fairy picture" by getting up "their best 'scenes and properties.'"

When the young clerk . . . takes [his intended] to the theatre, or for a little
excursion, all is poetry and romance; he has not had to consult with her before-
hand whether the few necessary shillings can be spared from their slender
store; and her wardrobe (supplied by her parents) is probably of elegant and
tasty description. The young man's eye is gratified, and he is proud to have her
by his side. But, after marriage, if they can only set aside £20 or £30 a year for
dress, it is impossible she can present the same elegant appearance as before;
the eye is no longer charmed; and, the stern realities having toned down the
romance, the excursion, visit to the theatre, or tête-à-tête is a very prosaic affair
indeed by comparison, especially if the pleasing accompaniment of a few crying babies is thrown in, for the care of a nurse cannot be afforded.[32]

One who has been lucky, *A Clerk*, writes from Liverpool, a great
centre of commercial activity, and known as a great gathering if not
nurturing place for clerks. He deplores the social stigma attached to
useful education, at least in large towns: the many young men seeking "a good 'house-managing wife'" see, when they "go 'a-courting,'" their intendeds employed only in "making artificial flowers,
playing the piano, &c." The swains are not allowed to enter the
kitchen to see them "making a pie, boiling preserves, or taking an
active part in any household arrangements," ironing a collar or
mending a garment. *A Clerk*, like many others, puts the blame on
mamma:

She will not allow Robert to come downstairs and see Emily in her undress. He
would think she was slovenly; he would notice what an old dress she had on;
and perhaps he might think Emily had no business in the kitchen, and thus be

disheartened in his wooing. Oh, no! this won't do; he mustn't come down stairs; Emily must amuse him in the parlour by playing and singing to him; she must not let him see her in the kitchen, or he may think her untidy and careless in her dress and manners, and unworthy a husband.

He himself fortunately was guided downstairs by a model mother, who gave him access to the one he intends "to call wife." She gets a character reference from him, as one who "can cook a joint of meat, scrape potatoes, darn stockings, and make bread as well as any woman in England, and she is but 21." "I speak this," he adds, "because I am proud of such a promising wife,[33] and have witnessed with my own eyes her industry, and the pains she takes to become well acquainted with every domestic arrangement. She is not ashamed of me seeing her at work in the kitchen. She knows I would sooner see her there than in the parlour, drawing or painting."

These young men evidently are as sensible as they are available, and one young woman (another lucky one) finds them not wanting. *A Real Help-Meet* is not like the foolish girls who "nowadays" see no need to go beyond dress and the reading of novels as allurements. They are much mistaken, for men are much more attracted to girls who can take their share of household duties. This proposition she nicely illustrates by a key passage in her own life:

My husband made up his mind to propose to me when he saw me washing up the breakfast things one morning when we were a servant short. He thought he would wait a few days before taking the eventful step. He did so, and caught me a few mornings after paring potatoes. "Ah! that's the wife for me; I'll propose at once." He did so, and I accepted him.

Another English Girl appears to be of similar mind but, after a *concessio* about the few actual "girls of the period," fears the best arrangements will act but as a booby-trap:

I think[34] that there are as many sensible, good-tempered, accomplished, and agreeable English girls as ever there were; but you must go to their homes to find them, and you will mostly find that they are thoroughly domestic. They are the girls who would make good wives to men either of moderate incomes or large ones; but where will you find the men who are good enough for them?

Comparable is the view of *A London Girl*: "it is only by seeing girls often and in their own homes that their good qualifications as wives can be discovered." Perhaps despairing of being thus discovered, she indulges in what would, had she enclosed her card, undoubtedly have been seen as self-advertisement:

I hope, if ever I marry, it will be to a man in my own position; and if I loved anyone I should be quite willing to begin on £120 or £130 per annum, as I am sure I could with a little management and economy (I do not mean pinching) live quite as happily, if not more so, than if my husband were possessed of £1,000. I think a good wife finds her pleasure and amusement in the well ordering of her husband's house, which cannot be unless the mistress herself superintends or lends a helping hand, particularly in cases where there are little ones to be seen after and cared for.

And indeed *A Lover of Home* treats this self-praise ironically. Some of the young girls "have written for themselves some unexceptional testimonials and recommendations," the "only drawback" being

that the private address of each is not placed in the left corner by the side of the date. Can you kindly, Mr. Editor, procure for some of us the interesting intelligence of their whereabouts when they are at home? for I think you will agree with me that any one with such a catalogue of excellencies as *A London Girl* . . . should be speedily introduced to some eligible bachelor, and commit matrimony with the least possible delay.

This precise note is sounded again by *An Old Married Man*, who thought the correspondence could much better dwell on the opinions of "old married men" on the marriage question than on advertisements for husbands by "English girls of 'the right sort.'"

Such responses, only partly humorous in intent, are neither typical nor fair; for young city people to meet one another in circumstances allowing for demonstration of character was increasingly difficult. Home was the best venue, but geographical, social, and cultural obstacles were genuine, and alternatives, such as churches, were less available (they are totally absent from the correspondence) to people for whom the parish was no longer the centre of group life. Once again, then, the solution to the marriage problem was clear, but not sufficiently available.

5 Not Enough Money

The final problem was of course the central one: given the facts of existence and the desire for human dignity, even assuming the best character and training in both sexes, there was just not enough money for prudent early marriage. Ample evidence of the reality and the perceptions has been given. Man's office was to supply the material support for the family, and for those in the lower middle class the prospects were not good. Wages were low, increments small, uncertain, and limited, and promotions rare; competition was intense for those in city employment, and loss of position an ever-present threat. The safety net provided only by personal insurance had large holes in it, through which those suffering from disabling illness fell sometimes to relative but also sometimes to absolute depths of poverty.

None of this was a secret, and no matter how hopeful and trusting people might wish to be, the question "Marriage or Celibacy?" seemed to have no answer both easy and happy. Even those who chose (or recommended) celibacy revealed that marriage was the proper answer, but the majority—including the leader writers of the *Daily Telegraph*—insisted on the qualification "prudent." The prudent choice then was between wait and emigrate. Waiting not being attractive, apparently the only way out was to take the way out.

CHAPTER SEVEN

Emigration or Starvation?

The *Daily Telegraph* series on marriage and celibacy changed emphasis, as explained above, in mid-July 1868. From the 17th on, the great majority of letters concentrated on emigration as the only available solution to the dilemma posed by the natural and divine imperative to marry and the natural and divine imperative to be prudent. Indeed one woman correspondent perceptively noted that the subject had changed to "Emigration or Starvation?" However, the editors continued to use the heading "Marriage or Celibacy?", and actually the marriage question was not ignored in the second half of the month and emigration had been referred to in the first half, twenty-one correspondents mentioning it in connection with the main dilemma. However, the demographic profile of the correspondents and the rhetoric changed with the main subject matter, there being a much smaller proportion of women and a larger proportion of bachelors. Public discussion of emigration was evidently the province mainly of single men—"private discussion" was certainly another matter, especially for married women. Also noticable is a shift in argument towards a concentration on non-rhetorical questions that prompt answers more purely descriptive than analytic with descriptive illustrations. The arguments are also simpler and less varied.

Like marriage, emigration was a grand British theme. Beginning with the enclosure movement in the eighteenth century, the economic and population pressures increasingly suggested that the comparatively empty parts of the world offered at least subsistence and hope for the poor, and greater opportunities for the "improving" classes. This history is well documented, not least in the published "home" letters of emigrants and in accounts of the government agents and entrepreneurs who assisted and profited from emigration. What is immediately apparent from these accounts, and leads to a puzzle over the correspondence in the *Daily Telegraph*, is that a great deal of information was available to intending emigrants, not only in Blue Books (always available but little read), but also in many popular and inexpensive forms, in books and periodicals, in pamphlets and newspaper stories and advertisements, as well as in the extremely important private "home" correspondence from family and friends who had emigrated.[1] And the fiction of the period often turned on or used incidentally the excitement, trials, and adventures of emigration: Dickens, Gaskell, Trollope come quickly to mind, but also minor novelists offered not only incident but opinion. For example, pertinent especially to the celibates in "Marriage or Celibacy?": "How narrow is the arena now left vacant in prosperous and overpopulated England for even the most energetic of her sons, when they possess no powerful influence to second them in the great struggle of life!"[2]

The periodical press had covered all the major issues repeatedly from early in the century. In the period of "Marriage or Celibacy?" it is indicative that the *Englishwoman's Domestic Magazine* which, it will be recalled, had recommended marriage as a way of "Getting Our Daughters off Our Hands," offered a different kind of advice in its companion piece, "Getting Our Sons off Our Hands." Noting that the traditional occupations were no longer easily available or profitable, and that examinations for public office (one of Trollope's *bêtes noires*) had ruled out that "refuge for the mentally destitute—a kind of 'cripples' home' for badly-nursed and rickety faculties," the author judged that "emigration and seeking a fortune in foreign lands became the venture which, as 'distance lends enchantment to the view,' seemed to smooth the rugged road of mechanical life."

The case of two youths is cited who, like the author, had not appreciated "the crowded state and eager competition for home appointments" until they consulted with "City friends."

"We don't like the sons of gentlemen for inferior employment," said one merchant; "they look out of heart and miserable where a tradesman's son looks happy." "More than average steadiness is required," said another. 'What we call 'the natural follies of youth' don't seem at all 'natural' in a house of business, where so many other youths are waiting to take the places of those who make a slip."

But what the youths themselves said was most stirring of all. "Why, here is a life of pens, and desks, and writing, and ciphering; and we know how we always hated those tedious school-ciphering afternoons; and this to go on for ever! No boating! no cricket! no fishing! no wandering in green fields! 'no nothing!'—but riding backwards and forwards on the knife-board of an omibus!"

The conclusion is hardly surprising after that anecdote: "Our experience is decidedly in favour of emigration"—though with sensible qualifications: youth, strength, health, unfixed habits, and freedom from luxurious tastes.[3]

One of the journals assiduous in reporting on emigration matters was the *Daily Telegraph*, and it is at first sight puzzling that its readers should feel the need to consult themselves in the correspondence columns for guidance on the issue. But, one may well say, the same was true *a fortiori* of the marriage question, though there opinion counted for more than in the emigration question. Whatever the reasons—and more will be said in conclusion—they looked to people like themselves, though better informed through experience, to tell the unvarnished truth. What they wanted to know, from travellers, returned colonists, even colonization agents, was which overseas lands offered the best hope of gradual improvement for those willing to work hard.

Driven by the stick of economic deprivation and pulled by the carrot of opportunity, these prospective emigrants were still not in the destitute and oppressed state of many then and since who must leave native lands willy-nilly to survive. So there was much to debate, and the latter part of the series includes a wide range of requests for information about opportunities overseas and replies varying in their geographical recommendations and enthusiasm, but generally rich in detail.

Illustrative is the help asked by one signing himself—without personal explanation of its relevance—*Perth (W.A.)*:

The first thing to consider, is where to go; and I would suggest that some returned settlers from Australia, South America, United States, and the Canadas should write to your journal and give us the benefit of their experience, naming particularly character of the occupation, nature of the climate, and chances of success, &c. We should then be able to compare, to a certain extent, the different countries and choose the best. Letters from closet theorists are of no use. What we want is the practical advice of old and successful colonists.

The one almost constant focus was on the identity of the group whose home prospects were most dismal, the young male office workers, who could not hope to fulfil divine and human injunctions and marry young. The inescapable dénouement of the clerks' tale was a voyage to a foreign land. And questions about supply on the trip and on landing, as well as about qualifications and conditions for survival and success, were imperative. The greatest variation was in queries and advice about the best place to find the homely grail or grange; considering these requests and replies provides an instructive and entertaining look towards the horizon seen brightly or dimly from among the often obscuring buildings of the city. For many, the enchanted distance could be anywhere. "America" was not here or nowhere in Carlyle's phrase; it was anywhere but here.

Consequently the specific targets in such comments as those by W.H.S. or J.F.H. are as vague as they are enthusiastic. The former remarks: "In America the 'land is wide and men are few.' This is just what *Benedick* says he wants in England. We agree as to the end, but disagree as to the means. He says, 'Refrain from marriage: don't trouble about duty or Divine law: society suffers.' I say, 'Marry or emigrate, or both; carry out each of the Divine commands, and benefit yourselves and society too.'" And the latter, after recommending "some of our colonies," opts for "the States":

I cannot understand why many of your correspondents wish to discourage the scheme of emigration. I would not recommend any man physically incapacitated to venture out of England to try his fortune; but, to young men of sound constitution and vigorous habits, I say by all means leave for some of our colonies. I verily believe that nine out of every ten will be in a much better position in a few years than they could reasonably expect had they remained in England. I myself intend "doing the States" as soon as I can arrange matters.

Others had the same impulse, but there were several "states"—where to go? they asked, and found answers.

Canada and the Rest of British North America

Of the far lands—and psychologically as well as geographically they all were far—the most commonly mentioned are the British North American colonies, cited by thirty-seven of the correspondents. Many of the prospective immigrants were, not surprisingly, somewhat vague about the political jurisdictions in the colonies, as well as about the geography, soil, and climate. The British parliament had passed in 1867, during the much more engrossing debates over the Second Reform Bill, the British North America Act, which had united as the "Dominion of Canada" the two provinces formerly known as Canada, Ontario (which had been called Upper Canada, and referred to also as Canada West) and Quebec (which had been called Lower Canada)—with Nova Scotia and New Brunswick. In the correspondence, almost all the references are to Ontario, though not under that name; there are no unambiguous mentions of Quebec, the dominantly French-speaking province. Of the other British North American colonies still outside the federation, the only one specifically discussed is British Columbia (which joined in 1870).

It quickly becomes evident that unlike later emigrants who flock to cities, the potential emigrants among the readers of the *Daily Telegraph* were attracted—or repelled—by agricultural life: the attraction was the hope of self-sufficiency, if not affluence, and the promise of one's own space; the repulsion was the fear of harsh and strange conditions in isolation. Indeed the hope and fear were normally mixed, so that the correspondence is driven principally by questions about the actual state of domestic economy in Canada and the other colonies. A typical inquirer is *Would-Be Emigrant*, who says: "I know many young men, who like myself, have a little capital, and wish to emigrate, but do not know where to go. Canada, Australia, South America, all present a wide field; but which is the best, I know not." Answers are given— often before the question has been asked—with strong assurance, but seldom with reference to the abundant printed information or to the major colonial schemes that had been operating for several decades.

The first mention of Canada in "Marriage or Celibacy?" arises directly out of the belief that marriage for the lower middle class in London was dangerously imprudent because necessary costs outran reasonable expectations of income. *Erastes*, whose early letter was, as indicated above, one of the most important in the series, scorns the notion that only "Belgravia" is habitable, and points out (in a passage quoted at length in chapter 3) that in a recent issue of the *Daily Telegraph* there was

a notice from the Toronto Government of land to be given away in hundred-acre lots for nothing. No lack of food upon the free and grand prairies, where the grain grows so thick for year after year without mending the soil that they light the kitchen fires with maize and feed the pigs with russet apples.

This met with a quick response from *W.J.W.*, who in derision blames the naïve opinion of *Erastes* on his reading romantic novels about prairie hunting,[4] as a prelude to his own experienced judgment about "the reality which . . . is often found much harder than those who pictured it thought it was." Food, he says,

is as difficult to get in Toronto prairies as it is in London shops; for, though

London shops are filled with food, we cannot always get it; and likewise, though Toronto prairies may contain many animals "good for food," the man who makes his home there cannot always "kill and eat." There is fresh air, no doubt, but one cannot live on fresh air alone. . . . *Erastes* would find, if he went out, that Governments do not generally give away land that yields so much good food, but land that they wish people to cultivate, so that it may in time yield something more than it does in its present state.

Women participated in the discussion of emigration much less than in that of marriage, but some wrote strongly and tellingly about the effect of emigration on family life. Most effective is the early participant who had lived for five years in British Columbia and appropriately signed herself *Colonista*.

As she knows, in the colonies women, like men, must work, and they have no time for "the weeping" supposed to be "a necessary feminine accomplishment" or for "fancied griefs." The tie between mother and child is strong, and though many English might not want to have children constantly with them, because there are no nurses or nurseries, "colonial children remain unspoilt—that is, they early learn the meaning of that excellent word Self-help, and, like their parents, are all the happier for it." If a colony is not flourishing, a woman with many children may be a drudge—but is it not so also in England? And living in a "tiny" house will not be "scandalising your nearest and dearest"; what is more, "society will actually survive the blow" if you come to the door with broom in hand. "In the evening, work done, and the children asleep, the sound of the piano may be heard in many households, and the magazines and books which have strewn the sitting-room table all day are opened and read."

This picture did not please another correspondent, *Clericus*, who claimed that *Colonista* had "very foolishly represented Columbian life in such guise" as to "quite enrapture" young women. While he favoured emigration, he objected to hiding the "many hardships" of "the wife of a backwoodsman." A girl should

weigh well, not only her willingness, but her ability to encounter deprivations (unheard of and unthought of in England) for a few years; and then, if victorious, will come independence. Happiness I cannot assure her of, either in Columbia or any other colony; that depends on the temper, disposition, and feelings of herself and husband.

That indeed is the general tone, captured succinctly by *Erastes*, who had commented: "I am not for sending damsels of gentle birth into the wilds of the Red River, nor am I for 'Love in a hut, with water and a crust.'"

But the main concern in this respect turned away from young girls to young clerks. The content and tone of the letter of *Roamer Returned* illustrates. A clerk with "a beggarly salary" and poor prospects, in 1862 he emigrated to Vancouver's Island with letters of introduction, seeking an office position. But in each of "the best houses in the colony" he got the same answer: "We do not need clerks, but we need skilled artisans, farmers, and capitalists." He found work "at what the colonists were pleased to term road-making," where in his "gang" he found twenty-three other young Englishmen, many of whom had attended university and one of whom had served a medical internship ("walked Guy's" six months). After some months he disposed of most of his "valuables," including all his clothes ("save what [he] stood in"), to set off for the gold fields to make his fortune—but alas for dreams.

At the end of a most miserable journey of 500 miles, over one of the roughest and most uninviting countries in the world, with weary limbs, a half-starved stomach, and a nervous apprehension of Chinook Indians lurking behind every nest of foliage, I landed in the British El Dorado. Some months of the hardest manual labour, together with a knowledge of the fact that I was not earning the salt I ate to my beans, convinced me that my best course would be to leave mining to those who liked it, and return to the pale of society.

So much for British Columbia. Another correspondent, *B.P.*, offered as warning his experience of the other side of the continent, a warning that will persuade many that, bureaucratically, *plus ça change, plus c'est la même chose*. Arriving in Nova Scotia some years ago he had applied for land to the Crown Land Department. The Commissioner sent him a letter stating the price for Crown Lands—£11 for 100 acres and under—and saying that he was seeking government instructions about any restrictions. However, a blank petition was enclosed, which he could now send. *B.P.* did so, but in reply was told that he could not get an order of survey until the fee was paid; however, the money should not be sent until he had received a judgment from "the committee of the executive council, which will meet in a day or two," after which the Commissioner would write again. "After the receipt of the above I waited patiently for more than two months without hearing further; then returned to England, a poorer but wiser man."

There was another view. Nova Scotia and New Brunswick are unambiguously recommended as "a fine field for the better class of emigrants who are not afraid of work," by *Canadian J.P.*, a resident for almost twenty years, with experience "as a trader, a large landowner, and an agriculturalist."

It has always been my impression that directly these provinces were settled with "Britishers" they would go ahead. There is the fish market and the timber market for the whole world. The taxes are merely nominal, while in the States they are crushing. . . .[5]

But *Canadian J.P.*, like *B.P.*, makes much of the governmental impediments.

The great bulk of the land of the eastern provinces is held in comparatively few hands, . . . [and the] Crown lands now offered to emigrants are merely wild lands in the interior, with absurd restrictions, at half a dollar an acre. Let emigrants beware of Government parties. . . . I was in frequent collision with the officials in connection with emigration parties. There was no preparation made to receive the emigrants, the Crown Lands Agent was without instructions; and altogether the "red tape" is better left out, and emigrants left on their own account.

One of the most nagging questions, relevant to almost any possible destination, had to do with the immediately practical issues. None of the inquiring correspondents mentions having family members to welcome them to the new land; the most plausible explanation is that if they had relatives they would not need to ask publicly for information. And none ask about travelling with a family, though that dangerous enterprise was a common one. Not that the value of companionship was ignored; one of the most commonly offered pieces of advice was not to go it alone, but to seek other like-minded young men who could jointly venture into the almost unknown.

A typical practical proposal is that of *Caution*: "Let some of your correspondents . . . form themselves into an emigration club, to collect information, &c. Let a couple of their number proceed, say, to Canada (if that colony should be approved), and do their best to establish themselves there." If successful, they can let others know of possible work and make arrangements for them; if they fail, they alone will suffer, and with "the assistance of their fellow-members" could return "wiser, if sadder, men." There is a condition, one found in other letters: "It is desirable that the pioneers should, if possible, be single men, in good health, and capable of hard work—steady, persevering, and stout-hearted."

An issue particularly important in the case of Canada was climate. L——S, who claims accurate knowledge of "the American continent . . . from Canada to Cape Horn," rates Canada fourth after the "western prairies of the United States," the "States of the River Plate," and Chile, largely because "the immense labour required to clear and prepare new land" had to be postponed during "the long and rigorous winter, when nearly all farm work must be suspended." Indeed, the winters, damned as "severe and protracted" by *Scotch Civil Engineer*, and "rigorous and protracted" by *Pioneer*, were seen as a major disqualification. Another correspondent, *Kentucky*, says with some authority:

I have a very great respect for the Canadians, but not so for their winters. It is absurd . . . to say that the winters in Upper Canada are little if at all worse than ours at home. . . . [I]n Toronto, or Hamilton, . . . the thermometer often finds its way down among the thirties in the lower zero range. I have known it 33 below zero. Then you are snow-bound and ice-bound for four months; for you must bear in mind that there are only three seasons in North America—summer, autumn, and winter.[6]

But there were those willing to chance their arms, including H.E.W.[7] Picking up an earlier suggestion, that someone "should organize fifty men"—fewer would be useless—"with £50 each, and start next spring to Canada," he has positive proposals as well as hopes. "It must be fully understood that . . . all sorts of home luxuries are left behind, and things will have to be taken in their primitive state." It is quite clear that, in his opinion, no clerks need apply: the fifty colonists should be made up of ten mechanics, ten agriculturalists, ten shepherds and herdsmen, ten hedgers, ditchers, fencers, and ten "as a foraging party, i.e., a hunting party in every sense of the word." His detailed account continues with the tasks of the "mechanical department": "shanties to be erected, fence rails made, timber sawn, household utensils made"—"glass and china being luxuries not to be thought of, and a good wooden bowl or platter, things indispensable." On arrival the group would make a selection from the government grant areas of land with "good water power" and easy access to a neighbouring township, by water if possible—to "save road-making, besides wear and tear of carts, &c." Upon arrival, the group labour (he is himself committed) should begin immediately on "a work and store shanty or shed, the mechanics entering upon their duties in erecting the sawing machines, and sawing and preparing timber whilst the remainder clear sufficient space for shanties." Land should be cleared immediately for planting potatoes or other crops. His sanguinity is shown in his estimate that within ten days of arrival twenty acres would be cleared and ten shanties erected, "sufficient to house the whole party, and the land fit for planting." Calmly but enthusiastically he concludes:

I consider that the body of men I propose, having made a code of the rules for their future guidance, and entering into a strict partnership for say three years, would be surprised at the benefit accruing therefrom, and I have no doubt would form the nucleus of a large and respectable class of emigrants from the mother country so far as regards the future.

One of the most enthusiastic endorsements comes from S., who thinks it "absurd in the extreme" to deride clerks and shop assistants as unadaptable weaklings—perhaps because he himself was formerly a draper's assistant. "An Englishman, however he is brought up, provided he enjoys good health, has little or no difficulty in entirely altering the whole mode of his life." And where better to do so than Upper Canada, "the most promising field for emigration in the world."

The soil is good, the climate healthy, magnificent lake and river communication with all parts of the world, enormous and unlimited water power, many valuable minerals, plenty of timber, and an excellent free government. . . . The seasons are most enjoyable, the much-abused winters being, in my opinion, the most enjoyable season of the year. Then is the time when hard work is not a burden, but a pleasure—when the bush farmer cuts his timber and takes his produce to market. I speak from experience, having spent three winters in Upper Canada, and although I did not succeed, but came back worse off than I went out, I attribute my failure entirely to having no settled object in view when I first went to the colony. I still have so much faith in Canada that I quite intend, as soon as I possibly can, going out again.

Many of the comments are based on comparisons with other possible havens, and not all of these favour the options. For instance, one correspondent in the *Telegraph*, signing himself *Professional*, in recommending the Western United States—he intends to emigrate to Nebraska—says simply: "emigration to Australia, New Zealand, or Canada is, to say the least of it, very doubtful."

Australia and New Zealand

Many, however, held firm for the outposts of empire in the Antipodes. Close behind Canada in frequency of mention in the *Daily Telegraph* series was Australia, with thirty-four references, about three-quarters of them generally favourable—but on condition that the emigrants had the right skills, which did not include a fine copper-plate hand. Australia was not yet a unified country; the six colonies, New South Wales, South Australia, Victoria, Tasmania, Western Australia, and (the newest, dating only from 1859) Queensland, did not federate until 1901. Five of these—all but Tasmania—are mentioned by correspondents,[8] many of whom have first-hand knowledge. Most of the references, however, are not specific to any colony, though on the whole the level of knowledge seems higher than in the case of Canada, perhaps because the gold rush of the late 1840s and 1850s was still remembered, and indeed mineral finds were still occurring. The writers knew, however, that agriculture provided, as in the case of Canada, the prime opportunity. But the cities were proudly growing: the grand town halls of Sydney, Melbourne, Adelaide, and Brisbane were all begun in the 1860s, signalling the diverse development of urban life and wider chances of employment, especially for artisans and merchants.[9] Transportation of convicts was no longer an issue, and questions about that "founding" population as well as the aborigines did not arise.

The dominant issue was the suitability of the clerkly class for Australian life. Thoughtful uncertainty is expressed by *L.H.J.*, a young, apparently single, clerk, who has looked into the matter, but remains hesitant. Australia is "supposed to be a good field," but he fears not not for clerks or for professional men. As in New Zealand, mechanics, labourers, and servants, and, in some cases, tradesmen may succeed. However, as in England, initial capital is necessary, such as will allow "an intelligent, industrious agriculturalist" to "realise a pretty comfortable position." But how few "London clerks are fit for such a life, which requires not only actual experience in farming matters, but very often the exercise of personal manual labour!" Further agricultural and mineral development depends on "strong able-bodied men used to country life," not—and here the series' main theme is recalled—by young "gentlemen," like "many of the young fellows are who are anxious at the present time to marry."

There were a few who would reassure him about the possibilities for those inured only to bench labour, including *H.H.F.*, a married woman with seven daughters, who knows the problem, having heard that very day "the same despairing vows from a young man who has been daily seeking for employment since March," but also knows of those in similar circumstances who "have been sent out to Queensland and New Zealand by the assistance of their friends and relatives as a last resource, and who have done well there, and settled down and married comfortably, and have blessed God for the happy day when they emigrated from home." Even more positive was *J.F.H.*, a young single man:

It is all nonsense to say that clerks cannot get a living abroad. Some friends of mine, who were City clerks, went out to Australia two years since on "spec." and without capital. Being steady, industrious, and willing to turn their hands to anything, after going through many hardships, they were in a much better position than when in England, and have never had cause to regret leaving.

Even they, however, did not say that the clerks had clerked their way to improvement—as Dickens's Wilkins Micawber in *David Copperfield* had so famously done[10]—and the general verdict was much more negative. It "would be absurd for a man, whose occupation is that of a clerk, to rush without capital or the knowledge of any trade, to Australia, or any other unsettled country" (*Lyn*); "for the lower middle class of clerks and struggling professional men" emigration to Australia "would be a jump from a cool frying pan into a very hot fire" (*Antipodes*); "Of what use to a City man is a hundred acres of land in the middle of the Australian bush or the Western prairie?—perhaps a hundred miles from the nearest market, very likely double that distance from a church, and city or town. Really it is no place for him, nor could he accommodate himself to it until he had everything that he now cherishes fairly knocked out of him" (*Five Years' Colonist*); "clerks . . . , as a rule, are the most useless emigrants under the sun" (*Mariner*).[11]

Nonetheless, some were emigrating, as witness the solemn note sounded by those pointing out that clerks are in over-supply in Australia—and in Canada[12]—as well (or ill) as at home. *A South Australian*, just returned after several years in "that distant land," reports that while South Australia is the best of the colonies for agriculture, to "the class of men who appear most desirous of emigrating, viz., City clerks enjoying a present income of £150 a year, it offers no inducement whatever. If such persons throw up their situations, and, without capital or influential introductions, proceed to Australia with a view of improving their positions, they will most certainly be disappointed." A recent instance illustrates: an advertisement from a district council near Adelaide for a clerk at £150 a year attracted more than a hundred applicants, among them "men of excellent birth, education, and ability—men who had once held good positions in society, but who had been reduced by the vicissitudes of colonial life to comparative indigence." Having gone through "years of toil and discomfort," they would have "gladly accepted what some of your correspondents effect to despise." In further illustration he mentions an Adelaide gentleman who advertised for six mechanics and two clerks, all at £3 a week each, and received replies from only three mechanics, but from over a hundred and fifty clerks.[13]

A *South Australian* then turns to the view that "agriculture offers a promising field for all classes," and so "a clerk who has been brought up to the desk may successfully turn his attention to the plough." South Australia, by perseverance, a liberal land act, and "Ridley's wonderful reaping machine, which is alone suited to the dry climate of this colony, . . . has established a large agricultural population, and exports wheat very extensively." But the drawbacks are not to be ignored: the weather is uncertain, and wheat, in the best years, does not yield more than fourteen bushels, while "in bad years, such as last, when red rust made havoc with the wheat, the average was the miserable one of four bushels." Failures eat up former profits, and the land becomes exhausted because crops cannot be rotated, the climate being too dry for anything but wheat. Indeed the climate, often described as beautiful, "with a temperature ranging from 100 to 115 in the shade for several weeks in the year, . . . can scarcely be considered perfection."

An inexorable conclusion is directed to those correspondents who complain of "the dreary and monotonous lives led by the London clerks, to the colourless routine which characterises their existence, and to the melancholy abodes in which they live"; let them distinctly understand that "their lot is by no means so sad as that of the colonial settlers whom they envy." Outside the large towns, life is monotonous; although "the solitudes of the bush" may charm some, they "tend to anything but cheerfulness or refinement." Indeed no class is "more to be pitied than that of the middle-class unsuccessful Australian colonists. They are too numerous everywhere, and I am afraid that the ideas of some of your correspondents, if carried out, would only tend to swell the list." Only a man with "a muscular frame inured to work, a sound constitution, and frugal habits," can expect success; "but if office work is his forte, and his pecuniary means small, London offers a better field for his capabilities than the Antipodes."

In knowledgeable agreement is *J.J.*, "an old emigration agent, who has sent many thousands to various parts of the world," and who recommends to the sedentary classes that if

they can earn but a bare subsistence in this country, whether they are Benedicks or bachelors, let them by all means stick to Old England, unless they are prepared to enter into an entirely new mode of working and living, and have stamina sufficient to stand the privations and hardships sure to be met with in founding new colonies. . . .

The system of free emigration, with which he has been "most connected" for eighteen years, limits its applicants "almost entirely to the agricultural and mechanical trades class"; this scheme, funded by the colonies, reflects their own view of reality, and so "it should be taken as a significant fact that all others must venture out on pure speculation, and at very great risk." He is constantly hearing that "the colonial towns are much overdone with the clerk and shop assistant classes, and many an one who threw up employment in the country to try their hand at the Antipodes would most gladly return and take their chance here again, overcrowded though it may be."

S.A.M. supplied the most informative letter on financial prospects. In towns, employment for bookkeepers or shopmen is hard to find, and wages are £50 per annum and keep. Say two hundred miles up country, employment is easy to find at shepherding, bullock driving, stockriding, overlanding with horses, cattle, and sheep, shingle splitting, cutting and drawing timber, fencing with split-rails, and stumping. For each he gives details of the work involved, and itemizes the wages, which roughly from £40 to £80—though some on piecework rates might get over £100, if they do "not die of sunstroke." Storekeeping is rewarded by some £80 to £100, with "good living, but the work lasts from 5 a.m. to 9 p.m., and no time allowed for meals, which is uncomfortable." Only these not "very intellectual" opportunities are open to clerks; still, having tried most of them himself, he admits that "for a single man the life has many attractions, and is infinitely to be preferred to trying to make both ends meet on £100 per annum." Even though the rations, "damper and beef during the week, with beef and damper on Sunday, by way of change," are monotonous, "the sauce of good appetite makes it very passable fare."

His closing offer of further particulars was not taken up in the *Daily Telegraph*, but those he had given provoked correction on exact detail from *A Colonial Clergyman*, who warned, on the basis of information about wages he had just received, that S.A.M.'s figures were too high by at least 10 per cent. Further, at least in South Australia, there is no shortage of labour; "bookkeepers or shopmen find it difficult at present to get any employment at all." Some of the occupations such as shingle-splitting, cutting and drawing timber, stumping, fencing with split-rails, &c., are no doubt "open to clerks," but "clerks attempting such work would certainly starve at it." Inexperienced newcomers cannot expect the same rate as "old hands," while even those accustomed to the use of tools need to "acquire the knack" for these kinds of work. Most will find only "disappointment or utter prostration of strength." Should no one then emigrate to Australia? Yes, but only those who have "at least a little capital to fall back upon," or are "regular farm servants or ploughmen," for whom the prospects are good.

That indeed is the general view, expressed for example by *Antipodes* (already quoted on clerks). Farm labourers and skilled mechanics need only find the means to emigrate. However, while for "those who can 'reap and mow, and plough and sow,' there is the great field of the Australian continent," in such "a new country the 'field' for the pen and its kindred is necessarily limited; . . . clerks, shopmen, and men of that class are a perfect drug in the labour market."

N.Z. (who recommends what his pseudonym suggests) concurs. He expresses concern because some correspondents, "very young ones, probably," appear "to think that the mere fact of emigrating ensures success; that it is only necessary to cross the seas in order to be in a position to support a wife, rear a family, and enjoy, indeed, most of the blessings this world affords." The pretty pictures drawn of colonial life are "utterly worthless as guides, lacking the one element of truth which alone could render them of service." In fact, only two classes should emigrate—the horny-handed son of the soil, accustomed to earn his bread by the sweat of his brow, and the capitalist.

Horny hands and sweat are obviously minimal desiderata in the view of *Civil Engineer*, whose detailed picture, based on experience in New South Wales and Queensland, is certainly not pretty. Most of the disappointed emigrants had been "carried away with the grand idea of becoming farmers," with a free land grant of "fine virgin soil that only required tickling with the hoe," and "magnificent timber with which they could readily build their cottages, out-buildings, and fencing." Having spent their all on the passage and a "bullock-dray and a few necessaries," they found up country some hundreds of miles away "the everlasting gum and iron bark," that could cost for felling as much as £7 per tree, ground that could not be broken until months later when the rains came, and heat that forbade the unacclimatized to work outdoors for nine months of the year. Rustic joys: "I have seen numbers of these families struggling for a bare existence, living in bark huts, a sheet of bark upon four stakes for a table, other stakes with sacking stretched over them for beds, and they are indeed well off if they can get a regular supply of the monotonous damper, mutton, and tea." Those in England now seeking emigration cannot cope with these conditions:

thousands have tried it and persevered bravely, but failed, and so they go back to the towns, sell their land grant to the first public-house, and then seek work on the roads. Just before I left Sydney I saw a mob of some hundreds of able-bodied men around the House of Assembly, appealing to the Government to start some work for them; and these men would receive 7s per day when at work, but the time expended in tramping from town to town, or from one station to another, would make their average earnings be even less than they could get at home at regular work.

Civil Engineer like others sees the great need for "men with large capital, and with brains to work it," not for "the class who cannot get a living at home"—or even for "the hundreds of engineers like [him]self who are now eagerly and anxiously seeking for work." So although he still believes "that the great remedy for the numbers of young pioneers and good practical men who are now struggling at home is to emigrate," he urges them on to "a country more like our own"—such as Canada.

Whatever the difficulties, however, the Antipodes cried out to such as the enthusiastic but realistic *O.E.S.* Look, he says, to Western Australia, to the Swan River Settlement, where, if "large fortunes are not to be quickly made," a "decent competence" awaits those willing to labour on the "well-watered," "kindly soil, under a temperate climate." Unwise initial decisions about land tenure now offer an opportunity, because the present proprietors are so impecunious that some "would let part of their lands rent free for a term of years to any tenant who would engage to stock them, with the view of increasing the value of the remainder." The area being suitable to sheep farming and near the seaboard, "whenever, as must come sooner or later, the great problem of meat preservation shall be solved, Western Australia, by virtue of its position as the nearest colony to England, must command the market."

O.E.S. closes on a theme important in fact as well as opinion: solo emigration was not the best kind. Any interested in forming emigration associations should look to Western Australia, where some of the landholders are so favourable to cooperation that "they would so far smooth the path of emigrants by giving, rent free for a certain period, their land, if others would provide capital and labour."

Indeed the fullest accounts of the value of cooperative ventures appear in letters dealing with the Antipodes, though the earliest suggestion in this correspondence (much referred to later) was to the Americas. *Ring* had proposed this solution:

Let several young men combine together, and (take their wives if they have any) organise a sort of expedition—the combination would make the expenses much less. Let them go to the far West or to some parts of South America, where land can be had for asking almost. If they all go together they will have that of which the want is mostly felt in those regions, namely society.

Lyn, moved by this suggestion, asked, "could not a committee be formed to see if any practical plan might be devised to establish societies or clubs for the furtherance of this object?" And *Independence* would soon join his brother, who, although "well educated and brought up to business," had been "fifteen months without employment" and so had just departed for Melbourne. But he would prefer to enlist in the "Middle Class Emigration Society," presenting, as it did to his mind, "the hope of enjoying the simple home life of our forefathers in place of the tormenting conventionalities of the present day." The only detail he suggests is that the "first cargo should consist of those who have a small capital sufficient to provide house accommodation, stock and till some part of the land, which should be granted by Government or purchased at a very low price; the poorer ones who might follow would then be more likely to meet with remunerative employment."

Much more detailed is the scheme of *T.W.*, "a practical man, and . . . an old Australian colonist of some considerable experience," who is greatly enthusiastic about the prospects of those "who possess or can command a sum of not less than £100," no matter whether "clerk, tradesman, or professional man." He proposes to form "a Co-operative Emigration Society," and, as soon as 250 adults join—each subscribing at least £100—"either to charter or engage a ship to embark them direct for Melbourne, Australia." His "meagre outline" deals with the cost of passage and outfit (£20 each), with cooperative examination and securing of suitable land ("open and entirely clear of heavy timber," though "a small quantity of light honeysuckle . . . is not objectionable"), and with obtaining "a depasturing licence to enable them to have the right of run [for cattle, sheep, horses, &c.] over many thousands of acres of unoccupied land." All initial costs should not exceed £15,000, "leaving £5,000 at interest in their bankers for working expenses, &c." There then being nothing left to do "but plough up and dig the purchased soil, put in the seed, &c.," any "clerk or other person, not physically incapacitated," may fearlessly "follow the avocation of a farmer in Australia." Indeed the judgments and apprehensions of others are topsy-turvy:

a clerk is sharp-witted, active, and intelligent, and I know many who are now most thriving settlers—some, indeed, more successful than many who have left this country crammed with their home agricultural knowledge, carrying with them to the Antipodes all old prejudices, &c., which often they are forced to unlearn and forget, and commence on colonial soil *de novo*.[14]

Such is also the attitude of *A Mother of Sons and Daughters*—one is happy to meet a parent with mixed-sex offspring and to hear a mother's voice on this subject. Anyone who has "£75 or £100 on landing," chooses one of "the many large and flourishing towns away from Sydney and Melbourne," and is not particular about the kind of employment, "will soon prove the wisdom of the change from the crowded anxieties of English town life to the cheerful prosperity of Australia." But the duties of office will be very different from "English ways":

the gentleman must not be above blacking his own, and perhaps his wife or sister's shoes, when they have blacking; cutting wood, grooming his horse, fetching water, digging in his garden, doing necessary carpenter's work, besides any regular office or other business he may obtain even in a store or shop. The lady must do all housemaid's work, and often all the cook's also, besides being able and willing to make every article of clothing needed in a family except shoes and strong tailor's work.

She is greatly grieved that only sons have been emigrating: the thousands of gentlemen "should each have taken a sister, if not a wife, rather than leave them dependent on others in England. . . . Society there would have been far different if English ladies had gone in anything like the proportion of gentlemen, and no sister need ever fear becoming a burden there upon a brother," for all will "at a proper time" find husbands and wives, "and many an anxious father and mother would rejoin their thriving families, and spend their last days happily in a beautiful climate and prosperous community."

Her point about the male surplus is taken up also by *O.E.S.*, who remarks on the reversal of the home proportions. In England, "all the evils aris[e] from a surplus of female population," whereas there "under proper management, numbers of women may be absorbed by the colonial communities, to the great advantage of both." And personal witness to the advantage when a match is found is offered by *Never Say Die*. In business of his own and with an income of nearly £200, he nonetheless felt unable to marry, and so, twenty years ago, emigrated—"a step never regretted"—though he has now returned to end his days. Finding on arrival in Australia "that to succeed, marriage was a necessity," and there apparently being no difficulty, he married and "acquired a competency by thrift and industry"—regrettably he says not how. He has messages for various groups: "ladies, refined ladies" will find that their like have easily adapted to colonial life and found "a freedom and contentment they would not like to exchange for the frivolous conventionalities they obtain in this overcrowded country." As to "all who are repining at their very sad state, 'Go and do likewise.'" And to young men "who do not know what to be at" he, like many a later advocate of "manly character," is equally forthright:

instead of whining and pining after that which in this country they cannot attain, by reason of every avenue being so choked, they [should] brace themselves up after a manly fashion, drop their sentimentalism about theatres and riding in the parks, and emigrate to one of the colonies determined to succeed—"leave their country for their country's good"—altered circumstances with legitimate prospects would dictate the desirability of taking a wife, and if a family, instead of proving a curse here, as it would almost appear to be by what is stated by more than one of your correspondents, it would prove a blessing and a source of consolation.

Another point made by *O.E.S.* also prefigures attitudes of the later century concerning the opportunities and ties of empire. Those who would seek "a new home and a better fortune beyond the seas" are "by no means the scum and refuse of an overpopulated country" but "on the contrary, some of the best and bravest of its young people." Therefore a wise policy would "facilitate the removal of the British subject from one part of the Imperial dominions to another," rather than encourage, as some correspondents have suggested, emigration to the U.S.A. or Brazil. "The time may come when the mother country may not be too powerful or too proud to need or accept the support of her children. Let, then, the young empire at the Antipodes be chiefly favoured. None can doubt its affection and loyalty."

This and almost all the other important themes are found in the most eulogistic account of all. *Kangaroo* offers at great length what he calls (in unconscious *litotes*) "a few words" that he hopes will "not be unacceptable to some" of the *Daily Telegraph*'s readers. First he allies himself with those who deprecate imprudent early marriage, such as would bring suffering and misery not only on themselves, but often also on "distant branches of their respective families." Then he turns to personal history: after "a moderate education" he compromised with his parents and, instead of going to sea as he wished, went to Australia, landing "a delicate youth," with but £5 in pocket. He mentions not his occupation, but only his "constant, steady application to business, without any 'slices of luck,' 'windfalls,' or any extraordinary chances or wild speculations," as giving him after eleven years an income of £350. Money not being his god, he has been home on holiday for a year or two, and now at thirty he is about to marry. His has been the wise course:

Well, Sir, on my return, what do I see among my old friends and schoolfellows, progression or retrogression? I am sorry to say most of the latter, and much of what I call dormant life, for many of them seem as though they might as well have been sleeping away their existence during my absence, for many of them are sitting at the same desks, living in the same make-the-two-ends-meet style, and have little or no hope of ever improving their positions, even if they have of holding their own in the battle of life; and yet I believe many of them have worked harder, and have had more unpleasantness to contend with, than I have.

Now the exhortation:

Young men of England, how can you stand it year after year, when there are so many fine fields of enterprise open to you, so much work to do in other lands, and so few hands to do it? Let your dormant spirit and energy have fair play, and remember that "in lands beside there's room enough for all."

But where to go? Australia, especially Victoria and South Australia, is much more promising than Canada, and as for the U.S.,

why give up your nationality by going to America, when we have these fine Australian colonies, peopled for the most part by our brothers and sisters, where you would feel at home, among your own countrymen, where you could hardly realise but that you were in another part of England, where personal and religious freedom and equality are to be found in all their fulness, where the Church is no longer fettered by the State, where political freedom is ensured by the ballot, where the climate is acknowledged to be one of the finest in the world, and where a man is valued for what he is, and where the "dignity of labour" is not sneered at, but duly honoured?

Success is not guaranteed anywhere, of course, and certainly not to those "young men of the period" of whom it is properly said, "unstable as water, thou shalt not excel," who "live in idleness, or wander from place to place, depending for subsistence upon remittances from 'the governor' at home, and when these cease they find their way back." Truly clerks are not in demand, but they should see it as an insult "to their manhood" to imply they cannot turn to "more manly, though it be more industrial, occupations" than "quill-driving." Falling into platitudes designed to touch the core, *Kangaroo* implores the desk-bound:

if still unmarried, go alone, fight your own battle, . . . remembering faint heart never won fair lady, and plant your own foot firmly on your adopted land; and then, when you see your way clearly, as you soon will, send or come for your lady love, who will thus be spared the first, which is the hardest, part of your upward struggle.

The married need wait only until they have saved £50 to £100. All a man need do is consult "the colonial newspaper files and books of reference at the Australian news rooms."

A stout individualist—"there is nothing like self-reliance"—he allows for combination between two or three like-minded friends, but has only scorn for the cooperative schemes of public companies and others. The old Australian colonists will willingly offer the helping hand to "new chums" that is "more valuable than any co-operative help can possibly be." And unlike others, he has a word for his "fair countrywomen":

Emigrate. Don't waste your time in an over-crowded country like this. Good as it is, there are many better for you; therefore if you meet with an opportunity of going in company with a respectable family to South Australia or Victoria, go, and I will answer for it you will find plenty of employment and also plenty of competition for your fair selves among men who have not to count your cost before proposing, and who think a fair loving English girl a most precious and priceless blessing, as he does who subscribes himself *Kangaroo*.

New Zealand, smaller and a newer "colony of settlement" than either Canada or Australia, prompted much interest and similar, if more ambivalent comments. There was less experience to report, with the settler population only about 100,000 in the early 1860s, and the six districts having been given collective legislative status in the late 1850s. Rather curiously, there is no mention of the fierce Maori wars, which ended in 1871. Of the fifteen brief references or more extended discussions, eight at least mildly favourable and four distinctly unfavourable, many link New Zealand with Australia.

The general comments range in tone from the optimistic report of *H.H.F.* (a married woman with seven daughters) that many of the despairing unemployed young men who, with "the assistance of their friends and relatives," went "as a last resource" to New Zealand or Queensland have "done well there, and settled down and married comfortably, and have blessed God for the happy day when they emigrated from home," to the pessimistic comment of *Ring* (a married man, civil engineer by profession) that his cousin, who went to New Zealand as many others have emigrated, "without an object, like a ship without a rudder," of course "came to grief."

The bulk of the comment centres on two discussions, one prompted by *Clericus*, the first of two using that signature, an unmarried priest, who early in the series scorned what he calls *Benedick*'s "selfish remedy, 'Become celibates,'" and is one of the first to say that the "best remedy is not celibacy but emigration." His proposal was brief but definite:

Let a number of the middle class form a society; let each male member marry a female of the same class; let each husband take out a healthy labourer, and each wife a stout, buxom servant girl (none of your would-be "like-mistress" damsels); and let Government give lands in New Zealand at moderate value. A colony is at once formed; and your humble servant will give up his present comforts to be their self-denying pastor.

This suggestion did not please *Antipodes* (another repeated pseudonym), who implies that *Clericus* is perhaps indulging in self-advertisement, as *A London Girl* had been accused of doing. He wants to ask *Clericus*

how on earth he thinks that men of small income could possibly afford, not only to take themselves and wives out to New Zealand (whither, with becoming modesty, he kindly proposes to accompany them as "their self-denying pastor"), but also "a healthy labourer," and "a stout, buxom servant girl," each into the bargain.

A colonist of experience, he advises those of modest means to go unattended, though the well-to-do may well take "helps." But go they ought, if they have "some definite object in view" and their "callings are suited to the requirements" of their destination.

J.N. was prompted to more vigorous and lengthy repudiation of *Clericus's* views. No colonists he has ever met, and he has met many, were "so disgusted with their fate as the middle-class settlers of New Zealand, despite its beauty and unequalled climate." Indeed the author of "a most romantic work on the country actually dare not visit the settlement of Taranaki for fear of his deluded victims taking vengeance on him." Only those who have large capital or the ability for hard work can expect any success, for all the grass land is already in the hands of large proprietors, and the rest is covered with "dense forests or fern." Would it not take up too much of the *Telegraph*'s "valuable space," he could tell "many a bitter story" of middle-class men who, induced by "the highly coloured accounts they had read of the country," brought their families out and are now "wandering about the forests with a woeful expression on their faces." Indeed, he tells one such pathetic story:

I once travelled for about three days through the forests with a young Manchester warehouseman, who had brought out his wife and family, and for whom he had been foolish enough to pay ten shillings a head for tickets in England which entitled each of the family to 20 acres of land in New Zealand. He was most enthusiastic about "life in the bush." After a good deal of trouble in the land office at Auckland, he was shown a part of the country (on the map) in which he might go out and make his selection. Poor man, I shall never forget the expression of his face the second day out; he was perfectly dazed. On the third day, after a considerable amount of "roughing it," we reached the spot where he was to make his "selection." I really did not know whether to cry or laugh, he looked so utterly miserable as he gazed around on his allotment. For all practical purposes he might just as well have had an allotment of 100 acres on the moon. It was miles from any sea beach or river, and there wasn't a road within fifty miles of it. All the available land was purchased by speculators years ago, and is not to be had now without paying a good price for it.

So he trusts that *Clericus* will reconsider before inducing people to go to a country "where they would be as much at home as a bull in a china shop."

A second debate about New Zealand concerned the history and prospects of Albert Land, a Nonconformist settlement founded in 1862 at the top of the North Island. The discussion was prompted by *D.B.*, who opened the question by asking for information about its partial success and was quickly answered by *N.Z.*, who had been there to see the complete shattering of the dreams of those immigrants who had "fondly imagined that Albert Land was to be simply another name for Elysium." Even better informed and rather more positive was the response of *W.P.*, a member of the second party that sailed in May, 1863, in the *Annie Wilson*. Having himself obtained a position in Auckland, he had not suffered the intense annoyance of those who had been bureaucratically delayed for six weeks from leaving for Albert Land. His second-hand information suggested, however, that it was now "a thriving little colony."

If *D.B.* was looking for more enthusiasm, he found it *S.B.*, so ebullient that one is not surprised to find that his stake was not theoretical. Identifying himself as a member of the founding committee, and subsequent manager of the Albertland Association, he summarizes the previous correspondence—*N.Z.* is a "croaker"; *W.P.* "speaks truly"—before going on "to deny *in toto* the charge of failure" against the "thriving little colony." Of course those "who can't live on less than £300 a year" will not succeed, but he has the "testimony, in the form of letters (since published)" of "men of purpose, fitness for colonial life, and determination to make their new home succeed in the bush," giving "beautiful descriptions of their lands and crops, of the splendour of the climate, and glowing with hope of a glorious future, from the fact of their present, though only early, achievements."

In the debates about New Zealand, as in those about Canada and Australia, the demands and opportunities for labour were central, and as in them, the power of hand and will was seen as crucial—and conquering, especially if a little capital was in pocket. *Traveller* is typical: "In Australia and New Zealand (if I mistake not), the labouring man, who brought nothing with him but his strong arm, and the man of considerable capital, represent the two classes who have, in their respective spheres, been the most successful."

And not unfamiliar is the message of *Colonial Tom*, whose view of emigration as a great blessing is founded on eight years' experience "in the back woods and gold fields of New Zealand," where he spent "four years working constantly on the diggings, and . . . two years in the bush as an axeman and woodcutter." If willing to "rough it" and put "his shoulder to the wheel," no youth, "gentle or simple, whatever his occupation in England may be," need fear colonial life. Only if he has a little capital and is sure of a "settled occupation" on arrival should he bring a wife; otherwise he should go alone and look about before sending for "the one he loves at home" to join him.

And *J.J.*, the "old emigration agent" quoted above, also repeats a common message: "I am continually hearing that the colonial towns are much overdone with the clerk and shop assistant classes, and many an one who threw up employment in the country to try their hand at the Antipodes would most gladly return and take their chance here again, overcrowded though it may be." *A.B.*, an enthusiast for the U.S.A., is more pressimistic: "I have been told by men lately returned from Australia and New Zealand that it is harder to get employment in those colonies than in England. They say that money is too scarce there."

On the hopeful side, the other correspondent signing himself *Clericus* (this one married) suggests for middle-class married people a plan like his namesake's but better developed. A committee of four resident near London and responsible for the initial expenses, with—what a nice touch for the *Telegraph*!—"a chairman appointed from among your responsible correspondents," should obtain a land grant from the government. They should then advertise their plan and invite participants—but only married ones with few or no children. He boldly shows himself one of the active clerisy: "Whatever is to be done must be done with energy and prudence. The less talk and the more action we have the better."

Once more it is appropriate to close the debate with an unabashed encomium, this from *Pioneer*, who certainly appears, on his own word, to be ideally qualified. First, a reason for everyone to choose New Zealand: it has "one of the finest climates in the world," to which "we owe our health and strength, [and] on the continued enjoyment of which greatly depend our future happiness and success."

Second, his personal qualifications, health and experience, which he mentions not out of pride, but "simply to show what a man can do, if he will only put his shoulder to the wheel." Strong and healthy, he is skilled both with clerks' and carpenters' tools,[15] and he can paint and glaze. While he has never "followed the plough," he was "reared amongst the Scottish hills" and so has some knowledge of agriculture; in any case, the British farmer has much to "unlearn (if the term can be used)," and it is not difficult to learn "colonial husbandry."

Third and at great length, an offer of and invitation to cooperation, here cruelly summarized. Taking up *W.M.P.Y.*'s suggestion, he offers a scheme for "a respectable body of middle-class English and Scotsmen, limiting the operations of the scheme to these two nationalities, without prejudice [sic] to our brethren in Ireland." Here too his opinions are based on special qualifications: "I am well acquainted with the formation of public companies, but my experience compels me to say that the operations of our scheme will be more economically and successfully conducted by private capital and enterprise." And he knows that the "first step is obviously to engage some temporary place of meeting." So his plan of course has noteworthy details: those only should apply who are under forty, in possession of £500, and ready for initial hard work. In "honour of our amiable Princess," the acquired area of some 5000 or 6000 acres should be called Alexandra Land. If those who have written letters on New Zealand would "confide their interests" to him in conjunction with "some other gentleman (if possible some experienced New Zealand colonist who may be at present in this country)," he is willing to be one of a pioneer party to choose and buy land, build houses, and arrange conveyance for the other participants in the scheme. Why wait?

I have letters of recommendation and introduction from influential persons in this country and connected with the colony, and I should be only too glad to have it in my power to say that my own humble efforts have in any way contributed to the success of the scheme, and to the future well-being of the Alexandra Land colonists.

It will be evident that most of the themes touched on by those commenting on Canada are also moot for the Antipodean questioners and answerers. All reflect the common concerns raised by placing the marriage question in economic terms: is there better hope elsewhere? if so, under what conditions? what is the labour market and what qualifications are needed? There is almost no reference to culture or to social life beyond that of the family; completely absent is consideration of what is essential for both, leisure. While there is some work for artisans (except perhaps in Australia, where town life gets more mention than elsewhere), the general assumption is that the immigrant's life will be rural: there is need for farmers and cheap uncultivated land is available (though much of it is not suitable for farming); long years of hard work are absolutely essential, work that is not suitable for those trained to sedentary jobs, especially clerks. Tales are told of inexperi-

ence conquered—but also of its being fatal, and there is general con-
cord that those who have some capital, which is in short colonial
supply, will be most welcomed. The move into the unknown was
daunting as well as challenging,[16] and so there is much interest in
cooperative schemes for emigration, though this common Victorian
theme conflicts with another even more dominant one, the demand for
self-responsibility that dictates self-help and avoidance of government
assistance. Though the discussions are male-dominated, there is some
attention to the quality of family life, with special attention to wives
and some to children and (through mention of colonial sexual imbalance) to the non-joys of male celibacy. That detailed discussions by and
about women are not dominant does not mean that the male correspondents were dedicated to a single life; emigration was seen as the
alternative not only to starvation but also to celibacy. Women were,
however, add-ons, relative creatures, defined by their roles as wives
and mothers. In the main, the prairies and outback had to be tamed
before these roles could be properly performed. Not surprisingly, then,
the judgments about wives are mixed: if, like the ideal male emigrants,
they (particularly in Canada and Australia) are content, nay happy, to
avoid demands to be "respectable" in the bad sense, they will succeed,
but they must be aware of the continual hard labour that to many will
seem mere drudgery. What little reference there is to children is unambiguous: they will benefit from wider opportunities and a less circumscribed life.

Probably little weight should be attached to the mention only in relation to Canada of one incentive—low taxes (as compared to the
U.S.A.)—and one deterrent—bureaucratic deadweight; it seems likely
that only by chance were they not dwelt on in the Antipodean
accounts. Historical circumstances seem more responsible for the lack
of mention in relation to Canada of town life, which figures in the Australian accounts, or of mining, which appears in both the Antipodean
sections. In relation to both Australia and Canada (and New Zealand
by inference), writers value the British connection, though not as much,
it seems probable, as they would have two decades later. Finally, one
topic allows for distinct contrasts—climate. For most (though not all),
Canada is simply too cold; for many, Australia is just too hot; only New
Zealand, with the best and not the worst of British weather, is right.

The United States of America

Writing when they did, during the great expansion of the American west, a popular theme in literature and journalism that was reported on by a stream of lecturers from both sides of the Atlantic, a large proportion of the *Daily Telegraph*'s correspondents referred, not surprisingly, to the United States. Some twenty-nine specific references appear,[17] only five recommending against (usually because they have another preference), while five merely ask questions or are equivocal. By far the most popular destination is "Western" U.S.A., attracting praise in no fewer than seventeen letters; the west coast (and specifically California) is mentioned three times; Texas and Kentucky once each—but ecstatically.

Given the maturity of urban life on the Eastern seaboard, when compared with the conditions in the British colonies of settlement, it is at first glance surprising that almost all the letters concerning the United States are preoccupied with agricultural matters, and especially the growing of grains. What needs to be recalled is that the great western expansion seemed to promise previously unattainable freedom from want. Was the promise reliable, asked some correspondents in the *Daily Telegraph*? and if so, how could it be turned into reality? *B.P.* (with unhappy experience in Nova Scotia) prudently asks whether the offer mentioned by *Professional*, that 150 acres can be had "from the United States Government for a nominal sum," can "be secured before starting?" *An Anxious Father*, a mercantile clerk with three little children to be anxious about, also asks about the Homestead Bill with its promise, as he reads it, of 160 acres for nothing. Willing to "undergo great hardship for the future welfare" of his children, he must find out if "a previous knowledge of farming [is] absolutely necessary to ensure ultimate success," or if it could be reached by "any intelligent man possessing an ordinary amount of health and strength, and a strong will to work for the good of wife and little ones, and possessing also sufficient money to make a fair start on his land."

Such questions met with a flood of answers, fuller of detail than those responding to questions about other possible havens, and rivalling those on domestic costs. Only a small sample can here be given, beginning with the contributions from one of those who signed with an actual name,[18] *George Francis Train*.[19] He reported, in reply to questioners, that

the entire cost of a homestead of 160 acres is about £3; that most of the land is taken up this side of the great rivers; that it will be necessary to move west of the Missouri, some 1,500 miles from New York; that it would cost about the same amount, say £6, to go to their homesteads from New York that it does to cross the Atlantic from England; that the land is the best, growing forty bushels of grain to the acre; and that thousands of families have gained a competency in a few years.

He gave information also on the nationality of immigrants in specific states, noting how they benefited by "association" in coping with problems. In a second letter, complaining that his first had produced so many telegrams and letters that he had to reply publicly, he dealt with several questions, including who properly receives land applications (the government land surveyors), whether there are houses on the properties available (no), whether the federal government assists immigration (no, except by "giving them almost a principality of land for a song"—and education is free during the five-year naturalization period), and whether there are other lands for sale (many, especially along the railways—he supplies considerable detail about location and cost, both much better than in Australia). Part of his message is familiar in content and style: "Bear in mind that kid gloves and patent leather boots are not wanted in a new country. You must take off your coat, roll up your sleeves, and get your living by the sweat of your brow. Where there is a will there is a way, and in the Far West the weakest go to the wall." But another part is more unusual at least in content: "Your neighbours will not ask your religion or your family history. In the Far West one man is as good as another, and sometimes a great deal better." These themes were not dominant in the expressed views of those asking the questions, whose overriding concern was economic survival.

Another enthusiast is *T.H.M.*, himself happy in Canada, but able to report that in "the Western States of America the fine prairie lands offer great inducements to settlers. It requires but little labour to bring the rich soil under cultivation," and there is land, lots of land. Drawbacks include the lack of trees for fuel and building, and the difficult climate, and no one should underestimate the time needed to find reward or the work needed for it. Also some capital is needed (he recommends cooperative schemes), especially for married men, because "it is cruel" to make a wife bear the hardships of landing "in a distant country, without friends or money."

Virtually every positive element in this account was challenged, and the negative ones elaborated, in the report of *J.C.L.*, "a native-born American" who had "lived and travelled in the extreme Western States for four years," and so "ought to know something of them." Quoting *T.H.M.* on the lack of trees, he agrees if Kansas and Nebraska are intended, and adds that coal is scarce also, and of poor quality. The climate is worse than *T.H.M.* thinks, being both "extremely cold" (the winter lasts six months) and extremely hot. If *T.H.M.* was referring to more than the nearly timberless Kansas and the miserably soiled Nebraska, that is, to Colorado, New Mexico, Utah, and Nevada, "he is going from bad to worse." Only mining, no farming in Colorado, and all provisions have to be brought in 650 miles, to Denver; New Mexico, with only a few fertile valleys surrounded by very high mountains, is a desert; so is almost all of Utah, with "plenty of saleratus and salt water"; and just so is Nevada, also a mining country. Before seeing these states, *J.C.L.* "thought they must be magnificent, and used to wonder why they were not settled," but now, having seen them, he judges the land "the most forsaken country I ever saw, and never wish to see it again." Public spirit alone leads him to make these remarks, "to save some weary traveller from awaking some 'fine morning' and finding himself out of the reach of fresh water."

His evidence was overborne, at least in volume, by that of others who feared not the absence of water, and agreed with *Professional*: "The Western States of America I most unhesitatingly affirm stand unrivalled as a field for emigrants." *L——S*, for instance, quoted above on Canada, ranks west as best "for men without any previous knowledge of country occupations," thanks to "Yankee ingenuity," which "has devised every possible description of labour-saving implements, so simple in management that any man of ordinary capacity can quickly learn their use, and be as efficient for nearly the whole work of the farm, at a minimum expenditure of toil, as the most experienced agricultural labourer." Initially cheap, land improves in value yearly at an astonishing rate, railways are spreading to all parts, and villages and towns spring "into existence as if by magic." What is the "only great drawback for many, that they must denationalise themselves," is not so for *L——S*, who believes the "idea of repatriation is almost always an idle dream," for quickly "the tastes and sympathies of the majority of new comers are assimilated with those of their neighbours, and as their children grow up, the last ties with the old country drop away, and they become permanent citizens of the Great Republic."

Pioneer, who has lived in the southern states for more than fifteen years, would now seem to have no such idle dream, whatever his initial thoughts might have been. Texas is without question the place for emigrants, "particularly for those who have to win their bread either by the labour of the head or hand, or who can only command a small capital [£100 to £300]." In eastern Texas, cattle and various harvestable crops, including the grape, thrive—he reports costs and returns—and the mild climate, with the cool breezes from the Gulf of Mexico, allows for "white labour." The western part, "with its lovely prairies, dotted over with the evergreen 'live oak,' and coated with the finest grasses," offers "great attractions to an Englishman," for "horses, cattle, and sheep increase and multiply, almost without outlay or care." The "Italian" climate, moreover, is "one of the most pleasant and salubrious in the world," the annual variation in temperature being only 22 degrees. Like several others, *Pioneer* hints at personal self-help as well as useful courtesy in closing: "Should you consider this worth a place in your widely-read paper, I may at another time present to your readers a plan by which a colony could be favourably located in Western Texas."

If "The Lone Star State" did not finally appeal, the adjacent lands were well promoted by *Kentucky*, a former naval surgeon who has seen even more of the world than the other promoters, having been in India, Mauritius, Natal, the Cape Colonies and Free State, as well as Brazil, the River Plate states, Chile, Bolivia, and Canada, before settling "in this beautiful region—the garden of the United States." But, presumably only because the land in Kentucky is "improved" and therefore high-priced, his recommendation for a man "prepared to make the necessary sacrifices—mental, social, and domestic"—is to look to Kansas and beyond (one hopes not those states so strongly condemned by J.C.L.), to the "range of country stretching from the Missouri River to Santa Fe and New Mexico, having a glorious climate, a fertile soil, connection by railway and river with good markets, free from Indian troubles." On easy terms clear title is available to cheap land, where already there are "good villages" and "plenty of schools and meeting-houses."

Returned Emigrant, a well-travelled clerk with views on Central and South America as well as the northern continent, is eloquent about California. He took up pen in response to *Roamer Returned*, another with wide experience in the Americas, who had reported that the only employment he, a single clerk, could find in San Francisco was "in one of the meanest and most plebian capacities."[20] Meeting others like himself, he concluded that, unless qualified by experience for hard labour, clerks were as well off at home. *Returned Emigrant* admits that while he also "underwent many unpleasant experiences" in California (as well as in British Columbia), he had held "no foolish ideas about the possibility of obtaining a clerkship in that distant colony," but was willing "to forsake the desk for the plough if necessary." He also met in San Francisco "dozens of disappointed and disgusted young Englishmen," carrying useless letters of recommendation. But actually work

was readily available, and he soon "stepped into a lucrative situation
. . . in the golden city." So, though the eastern states are as crowded as
the U.K. with young men who "sit down in a saloon or wander use-
lessly about waiting for something to turn up," and in New York are
lucky to find a clerkship that "in nine cases out of ten is rewarded with
a starvation salary,"[21] there is hope elsewhere, and especially for those
willing to labour—or with a small amount of capital. And nowhere
better than the interior cities of California, where there is plenty of
room, and if clothing is expensive, living is cheap. The climate is magnificent: "Eternal summer reigns," while "the serene and cloudless sky
and pure clear air remind the Continental traveller of Italy." Look no
further: "Along the line of the Pacific railroad dozens of small towns
are springing up as if by magic, and these are the places to find elbow-
room, a fair field and no favour."

The useless clerk theme is developed by other commentators on the
U.S., including *Five Years' Colonist* (where he does not say), who dwells
on "the unsuitableness of a certain class of delicately-reared young
men, who ignorantly suppose that 'society' in the Western States or
South America is better or will be more to their taste than society at
home among friends and equals, and at which they grumble so much."
Of what use to a "City man is a hundred acres of land in the middle of
the Australian bush or the Western prairie?[22]—perhaps a hundred
miles from the nearest market, very likely double that distance from a
church, and city or town."

Equally blunt is *Benedick*, who wants to "realise an America at
home," by limiting population so that "men should be few in proportion to the land." Successful emigration, he points out, requires that
which allows successful marriage at home, namely capital. And the
clincher for him: "emigrants must become tillers of the soil—there is no
room for men of other callings—and a tiller of the soil is not the highest
animal in the world."

For the majority, the highest animal is social man, and cooperative
ventures would lead him—and eventually woman—to the best of all
possible worlds. The instigator of this discussion in the *Daily Telegraph*
was *Ring*, already quoted, whose suggestion was vague:

Let several young men combine together, and (take their wives if they have
any) organise a sort of expedition—the combination would make the expenses
much less. Let them go to the far West or to some parts of South America,
where land can be had for asking almost. If they all go together they will have
that of which the want is mostly felt in those regions, namely society.

This proposal struck a chord in the hopeful breasts of such as *Nil Desperandum*, who is

happy to combine with those who have for their object such a scheme as this, and would gladly render what aid I can to establish "homes," not only for ourselves, but for those whom many of us have to think about, and for whom with ourselves we picture a bright future of happiness, but which, apparently, under existing circumstances, we cannot realize in this the "mother country."

Also stimulated by *Ring*'s proposal for "combined emigration," *Veritas* assured the editor that "hundreds of your readers, though silent observers, are anxiously looking forward to *The Daily Telegraph* for further information,[23] expecting no doubt a project will be started for the benefit of those married or single individuals desirous of adventuring their prospects abroad." *A.B.*, offering "All honour" to *Ring* for his initiation of the idea, and stimulated by a request by *Independence* for someone to make a proposal, is sure (on no presented evidence) that the U.S. government would do everything "in its power" to encourage "temperate, well-educated, industrious, and law-abiding English men and women" to move to "the fairest portion of the globe, the pride of the nineteenth century, and the glory of the Anglo-Saxon race," a land "abounding in every kind of produce, peopled by Anglo-Saxons, and governed by laws identical with those of England in all matters of importance."

So impressed by *Veritas*'s encomium was *Scotch Civil Engineer* that he quoted it from "fairest portion" to "laws identical"[24] as preliminary to a detailed scheme of "co-operative emigration," typical of others.[25] In his view, some twenty families with capital of £500, no more than five in each, and the eldest member under forty years of age, should agree on terms of co-partnership. Two then should go as a pioneer party to the States, and acquire 5000 acres of good land from one of "the great railway companies, getting a station on the railway for the settlement." After three-apartment residents for each family, and a meeting-house that would double as a schoolroom, had been made "ready for their reception," a "special vessel" would be commissioned "at a cheap rate." Among those arriving must be "a clergyman, who would act also as schoolmaster; a surveyor, to superintend the clearing of the land, construction of the roads, and cultivation of the soil; also a storekeeper." The shared fund of capital would be applied to the costs of land, houses, passage, stock and seeds, and tools, "and also wages for the work of each emigrant at the current rates of the country for the work performed"; it would be replenished by the sale of "produce, stock, and timber."

When lots of 250 acres had been cleared, each family would receive its portion of the general fund, and then the man would cultivate the farm on his own account, but contributing to the community his work as a labourer "until the whole land was cleared, and all the families had got their allotments; he meantime receiving current rate of wages for the labourer's services out of the general fund." Under this scheme, land bought cheaply and on easy terms would rapidly increase in value; "comfortable homes and pleasant society" would be immediately available, and labour would be rewarded by good wages until allotments were available.

Finally showing his full interest, in welcoming the "sensible letter" with a similar proposal from *A Minister of Religion* (who actually recommended Canada), *Scotch Civil Engineer* also offers to "assist" and "share" in such an adventure, being willing with him to "be one of a pioneer party, if a company can be formed, to visit and select the land, and make arrangements for the accommodation and reception of the emigrants, as well as afterwards give my professional advice and assistance in clearing the land and bringing it into cultivation."

One of the two signing *Antipodes* brings out explictly what is implied by *Scotch Civil Engineer*: a telling though not much discussed point, namely that in a cooperative society not all should be soil-tillers, for a full range of talent would be needed, including builders of houses (which need not, he comments, necessarily be " 'pigstyes,' as suggested by your correspondent *W.E.W.W.*, unless made so by the taste and habits of their occupants"), "bakers, grocers, butchers, and other suppliers of the daily wants, to say nothing of doctors, lawyers, and numbers more besides."

Promotional fever is more evident in those recommending the U.S.A. than anywhere else, with pulse running high in and details pouring out of *George Francis Train, Professional* (two letters), and *W.J.I.* The accounts are so detailed, including lengthy passages from reports of conditions, that summary would be misleading while full quotation is impracticable. What can be given here is a sampling from the most unqualified appeal from the new world to the old.

Traveller, writing from the New University Club, St James, gestures grandly in the style of "westward look, the land is bright." The "rapid advances westward of the two great Pacific railways"—seen by him personally in the last nine months—have opened opportunities of land and employment for "settlers, clerks, traders, &c." as astonishing to

New York and Philadelphia as they would be to London. And further south there are even greater chances, witness the conversion of Eastern Kansas into "a garden" by the Union Pacific Railway. "Want is unknown there; schools, churches, and, to speak truly, theatres and many other practical signs of prosperity, are fast multiplying and extending westward." Ever-greater demand will be felt for "that latent energy which is going to waste here as a drug on the market."

Traveller's warmest encomium is for New Mexico, where in a few months the bracing summer climate "made a man of the delicate Londoner who now writes this letter." There are found first-quality coal, iron, and lime, abundant reserves of gold, silver, and other metals, and hundreds of square miles of fine pasture land. In valleys as fertile as those of California, colonies of agriculturalists, "by uniting their strength for purposes of irrigation, could raise enough produce of all kinds to supply the mining populations of other districts." Most exciting is the potential for vine cultivation of 256,000 acres in the Rio Grande Valley, which could produce at least 50,000,000 gallons of wine. Surely more than disinterest lies behind Traveller's account of this unexploited treasure:

the few vineyards that at present exist belong to Pueblo Indians and a few Mexicans, and the wine produced is so small in quantity and so highly prized that it is almost impossible to obtain it at any price. The greater part of the population of America are almost entirely debarred from this luxury on account of the high price of the imported article. The wines of California have not increased in reputation, but there can be only one opinion about the El Paso wine of the Rio Grande. The grapes are there, the land is there, the market and at last the means of transportation are all ready; even labour is on the spot, but for the motor power, knowledge, energy, and capital, we must look to emigration.

From his viewpoint—displayed at great length—the accounts stressing the necessity of capital and labouring experience are greatly exaggerated: "The very classes who find it hardest to get on here are the most required in the Far West"; indeed, "Middle-class emigration is what is required there." What is needed is "a middle-class emigration company, whose office it would be to give reliable information, cheapen the cost of transportation, and to lessen the risk of those who seek their fortunes in distant lands." And the need is immediate, for an American company is now preparing to send recruiting agents abroad for just such purposes; however, Traveller believes that if given the chance, few would wish "to intrust their fortunes, at the turning-point of their lives, to a foreign company, of which they know nothing." So let there be formed a home company, with benefit to all concerned: "It would facilitate the enlistment of persons willing to emigrate, it would furnish them with accurate information, it would facilitate contracts for cheapening transportation, and it would form a very effectual check on the misrepresentation that companies having land to sell and districts to settle might be induced to make."[26]

The Rest of the World

Horizons and hopes enough? Not so, for some correspondents had visited and some dreamed of other, seemingly more exotic, shores.

South and Central America

Of these, the most often mentioned were the other Americas, south of the U.S. border. Eight of the twenty-four references are only to "South America," many others, apparently specific are in fact either perfunctory or vague, and some correspondents mention several locations. Though there is considerable enthusiasm and some boosterism, a higher proportion of the correspondents (more than a third) are hostile or contemptuous. Brazil is the most frequently cited, with six comments. Next come the "states of the River Plate," collectively so called three times, with specific mentions of Uruguay four times (once as "Banda Oriental"), and Argentina and Paraguay thrice each. Chile is also referred to by three correspondents; Bolivia and Peru each by one. Of the Central American states, Mexico (twice) and Nicaragua (once) are mentioned. Only Brazil and the states of the River Plate are treated at any length, however, and of the other accounts, the accolade of Nicaragua alone merits quotation. "On my way eastward," reports *Returned Emigrant*, "I passed through Nicaragua, from the Pacific to the Atlantic, a distance of nearly two hundred miles. I have never seen a finer country—splendidly wooded, beautiful streams, game in abundance. I believe the Nicaraguan Government gives encouragement to emigrants."

Once again, as in that passage, so in almost all: land is the main question, with the need for hard labour and the clerks' suitability intertwined. The comments of *Ring* cited above led to a less than committed query by *L.H.J.*, a clerk, who would "like to know more of the advantages to be derived from emigration to such uncivilised countries"[27] before venturing "to take a wife there"; *Delta*, however, was induced by *Ring* to "hail with pleasure the scheme" of combining with "any respectable young men who have for their object emigration to South America," which appears best "for the exercise of enterprise and industry."

Brazil evoked most contention. *An Old Colonist* mentions no other option, not surprisingly in view of his eulogy, based on four particular reasons: first, the climate, particularly in the south, is the best in the world; second, the soil is fertile in the extreme; third, the Brazilian government, "anxious to attract industrious settlers," offers assisted passages, cheap land on good terms, a temporary house, and "seeds, implements, &c., on credit to those without means"; and fourth, many emigrants have written home to induce friends to join them.

He dismisses scornfully one main contention of correspondents, that "a man unacquainted with agriculture is not likely to succeed in the colonies." Actually, English farmers are less successful than the inexperienced because they are "generally prejudiced, and slow to take advice on subjects they consider themselves authorities on"; so, "while a clerk, professional, or tradesman works his hand as the old colonists recommend, the farmer goes on as he did in England, forgetting that here land is dear and labour cheap, while in his new home land is cheap and labour dear, and so often makes a failure."

For those still hesitant, he remarks in conclusion that "life and property are as safe in Brazil as here." But in fact that is not quite the conclusion, for he has another bit of information that again suggests more than disinterest: "The Brazilian Government emigration commissioners are Messrs. Meadows and Christopher, 32, Clement's-lane, E.C., to whom some friends of mine were referred by the Consul, and who afforded them such satisfactory information that I hear they start by the first vessel."

G.S.R., a clerk, agrees with *An Old Colonist* about the "rare attractions" of Brazil, which include easier access than Australia, and better climate than North Ameria. The soil is among "the richest and most productive in the world"; "irrigation and internal communication are rendered comparatively easy by the large and beautiful tributaries of the Amazon and La Plata"; and there are many productive mines. There is, however, a serious problem not mentioned by *An Old Colonist*: "The only drawback of the country, for emigration purposes, appears to be the difference of race, and the consequent unpleasant feelings that may arise between English emigrants and the Portuguese or Spanish settlers." Just this problem, *G.S.R.* says, caused *A.B.* to describe the inhabitants as "half-civilised, bigoted, and lawless"; however, he seems personally assured by the apparently better-informed judgment of *An Old Colonist* that life and property are as safe in Brazil as in England.[28]

Even more informed are *M. and C.*, who certainly qualify as agents of the Brazilian government, paid or unpaid. Advocates of "association," they presented the Brazilian government with a plan designed so that "English families with small means (say £100) might settle near one another for mutual aid, comfort, and society," and be granted 250,000 acres for their exclusive use. They proceed in the style of a brochure. The grant is "in the province of Parana, specially recommended for English settlers, the climate being cool, and not so trying as we have lately experienced here." Without benefit to them, the projectors, emigrants would be ceded blocks of 250, 500, or 1000 acres at 1s per acre, with five years allowed for paying the first instalment covering 250 acres, and, in the case of the larger lots, three years for the second 250; for the final 500 acres of the largest block, "the Government requires cash to be paid."

They go on to offer another deal—with which they are also connected—"designed by the Brazilian Government" for those with little or no capital. A farmer, or even a farm labourer or gardener, granted 75 acres at about 3s 9d per acre, payable in five years, will be assisted by "the municipal body, under the express sanction of the State."

On his arrival he finds a primitive house built for him, about 1 1/4 acres (not less), prepared for him; farm implements are lent him, and seed given to him; and, besides his passage being reduced to £7, he is presented as a gift with £2 5s to commence housekeeping. If he has no money, and the emigrant shows industry, even a small loan may be obtained from the municipal committee for improvement of the emigrant's lot; and employment is also given for the general improvement of the colony at about 2s or 2s 6d per day, when the emigrant is not working on his own lot.

Should one believe these wonderful promises? Not according to *Returned Emigrant*, who has encountered "many returned adventurers from that country, . . . and if half the tales they told be true it is not a very inviting place for an emigrant." And *A.J.S.*, as rich in prejudice as in judgment, provided just such a tale about Brazil. He is greatly disturbed at descriptions of it as a "promised land," by such as *G.S.R.*, with his eulogy of "the large and beautiful tributaries of the Amazon and La Plata." Only those with a few years' experience of the climate, people, and means of communication within a country should write of it, and *G.S.R.* does not qualify; otherwise he would not write such nonsense about the "easiness of communication." *A.J.S.*, as a "resident in the capital and a regular traveller through the interior," knows better; he knows, for instance, that "the large and beautiful tributaries are mountain torrents," are so broken into rapids and falls that, no matter how full of beauty and interest "to the eye of a traveller," they are "perfectly impracticable" for transporting produce and merchandise. As to the climate, it is tropical in every sense: one can hardly bear it indoors in Rio de Janeiro, but for "an English labourer, much more a City clerk, turning out into the fields and performing manual labour under a sun that at times even the African nigger shrinks from, the thing is quite preposterous." After a few months, "the religion, the people, the language and customs, the food and the climate," all "opposed to English ideas," would result in disgust. So it is that only those who can prosper without knowledge of the country, the people, and the language, should try Brazil, "viz., the men possessed of large means."

In case the "yeas" did not carry the motion against such a thunderous "nay," readers might wish to consider the "pampas" of the states of the River Plate, where probably many more than *Ring*'s "hundreds of people" would be able to profit because "a new mode of preserving South American beef by freezing has come into vogue."

The remarks of *J.N.* so stirred one correspondent that he had "fully made up [his] mind that the Pampas of South America" should be his "future field of operations," and indeed signed himself *Pampas*. What had been said by *J.N.*, "lately the manager of a large cattle and sheep station on the pampas or plains"? He offered an opinion "especially for the information of the following classes, viz., poor gentlemen, clerks, or shopkeepers, in fact for any man who has led a sedentary life until manhood, and is therefore unfitted to begin a life of manual labour, and who, having a small fortune of £400 or £500, and seeing little or no prospect of improving his condition in this country, has determined to try his fortune in a new land." What was the opinion? For them South America is simply "the finest country in the world." While life on the pampas lacks much found in comfortable London lodgings, you have "many sources of pleasure" unavailable in London to "a comparatively poor man." Among them, apart from cheaper tea, tobacco, and bread, and the "magnificent" climate, is freedom from "taxes, bills, rent, and all the other worries of middle-class life in England."

Not all is ideal; indeed life on the pampas has "its dark as well as its bright side."

I have many a day worked about the station until I felt dead beat; I have shorn sheep until I thought my fingers would crack; I have dug wells and worked at brickmaking under a hot sun until I thought I would faint. Now all of these occupations, and others I could mention, were trying to a town-bred man, but none of them constituted what I call the dark side of life on the pampas.

And what then was the "dark side"? "What I wanted was a good wife." How to repair this deficiency he alas does not say, but perhaps his final urging might cover even that matter: "By applying at the Consul's office (I think in Westminster-street) I have no doubt inquiries will meet with every attention."

Readers of the *Daily Telegraph*, however, did not have to travel to Westminster Street for information; they could stay at their breakfast tables to read a long letter from L——S, who, it will be recalled, rated the states of the River Plate next after (but well after) the western prairies of the U.S.A. (and still ahead of Chile and Canada) as "fulfilling the necessary conditions of good climate, need of labour, and abundance of fertile land." He openly sets up his ethical appeal: because he owns a small tract of frontier land in the area, he has been "careful to understate (if anything) much in the following remarks," lest they "appear too favourable" to the suspicious.

And favourable they are. Excluding that lying along the 600 miles of railroad, there are "fifteen million acres of fertile land within twenty-five miles of port of shipment direct to Europe." Rich in "runs" carrying cattle, sheep, and mares, land has a "fee-simple value" of from 8s to £1—no comparable opportunity can be found anywhere in the world. Though the country could rival the U.S. in supplying grain to Europe, at present it imports "breadstuffs"; why? "the dearth of hands." The "gaucho," the native peasant, will not leave the saddle even for more lucrative shepherding, let alone the labour of farm work. It falls to Italian and Basque immigrants who, after a year or two, buy patches of land near a town, and grow produce so successfully that they can before many years return home in "good circumstances." (For evidence, L——S refers readers to statistics lately published by the Italian government.) The field is then open not only to "capitalists and men of small means in the middle class," but to the body of poor unskilled workers

which so keenly suffers through every slack period, and which, even when the industries of the country are in full swing, cannot put by sufficient from its earnings for the hour of need, and is constantly living on the verge of that pauperism into which dull times have plunged so many thousands during the past year.

The field is, however and alas, not wide open. Because of a costly foreign war, "the public finances of the Platine States do not at present admit of pecuniary assistance on any scale to immigration, and there is no law of contract securing the individual settler who may send home and engage labourers on his own account." As a result, since "the less scrupulous among the immigrants" soon leave their employers without means of recovering passage costs, few settlers are willing to seek labour abroad.

Still, L——S was favourable. Not so another copious correspondent, *J.R.*, who went on the attack against *J.N.* The enthusiastic glow of his account came from a false fire, luring "young men of education with a small capital" towards "bitter disappointment." One of *J.N.*'s suggestions is particularly astonishing to *J.R.*, "that it is desirable for the small sheep-farmer of the Argentine Republic to get married."

The manager of a South American sheep-farming company, with a liberal salary and a comfortable brick house to live in, may please himself in the matter; but how a poor "puestero" or "medianero," living in a mud hut swarming with flies and fleas, can dream of asking the girl he loves, brought up, presumably, with English ideas of comfort, to share his wretchedness, I do not know.

The profits from sheep-farming are so slight that even building an "unpretentious brick dwelling-house" is out of the question for those even with a few hundred pounds. A capital of £300 or £400 will produce annually merely £30 or £40, hardly enough for "biscuits, tea, coffee, sugar, and such-like necessaries of camp life." If—a rare event— one became "manager of a sheep-farming company, . . . to marry or not to marry would become a question of choice." To him, "the idea of a young and educated Englishman taking out his wife to the deserted pampas of the Argentine Republic, there to share his wretched mud-built 'puesto,' and to enjoy the society of sheep and 'biscachos,' seems preposterous." In an appeal to authority, he mentions that "numbers of [his] friends can corroborate these statements," and he himself has "tried sheep-farming life in Entre-Rios, Cordova, Santa Fe, and other 'rising' places, and so ought to know something about it."

Such a negative view is indeed shared by most of those who claim to know, including *Kentucky*, whose signature locates his residence and his enthusiasm, but who has seen the world. Truly, he admits, "there is a very beautiful section of country stretching from the Parana to the Andes. Carientes, Cordova, and the Banda Oriental, of which Monte Video is the capital, are fertile provinces." They are not, however, welcoming to all. European emigrants—though he does not say so, he means Protestant ones—are met by "distrust and suspicion" by the Catholic residents. In the grazing districts, droughts are severe at times, while water and timber are always scarce. While some Scotchmen have done well in sheep-farming on a share system, their life is a solitary and "semi-savage one." The dry summers and their migratory sheep-herding lives mean they cannot even cultivate gardens, so their fare is almost entirely "mutton and hard biscuit." "Believe me," he says—and why should one not?—"this is no life for a rational Englishman" (and one may conclude what one wishes about the Scots).

In concurrence is *A.J.S.*, whose knowledge is only second-hand but founded on reports from worn-hands who are "better judges of the state of the country than those who sit comfortably at home, and form ideal and romantic notions of camp life." He reports not only difficulty but danger. In Monte Video there has been no protection for life and property since the assassination of Flores, and in Argentina, though the presence "of the English element" makes things better, the essential wool trade is "completely paralysed" because of the recent protective U.S. import duties, and "the long and desultory warfare with Paraguay."

All in all, it would seem that the poor clerks had better stay in suits and soot, for even the voyage home, as reported by *Roamer Returned*, was vile. After he had spent hard days in British Columbia and California, he "visited Chile and Peru,"[29] where he "experienced the same difficulties in obtaining employment," with "the additional obstacle of . . . ignorance of the Spanish language."

After many weeks of privation and severe hardship I thankfully accepted a berth as steward of a homeward-bound English vessel. Talk of the grievances of City clerks! Why had any of them to submit with patience to the indignities continually imposed upon me during my voyage home, they would sit down to their desks with a firm determination to do their duty in the condition it had pleased God to place them, and leave the roaming to those who know what it means, and the many inconvenience attendant upon such a course.

South Africa

Correspondents mention four locations in what was later to become a united South Africa, namely, the Cape Colony, the Transvaal, the Orange Free State, and Natal, but apart from the last, all but one of the specific references are perfunctory.[30] Though *L.H.J.* thought that, like Canada, South Africa held out prospects in manufacturing and commerce, the general themes were agriculture—and mining, the gold fever then heightening in yet another part of the southern world.

But the opposite of perfunctory is *W.D.A.*'s enthusiastic account of the Transvaal Republic, which, he says, is arousing "great attention in the United States, in Germany, the Cape Colony, and Natal." It has the attractions of Australia in its early days for "young and energetic men with limited means," who should, however, avoid the allure of the newly found gold fields, and dedicate themselves to "the more certain occupation of sheep or general farming," because there will be an increasing demand for food as "the great influx of emigrants" settles in. *W.D.A.* has particular information (once more suggestive of agency). Excellent sheep and wheat lands are available in New Scotland and "the flourishing settlements of Industria" at from 2s 6d to 3s per acre, on easy terms. Association is the means:

Co-operation ... would largely secure economy in passage and other expenses; it would also secure society, and afford opportunity for some of the number to alternately make trading trips, bartering beads, brass wire, and English goods for ivory, skins, ostrich feathers, &c., or making hunting excursions, which is a favourite sport, and, at the same time, a remunerative occupation common to the country, and thus break the monotony of pastoral life.

Perhaps disingenuously, he disavows knowledge of relevant literature, "except a small pamphlet issued gratis at the Consulate, where also," he believes, "maps of the country may be seen, and general information obtained."

As to Natal, the enthusiasm was almost unmixed, from the brief letter signed *Natal*, mentioning the free grant of fifty acres of land to those paying their own passage, and offering cooperation, to the longer letters of *Kentucky*, *An Intending Emigrant to Natal*, and *S.C.H. Kentucky*, it will be recalled, is most fervent for his part of the U.S.A., but he has an informed judgment about and kind words for Natal, especially in comparison with the Cape Colony and the Orange Free State. Land prices are high, but it has fertile soil, and produces a wide variety of goods from sugar to sheep, cotton to coffee, cereals, maize, indigo, arrowroot, oranges, grapes, pines, bananas, and figs. As to the present population, the colonists are "either English or Scotch, shrewd but genial," and "black labour [is] abundant." The costs of clothes and staples are low. For whom is there opportunity? "Natal promises a prosperous future to mechanics; clerks and shopmen have no business there. Small capitalists, too, often lose all their money before they have cut their eye teeth." *Natal* had said that passage cost £6; *Kentucky*, better informed, gives the cost of "second cabin, about £28," otherwise ("by ship"), £16. The only drawback in Natal is the lack of navigable rivers along its coast.

The information given by *An Intending Emigrant to Natal* is compatible, though the comparison is with Australia, about which he is trying to disabuse *W.M.P.Y.* Australia already has enough population, and land in Natal is "just five times cheaper—the Government upset price being 4s instead of £1—and quite as good." He mentions occupations "in the uplands" as horse, cattle, sheep, and goat breeding; on the coast the production of "coffee, sugar, tea, arrowroot, cotton, &c."; and "all over the colony" wheat and "mealies (maize)" are grown. As a stake "£150 would go a long way where a man lives on his own farm, kills his own game, mutton, &c., grows all the wheat, &c.," and has no expenses, except for "clothes, &c." Once more an interest may be hinted at: "The Natal Government agent is now in England, and he will be happy to give every information concerning the colony."

The final letter on Natal was prompted by this last, as *S.C.H.* (also knowledgeable about the Free State and Transvaal) offers yet more encouragement. He mentions, to set the proper tone, that "there has been a fearful monetary crisis in Natal, the tail end of the same wave sweeping over it that swept over us when [the firm of] Overend and Gurney broke," but it "has now nearly passed over." Indeed "those who can go out there now with money in their pockets and brains in their heads cannot fail to make a thoroughly good thing of it," being able, "so to speak, [to] sell their money for goods and stock to an extent almost incredible." The manner in which *S.C.H.* presents his authoritative detail is unusual for his time and now unheard of in correspondence columns: he quotes at great length extracts from a letter sent by a friend in Natal. Here only hints at the tone and message can be given:

At this moment we are on the tiptoe of expectation looking for our salvation; all eyes are turned towards the centre of South Africa in an eager manner, whence we hope cometh our help. Gold! gold! gold! that is the word in everybody's mouth.

This will never be much of a place until the Home Government wake up and extend the protection of the British flag throughout the whole of South Africa. All things point that way. The Boers have made themselves so obnoxious to the natives by their dastardly conduct that the latter are praying the Cape to take them over.

If the gold turns up trumps I don't intend to remain here a poor man; indeed, I have a mind to send to some firm to send out requirements for diggers, as for the first year there will be lots of money made.

If a man is content to vegetate here there are few places which offer such facilities for an easy life. . . . With our climate and productive soil a few hours' work a month would give him all that he would actually require for a year. For the rest his gun will do all he wants. . . . Are you fond of fish? Half an hour will supply you amply.

We want nothing in this highly-favoured land but money. As I have said, should the gold turn up trumps, there will be a rare kick-up in Durban, and he who is wide awake will pick up lots of chips.

This picture of "mixed good and evil" on the "eastern side of the Natal colony" is more complex, in its blend of political hopes with economic facts and dreams, than any other of the emigration letters, and is of special interest as coming immediately from someone both in a colony and committed to a colonial future.

India and Interior Africa

These are the only other destinations mentioned, but not positively or in detail. The well-travelled *Kentucky*, who as a surgeon had visited India (in addition to Mauritius, Natal, the Cape Colonies and Free State, Brazil, the River Plate states, Chile, Bolivia, and Upper Canada), is unqualified in his judgment: "India will never be extensively settled by Europeans; that is a fact. It is too hot." The other reference is quite odd: *Returned Emigrant*, who is keen on various parts of North America, says without previous reference to the great subcontinent: "For myself I intend to start shortly for India." (Could this be a misprint for Indiana?) And finally, in passing, *Nobody In Particular*, who is for nowhere in particular except home, is scathing about the eccentricity of proposing a new life in Canada or Australia, let alone Mexico and Paraguay, and comments with unconcealed irony: "We may as well add the interior of Africa, perhaps, which is surely almost as eligible for colonisation as the last-mentioned territory."[31]

In the emigration letters, two debates emerge. The first concerns the advisability of emigrating. Both sides assume that economic circumstances are bad and prospects grim at home; their disagreements are fundamentally about whether distant prospects are any more rosy, and if so, for whom. Unlike some—such as Dickens and Carlyle—who would have private agencies or government light home fires, the letter writers on the near side of the ports who generally claimed personal experience of the colonies called for no action except that of the responsible individuals themselves, especially in association with the like-minded, and indeed they concentrated mainly on the dangers and trials of emigration. For them, with some innuendo and sarcasm, the main argumentative tool was personal judgment based on factual assertion.

The other debate was engaged in by those who favoured emigration: where is best? The overwhelming conclusion was for European settlements, especially those with British antecedents and polities; here there was no true disagreement, even the young adventurers not being specially romantic in urge or language. Not surprisingly, the opinions correlate closely with the actual practice of British emigrants, the great majority of whom chose North America or the Antipodes. The main argumentative path is through question, actual and implied, and informed answer; the facts reported of course embed judgments, both favourable and unfavourable to particular countries. The seekers after fact are young and restless, city-bred and city-employed; the answerers are more varied in experience, of course, and proud of their funded knowledge. Several of the most fulsome are evidently agents for emigration companies or governments.

One other element complicates and saddens the debates: those who need and desire better opportunities, typically the city clerks, could not be encouraged by the general themes of those who purported to know the circumstances abroad. Almost all the detail dealt with agriculture, and consequently with rural society—or non-society. It might even be complained that the series, judged as a literary/sociological work, lacks interest because the heavy bias towards farming excludes what the twentieth century has come to associate even more exclusively with cities, that is, cultural and social life. The absence is noteworthy in the cases of Canada and Australia, and striking in that of the U.S.A., which had more than a century of urban experience.

The collective consensus could not well be overlooked: though prospects for agriculturists (including labourers), artisans, and those with at least small amounts of capital—especially if not exclusively those still single—were pleasing almost anywhere but at home (except perhaps for the capitalists, whose advantage was only comparative in degree), clerks could hope for nothing but a chance to become something other, and that other was not, on the established grounds of the marriage debate, as respectable as their current state. A punishing remodelling of body and psyche, only by hazard and hope successful, held little promise. History tells us that nonetheless decisions for distant dreams were made, and many of them fulfilled. But history also tells us that the vast majority, as the majority of the correspondents in the *Daily Telegraph* suggested they should, voted inertially and stayed home. What historians have not perhaps sufficiently told us is that they too survived and indeed prospered in their own ways which, if not our ways, may in the long view suffer little in comparison.

CHAPTER EIGHT

Conclusions

The compliment to its readers and itself that graced the final leading article on marriage or celibacy in the *Daily Telegraph* remains a just judgment: "A public discussion more remarkable in many respects has seldom been conducted; and we are glad to have furnished the arena for so much good sense, liveliness, practical wisdom, and hearty humanity as have marked the greater portion of the controversy."

The remarkable respects include two of special importance: first, the series was a "public discussion" of a rare kind, conducted in the "arena" provided by the *Daily Telegraph*; in this respect—perhaps intuited by, but certainly not fully apparent to the proprietors and editors of the *Daily Telegraph*—the series adumbrated if it did not initiate developments in the history of popular journalism and indeed of mass communications. Second, it revealed, through "good sense, liveliness, practical wisdom, and hearty humanity," previously muted lower middle-class attitudes to essential aspects of their lives; these attitudes resembled in many respects those of earlier times and other classes, but in their particulars, and especially in the way those particulars were expressed, they intimate major social and economic shifts that transformed British life in the next hundred years.

A brief comparison of the thematically similar series in *The Times* and the *Daily Telegraph* helps elucidate some aspects of these and subordinate issues, and assists understanding of the argumentative strategies of the leader writers and the correspondents in the *Telegraph*.

Initially, and not entirely superficially, there are both formal and thematic similiarities between the series in the two newspapers, as indicated in chapters 2 and 4 above. Formally, the series were initiated by a leading article and/or a news story on evils relating to prostitution, and a connection was posited between prostitution and the economic and social difficulties preventing early marriage. The editorial staff had opinions, usually strong ones, as did the correspondents, who often adopted the tone of debate, not only commenting on but attacking and refuting one another. Similar kinds of evidence were offered in both journals, such as reports of income and budgets, personal experience, and contrasting fictional cases.

Thematically, there are similarities in the general avoidance of debate on moral and religious issues, on which there is a tacit assumption of basic agreement; exhortation on moral grounds is common, however, while religious exhortation is rare. Marriage is seen as a natural and moral imperative by both sets of correspondents; there are a few who argumentatively (if not factually) opt for celibacy, but only because of the insurmountable obstacles to prudent marriage. Prudence to prevent cares and vexations is indeed assumed, and so the marriage question is never free from economic variables. Individual character, upbringing, and circumstances are admitted to be important in determining where prudence in marriage begins and ends. And there is comment in both journals on the difficulty of suitable young marriagables meeting and courting.

In almost all respects, however, just these similarities reveal, on analysis, significant differences, two of which have major importance. First, the difference in the amount of correspondence and editorial comment amounts to a difference in genre, with the bulk of material and coherence making for a more complex narrative line and richer "story" in "Marriage or Celibacy?" In The Times, the outside limit was about ten letters, with at most two leading articles, while the Telegraph ran to nearly three hundred letters, with five major and one minor leading articles. Second, in The Times the social level implied, both in joke and earnest, is aristocratic and upper middle-class, and so the nuances and necessities are not in parallel with those found in the letters of the Daily Telegraph's middle- and lower-middle-class correspondents. The absolute minimum for marriage in The Times of £300—which is certainly not a wage but an upper salary or investment income—signals a social level, often in the sense of the "Upper Ten," above all but a few of the Telegraph's readers, for whom the threatened deprivations are of necessaries, not of Broadwoods and broughams. Indeed the term "respectability" is not prominent in The Times because life without it is not contemplated.

Other differences, partly entailed by these two, are only slightly less important. For example, there is much less detail in the series in The Times, even when their comparative brevity is taken into account.[1] And, allowing for the fun of the Telegraph's correspondents, there is less facetiousness than in The Times. As to spoofs and verisimilitude, in

The Times fictions (such as those by Higgins) are presented as fact, whereas in the *Daily Telegraph* examples are most often set up as obvious fictions.[2] Further, and again not ignoring the difference in bulk, in the *Telegraph* the range of topics (especially in the turn to emigration as theme) and the intensity of feeling are wider and stronger. Finally, though *A Mother* and the "Belgravian" mothers appear in *The Times*, and female folly is excoriated, in it the point of view on marriage is much more controlled by male preoccupations. There is also much less warfare between the sexes than in the *Telegraph*, and, though in both the decision is anti-utopian, the value of "romance" is much higher in the *Telegraph*—among men as well as women.

Further analysis demonstrates again and again that "Marriage or Celibacy?" reflects the new importance and self-awareness of the lower middle classes, and shows their determining attitudes. That the middle classes generally were (as so often in history) in the ascendant is abundantly documented, even if one does not go into the metaphoric contortions of Duncan Crow, who says, "Like a worm in motion, the middle part of society was thickening as it closed up towards the front part and drew away from the tail."[3] And by definition, the lower middle classes were part of the middle classes; though in much more intimate contact with the tail and less proximate in all ways to the head, they were with the bunching middle in many respects. In particular, though the cost of living had risen and was rising very little, collectively they felt under greater economic pressure,[4] for reasons outlined by W.R. Greg, who held that the *"style of living"* had "advanced in an extraordinary ratio," so that

however frugal, however unostentatious, however rational we may be, however resolute to live as we think we ought, and not as others do around us, it is, as we shall find, simply *impossible* not to be influenced by their example and to fall into their ways, unless we are content either to live in remote districts or in an isolated fashion. The result is that we need many things that our fathers did not, and that for each of these many things we must pay more.[5]

Banks, locating the change in attitude in the 1850s and 1860s, comments that the "range of satisfactions considered appropriate for civilized existence expanded at an alarming rate and involved all those who numbered themselves among the middle classes in habits of expenditure which they would not find it easy to give up should they be called upon to do so."[6] That is, in Crow's words, there was a significant rise in the "standard of living, regarded both as a norm to which the middle classes aspired and as a level which they attained."[7] But for the lower middle class the aspiration was more available than the attainment.

Persuasion

Attention to the rhetoric of leading articles and letters helps illuminate the distinctive qualities of the series. The rhetoric is not unique, of course, sharing basic elements with other examples of the genres earlier and later, and indeed with all communications. But the special qualities of the series in the *Daily Telegraph* are revealed by examination of the types of narrative and argument developed, the kinds of authority and evidence adduced, the relations with the assumed audience posited and developed, and the writers' intentions; and this examination also enables an analysis of beliefs.

The distinctiveness is evident in the leading articles, which are rich with material inviting rhetorical analysis. The *Telegraph*, like other newspapers, distinguished among kinds of leading articles. The "first" leader, political in nature, during the parliamentary session normally followed the report of debate in the Houses.[8] Another type, often occupying the "second leader" slot, touched on "literary, artistic, social, or biographical" topics, so described by one of the main leader writers, George Augustus Sala, who may well have written the first two in the *Telegraph* series, which fall into the "social" category.[9] Such leaders were part essay on a topical theme (usually related to an active news story), and part sermon on evils (of varying degrees) displaying a prophetic anger at the disobedience of moral maxims by identified villains (including the populace as a whole, excepting only by implication the writer and the readers), warning of great danger, and exhorting to shun evil and cleave to good.[10] "Third" leaders might touch on any issue of the day, while the fourth slot was generally reserved for more facetious comment.

The major leaders originated in discussions between the proprietors and the editorial staff,[11] who acted (in modern parlance) as "gatekeepers," determining subject and approach.[12] They were written quickly to order, but on well-established patterns, such as those seen in the leaders of 16 and 19 June, 1868, which both have the same goal—action against the great social evil—and employ similar demands and devices. In them, as is normal, the editorial eye sees all, and comprehends everything but continued inaction in the face of evil.[13]

Like other authors, the editorial writers were attempting to modify or strengthen their readers' beliefs as a means to induce better or to maintain good behaviour. Their attempts encompass the traditional three kinds of appeal, from character, to reason, and to emotion. The appeal from character (the "ethical" appeal) is most obviously embedded in the "editorial we," which assumes general authority, but also draws the audience into agreement; as well it gives the paper opportunities for self-reference and occasionally self-celebration ("we have forced the public mind to be aware"). Also, it makes easier of acceptance any assertions of good qualities (either rational or emotional) that are by assumption shared with their "good" readers—and there are of course no others, all villains being outside the *Telegraph* family. The praise of the correspondents and the detailed summary and quotation from their letters, both of which serve to unite the newspaper and its readers, further develop the *ethos*. Also, there is a reflexive ethical power in forceful rational and emotional devices, especially once a commonality of belief is established or assumed.

Editorialists must employ (and seemingly enjoy employing) abbreviated forms of rational proof, but in this they are not different from others limited to brief communications—or indeed to most writers. Their inductions must depend on limited examples, supported by assertions of their typicality, as was seen in the first two editorials' discussion of individual cases of procurement and seduction, as well as of such lax authorities as the Lord Mayor. Another inductive device is the series of assertions, questions, solutions, which, if persuasively complete, implies a total induction, as well as (ethically) a resolute determination to examine all the facts. Deductions are perforce often dependent on suspect transitional inferential words ("therefore," "because," "since," etc.), though occasionally "if . . . then" (sometimes in a series) signals a hypothetical proposition. Among the suspect kinds of rational proof are analogy, most strongly evidenced in the leader comparing the Coles and Belgravians, and the citation of authority, which is objectively a fallacious or emotional appeal (especially when the authority is a clichéd maxim or quotation, both perdurable workhorses of the editorialist), but can properly be viewed as a collapsed appeal to reason, claiming but not displaying its epistemic base. Classification, evident for example in the early references to both legal and medical "treatment" as part of the crusade against sin, also has the rational appeal of systematic investigation. The main rational proof, however, is one that minimally falls into the rational category, namely, strongly assertive sentences, particularly to begin the exordium and to follow criticism of belief and action: they typically take the form of "the fact is that" ("we all know that," "no one will question that"), in which the sceptical and cynical will see assumption of the conclusion. The matching device towards the end of leaders is the rhetorical question, which has a similar rational status and performs the dispositional function of introducing a call to action.

There can be little doubt, however, that the greatest appeal in these leading articles is emotional, most evident in the first two leaders. The strong condemnation of the "merchants" of crime and disease is carried by labelling, or what may be called epithetical argument, in which the cumulative effect of the diction of damnation is the urge to action, essential if exhortation (the leader's mode) is to succeed. In contrast, there is some positive labelling (allied to sloganeering), as when reference is made to a "true man's pity and reverence for woman." That the procurer-traders are vile beyond normal measure is established by powerful appeals *ad misericordiam*, in which the innocence and frailty of the victims are stressed, not least by associating them with the unsophisticated rural poor. The judgment is supported by heavy irony, such as clearly inappropriate characterizations given in quotation marks— "Christian," "value-received," "commodity." As indicated above, these, along with the appeals to patriotism and to popular sentiment, work also to strengthen the ethical appeal of the newspaper, a guarantee of rectitude in the future as well as the present. Other minor devices that heighten affect (in part apparently by stimulating physical reactions) are seen throughout the leaders in alliterative and semantic doubling, the tripling in series with *anaphora*, a breathless or angry breaking off (*aposiopesis*), the similar rushing along without marked punctuation (*asyndeton*), the use of exclamation marks (known also as "marks of admiration").

In general, editorials are one-shot affairs, presented as novel (i.e., still essentially "news"), even though the shoot-out is often repeated without reference to earlier instances. Such is the major impression given by those that I have here treated as a series when they are read individually, except for the first two, which appeared only three days apart, and found their origin in the same news story. But certainly no one could know that the article of 16 June was an initial move in what became the series "Marriage or Celibacy?" The final three editorials, however, while not making reference to the preceding ones, are responses to the letters, and give the series shape, though only the final one explicitly does so by drawing the curtain.

The leaders then frame the series, but its narrative line is determined by the letters. Patterns in their rhetoric are revealing of assumptions and tendencies. In summary, the opening *exordia* establish the relation between medium and writers: the newspaper (this particular newspaper) is seen as aiming at the general good, specifically by allowing space, characterized as "valuable," for this discussion, which is of (a) significance, (b) utility, (c) interest: the praise encourages the continuing of the series, and initially justifies the individual correspondent's contribution.

Further justification depends on the assertion of authority to support the expressed beliefs. In the early letters, given that marriage with family is accepted as the normal state, there is virtually no room for questioning its validity as the norm. Major issues in every life are the marriage question, and how and where to live. The subjects being universally interesting (to those married, to those who may and/or wish to marry, and even to those who have forsworn marriage), and in their abstract form timeless, there are general authorities: the word of God and the church as rule-setting, and group experience as factual guide. Group experience is found in maxims and also in literary quotations that can be seen as classic (and therefore as having achieved the status of wisdom literature): these therefore appear abundantly in the *confirmatio*. Specific authorities are useful for specific judgments about present conditions as refining and giving force to universal injunctions: so individuals' observations are needed—this is the special justification, worded to reveal the qualification of point of view (status, age, occupation), not of commanding insight (usually the claim is modest in extent and wording). These elements constitute the *exordium*: an initial *pro forma* "Dear Sir," accepting and asserting the relation of writer and recipient (who is of course only a mediator); praise of the *Daily Telegraph* (personified as "you," the Editor who is also "Dear Sir"); and assertion of point of view. All of these constitute elements of the ethical proof, building on the recognition that one who plays by the rules is a good person, deserving an audition.

The next essential element is a placing of the following discussion in context, or letting the readers know what they need to know to understand (known in classical terms as *narratio*). Typically one finds, first, a brief statement indicating that the correspondent has followed the series thus far, with an equally brief judgment about one or more of the correspondents as providing an entry for a statement of thesis, and a description of self to justify the point of view. (Sometimes the modesty takes the form of saying of course the point of view is limited—but still valid.) There is usually not much room for a clear outline of the following argument (*divisio*), but adumbration is handled adequately.

The main part of the letters is given to proof, argument for and against (*confirmatio* and *refutatio*). Here is easily accommodated some anecdotal material, which also energizes the account and allows for the play of dialogue, characterization, and various forms of humour. Indeed the main proof derives from this kind of material, supported by loose deductive arguments; induction is greatly varied, as will be explained below, but may be summarized as depending on assertions of the "everybody knows" kind.[14] Refutation is directed against earlier correspondents on the basis of asserted fact and undermining of their authority as biased or limited or simply mistaken (sometimes their cited authorities are dismissed, often by sarcasm or by counter-authorities of higher status). An alternative is to present straw-folk who hold views reprehensible because of their folly, silliness, or evil nature (often portrayed as selfishness): these include such targets as Belgravian mammas, girls of the period, young men of the period, romantic idealists, and heartless cynics—of course some of the straw is used with the mud of actual correspondents to make bricks.

The conclusion (*peroratio*) is typically short, consisting of a reiteration of the thesis, reinforced by a maxim or pithy restatement, with some attempt at ethical appeal, not using new material, but repeating some from the *exordium* or *narratio*, and frequently incorporating, like the leading articles, an appeal for action. The final rhetorical appeal is in the signature that often explains or emphasizes the point of view; in more than a few cases, an apt signature is integrated with the syntax of the final sentence to form a telling period.

These comments are descriptive of the correspondence as a whole. Some qualifications are needed for the letters dealing predominantly with the desirability of and prospects for emigration, because the kinds of expertise needed for successful marriage and successful emigration were quite different. On marriage there was a generally shared body of experience, even those unwed having first-hand experience of family life; many writers ask for details about budgets, but nothing exotic was expected by way of answer. The atmosphere was that of debate, not of question-and-answer. On emigration, however, there were those who did not know much that was needed, and their appeal to the knowledgeable is more dominant: "Would someone please inform me . . . ?" And the answers are suitably detailed, presented as factual narrative, without any of the fancy that marks some marriage narratives. There is indeed throughout a sense of "fact," even when there is controversy about the accuracy of some of the reports from abroad. The move into the main body of the letter is more abrupt, though courtesy is not for-

gotten and accolades of the *Telegraph* continue; there is almost no literary allusion or reference, and the few quotations are from experts who
give facts as the basis for opinion. There is, therefore, a much narrower
basis for authority, though that basis is (for the empiricist) much
firmer.

What merits more attention is what holds both kinds of argument
together: the positive authority associated with one's own side and the
negative authority of one's opponents in a debate. The matter of
authority is best approached through consideration of the form of
debate.

That there is debate is established by the many allusions to other
participants in the series; indeed these hold the series together just as
much as the commonality of topic. The normal argumentative tactic is
a soft one, for often the references to allies and opponents among the
other correspondents are general; however, ignoring these,[15] no less
than 60 per cent of the letters mention, commend, or criticize other correspondents singly or in groups, sometimes tellingly quoting actual
words or summarizing arguments, usually so that they can be controverted. In all, 93 correspondents are cited,[16] some repeatedly; looking
at the citations as debate, one can identify 35 correspondents who are
mentioned neutrally, 48 who are controverted, and 54 who are supported by others.[17]

While it might be thought that the debate on emigration could be
decisive, settling whether Canada or Natal or the States of the River
Plate was the best destination for clerks, reflection suggests that the outcome was in actuality not very different from that of the marriage
debate. Quite possibly someone here or there may have acted on what
the *Telegraph* said was the majority vote, that is, no marriage for clerks on
less than £200, but it cannot be pretended—and the *Telegraph* did not
pretend—that the question had been resolved. It is quite apparent that
the lower middle class continued to marry (and be given in marriage) on
lesser amounts. Not all of them read the *Telegraph*, but one can safely
assume that even among that not inconsiderable group most ignored
the apparent decision. I would not say "went against it," for that would
imply that they consciously took what was judged to be the losing side,
thus making it the winning side in the active world if not in the printed
word. The practical point is that for individuals, and especially for those
moving, as human beings will, into marriageable age, the question
remained open. From the newspaper's viewpoint, all the better, as it
would never be short of "marriage copy." And, similarly, for "emigration copy." So this debate, intense and serious as it was for many, if light

and frivolous for a few, was just a debate like any other. No vote could conclusively terminate either issue, just as there is no potential end to "Resolved that the world is going to hell in a hand-bucket."

Debate lives on evidence, and evidence depends on authority to establish, bolster, and illustrate arguments. As seen earlier, the correspondents generally assume that the venue gives validity to the debate: not that the *Telegraph* is itself infallible, but the "forum" it provides authenticates the views expressed—even though they are often in opposition to one another, they have the force of "authenticity," of "sincerity." Those attributes are also, by assumption, typical of the *Telegraph*, as is implied in the complimentary openings of so many of the letters: such valuable space would not be given to this series were it not in itself (and hence in its components) valuable.

In this respect the two parts of the series differ: among the letters concerning marriage, as argued above, are some whose authenticity and sincerity are open to question. Indeed a few appear to be the kind of spoofs to which all newspaper readers of the period should have been alerted.[18] Some may even say—though I do not—that because almost all the letters are signed by pseudonyms, and to that extent written "in character," they are unreliably "fictitious." However, their contents have validity, because even if the origins are suspect, the newspaper must have believed that the opinions and experiences related would ring true, through what may be called a willing suspension of belief. Moreover, even though most of the correspondents on emigration are also pseudonymous in the fashion of the time, suspicion about them generally seems silly; the self-interest of the emigration agents is self-evident; and while there is some obvious stretching of the facts, and some episodes are aesthetically shaped, the question of "authenticity" does not arise.

Other interesting contrasts between the two sets of letters emerge when, accepting that persuasion is an abiding concern, one considers the kinds of authority used and cited. In both parts there is very little overt reference to reason as authority for belief; indeed, as in most persuasive communications including (as mentioned above) editorials, deductive inference is almost never hinted at, though there are a few "if . . . then" sequences, and the normal logic words appear frequently though casually. Contents of the great inductive basket are of course common property in their normal miscellaneous fashion, paralleling and absorbing such *topoi* as comparison (what are the conditions and effects of French marriages?) and analogy ("savages" and "Irish," for example).

But what dominates throughout is the appeal to empirical "facts" as settling questions: the search for, and assertion of, this kind of authority (the expert, the experienced) is evident in both parts, particularly in the demand for and supply of actual budgets in the earlier letters and the reports of actual conditions overseas in the later ones. Both kinds have been extensively illustrated above, but a few additional comments assist conclusions.

One well-regarded source of opinion appears only in the correspondence concerning emigration, that is, mention of and quotation from private letters. For instance, *E.C. Booth* says, "I have just received a letter from a settler with whom I am well acquainted."[19] Quite often, this kind of information has derived additional authority from publication: *Professional* refers to the Rev. Richard Wake, of Chicago, who "wrote a series of letters, published in the columns of the *Christian World*, advocating emigration of the middle classes to the Western States of America, and so numerous were the inquiries made at the time that he arranged to come to England, and publicly meet those desirous of information."

Sometimes in emigration letters the personal authority is no more than that, not in itself inconsiderable, of a reference librarian, directing inquirers to established sources. They are seldom, however, as free from bias as such librarians. For example, *Kangaroo* directs prospective emigrants to "the colonial newspaper files and books of reference at the Australian news rooms";[20] and *An Intending Emigrant to Natal* tells the like-minded (and those who should be like-minded) that the "Natal Government agent is now in England, and he will be happy to give every information concerning the colony."

The most elaborate account of evidence in these letters is that of W.J.I., who presents (in lengthy passages, seemingly more appropriate to a pamphlet, that would certainly preclude the publication of such a letter in modern newspapers) the information supplied by Mr Frank Ruffin, of Summer-hill, Chesterfield Co., Virginia, which includes facts from the *Massachusetts Plowman* of May or June, 1857, and a "Report on Farms" of 1856 by a committee of the Seaboard Agricultural Society, and gives as well the views of his friend, Mr William Sayre, who lives near Norfolk, Virginia.

The appeal of authentic personal experience is awarded strong status: I have seen this, done that; I have no reason to lie; you should believe me. Counter-arguments do not challenge the basic assumption about the validity of the first-hand; they take issue with the accuracy of the report and more often with the inferences drawn from it. In an increasingly democratic age, the individual's account is *prima facie* valid, at best but with difficulty dismissed as "it may be so for you, but you are not typical, and/or your perception is distorted." In the letters on marriage and family, who indeed could know better than those who tell their own tales? (And perhaps most so if an anecdote is told in dialect, as by the Scot, *Hannah*, quoted in chapter 5.)

In the letters on emigration, there is a similar dependence on personal experience. For example, *N.Z.*, countering *D.B.*'s views on Albert Land, establishes his authority simply by saying "I was in the colony at the time"; *W.P.* asserts that, as "one of the second party that sailed in May, 1863, in the *Annie Wilson*, I can give . . . a little information"; and *Veritas* feels "considerable confidence, from the varied experience" he has had "of North America and Colonial life," and obviously expects his readers to think his confidence well placed. The qualification in *Canadian J.P.*'s comment—"I only speak from my own experience (from small beginnings) as a trader, a large landowner, and an agriculturalist"—is an instance of the ironic appeal from humility, not offered or to be taken at face value.

Some already cited offer further authentication of their views by indicating that they have had wide circulation or acceptance, *W. Parker Snow* being the prime example: "About ten years ago I lectured and also wrote much upon this question. . . . The plan I submitted in my little work on the subject would effect much at little cost." Compare *M. and C.*: "Believing in that principle [of mutual aid and cooperation], we laid our plan before the Brazilian Government, . . . and we have consequently had 250,000 acres placed in our name for this express purpose of association, to which our emigrants alone can proceed."

Sometimes one can detect an interesting variant when the empirical authority of others is not only cited but quietly transferred to self. This tactic is especially evident when family members' opinions are relied on. Here the difference from the letters on marriage is less in reliability than tone: compare *Benedick*—"I recently suggested to my wife that we should keep fewer servants, and she replied that if I did not mind the rooms being rather dusty, and the cook looking a little dark about the nose when she went to open the door, she saw no difficulty in the way"—with *W.L.*—"my brother is at present engaged in making arrangements for a party to go out"—or with *Ring*—"I have a cousin who went to New Zealand under similar circumstances." However, fact more than opinion is implied in the reports quoted above of *Roamer Returned*, and those given by "near and dear friends in Canada West" (*Pioneer*), or by "some friends of mine, who were City clerks,

[who] went out to Australia two years since on 'spec.' and without capital" (J.F.H.). Perhaps less powerful, as depending on remembered oral testimony, but still associated with the self is the account of A.J.S., who, concerning the River Plate, "can only speak from information derived during my return voyage on board the packet," but attempts to add force by saying that the men he listened to "were better judges of the state of the country than those who sit comfortably at home, and form ideal and romantic notions of camp life." And the probative power of iteration is asserted by *Canadian J.P.*, who has not just heard but "repeatedly heard" the views on Canada of "Americans of the extreme north"—who also have the authority derived from proximity to evidence.

The empirical appeal is even more prevalent than this surface evidence shows, for it is often disguised. For instance, references to elements of common knowledge embed personal ethical, moral, and rational authority drawing on fact. Though the implications need not be drawn out, allusion and judgment meld to show that the writer is the right sort. For example, the most common of the citations, to the "Girl of the Period," appears in twenty-five letters, always embedding a judgment, such as that of *A Bachelor Curate*, whose beloved is "as brave a girl as ever stepped, honest and true, with nothing of 'The Period' about her." Both argument and conclusion are clinched by epithet: the implication is that anyone who disagrees with the negative assessment of the Girl of the Period is uninformed or vile. Similar in kind is the allusion to the Madame Rachel affair by *A Few True Girls of the Period*, who think no extended comment is necessary on "the two old women who have cut such a sorry figure in the eyes of the public lately"—"sorry figure" is sufficient empirical argument.[21]

It can also be argued that the appeal to "great names," authority pure and simple, while normally disconnected from any epistemic evidence, rests on the belief that they should be listened to because they have fully examined the facts and properly pronounced in an *authoritative* way. This tactic is most commonly employed in the series with reference to recent writers, though there are some allusions to the Classics. The most prominent hero (or villain, for authority is a debating device) is John Stuart Mill, who appears as author of the *Principles of Political Economy* and/or "the honourable member for Westminster" in nine letters extolling his wisdom on imprudent marriage or calling for dismissal of his "pack of trash."[22] There are about five references to Malthus, and two to each of Darwin and Talleyrand. Disraeli and Cobden are each mentioned once, the citations illustrating the soft and hard ends of such authoritative appeals: *Paterfamilias* refers scornfully to those who have "no more confidence in the Almighty than in Mr. Disraeli," while *E.C. Booth* (disguised slightly as *E.C.B.*) need say only that the Illinois Central railroad system was "much praised by Mr. Cobden." It may be noted that in most cases only the name need be invoked, without any quotation or specific detail; exceptional is even such a reference as that of *J.A.C.V.* to the Malthusian phrase "preventive check," knowledge of which has notoriously "long prevailed in this country."

Other allusions to well-known names associate the writers with the virtues of the models,[23] and the few allusions to recent history and contemporary events are essentially illustrative, though they also bolster the authority of those who cite them,[24] especially in such cases as *Benedick*'s very mixed notice of Allan Gardiner, "the noble soldier of the cross in Patagonia," whose folly brought on his death.

Much the same is true of citation of the Classics. In high cultural works, of course, the Victorian period continued in only somewhat abated bulk the bolstering of argument and *ethos* by citation of classical tags, frequently obscure; and authors often used the classics for narrative frameworks, themes, or analogies, in all cases implying a careful and detailed study designed to impress, and to inscribe the writer's name in the company of the learned. In this series, where almost all the references occur in letters relating to marriage, the echoes are seldom heard and comparatively vague, and the reverberations slight: though still intended to impress, the allusions imply an audience much easier to impress in this respect at least. They include single mentions of Homer, the Aristotelian "golden mean," Scylla and Charybdis, Strephon and Phillis, Arcadian life, the charms of Venus and the wisdom of Minerva, the altar of Hymen, "Glorious Lucrece,"[25] and the Roman who lost the world for love (borrowed from Shakespeare's Antony). On the historical side, there are references (ironical) to Augustus's folly in taxing the bachelors, and (sincere) to the women of Carthage cutting off their "raven, golden, and chestnut locks" so that they could be made into rope and cord for the besieged navy. Caesar is adapted by *D.F.P.* to read "Par l'amour je vins, je vis, et je vainquis," and *J.P.M.* quotes what he calls "the old song" that each should "learn to know himself."

The numerous citations of English literary figures can be described similarly. In some of the early letters (when the debate is still sited in Belgravia) there are high cultural references,[26] but gradually the emphasis turns to more broadly available authorities with a general rather than a special appeal. Typical of the early ones are quotations from Shakespeare, not arcane but not in common currency, as from *Macbeth* by *Benedick* and *Erastes* (the "pale fears and half-nerved manhood" which "lets the dare not wait upon the would"), and also *Paterfamilias* ("to prick the sides of his intent").[27] More typical are the simple allusion to *King Lear* by *Single Man* and the echo of *Hamlet* by *Colonist* ("there is something rotten in the state of" society), as well as all the allusions to *Much Ado about Nothing* through the name Benedick, whether in signature or text—"my Benedick life" (*A Clergyman, Aetat 47*), "Benedicks or bachelors" (*J.J.*).

It hardly matters whether the sources are known to letter writers who ask, after Sterne, "Do they manage these things better in France?", follow Goldsmith in deploring those who love "not wisely, but too well," or repeat after Milton the call to "pastures new" or sign a letter with his *"They Also Serve Who Only Stand and Wait."*[28] Most readers are, unlike the too nervously guilty scholar, willing to read authority from familiarity. This at least seems to be the case with the fully anonymous parallel citations, signalled by quotation marks but graced by no identities: "Possession is the grave of love!" (*Jane*), the "chartered libertine" of home (*Benedick*), their best "scenes and properties" (*T.T.*), "purple and fine linen" and "fare sumptuously every day" (*Bunny*).[29]

Nineteenth-century literary figures are also called into service, once more with the less obvious and more precise references occurring early in the series. Dickens, at the height of his fame, is first in their minds: *Benedick* mentions his *All the Year Round* and makes use of his "old lady who never went to sea" who consequently "dies triumphantly in bed," and others allude to *The Chimes* (*A Young Briton*), *Martin Chuzzlewit* (*Lucy*), and the edition of his works currently available in instalments (*Paterfamilias*). *Benedick* with cultured ease also produces allusions to Macaulay and Artemus Ward, while his foe in the lists, *Erastes*, chimes in with Browning and Tennyson.[30] Carlyle merits two quotations, one brief and one in this setting very extensive.[31] Only John Ruskin receives the compliment (from *Paigntonians*) of a similarly extensive quotation.[32] Much more typical are such brief hints as are provided by *Antipodes'* offhand reference to Goethe ("Faust's Margaret and the everlasting 'loves me, loves me not'"), and *Humanus's* mere allusion to Cobbett, his assumption clearly being that anyone worth sharing a belief with him will understand it.

These references to great names bear upon authority in different ways, some ethical, some emotional, and some rational, and while most correspondents try to associate the established writer's authority with themselves, others dissociate themselves from fallacious authority. Something of the range is revealed when *An English Girl* establishes her credentials by mentioning that she subscribes to Scott's novels, and *W.J.W.* places himself by ironic reference to Captain Mayne Reid's novels; *E.F.H.* alludes to "a kind of Claude Melnotte description," while *Colonista* dismisses Charles Kingsley's view that "weeping" is "a necessary feminine accomplishment." Froude's "Cat's Pilgrimage" has an admirable and timely message, says *Paterfamilias*.

The overlap in readership between the *Daily Telegraph* and one of its Liberal but "facetious contemporaries" is signalled by the three references to *Punch*, by *Spes*, *Pegging at It*, and *A Draper*, the last two of whom play on that running punch-line, quoted above, given as advice to the foolhardy, "Don't!"

Other easily identified allusions are properly classed with maxims and folk-sayings, for it seems likely that those who made them had no specific sources in mind. The most prominent of these is "love in a cottage," cited with varying degrees of scorn by no fewer than ten correspondents, who probably had no notion of its appearance in George Colman's play *The Clandestine Marriage*: "Love and a cottage! Eh, Fanny! Ah, give me indifference and a coach and six!" Similarly, no close knowledge is needed to appreciate Longfellow's "Life is real— life is earnest," quoted by *W.J.W.* and *An Eldest Daughter*; to understand *Colonista's* mention of Mrs Grundy; to take the point of *Caution's* oblique hint at Coleridge's "Ancient Mariner" ("wiser, if sadder, men"); or like *Prudens* to use the phrase "Coelebs in search of a wife" not as the title of a novel.

The effects of the common appeals to religious authority are similar. Most of them depend on simple citation of familiar passages in the Bible and the Book of Common Prayer. Nothing more than the citation is usually thought necessary, the invocation itself being sufficient proof: "Go and do likewise" (*Never Say Die*); "I say ... and a greater than I says ..., 'It is better to marry than to burn; don't be afraid—trust in God'" (*Paterfamilias*); "having nothing," to expect to marry a man "Possessing all things" (*A Young English Governess*); and perhaps most direct, "God said, six thousand years ago, 'It is not good for man to be alone'" (*Humanus*).[33] As with classical authorities, sometimes only a token is needed: *L.C.J.* refers to the golden calf, *A Plain Man* to Tobias and Sarah, and *C.L.W.* to Dives.[34]

A telling quotation is earnestly offered by *A Disciple of Malthus*, who denigrates selfish views by citing their source in the maxim of an archetypically bad man: "Cain pithily embodied them in the inquiry,

'Am I my brother's keeper?'" Similar instances include the good housewife's creed, "She looketh well to the ways of her household and eateth not the bread of idleness; her children rise up and call her blessed; her husband, also, he praiseth her" (*A Draper*), and the traditional warning, "the fathers having eaten sour grapes, and the children's teeth being set on edge" ("*They Also Serve Who Only Stand and Wait*").[35]

One obvious text in the matrimonial debate, "be fruitful, and multiply and replenish the earth," used by *Paterfamilias* and *Another Mechanic*, is also opened by analysis to a different conclusion when W.H.S. speaks of those who "'increase and multiply' to an enormous extent," but "do not 'replenish and subdue the earth.'"[36]

Sometimes authorities are combined, as by *Bread-Winner's Wife*: "An Englishman's house is his 'castle,' but for the sake of those dependent upon him he is obliged to take the stranger within his gates." Here the religious sanction is united with that most obvious in these letters, that is, proverbs, traditional maxims, aphorisms, old saws, usually placed in quotation marks, that condense folk wisdom in what appears under analysis to be mere clichéd assertion, but in fact carries in common communication tremendous weight.[37]

This too is at root an epistemic appeal, authenticated by unstated agreement that what condenses common experience expresses the truth about it. It is seen especially though not exclusively in letters dealing with that most common of experiences, family life. The most popular aphorism catches the message of the dominant prudent group: "When poverty comes in at the door, love flies out of the window." This is used, with minor variations, by eight correspondents, and no one disputes directly this "evidence," except by implying, without reference to the proverb, that such flighty love is not truly love. Aligned with this wisdom is "marry in haste, repent at leisure," cited by *A Matron*, *Pegging at It*, and *George*, the last uniting it with another popular warning, "Don't marry in haste, but look before you leap," also issued by the aptly named *Prudentia* and *A Woman*. Beware, say *Pegging at It*, *Cassio*, and *A Chief Clerk*, of the wolf at the door, while for *Three "Girls of the Period"* to enter marriage injudiciously would be "to jump out of the frying-pan into the fire," and *Antipodes* simply cautions that emigration for the unfit "would be a jump from a cool frying pan into a very hot fire." Similar advice comes from *Two Plain English Girls*, who know that one cannot "live upon love," while *Pro Bono Publico* reminds readers of "all the ills that married life is heir to." A slightly stronger effect is produced by "*They Also Serve Who Only Stand*

and Wait," who foresees "Nature's retribution on the direct infraction of her rule that 'food and feeders must be in equal ratio.'" An air of confident judgment is exuded by the comments of *A Woman, But Not a Slave,* who perhaps hardly needs say "that it is not all gold that glitters"; of *Home-Made Bread,* who notes that "the gilt wears off the 'gingerbread'"; and of *Beta,* who is pleased to say that "there are just as good fish in the sea."

As always, proverbial wisdom can be cited on the other side, and so it is not surprising that *A Woman* notes that "Providence does help those who help themselves," that *One Who Speaks from Experience* mentions the belief that "two can live as cheaply as one," that *G.L.M.* rhetorically asks, "Is it not better to wear out than to rust out?" and *Fabius* encourages bold action because "where there's a will there's a way." *Geo. Francis Train,* for potential emigrants, advances the last position by negative reinforcement: "Where there is a will there is a way, and in the Far West the weakest go to the wall." *Antipodes* is of like mind: "We must obey the policeman's behest; we must 'move on.'" As in that instance, such general moral advice pervades the calls to emigrate: "share and share alike" (*Five Years' Colonist*), "a stout heart to a stae brae" (*Fabius*), put your "shoulder to the wheel" and remember that "faint heart never won fair lady" (*Kangaroo*).

Some aphorisms seem designed mainly to maximize the appeal from character, suggesting a repository of wisdom by letting out bits of it *ad libitum,* but not specially giving authority to any particular belief: "Let him laugh most who laughs last" (*Clericus*), "verbum sap, &c." (*Vieux Moustache*), "The proof of the pudding is in the eating of it" (*A Woman*), and so on.[38]

What may be detected here is a subtle and gradual but determining shift in authority. Traditionally, great if not exclusive weight has been given to named and established authorities; to know, you go to those who are known to know. These are not forgotten or discredited in this series, but new force is being given to common agreement, to democratic coherence of views nicely summed up by *J.A.C.V.* in a maxim that itself sounds traditional: "What everybody says must be true." Sometimes the basis of belief emerges, not as Macaulay's notorious "every schoolboy knows," but in more equalizing variants on "everyone knows":

It is a well-known fact that one gentleman who wrote a most romantic work on the country actually dare not visit the settlement of Taranaki for fear of his deluded victims taking vengeance on him. (*J.N.*)

As everybody knows, Australia has quite enough population. (*An Intending Emigrant to Natal*)

[I]t is familiarly said, "A French family will live in comfort on the value of what is wasted in an English family of the same social position." (*T.C.C.*)

Without being as manifest as it is in these passages, the assumption that what "everyone knows is so" has great power in forcing those who don't know into making an embarrassing denial or nodding themselves into membership of the majority. And its effect is compounded by the strongly attractive force of the personal statement. This indeed is one of the main qualities that give this series a significant place in the history of popular media.

Messages

In summation of this rhetorical analysis, it is fair to say that the *Daily Telegraph* in 1868 was necessarily a child of its times, but also a recognizable parent of ours. It is not news that the virtually universal acceptance of economic and political democracy, at least as an ideal, has had profound effects—some disturbing—seen in journalism, caught essentially in the term "mass media," and in the recent vogue for "popular culture." And the 1860s in Britain were pivotal years.

With the lowering in price, newspapers were being bought by more people, and most of the new readers had lower middle-class attitudes, habits, and aspirations. It seems in hindsight obvious that newspapers would change in style, content, and utimately in format to accommodate—exploit if you will—that change. The proprietors of the *Daily Telegraph* were among the first to sense the need for change, though they did not fully or finally adapt to it. Certainly the paper of the 1860s looks to modern eyes, and on analysis is in fact, more like its daily competitors than like modern tabloids, but to readers then (witness Matthew Arnold) the style and content revealed shifts towards what came to be called populism.

The aptness to the times of "Marriage or Celibacy?" is even more apparent in this context. The editors were not ignorant of the fact that people are likely to buy newspapers that print their letters, and that are read by people like them (or like their image of themselves). As to the editorials, the obvious criteria are that they should speak to people like themselves in their language, slightly elevated in rhetoric and firm in authority, should deal with everyday concerns and place blame liberally but not on the readers. The general attitude is well expressed in a letter from *Moderation*, who praises the *Telegraph* for giving space to "Marriage or Celibacy?", a topic that has "at least a thousand times more real importance than any of the 'great questions' of the day, though smug Philistines cannot see it, and would prefer that your space were devoted to reports of vestry speeches, or letters on the rival railway lines from Pilegorskaia to Nerpinski."

As argued in chapter 2, the *Telegraph* was forwarding a revolution by this addition of "opinion" from its readers—moving authority from Leaders to Readers, and, by encouraging the readers to feel part of the enterprise, giving them the power to signal public attitudes. Another tendency was thus forwarded, to exalt opinion, valued as individual but judged more powerful the more widely shared.

In a perceptive description of the invention of another forerunner of what can be called participatory journalism, J. Paul Hunter says of a late seventeenth-century journal that entertained questions from its readers and answered them in print: "Like late twentieth-century 'two-way' radio programs that are networked, syndicated, and rebroadcast, *The Athenian Mercury* found a free source of material and a public that would pay to hear itself puzzle aloud."[39] In fact, the most popular television broadcasts of a similar kind, as well as columns and pro-grammes given over to "advice," involve not so much puzzlement as debate and assertion, and I feel justified in adapting Hunter's remark, saying that like late twentieth-century popular programmes, the *Daily Telegraph* found a free source of material and a public that would pay to listen to themselves. *Vox populi, vox Telegraph*—and finally *lex patriae*.

Thus may be explained the apparent paradox that correspondents were asking for opinions from people like themselves on matters where more authoritative information was available: the goal is expo-sure, not resolution, of issues. The rhetoric of urgency can accommo-date the repetitions of participatory journalism for our advice-giving species, whose members like to talk and hear talk about themselves, and hear themselves talk and see themselves heard.

Other conclusions arise from consideration of major themes in "Mar-riage or Celibacy?" As has been demonstrated, the letters are both descriptive and prescriptive: they show how their authors saw their own situations, their problems, morals, dreams. In many ways, espe-cially to those who find no greater pleasure than in scorning bourgeois values, the series might be thought merely to emphasize what is already known about the high Victorian middle class. But in addition to providing more and sometimes surprising information of a different kind from otherwise muted voices, the series certainly offers important implications that suggest if not shattering, at least remoulding of stereotypes.

Some of the implications need little further exposition. The series makes evident the widespread awareness—in some circles hopeful and in others fearful—of the imminent effects of bringing the lower-middle-class males within the political pale; having been given the right to vote in 1867, they were about to exercise it for the first time in an election. In the earlier Victorian period there was much discomfort—to use a mild term—about giving the franchise to the uneducated, and certainly for more than a few in the 1860s the proposal still seemed utter folly;[40] what this series suggests is that if education can be measured by easy yet controlled fluency, direct yet witty statement, focused yet ranging argument, then those who wrote these letters, and those like them, fully merited the vote. Focus on the Education Act of 1871 tends to underplay the level of literacy that is evidenced not just by letters like these but by the huge circulation of the *Telegraph*.

This conclusion runs in parallel with another that the series establishes. Concentration on both high and low Victorian culture often hides the social significance of the mushrooming of the commercial and financial industries, running alongside the growth of government agencies—an amazing growth in the clerkly class. (In the 1860s and into the 1870s, the clerks were male; only in the 1881 census did female clerks and secretaries begin to appear, and thereafter their numbers grew rapidly.)[41] If the French characterization of "a nation of shopkeepers" is acceptable for the early years of the century, it seems equally apt to see by its end a nation of clerks. In any case, appreciation of their *mentalité* is central to understanding the age. And it is not captured by generalizations based on social-control or economic-base theories.

For instance, this series gives examples, both negative and positive, of the perceived power of emulation, whether social and pernicious or moral and refining, and so helps explain why revolutionary changes were not forthcoming. There is little or nothing here of the deference that has been debated as a staying force, but there is much evidence of the social adhesive resulting from perceptions, attitudes, goals, and apprehensions shared across economic class boundaries. That conclusion seems firm, even though to these folk the boundaries did not have many gates allowing considerable material improvement.

One illustration is seen in the expressed attitudes to respectability and decency. A generation earlier, Thomas Love Peacock gave satirical voice to prevalent notions:

CAPTAIN FITZCHROME Is it come to this, that you make a jest of my poverty? Yet is my poverty only comparative. Many decent families are maintained on smaller means.

LADY CLARINDA Decent familes: aye, decent is the distinction from respectable. Respectable means rich, and decent means poor. I should die if I heard my family called decent. And then your decent family lives in a snug little place: I hate a little place; I like large rooms and large looking-glasses, and large parties, and a fine large butler, with a tinge of smooth red in his face; an outward and visible sign that the family he serves is respectable; if not noble, highly respectable.[42]

When this is compared with the statements in the *Daily Telegraph* in 1868 one sees not just differences in time but also in perception of class. The lower middle class was appropriating and redefining respectability in their own terms. Also, and here time was on their side—they were associating it with decency, and strove for both, while, as the series in *The Times* indicate, the upper middles took both for granted—and worried about gentility, a condition that was becoming outmoded and was in any case beyond the range of the lower middles.

They in fact deplored too great expectations as sheer folly, and yet they displayed in this forum no class hatred, just as they looked for no state aid. To a few, self-sufficiency entailed stern and unrelenting competition, but to more it was easily compatible with cooperation: social beings help themselves by sharing tasks with non-competitors, but help themselves they must.

From nature they expected no assistance. What can be read here is not just Darwinianism, though it is evident, but what lay behind Darwinianism, Malthusianism. To the direct references to the pessimistic parson can be added those to J.S. Mill, which are infused with cautions against imprudent breeding, but the evidence goes beyond explicit allusions. The effective silencing of neo-Malthusians, those who advocated contraception, made some wary of even mentioning Malthus, but his views were widely known. It has been said that Malthus "was the 'best-abused man of the age.'. . . For thirty years it rained refutations."[43] But the rain only germinated the seed, to use a perverse metaphor. It is not an exaggeration to say that Malthus provides the texts for these sermons, even if chapter and verse are not given. Probably, indeed, they could not be given precisely, for such are the perils of reputation.

Without, then, claiming that the correspondents were in general aware that coincidence if not causality was involved, one may cite key passages in Malthus that lie behind the assumptions and words of the readers of the *Telegraph*. First, with reference to general attitudes towards economic motives, he identifies the principle "by which population is kept down to the level of the means of subsistence" as "the grinding law of necessity, misery, and the fear of misery."[44] As a result, the wise are prudent, Malthus observes, calling in an even greater authority: "Dr Adam Smith has very justly observed that nations as well as individuals grow rich by parsimony and poor by profusion, and that, therefore, every frugal man was a friend and every spendthrift an enemy to his country."[45] Consequently for Malthus (as for Mill in the passages quoted from him) moral responsibility is entailed:

[Those who had turned their attention to the true cause of society's difficulties would urge] that some check to population . . . was imperiously called for; that the most natural and obvious check seemed to be to make every man provide for his own children; that this would operate in some respect as a measure and guide in the increase of population, as it might be expected that no man would bring beings into the world, for whom he could not find the means of support; that where this notwithstanding was the case, it seemed necessary, for the example of others, that the disgrace and inconvenience attending such a conduct should fall upon the individual, who had thus inconsiderately plunged himself and innocent children in misery and want.

The institution of marriage, or at least, of some express or implied obligation on every man to support his own children, seems to be the natural result of these reasonings in a community under the difficulties we have supposed.[46]

One of Malthus's strongest points is fundamental in "Marriage or Celibacy?", namely the connection between early marriages and improvidence, entailing social degradation:

I think it will be allowed, that no state has hitherto existed . . . where the manners were so pure and simple, and the means of subsistence so abundant, that no check whatever has existed to early marriages, among the lower classes, from a fear of not providing well for their families, or among the higher classes, from a fear of lowering their condition in life.[47]

Can a man consent to place the object of his affection in a situation so discordant, probably, to her tastes and inclinations? Two or three steps of descent in society, particularly at this round of the ladder, where education ends and ignorance begins, will not be considered by the generality of people as a fancied and chimerical, but a real and essential evil. . . .

These considerations undoubtedly prevent a great number in this rank of life from following the bent of their inclinations in an early attachment.[48]

With changes in the times, by the 1860s these passages more closely resembled the attitudes of the upper than the lower middle class; the latter would not (and properly would not) consider themselves below the point where "ignorance begins." Though seemingly more exposed to this kind of degradation, they were less concerned about "steps of descent" than the upper middles.

Perhaps more surprisingly, Malthus advances the key relation between delayed marriage and prostitution that impelled the series.[49] Arguing that "the preventive check" operates in "all old states" and "through all the classes of the community," he notes that the effects of "these restraints upon marriage are but too conspicuous in the consequent vices that are produced in almost every part of the world, vices that are continually involving both sexes in inextricable unhappiness."[50]

To point to these parallels is not to assert that middle-class marriage had not changed in a half-century. The terms of real and earnest life were not so stringent as they had been, for poverty was not, in absolute terms, so prevalent, even if people had genuine reason to fear it. The improvement is masked for late twentieth-century commentators by the dominance now of notions of relative poverty, which control definitions of "the poverty line," usually ignoring the relation of income and expenditure to age.[51]

With the distinction between absolute and relative poverty in mind, one wishes that, with so much detail about budgets, the series provided firmer evidence about differences in typical expenditures between those with low and those with high incomes.[52] It is not surprising that a higher proportion of income went on food and shelter for those at the lower end of the wage scale (there is about a 10 per cent difference), or that less was spent by them on servants. What needs emphasis is that what many then and almost all now view as "necessaries" were to them luxuries—and luxuries were not to be thought of. The coming changes are hinted at, however, in attitudes towards seaside vacations, indicating perhaps less a different attitude towards the good life than the decreased cost of travel. That is, "affordability" plus habit makes necessaries of luxuries.

What is abundantly evident is that for the majority in this group it was thought proper—i.e., rational and moral—for sense to rule over sentiment, and, consequently, they put a premium on foresight and caution. That economic considerations were central in their lives points not to selfishness but to realism, there being few external supports for the indigent, and those that were available sullying the dignity that was imperative for self-respect as well as respectability.[53] Another key text for the times was available in Mill's *On Liberty*: "The term duty to oneself, when it means anything more than prudence, means self-respect or self-development."[54]

In other times work may be seen as a matter of choice or a sign of grace, but for them it was primarily a means of survival. This reality granted, regularity and routine are not only insurance against dismissal and disaster, but also means of giving value to life. Dickens, who aimed to present the romantic side of familiar things, was brilliantly able to satirize their unromantic side, as in his portrayal of Dombey and Podsnap—but Dickens's fear of poverty and disgrace was evident in his own life and business dealings. Like all geniuses, he was not a model, and his satire is more effective at indicating excess than at presenting clear alternatives. For most in his times—and a large number since—routine gives meaningful structure, and separates the elect from the reprobate. Podsnap epitomizes for spectators a denial of spontaneity and freedom; for players in the game of life (when he never kept anyone waiting) he was illustrating a necessary if regrettable reality.

Heightening such attitudes was the view taken of marriage, which was not a relation like any other. It was the "natural" and religiously ordained state for humans, and so entailed—indeed was defined by—obligations and duties that forbade the foolishness and selfishness that imperilled others.[55] These correspondents generally held the same view as the *Englishwoman's Domestic Magazine*:

to be deterred from marrying by reasons of fear for the comfort of those you love, cannot, gentlemen, be otherwise [than] proper. . . .

Selfish old bachelors may warn their young friends of having to give up "the club," eschew dress-coats from Poole's, smoke inferior cigars or the humble pipe, as the consequences of matrimony; yet perhaps they will seldom or never deter any except those who, for the happiness of others, it is better should remain single.[56]

No wonder Felix Holt was seen as "a radical" when he gave other reasons for celibacy:

I'll never marry, though I should have to live on raw turnips to subdue my flesh. I'll never look back and say, "I had a fine purpose once—I meant to keep my hands clean, and my soul upright, and to look truth in the face; but pray excuse me, I have a wife and children—I must lie and simper a little, else they'll starve!" or, "My wife is nice, she must have her bread well buttered, and her feelings will be hurt if she is not thought genteel."[57]

But George Eliot, no radical in this sense, had other ideas—and Felix does marry and have children. Perhaps Felix was foreseeing Lydgate's problems in Eliot's *Middlemarch* (1871–2), when his wife has over-genteel notions.

Once more, it is essential to remember that the fiction normally portrays a higher level of income than is the case with Felix, who is an artisan; however, he has been educated as a doctor, and chosen the "lower" vocation. There is a tendency in the novels of the time to portray male aspiration as foiled by female ostentation;[58] "Marriage or Celibacy?" supplies a picture of the lower middle class where such marital conflicts were less probable and less damaging, the desires for status in both sexes being more moderate.

Just because marriage had stronger sanction than other relations, attitudes towards home and what has come to be called the nuclear family[59] were strongly fixed. Separate roles, separate spheres, for women and men seemed obvious, and came to be morally justified, because in all ages and times what seems to be permanently the case is more acceptable if seen also as all for the best: whatever is, is right—or at least, 'twould be better so.

Two transitions, one underway and one to come, are intimated but not dominant in the series. First, the separation of paid work from home resulting from the industrial and commercial revolutions had prompted much of the current attitude to women's roles. Also, however, the move was affecting male morality as well, for men had to discover a novel role as they found or were expected to find personal satisfaction in the new private world. The double standard was becoming not just an injustice to women but a challenge to men; the dilemma for those like J.S. Mill who promoted sexual justice was that women were not only equal to but better than men. Therefore the man should "stick his beans" so that the angel in the house could cook them—or at least supervise their cooking by a not-yet angelic skivvy.

Second, women of the better-off classes were challenging the model of marriage and separate spheres. There was a change of emphasis from the rights of man (the abstract singular) to the rights of women (the living plural), prompted in part by social changes. A few of the young women who wrote to the *Telegraph* were "in business," though still probably as a preliminary to being "at home"; their younger sisters, however, would increasingly labour in the market, by choice as well as necessity, a necessity not only economic but demographic because of the "surplus" women. And a few, again in the better-off classes, were beginning to repudiate marriage privately and practically,[60] sometimes in terms that had been associated with selfish men. A contemporary diary records a conversation between two female friends in which they "fell to talking about love and marriage. We agreed that people—ladies at least—ought to be educated to do without it and then they would be less inclined to marry unless the very best were offered to them."[61]

Thematically, the strongest impression left by the series is the stress imputed to and undoubtedly felt by young men of the clerkly class. Some were moved by the call of adventure sounded by the trumpets of emigration, but responding to it did not then any more than now imply a lifelong commitment to life elsewhere and other. And most revealed that leaving would be a tearing away. An almost universal home-land centredness is seen in the use throughout the series of "emigration" rather than "immigration"—the focus is clear, even when the proposed move is to a "colony of settlement." There is perhaps less insistence on British traditions than one might expect, but the bias is there in nuance as well as statistically in the suggested choices of destination. In the event, of course, most of these prospective emigrants did not leave; they were not in the hopeless position of earlier Irish and later eastern-European and Third-World people who were, if lucky, choosing between death and elsewhere.

That, however, is not the resolving note on which to quit "Marriage or Celibacy?" for it fails to encapsulate the spirit or letter of the series. Once more, the *Daily Telegraph*'s judgment is quintessential:

A public discussion more remarkable in many respects has seldom been conducted; and we are glad to have furnished the arena for so much good sense, liveliness, practical wisdom, and hearty humanity as have marked the greater portion of the controversy.

APPENDIX A

The Correspondents

Who were the readers of the *Daily Telegraph* who, on the subjects covered in the series, felt either that they had something to say or (to use a distinction made by John Stuart Mill) that they had to say something? There is almost no evidence outside the letters themselves, and most of them, like almost all of the newspaper letters up to this point in the century, were signed by initials (often suggesting attitudes or allegiances) or by pseudonyms that invite inferences. Although 281 letters appeared, some correspondents had more than one letter printed; subtracting the duplicates and probable duplicates, I conclude that some 267 different signatures are involved, but even that is not the number of correspondents, for a few letters are conjointly authored (one, signed *Paigntonians*, being ostensibly from four people).

Rarely are letters signed with obviously actual names, and such names are associated either with the early attempt to incriminate Miss Page or the later encouragement of emigration: in the first group, *John W. Miller, Mr. Nicholas, Harriet Barnett*; in the second, *Edwin C. Booth, George Francis Train, W. Frank Lynn,* and *W. Parker Snow; Therese Picot,* the first of three correspondents writing in French (in itself a rather surprising fact), may or may not be using her name. Indeed, she, and some of the others who use pseudonyms or initials, are probably fictions or at least not *propriae personae*. As indicated above, the practice of Victorian newspapers—one need not speculate about later epigones—makes it dangerous to assume that no letters were written by the *Telegraph*'s staff (or their friends), engaged in stirring the pot while filling it; however, it seems absurd to assume that a large number were faked in that way, for the staff would have been pressed beyond even their practised logorrhea to write all the published letters. The possibility, however, makes even more shaky unqualified inferences about the actual authors; on the other hand, the editors seem to have had a very acute sense of the attitudes and desires of their readers, and so it could be said that even if some of the productions are dramatic, they are realistic drama. And scepticism is less apt as the series progressed; both in content and tone the letters become less sophisticated and more matter of fact, and there would be little reason for pretence.

The pseudonyms are generally typical of the period and genre,[1] but there are particular differences suggestive of democratization as well as the subject. The largest number are apt to the status, themes, and tone of the correspondent. With reference to the central controversy about prudent marriage, for example, status is signalled, among others, by *Benedick* and *Cassio* (Shakespearians both), *One Who Has Tried It*,[2] *Materfamilias* and *Paterfamilias*, *One Who Married on £120 a Year*, *A Happy Nine Years' Wife*, *A Few True Girls of the Period*, and that constant supplicant, *A Bachelor Curate*. Those implying attitude and tone include *Nil Desperandum*, *Home-Made Bread*, *A Disciple of Malthus*, *A Would-Be Reformer*, *Plain Truth*, *A Philanthropist*, *Pro Bono Publico*, *Self-Help*, *Vestigia Nulla Retrorsum*,[3] *Caution*, and *The Best of Things*. The second theme of the series called forth parallel types, represented, for instance, by *Antipodes*, *Perth (W.A.)*, *Colonial Tom*, *Roamer Returned* (a pessimist), *Pampas*, *Huron*, *Kangaroo*, *Kentucky* (a fine enthusiast), and *Canadian J.P.*

The hints in some of these of occupational status are overt in a few—and here the new voices of the *Daily Telegraph* become more evident—such as *A Young English Governess*, *A London Mechanic*, *A Draper*, *Professional*, *Hammer and Nails*, *Accountant*, *A Married Priest*, *Mariner*, and (alas) *A Poor Tutor*. Finally—excluding a miscellaneous group[4] and the large number signed with initials or letters of the alphabet (including such Greek contributors as *Alpha*, *Beta*, and *Delta*)—come those not characterizing individuals but suggesting the new circumstances and authors, signatures consisting of forenames and nicknames, real or fictional, such as *Lucy*, *Flo*, *Penelope*, *Jane*, *Allie*, *Hannah*, *Joseph*, *Nellie*, *Miles*, and *Bunny* (!). *Penelope* may, of course, be a learned literary allusion, as are some implying attitudes, such as *Erastes*, *Enemoplem*, and *Emolas* (both to be read in reverse),[5] *Giglio*, *Nachod*, *Fabius*, and perhaps *Joseph*. Of considerable interest as an epistoleer, but of unknown antecedents, is *Solon Smiff*, *M.E.*[6]

Though it is impossible to identify the correspondents, some interesting groupings can be inferred from the contents and signatures.[7] Analysis is greatly blurred by the need in many cases to deduce, for example, sex and marital status, and even the place of residence; however, the general picture can be drawn in wavy and dotted lines. After the initial 7 letters (2.5 per cent of the total) printed under the heading "The Procuress," the series until 16 July was mainly concerned with the exigent conditions of middle-class marriage and after that mainly with emigration: during the first part, 147 letters (52.3 per cent) appeared; in the second part, 127 (45.2 per cent). That division marks some signal differences.

One of the most interesting is seen in the distribution of letters by women and by men. Of the 281 letters, 209 (74 per cent) are from males, 64 (23 per cent) from females. Only a few of the correspondents (some 3 per cent) provide no clue as to their sex.[8]

Marital status is less frequently, though not rarely, signalled. Of the men, 80 are identifiable as single;[9] 41 of their letters were published before 17 July (i.e., when the main subject shifted to emigration), 39 subsequently. Just over half as many, 42, are married men; 1 of their letters appeared under the heading "The Procuress"; of the 41 that appeared under "Marriage or Celibacy?" 28 were published before 17 July; 13 subsequently. No marital status is indicated in 87 other letters by men; of these, 4 appeared in the series labelled "The Procuress," in "Marriage or Celibacy?" 27 appeared before 17 July, and 56 subsequently.

Of the female correspondents, 30 appear to be single; of their letters, 26 were published before 17 July, and only 4 subsequently. There are letters from 27 married women, 20 of them appearing before 17 July, and 7 subsequently. There are only 7 from women whose marital status is not inferable: 2 of them appeared under the rubric "The Procuress"; under "Marriage or Celibacy?" 4 were published before 17 July, and but 1 subsequently. In tabular form:

Table 1
Sex and Marital Status of the Correspondents

	Men	Women	?	Married		Single		?	
				M	W	M	W	M	W
"The Procuress"	5	2		1		1		4	2
"Marriage or Celibacy?":									
Before 17 July	95	51	8[a]	28	20	41	26	27	4
Subsequently	108	12		13	7	39	4	56	1
	208	65	8	42	27	80	30	87	7

[a]The one who is single is not counted in the final columns.

It will be seen that in these two respects there is a marked difference between the two halves of the series: in the first half about one-third of the letters are from women, as against less than one-tenth in the latter half. Another striking but not surprising fact is that while a large number of men give no indication of their marital state, almost all the women do; the inference that they saw themselves as "relative creatures" is only slightly lessened by observing that most of the letters from men in which there is no mention of marriage come in the part of the series on emigration, when few letters from women were published. Assuming that the editors of the *Daily Telegraph* chose indifferently as to sex and marital status, these variant views can be seen as related to the switch in topic in mid-series; emigration seems to have been taken almost universally to be a topic on which the weightiest opinions were those of males, and especially single males—or, less tendentiously, that the option of emigration was more clearly open to single males than to any others. On the other hand, opinions on marriage were equally open to all, the sexual imbalance being explained simply by the combination of factors that led to the predominance of males in all editorial correspondence of the period. Most of the letters signed by initials (and so not indicating any special attitude) involve emigration, and particularly questions about its practicability, and most were evidently written by single men.

Judgment about the amount of money necessary for marriage, the basic initial issue that persisted in weakened form into the second part of the series, was influenced by sex and marital status. (Not all those who engaged in this debate expressed an explicit or clearly implied figure.) Taking the minimum at the rather high figure of £200 (somewhere between £200 and £150 would come closer to averaged opinion), one finds the distribution shown in table 2.

The age of the correspondents is surely significant on these points, yet very few of them give even such minor clues as "young." However, while defensible generalizations are not available, some comments about individuals that have implications for groups will be found in the text, especially in chapters 3, 4, and 7.

The *Daily Telegraph* did not bother to indicate where a large number of the letters were dated from, though it seems very likely that all of them had some postal address. From the contents as well as from the datelines (when they appear), one may conclude that some three-quarters of the correspondents were resident in London (including its suburbs), where it is certain that most of the readers of the *Telegraph* lived, though it circulated widely through the country. Of the other

Table 2
Can One Marry on Less than £200 a Year?

	Yes		No		
	M	S	M	S	Perhaps
Males[a]					
Before 17 July	7	2	20	23	20
Subsequently	1	1	6	15	4
Total (males)	8	3	26	38	24
Females[b]					
Before 17 July	8	12	10	7	9
Subsequently	0	0	10	0	1
Total (females)	8	12	20	7	10

[a] Through 16 July, a total of 52 males say no to marriage on these terms, but the marital status of 9 of these cannot be inferred; after that date, the one male nay-sayer may be either single or married.
[b] The marital status of all the women can be inferred. Here again the importance of marriage as defining women is evident.

quarter, comprised of 70 letters (from 67 correspondents), 25 give no sound clue, and may have come from London.[10] In addition, some 11 correspondents, while they normally live elsewhere, say they are visiting England, and, one may reasonably assume, are writing from London, while 3 letters (2 correspondents) come from seaside resorts, and may well represent London views.

That leaves only some 31 correspondents from elsewhere in the United Kingdom, and 1 from Europe,[11] 7 (9 letters) from unspecified places in the "country" (2 of them visiting London), and 2 from country towns. The British correspondents are scattered, with more than one letter coming only from Manchester (4 letters) and Liverpool (2).[12] Attitudes and experiences relevant to the main themes emerge from these non-Londoners, especially concerning cost of living and manners as well as conditions for emigrants; what needs to be emphasized is, however, the unsurprising dominance of London views.

An even larger majority may with confidence be located in that amorphous, constantly expanding and not so obviously contracting group, the middle class, the main contribution coming from what may equally confidently be designated the lower middle class, that is, the families and individuals living on the salaries and earnings of the lower professional ranks, the clerks, and petty tradesmen. A not inconsiderable number of the correspondents state, or give good evidence of, their occupations and incomes. Not surprisingly, almost all of the women (including several of the single girls) keep house for their families: the 5 identifiable exceptions are *Charlie's Wife* (a housekeeper who shared a business with her husband—though it failed), *A London Girl* (who says she is "in business"), *An Anxious Worker* (who has her own retail business),[13] *A Daily Governess*, and *The Best of Things* (also a governess).

The men earn the families' daily bread (and not inconsiderable amounts of what goes on and with it) in a range—but certainly not an unrestricted range—of ways. Here again, if one bears in mind the kind of correspondents who wrote to *The Times*, the contrast is quickly evident. The professions are not absent from the series—a surgeon (two letters) and a barrister in the first series on "The Procuress," and later 8 clergymen, another barrister and a surgeon, an author and lecturer, and 8 identifiable generally as professionals. But most of the clergymen are (or see themselves as) poor, and usually ready for emigration, and the others who may be seen as professionals are not typical of *The Times*'s correspondents: a mechanical engineer, 3 civil engineers, an architect, a tutor, an insurance agent, and an accountant. Among those who might well write to *The Times* as well as the *Telegraph* are the 3 emigration agents, and the "Late Inspector of Settlement to the Government of Victoria," who had special messages for the *Telegraph*'s readers. The differences between the newspapers' readerships are more obvious when one turns to trade, the representatives in the *Telegraph* being a draper, an independent businessman, and a merchant trader. But the dominant group is made up of clerks, of whom no fewer than 31 can be identified, and with whom may be included a few of the lower professionals listed above, as well as 1 "civil servant," 2 shopmen, and 1 "student."

The predominance of cityfolk is challenged, on the question of emigration in the latter half of the series, by 6 farmers and pastoralists (mainly with colonial experience, one having also been a trapper), one with multiple experience as "a trader, a large landowner, and an agriculturalist," and a mariner.

And finally, the middle-class voices are joined by 2 artisans (self-identified), 3 mechanics, a carpenter, a colonial farm labourer (but he had been a clerk at home), and 1 male who describes himself as unemployed (almost certainly also trained as a clerk).

Such are the players, almost all pseudonymous, who stepped forward out of obscurity to speak their minds and then disappear from history. What they left were their views, initially and especially on money, marriage, and mores.

To facilitate further research and to save clutter in the text, I here list the correspondents, ordered by date of publication. Only information that can be reasonably inferred is given; if there is no indication of sex or marital status, income or occupation, or residence, no evidence has been discerned. Attitudes pro and con emigration are indicated, with the places mentioned. Duplicate signatures that are assumed to signal the same person have the inferences listed in their first citation. The first 7 letters appeared under the rubric "The Procuress." The following abbreviations are used: day and month are given as, e.g., 17/6 for 17 June; M and F are used for male and female; S and W for single and wedded (married); L for London; ? indicates a degree of doubt about the inference. E signals a discussion of emigration, with + indicating approval and   disapproval; Q and A indicate that the primary intent in this regard is seeking information (by question) or supplying it (by answer). AUS = Australia, CAN = Canada, NZ = New Zealand, UC = Upper Canada (Ontario), USA = United States of America; other potential destinations are spelled out.

1 *John W. Miller* (2 letters), 17/6, 19/6. M, surgeon, L.
2 *Mr. Nicholas*, 19/6. M, L.
3 *Harriet Barnett*, 19/6. F, L.
4 *John W. Miller*, 19/6. 2nd letter; see 17/6 above.
5 *One Sorrowing For Her Sex*, 20/6. F, L.
6 *A Barrister*, 24/6 (dated 23/6). M, barrister, L (Chancery Lane).
7 *R.P.C.*, 26/6. M, W, middle class (income £130 on marriage), L?
8 *Benedick* (2 letters), 27/6, 9/7 (dated 26/6, 6/7). M, W, L. E: USA .
9 *One Who Has Tried It*, 27/6 (dated 26/6). M, W, L?
10 *Materfamilias*, 30/6 (dated 29/6). F, W, middle class (she had £80 in her "office" before marriage; her husband had £150 on marriage), L?
11 *Solon Smiff, M.E.*, 30/6 (dated 28/6). M, S, age 32, mechanical engineer, income £300?, L (Westminster).
12 *Erastes*, 1/7 (dated 30/6). M, L. E: UC+, Canada West (the Red River).
13 *An English Girl*, 1/7 (dated 30/6) (cf. 8/7; probably different person). F, S (engaged), housekeeper (for mother and self), income £80 (fiancé's £130), L.
14 *A Young Man*, 2/7. M, S, L.
15 *Never Say Die*, 2/7 (dated 30/6). M, W, age 50+, L?. E: AUS +.

16 *W.J.W.*, 2/7 (dated 1/7). M?, L. E: UC .

17 *Nil Desperandum*, 2/7 (dated 30/6) (cf. 14/7; probably different person). L?

18 *Another English Girl*, 3/7 (dated 2/7) (cf. 8/7; probably different person). F, S, L?

19 *A Matron*, 3/7 (dated 2/7). F, W, L?

20 *P.C.L.*, 3/7 (dated 2/7), M?, L?

21 *A Young Briton*, 3/7. M, S?, "limited means," L?

22 *One Who Married on £120 a Year*, 3/7. F?, W, income on marriage £120, L?

23 *Single Man*, 3/7 (dated 30/6). M, S, L?

24 *G.J.L.*, 3/7 (dated 30/6). M, S, architect, L?

25 *Preceptor*, 3/7 (dated 30/6). M?, S?, L.

26 *J.W.J.*, 3/7 (dated 2/7). M, W, income £150, L ("respectable locality").

27 *Therese Picot*, 4/7. F, S, age 20, Royal Crescent, Ramsgate.

28 *J.P.M.*, 4/7 (dated 2/7). M?, L.

29 *A Happy Nine Years' Wife*, 4/7 (dated 1/7). F, W, income £100 on marriage, Brighton.

30 *E.F.H.*, 4/7 (dated 1/7). M?, S?, clerk?, L?

31 *Colonista*, 4/7 (dated 2/7). F, W (widow?), income "small," L? E: British Columbia+

32 *Paterfamilias*, 4/7 (dated 2/7). M, W, age 37, professional, income £120 on marriage, now £300, L?

33 *A Plain Girl*, 4/7 (dated 2/7). F, S, "middle class," L?

34 *Charlie's Wife*, 6/7 (dated 1/7). F, W, age ca. 35 (married 15 years), husband "professor" (of music?), started business together and failed, income on early marriage £120, £250 for last three years, "country" house.

35 *A Bachelor*, 6/7 (dated 3/7) (cf. 10/7; different person). M, S, age "not old," 10 years as chief clerk in a London establishment, now unemployed, L.

36 *A Would-Be Reformer*, 6/7 (dated 2/7). M?

37 *A Simple Country Girl*, 6/7 (dated 2/7). F, S, country.

38 *Z.Y.X.*, 6/7 (dated 3/7). M, S, age 26, income £100–300, L.

39 *An English Wife*, 6/7 (dated 3/7) (cf. 15/7; probably different person). F, W, "a matron of some years' standing," income £350, L?

40 *A Welsh Bachelor Pro-Tem* (2 letters), 6/7, 11/7 (dated 3/7, 9/7). M, S, clerk, income closer to £100 than £200, L (on holiday in Tenby, South Wales).

41 *Lucy*, 6/7 (dated 3/7). F, S.

42 *A Pilgrim of Love*, 6/7 (3/7). M?, S?

43 *Plain Truth*, 6/7 (dated 3/7).

44 *A Few True Girls of the Period*, 6/7 (dated 3/7). F, S, L?

45 *One Who Looks before He Leaps*, 6/7 (dated 3/7). M, S?, L?

46 *C.S.C.*, 6/7 (dated 3/7). M, W, clerk?, income ca. £200, L.

47 *Moderation*, 7/7 (dated 6/7). W?, L?

48 *One of England's Daughters*, 7/7 (dated 4/7). F, S, fiancé has £150, L?

49 *Vieux Moustache* (3 letters, possibly not all from the same person), 7/7, 11/7, 16/7 (dated 4/7, 8/7, 14/7). M, W, professional (military?), in 2nd letter mentions expenditure of £370+ (in 3rd letter says £336+ in 1867), provincial town.

50 *Flo*, 7/7 (dated 4/7). F, S, age 18, Birkenhead.

51 *Spes*, 7/7 (dated 4/7) (cf. 17/7; different person). M, S?, civil servant, Burton-on-Trent.

52 *A Real Help-Meet*, 7/7 (dated 4/7). F, W, age +24, probably in 30s (married at 19), income £200 at marriage, subsequently less, now £1300, L (Hampstead).

53 *Humanus*, 7/7 (dated 4/7). M?

54 *Enemoplem*, 8/7 (dated 6/7). F, age "woman's estate."

55 *Pegging at It*, 8/7 (dated 5/7). M?, Derby.

56 *Public School Man*, 8/7 (dated 5/7). M, S?, upper middle class, Hertfordshire.

57 *W.E.W.W.*, 8/7 (dated 6/7). M, S, income £150, L.

58 *Un Francais qui n'a plus 20 ans, et qui a fini ses etudes*, 8/7. M, S, age 20+.

59 *An Ordinary-Looking English Girl*, 8/7 (dated 6/7). F, S, age 19.

60 *Another English Girl*, 8/7 (dated 6/7) (cf. 3/7; probably different person). F, S.

61 *R.O.*, 8/7 (dated 6/7). M?, L?

62 *One Who Speaks from Experience*, 8/7 (dated 5/7) (cf. 16/7; different person). M, W, married 10 years, income £150 on marriage, now £250, L?

63 *An English Girl*, (8/7 (dated 6/7) (cf. 1/7; probably different person). F, S, L?

64 *A London Girl*, 8/7 (cf. 9/7; different person). F, S, age 19, "in business," L.

65 *Cassio*, 8/7 (dated 6/8). M, S, barrister?, income £350, L (The Temple).

66 *Penelope*, 8/7 (dated 5/7). F, L?

67 *A British Matron*, 8/7 (dated 6/7). F, W, income £200, L?

68 *3*, 8/7 (dated 6/8). M?, L?

69 *Jane*, 8/7 (dated 4/7). F, W, L (Old Brompton).

70 *D.F.P.*, 8/7 (dated 5/7). M, S, writes in French.

71 *Two Plain English Girls*, 8/7 (dated 6/7). F, S, L?

72 *Benedick*, 9/7. 2nd letter; see 27/6 above.

73 *A Young English Governess*, 9/7 (dated 4/7). F, S (engaged), governess (since age 18).

74 *Beta*, 9/7 (dated 7/7). F?, W?, L?

75 *Lover*, 9/7 (dated 7/7). M, L?

76 *A Lover of a Quiet Home*, 9/7 (dated 7/7). F?, W?, L?

77 *S.A.L.T.*, 9/7 (dated 7/7). M?, L?

78 *A London Girl*, 9/7 (dated 7/7) (cf. 8/7; different person). F, S, age 22, housekeeper (mother dead), father (professional) has income of £150–200, L (suburb).

79 *Home-Made Bread*, 9/7 (dated 7/7). F, S, age 20, L?

80 *Ring* (3 letters), 9/7, 18/7, 25/7 (dated 6/7, n.d., 24/7). M, civil engineer, L? E: A; "far West"+ [USA], South America+, NZ.

81 *L.C.J.*, 10/7 (dated 9/7). F, S, L?

82 *A Country Girl*, 10/7 (dated 9/7). F, S, "country village" (in L for a few weeks).

83 *Comfortably Single*, 10/7. M, S, "small income" "upper middle" class (£150?).

84 *A Bachelor*, 10/7 (dated 8/7) (cf. 6/7; different person). M, S, income £100–200?, L?

85 *A Happy Married Man*, 10/7 (dated 8/7). M, W (7 years), income ca. £100, L?

86 *H.B.*, 10/7. F?, L?

87 *A Match-maker (Matrimonial, not Lucifer)*, 10/7. M, W, in an "office" (probably in the City), expenditure ca. £186, L.

88 *G.L.M.*, 10/7 (dated 8/7). F?, W?, L.

89 *A Philanthropist*, 10/7 (dated 8/7). M, W?, L?

90 *S.R.H.*, 10/7. M?, Manchester.

91 *An Eldest Daughter*, 10/7 (dated 8/7). F, S, age 19, family of "small means," L? (has experience of L and of country).

92 *Giglio*, 10/7 (dated 8/7). M?, L? (has experience of provincial France).

93 *Allie*, 10/7 (dated 7/7). F?, S?, L?

94 *M.T.M.*, 10/7 (dated 6/7). M?, S?, L?

95 *A London Mechanic*, 10/7 (dated 8/7). M, W, mechanic, L.

96 ***, 11/7 (dated 10/7). F?, W?, L?

97 *Prudens*, 11/7 (dated 8/7). M?, W?, L?

98 *Vieux Moustache*, 11/7 (2nd letter; see 7/7, 16/7).

99 *B.*, 11/7. M, S, "old bachelor" (young man 20 years earlier), L?

100 *One Who Would Be a Good Deal Happier If He Had It*, 11/7. M, W (4 years), clerk?, income ca. £180?, L.

101 *A Plain Man*, 11/7 (dated 8/7). M, S, age 30, clerk?, income +£200, L.

102 *C.A.J.*, 11/7 (dated 9/7). M, S, income £150?, country.

103 *Prudentia*, 11/7 (dated 9/7). F, S, age 19, L?

104 *Another Benedick*, 11/7 (dated 9/7). M, S (concludes by hoping that he will become "Another Benedick"), clerk (unemployed), L? E+: Q.

105 *A Young Bachelor*, 11/7 (dated 9/7). M, S, income "moderate," L (Regent's Park).

106 *A Clerk*, 11/7 (dated 8/7). M, S, clerk, income "small," Liverpool.

107 *A Welsh Bachelor Pro Tem*, 11/7 (2nd letter; see 6/7).

108 *A Prudent Bachelor*, 11/7 (dated 9/7). M, S, government clerk (was a city clerk for 5 years), L.

109 *Delta*, 11/7. M, S, unemployed (eldest son of officer, 7 years college). E: Q; South America+.

110 *Alpha*, 13/7 (dated 9/7). M, W, professional lower middle class?, L?

111 *Hannah*, 13/7 (dated 10/7). F, S (fiancé died 2 years ago), Scotland ("country" girl visiting L).

112 *W.H.S.*, 13/7 (dated 10/7). M, S, L? E: "America"+.

113 *T.T.*, 13/7 (dated 11/7). M?, clerk?, L? E (mentioned only).

114 *Nachod*, 13/7 (dated 11/7). M?, L? (experience of Germany).

115 *Emolas*, 13/7 (dated 10/7). M? (in spite of signature). E: AUS, Mexico, Paraguay, &c.+.

116 *One Who Is Content to Wait*, 13/7 (dated 10/7). M, S (lives at home), income £150, L?

117 *A Lover of Home*, 13/7 (dated 10/7). M, S?, clerk (Admiralty), L.

118 *An Old Married Man* (2 letters), 13/7, 16/7 (dated 10/7, 12/7). M, W, age ca. 51 (30 years of experience in marriage; married at 21), clerk, income has varied between £200 and £300, L?

119 *Prudence*, 13/7 (dated 10/7). M, S, L?

120 *Veritas*, 13/7 (dated 9/7) (cf. 14/7 and 27/7; probably different people). M, S?, L? E+.

121 *Plain Fact*, 13/7 (dated 10/7). M, W, expenditure £232+.

122 *R.F.H.*, 13/7 (dated 10/7). M, W, age 25, income £200, L (Islington). E+.

123 *C.L.W.*, 13/7 (dated 10/7). L?

124 *F.M.*, 13/7 (dated 9/7) (cf. 22/7; different person). M?, W, income £150?, L?

125 *A Young Englishman*, 14/7 (dated 11/7). M, S?, L?

126 *Another Mechanic*, 14/7. M, S, income ca. £70? (less than 1/4 *Solon Smiff*'s), L?

127 *Clericus*, 14/7 (dated 11/7) (cf. 28/7; different person). M, S, age 27, Church of England clergyman, L. E+: British Columbia.

128 *H.H.F.*, 14/7. F, W, has 7 daughters, L. E+: AUS (Queensland)+, NZ+.

129 *A Dutchman*, 14/7 (dated 11/7). M, W, age 35 (married at 25; wife then 18), professional, income £350 (£200 when married).

130 *Nil Desperandum*, 14/7 (dated 11/7) (cf. 2/7; probably different person). M, L? E+: Q; USA ("America")+.

131 *Veritas*, 14/7 (cf. 13/7 and 27/7; probably different people). M, L? E+: USA ("America")+.

132 *Joseph*, 14/7 (dated 11/7). M, S, L?

133 *An Anxious Father*, 14/7 (dated 10/7). M, W, has 3 little children, mercantile clerk, expenditure £223+ (earns a little more), L. E+: Q; USA.

134 *B—*, 15/7 (dated 13/7). M?, above clerkly class, Penshurst.

135 *Precaution*, 15/7 (dated 11/7). F, S, age 21, family income £400–600, Brussels.

136 *An English Wife*, 15/7 (dated 13/7) (cf. 6/7; probably different person). F, W, several children, L?

137 *Three "Girls of the Period,"* 15/7 (dated 13/7). F, S, income "small," L?

138 *Foreigner*, 15/7 (dated 11/7). M, clerk?, L? (educated on Continent, "foreign").

139 *A Clergyman, Aetat 47*, 15/7. M, W (10 years), age 47, clergyman, married on £200 (has always spent more than stipend, made up by extra work).

140 *Lyn* (3 letters, the others signed *W. Frank Lynn*, 21/7, and *W.L.*, 27/7), 15/7 (dated 13/7). M, L? E+?: Q; AUS.

141 *Philos.*, 15/7 (dated 13/7). M, W, upper middle class?, Norwood.

142 *Unit*, 15/7 (dated 13/7). M?, S? (by signature), L?

143 *Young England*, 15/7 (dated 13/7). M?, L? E+.

144 *Vieux Moustache*, 15/7 (3rd letter; see 7/7, 11/7).

145 *A Woman*, 16/7 (dated 14/7). F, middle-aged, L?

146 *An Old Married Man*, 16/7 (2nd letter; see 13/7).

147 *L.H.J.*, 16/7 (dated 13/7). M, S?, clerk, L? E+: Q; AUS?, NZ?, CAN?, South Africa?, South America?

148 *Espero*, 16/7 (dated 13/7). M, W (less than 6 years), clerk, income £250, L.

149 *Nobody In Particular*, 16/7 (dated 13/7). M, S?, professional, L? E : CAN , AUS , Mexico and Paraguay (might as well add interior of Africa).

150 *M.B.E.*, 16/7 (dated 11/7). F, W?, income £150+, L?

151 *A Wife and Mother*, 16/7 (dated 13/7). F, W, left school 17 years ago, income £150, country.

152 *One Who Speaks from Experience*, 16/7 (dated 13/7) (cf. 8/7; different person). F, W, mother for many years, slender means, L?

153 *Fabius*, 16/7 (dated 14/7). M?, L? E?: A (in form of Q).

154 *One of the "Girls of the Period,"* 16/7 (dated 14/7). F, S, L?

155 *J.A.C.V.,* 17/7 (dated 14/7). M, S, middle-aged, son of army officer, and "well connected."

156 *Bread-Winner's Wife,* 17/7 (dated 16/7). F, W, married 18 years, husband government clerk, income on marriage £100 (now after 23 years' service £220), L (suburb). E+?

157 *A Draper,* 17/7 (dated 16/7). M, W?, middle-aged, draper, L?

158 *A Young Man of the Period,* 17/7 (dated 16/7). M, S, of non-aristocratic "county family," income £200+, L.

159 *An Active Wife and Mother,* 17/7 (dated 15/7). F, W, married 15 years, income £150 when married (and for at least 3 years after, now great change for better), L?

160 *J.W.H.,* 17/7 (dated 15/7). M, L? E+?: Q.

161 *A Disciple of Malthus,* 17/7 (dated 15/7). M, S, clerk or professional?, L. E (for middle classes).

162 *A Woman, But Not a Slave,* 17/7 (dated 15/7). F, W, married 8 years, parents wealthy (ca. £300+?), L? (since marriage has lived in Germany as well as England).

163 *Independence,* 17/7 (dated 15/7). M, S?, middle class, L? E+: Q; A; AUS (Victoria).

164 *Spes,* 17/7 (dated 14/7) (cf. 7/7; different person). M, W, clerk?, married (a few years ago) on £120, L? E+.

165 *A Chief Clerk,* 17/7 (dated 15/7). M, W (5 years), clerk, L?

166 *Pro Bono Publico,* 17/7 (dated 15/7). M, S, income ca. £100?, L (Harrow Station). E+: Q.

167 *A Widower,* 17/7 (dated 14/7). M, W (widower), unnamed town of 12,000 inhabitants. E+: Q.

168 *A Rural Bachelor,* 18/7 (dated 16/7). M, S, neither very young nor very old, unnamed agricultural county.

169 *One Who Waits and Hopes,* 18/7 (dated 15/7). M, S, age 23, 1st assistant clerk in professional office, income £105, Torquay.

170 *Antipodes,* 18/7 (dated 16/7) (cf. this date below; different person). M, AUS or NZ. E+: Q; A; NZ, USA ("America"), British Columbia (concerning *Colonista*), AUS or NZ (by signature).

171 *T.Z.,* 18/7 (dated 16/7). M, W, had sold farm before 1854, farmer (retired), invested in house property and land, income £150–200 (from investments), Norwich (farm was in Norfolk).

172 *Ring,* 18/7 (2nd letter; see 9/7, 25/7).

173 *"They Also Serve Who Only Stand and Wait,"* 18/7 (dated 14/7). M?, S?, L?

174 *An Anxious Worker,* 18/7 (dated 16/7). F, W (7 years), age 32, owns retail business, L (country bred). E+: Q.

175 *Professional* (2 letters), 18/7, 25/7 (dated 16/7, 23/7). M, S?, L? E+: A, Q; USA (West; intends to emigrate to Nebraska)+, AUS , CAN , NZ .

176 *Antipodes*, 18/7 (dated 14/7) (cf. this date above; different person). M?, clerk?, Liverpool. E: A; lower middle class and professional , labourers and skilled mechanics and farmers+; "Australias."

177 *Amicus*, 18/7 (dated 16/7). M, Church of England, L? E+: North and South America, AUS.

178 *Would-Be Emigrant*, 18/7 (dated 15/7). M, S, Manchester. E+: Q; CAN, AUS, South America.

179 *One Who Can't Help It*, 18/7 (dated 15/7). M, S, clerk, income £100, L?

180 *Perth (W.A.)*, 18/7 (dated 15/7). M. E+: A, Q; AUS+, South America, USA, and "the Canadas."

181 *Edwin C. Booth* (2 letters), 20/7, 28/7 (dated 17/7, 25/7). M, Late Inspector of Settlement to the Government of Victoria (for 15 years), also journalist and gold-digger, L (Wandsworth). E+ (with caution): A; AUS (Victoria)

182 *M.B.*, 20/7 (dated 18/7). L.

183 *Self-Help*, 20/7 (dated 17/7). M?, L?. E+.

184 *George*, 20/7 (dated 17/7). M, S (engaged), late 20s, has independent business, income ca. £600, L?

185 *A Widow*, 20/7 (dated 17/7). F, W (widowed 2 years), age 30s?, income £200 (£150 when widowed; no explanation), L?

186 *D.B.*, 20/7 (dated 17/7). M?, L? E: Q; NZ.

187 *Hammer and Nails*, 20/7 (dated 17/7). M, S?, artisan (carpenter?), L (Bermondsey).

188 *Vestigia Nulla Retrorsum*, 20/7 (dated 17/7). L? E+.

189 *Caution*, 20/7. L? E: capitalists and labourers+, clerks ; CAN+, "banks of the Parana" .

190 *Life Assurance*, 20/7 (dated 17/7). M?, insurance agent?, L?

191 *One Who Is Waiting Patiently*, 20/7. S, income £200?, L?

192 *A.B.*, 20/7 (dated 17/7). M?, middle class, L? E: A; AUS , NZ , CAN , South America , USA+

193 *An Old Colonist*, 20/7 (dated 18/7). M, L? E+: A; Brazil.

194 *Colonial Tom*, 20/7 (dated 18/7). M, clerk, L? (lived in NZ 8 years). E+: A; NZ+, AUS.

195 *A Contented Old Maid*, 20/7 (dated 16/7). F, S, income small but sufficient for gentlewoman, L? (but see difference between date on letter and publication date).

196 *Traveller* (2 letters), 20/7, 25/7 (dated 18/7, 24/7). M, S, L (New University Club, St James's-street). E+: Q; India, AUS (New South Wales, Queensland), NZ, USA+.

197 *George Francis Train* (2 letters), 20/7, 28/7 (dated 16/7, 24/7). M, L (Dublin Four Courts, Marshalsea). E+: A; USA+ (West), AUS.

198 *Roamer Returned*, 21/7 (dated 18/7). M, W (S in 1862 when emigrated), clerk, income in 1862 "beggarly," L. E: artisans, farmers, capitalists+, clerks ; A; British Columbia, USA (Washington Territory, San Francisco), Chile, Peru.

199 *W. Frank Lynn*, 21/7 (dated 20/7) (2nd letter; see *Lyn*, 15/7, and *W.L.*, 27/7). M, L? E+: A; CAN (UC? and Canada West)+.

200 *Miles*, 21/7 (dated 19/7). M, L? E+: Q.

201 *Accountant*, 21/7. M, accountant, L? E+: A.

202 *A Mother of Sons and Daughters*, 21/7 (dated 18/7). F, W, L?. E+: A; AUS (New South Wales, Victoria).

203 *A Minister of Religion*, 21/7 (dated 18/7). M, W, clergyman, L?. E+: A; UC.

204 *B.P.*, 21/7 (dated 18/7). M, S, Hemel Hempstead. E: Q (USA), A (Nova Scotia); USA+, Nova Scotia .

205 *Civil Engineer*, 21/7 (dated 17/7). M, civil engineer, L? (but see difference between date on letter and publication date). E : AUS (New South Wales, Queensland).

206 *Unfortunate Husband*, 21/7 (dated 17/7). M, W, married at 27 (in early 30s now), clerk (when married), income £150 (when married), then unemployed, now £170, L?

207 *P.*, 21/7. M?, Wales? E+: A.

208 *A Would-Be Benedick*, 21/7 (dated 17/7). M, S, income under £300 (claims to be upper middle class), Newbury, Berkshire.

209 *W. Parker Snow*, 22/7 (dated 20/7). M, W, author and lecturer, L? E+: A.

210 *F.M.*, 22/7 (dated 20/7) (cf. 13/7; different person). M, S, age 22, clerk, income £90, soon to be £100 (top for his grade), L (Railway Clearing House, Euston-square).

211 *J.J.*, 22/7 (dated 20/7). M, age 40s?, emigration agent (for 18 years), L?. E: clerks ; AUS, NZ.

212 *N.Z.*, 22/7 (dated 20/7), M, L?. E: farmers (labourers anyway)+, capitalists+, clerks ; A; NZ, AUS.

213 *W.P.*, 22/7 (dated 20/7). M, S (at least in 1863), L? E+: A; NZ.

214 *J.N.*, 22/7 (dated 18/7). M, lately manager of sheep and cattle station in pampas, L. E+ : A; AUS (except capitalist) , NZ (except capitalist, artisan, labourer) , pampas of South America (even for poor gentlemen, clerks, shopkeepers—though they seem to need £300-400 to begin)+.

215 *T.H.M.*, 22/7 (dated 20/7). M, S (seeking wife in England), left England

12 years ago, clerk before emigration, income before emigration £50,
UC. E+: A; AUS, CAN, USA.

216 *T.W.*, 22/7 (dated 20/7). M. E+: A; AUS.

217 *L——S.*, 23/7 (dated 21/7). M, Hull. E+: USA (western prairies), the
States of the River Plate, Chile, UC, British Columbia, California; +1st 4
in that order.

218 *A Married Priest*, 23/7. M, W (just), clergyman, income £200, L?

219 *Pioneer*, 23/7 (dated 22/7) (cf. 27/7; different person). M, agriculturist?,
Texas? (lived there 15 years). E+: A; USA (Texas), CAN.

220 *Five Years' Colonist*, 23/7 (dated 21/7). M. E: clerks , labouring
classes+; A; USA (West), South America, AUS.

221 *A South Australian*, 23/7 (dated 21/7). M, L (just visiting?). E+: A; AUS
(South Australia, New South Wales, Victoria).

222 *An Undergraduate*, 23/7 (dated 21/7). M, S, student, L? E+.

223 *H.C.*, 23/7 (dated 22/7). M, has been farmer and trapper (in Canada
West), L (just visiting?). E: clerks , clergymen (and others)+; A;
Canada West (and British Columbia?)+, USA , Gaspé .

224 *Road*, 23/7 (dated 21/7). M, Manchester. E+ (even for clerks): Q, A.

225 *A Daily Governess*, 24/7 (dated 22/7). F, S, governess, income £20?, L?

226 *J.A.B.*, 24/7 (dated 22/7). M, W (no children), age 30, works "behind
a counter," income £150. E+: Q; CAN.

227 *Pampas*, 24/7 (dated 22/7). M, S, educated middle class, L? E+: Q;
South America (Pampas)+.

228 *G.S.R.*, 24/7 (dated 22/7). M, S?, clerk, L? E+: A, Q; Brazil+, USA +,
CAN .

229 *Another Returned Roamer*, 24/7 (dated 22/7). M, clerk (public school
education), income £100 when emigrated 10 years ago, Lincoln. E: A.

230 *S.R.C.*, 24/7 (dated 21/7). M, L. E: A; USA, CAN.

231 *S.A.M.*, 24/7 (dated 22/7). M, L (Oakley-square, NW). E: A; AUS.

232 *Mariner*, 24/7 (dated 21/7). M, mariner. E (clerks); AUS, CAN+.

233 *S.B.*, 24/7 (dated 22/7). M, L? E: A; NZ.

234 *Nellie*, 24/7 (dated 22/7). F, S, had to leave home of comparative
luxury, L? E: Q.

235 *W.M.P.Y.*, 24/7 (dated 22/7). M, S?, can use tools, could raise needed
capital (ca. £100?), L? E+: Q; AUS, CAN.

236 *Bunny*, 24/7 (dated 23/7). F, W (9 months), age ca. 23?, income £500
(husband's was £250 when fell in love, waited 4 years), L (suburb).

237 *J.R.*, 24/7 (dated 23/7). M, has sheep-farmed, L? E: A; Argentina
(Buenos Ayres, Monte Video).

238 *Ring*, 24/7 (3rd letter; see 9/7, 18/7).

239 *Traveller*, 24/7 (2nd letter; see 20/7).

240 *Huron* (2 letters), 25/7, 27/7 (dated n.d., 25/7). M, S, age ca. 25, farm labour in CAN for 3 years (formerly clerk?), L? E+: A; CAN [UC]

241 *Elgo*, 25/7 (dated 24/7). M?, middle class, L? E+: A.

242 *Colonist*, 25/7 (dated 23/7). M, farmer?, L? (visiting from Canada where he has lived 35 years, probably in Upper Canada). E+: A; CAN.

243 *Kangaroo*, 25/7 (dated 23/7). M, S (about to marry), age 30, income £350, L? (home in UK for ca. two years). E+: A; AUS (Victoria, South Australia)+, CAN , USA .

244 *Professional*, 25/7 (2nd letter; see 18/7).

245 *Scotch Civil Engineer*, 25/7 (dated 24/7). M, civil engineer, L? (visiting from Scotland?). E : A; Queensland , Cape of Good Hope , South America (the Argentine Republic, Banda Oriental, and Uruguay), CAN +, USA+.

246 *O.E.S.*, 25/7 (dated 24/7). M, S?, L (Army and Navy Club). E+: A; AUS (esp. Western Australia)+, Brazil , USA .

247 *Kentucky*, 25/7 (dated 24/7). M, surgeon (formerly naval), Kentucky (not citizen). E: clerks , artisans and labourers+; A; USA (Kentucky, Kansas)+, India , Mauritius?, Natal+, Cape Colonies and Free State , Brazil?, River Plate (Carientes, Cordova, and the Banda Oriental) , Chile?, Bolivia?, UC+ .

248 *J.C.L.*, 25/7 (dated 23/7). M, visiting London? (native of USA). E: A; USA (West: Kansas, Nebraska, Colorado, New Mexico, Utah, and Nevada) .

249 *Pioneer*, 27/7 (dated 25/7) (cf. 23/7; different person). M, S?, age under 40 (20s?), carpenter (can manage other trades), can raise over £500 capital, L? (born and raised in Scotland). E+: A; Canada West , NZ+.

250 *H.E.W.*, 27/7 (dated 25/7). M, W (12 years, 8 children, 5 of whom died), age 34, mechanic? (claims to have various abilities, including "scientific"), keeps a shop with wife in addition, income £100 plus a bit, L? E+: A; CAN+.

251 *W.L.*, 27/7 (dated 25/7) (3rd letter; see *Lyn*, 15/7, and *W. Frank Lynn*, 21/7). M, L. E+: A; CAN+.

252 *An Intending Emigrant to Natal*, 27/7 (dated 25/7). M, L. E+: A; AUS , Natal+.

253 *Lex*, 27/7 (dated 23/7). M, S, age 20s?, articled clerk to solicitor, £200–300 anticipated when admitted next year, L?

254 *J.F.H.*, 27/7 (dated 23/7). M, S, age 20s?, L? E+: A; AUS, USA.

255 *Veritas*, 27/7 (dated 24/7) (cf. 13/7 and 14/7; probably different people). M, L? E: A; Newfoundland, Nova Scotia, Prince Edward Island, New Brunswick, and CAN, including Gaspé, all+.

256 *T.C.W.*, 27/7 (dated 23/7). M, S?, age 20s?, capital £100–200, L? E+: Western USA+.

257 *M. and C.* (implies two people), 27/7 (dated 24/7). M, agents of
Brazilian Emigration Office, L. E: A; Brazil+.

258 *A.J.S.*, 27/7 (dated 24/7). M, merchant trader?, L? E : A; Brazil ,
River Plate , Argentina .

259 *Canadian J.P.*, 27/7 (dated 25/7). M, age 60s?, retired (formerly Justice
of the Peace, "a trader, a large landowner, and an agriculturalist"), L?
(may return to Canada). E+ (but with qualifications): A; Eastern
Canada (Nova Scotia and New Brunswick)+, USA (Maine) .

260 *W.J.I.*, 27/7. M, "old" emigration agent for Cape Colony and Natal, L?
E+: A; Southern USA (Virginia)+, Rhode Island.

261 *Huron*, 27/7 (2nd letter; see 25/7).

262 *One Just Above Water*, 27/7 (dated 24/7), M, L? E+: A.

263 *E.C.B.* [Edwin C. Booth], 28/7 (2nd letter; see 20/7).

264 *W.D.A.*, 28/7 (dated 24/7). M?, L? E+: A; Transvaal Republic (New
Scotland, Industria),+ AUS.

265 *T.C.C.*, 28/7 (dated 24/7). F?, L? E: middle class , artisans and
labourers+; AUS.

266 *A Poor Tutor*, 28/7 (dated 24/7). M, S, tutor, income "meagre," L. E: Q.

267 *A Bachelor Curate*, 28/7 (dated 26/7). M, S (engaged), clergyman,
income £105, L?

268 *Viator*, 28/7 (dated 24/7). M, Manchester. E+: Q; USA (California, San
Francisco, Oregon, and the Pacific generally)+.

269 *The Best of Things*, 28/7. F, S, age 25, governess, income certainly more
than £20, L?

270 *H.T.A.*, 28/7 (dated 24/7). M, S, "middle class," L? E+: Q.

271 *Clericus*, 28/7 (dated 24/7) (cf. 14/7; different person). M, W,
clergyman, L? E+: A (organization only); NZ.

272 *Natal*, 28/7 (dated 25/7). M, L? E+: Natal+, USA.

273 *Paigntonians*, 28/7 (dated 25/7). F,F,F,M, W,S,S,S, age 24 years married,
daughter, daughter, fiancé of daughter?, seaside near Torquay.

274 *Geo. Francis Train*, 28/7 (2nd letter; see 20/7).

275 *H.J.*, 28/7. M, L? E+: A.

276 *U.C.*, 28/7 (dated 25/7). M, S?, L? E+: Q; UC (cf. pseudonym).

277 *A Colonial Clergyman*, 28/7 (dated 25/7). M, clergyman, L (visiting from
AUS?). E: (except for those with some capital, and single farm
labourers) ; A; AUS (esp. South Australia)+.

278 *S.*, 28/7 (dated 24/7). M, S?, formerly draper's assistant, "middle
class," L? E+: A; UC (3 years' residence)+ and "the vast country out
west"+.

279 *Returned Emigrant*, 29/7 (dated 27/7). M, S, clerk, L (Chelsea; several

years abroad, 3 of them in California). E+: A; British Columbia+, USA
(California+, Eastern States), Nicaragua+, Brazil .
280 S.C.H., 29/7 (dated 27/7), M, L? E+: A; Natal+, Free State, Transvaal.
281 C.K., 29/7 (dated 27/7). M, Sheffield. E : A; USA, AUS, CAN, NZ.

Budgets

OTHER SOURCES

Economy for the Single and Married

£50 Single (p. 11):

Bedroom (5s/wk)	£12	0	0
Breakfast (coffee house) coffee, roll & butter			
4d = 2/6 wk	5	12	0
Dinner—small plate boiled beef @ 4d, potatoes			
& bread @ 2d = 6d	8	8	0
Tea-room, bread & butter 3d	4	4	0
Supper occasionally (a-la-mode beef, etc.)	2	10	0
Washing	5	0	0
Clothes	5	0	0
Church	0	15	0
Extra	2	1	0
Surplus	4	10	0
	£50	0	0

£50 Married (p. 12):

House rent & taxes	£24	0	0
Let off a furnished room	18	0	0
	6	0	0
Coals, candle, wood	7	0	0
Tea & sugar	8	0	0
Butter	3	0	0
Meat	12	0	0
Vegetables	5	0	0
Church	1	0	0
Dress, Extras, & washing at home	8	0	0
	£50	0	0

Walsh, *A Manual of Domestic Economy* (1857) (p. 606)

Table of Expenditure
Annual Income

	No. 1 £1000	No. 2 £500	No. 3 £250	No. 4 £100
Housekeeping:	£ s	£ s	£ s	£ s
Butcher's meat & bacon	75 –	40 –	30 –	18 –
Fish & poultry	30 –	10 –	7 –	—
Bread	20 –	16 –	14 –	10 –
Milk, butter, & cheese	20 –	18 –	16 –	8 –
Grocery	30 –	20 –	18 –	8 –
Italian goods[a]	8 –	5 –	3 –	—
Greengrocery	20 –	12 –	10 –	6 –
Beer	20 –	12 –	10 –	5 –
Wine & spirits	50 –	15 –	8 –	1 –
Coals	25 –	15 –	12 –	5 –
Chandlery	12 –	7 –	7 –	2 –
	350 –	200 –	150 –	65 –
Carriages & horses	150 –	50 –		
Rent & taxes	125 –	62 10	31 5	12 10
Clothing	125 –	62 10	31 5	12 10
Wages & incidental exp	125 –	62 10	18 15	5 –
Illness & amusements	125 –	62 10	18 15	5 –
	£1000 –	£500 –	£250 –	£100 –

[a] Italian goods = olives, anchovies & sardines, vinegar pickles, etc., but not pasta.

Walsh, 1873

Income range changed from earlier version to reflect altered circumstances (p. 677)

Table of Expenditures
Annual Income

	No. 1 £1500	No. 2 £750	No. 3 £350	No. 4 £150
Housekeeping				
Butcher's meat & bacon	110 –	60 –	50 –	30 –
Fish & poultry	45 –	15 –	12 –	—

Bread	25	20 –	18 –	12 –
Milk, butter, & cheese	25 –	22 –	20 –	10 –
Grocery	35 –	28 –	22 –	10 –
Italian goods	10 –	7 –	5 –	—
Greengrocery	25 –	15 –	12 –	8 –
Beer	25 –	15 –	12 –	8 –
Wine & spirits	80 –	20 –	10 –	1 –
Coals	40 –	25 –	20 –	10 –
Chandlery	20 –	10 –	9 –	3 –
Washing	50 –	40 –	30 –	3 –
Repairs & extras	65 –	18 –	—	—
	555 –	295 –	220 –	95 –
Carriages & horses	205 –	75 –	—	—
Rent & taxes	185 –	95 –	45 –	17 10
Clothing	185 –	95 –	45 –	17 10
Wages & incidentals	185 –	95 –	20 –	10 –
Illness & amusements	185 –	95 –	20 –	10 –
	£1500 –	£750 –	£350 –	£150 –

Eliza Warren, *How I Managed My House on £200 a Year* (1864) (p. 12)

Rent & taxes per annum	£25	0	0
Coals, candles, & living for ourselves, our little one & servant, 27s. per week	70	0	0
Wages for servant—only one, mine[a]	10	0	0
Insurance for £1000	25	0	0
Clothes for myself	20	0	0
Clothes for wife	15	0	0
Clothes for babe	5	0	0
For washing	10	0	0
	180	0	0
For doctor's bills, unforeseen sundries, or exigencies	20	0	0

[a] Sic, though this account is drawn up by the husband; but surely he means the same servant as in the previous entry.

The husband, not the wife, is responsible for rent, taxes, clothes, and servant's wages. She has control over 27s per week, and he lays out exactly how she should expend it: grocery, 3s 6d; bread, 3s; meat and bacon, 10s; servant's requirements, 2s 8d; beer, 2s 4d; vegetables, 1s 8d; coals and wood, 2s 4d; lights and gas, 1s 6d (p. 82).

"How I Manage on £200 a Year," *Girl of the Period Miscellany*, 1, no. 7 (Sept. 1869), 236

The "realistic budget" of the married "Girl of the Period"

Billiards, bets, cigars, theatres, newspapers, periodicals, etc.	£52	0	0
Tips to servants	8	0	0
Travelling expenses	30	0	0
My millinery—paid on account	60	0	0
Tom's clothes—also " "	30	0	0
	£180	0	0
Surplus to be devoted to renewing accommodation bills, and staving off other difficulties	20	0	0
	£200	0	0

"Espoir," *How to Live on a Hundred a Year, Make a Good Appearance, and Save Money* (1874)
(London: Ward, Lock, and Tyler, 1874), pp. 27, 51

Expenses for January	£	s	d
Rent & taxes	1	3	0
Wages	0	12	3 1/4
Meat & poultry	1	9	4
Brandy	0	2	6
Bacon	0	6	0
Butter	0	2	8
Wine	0	3	1
Beer	0	3	0 3/4
Cheese	0	2	0
Tea	0	5	0
Sugar	0	2	8 1/2
Flour	0	1	3
Eggs	0	1	0
Milk	0	1	0
Lamp Oil	0	1	6
Biscuits	0	0	6
Crust	0	0	6
Soap, Soda & Blue	0	1	6
Coals & Wood	0	15	6
Bread	0	7	6
Sage, Split Peas, etc.	0	0	8
	£6	2	6 1/2

Her 12-month budget added less frequent expenditures:

	£	s	d
Annual expenses	73	10	6
Garden	5	2	0
Dress	7	16	0
Seeds (garden)	0	10	0
Subscriptions (charity)	2	0	0
Flannel	1	16	0
Blankets	1	4	0
Sundries	1	0	0
	92	18	6
Income	£100	0	0
Balance to place at bankers	£7	1	6

In addition, she mentions buying a new silk dress every three years out of her savings.[1]

A Happy Man, The Times, 15 Jan. 1858, p. 8

	£	s	d
Baker	8	0	5
Butcher	22	8	1
Beer	5	17	7
Cheesemonger	5	4	7
Coals & wood	8	18	8
Fish	1	6	2
Greengrocer	8	1	4
Grocer	13	11	11
Milk	2	7	7
Rent	25	0	0
Taxes	3	12	7
Railway ticket	8	0	0
Tallowchandler	6	3	7
Wages	12	6	0
Washing	3	7	2
Wines	2	0	4
Total	136	6	0

Add to this an estimated outlay for—

Clothes for self, wife, & child	40	0	0
Insurance, life & fire	12	0	0
Medical attendance & monthly nurse	12	0	0
Travelling expenses, cabs, books, & newspapers	10	0	0
Church & charity	20	0	0
[Subtotal]	84	0	0
Would amount to a total of	230	6	0
Leaving a balance on £300 a year of	69	14	0

THE "DAILY TELEGRAPH" SERIES

Prepared by the intended of *E.F.H.*'s "Old And Valued Friend"

House rent	30	0	0
Living for three people, at 4s per day	72	16	0
Dinners for you in town	25	0	0
Expenses to & from town	10	0	0
Servant	10	0	0
Laundress	15	0	0
Taxes	5	0	0
Gas	5	0	0
Coals	5	0	0
Dress for both	30	0	0
Sundries	5	0	0
Water rate	5	0	0
	£217	16	0

Vieux Moustache's calculations of the costs for *Paterfamilias*'s admitted outlays:

Rent, as *Paterfamilias* states	£45	0	0
'Bus—daily, 3d; per annum	3	18	0
Theatre thrice a year	0	18	0
Trip every second year, per annum	10	10	0
Royal Academy, &c.	0	6	0
Daily governess	18	0	0
Daily Telegraph	1	6	0
Denominational paper	0	8	4
Magazine	0	12	0
Charles Dickens	0	12	0
Benefit Societies	1	10	0

Premium of Insurance—Furniture	0	7	0
Life	5	0	0
Building Society	9	0	0
Hire of piano	12	0	0
Sitting in church	3	0	0
Total	112	7	4

To which he adds "the other expenses to which a married man with a family of children must be subject":

Dress for pater, mater, & family (£58)[a]	£45	0	0
Wages for servant	14	0	0
Coals, wood, & gas	12	0	0
Medical attendance & medicine	8	0	0
Paper, postage, &c.	2	0	0
Taxes, water, & the poor's rates	12	0	0
Sweep, clearing bin, breakage, materials for cleaning house, table linen, & carpets, brooms, &c.	10	0	0
Charwoman for washing once a week, soap, soda, &c.	12	0	0
Living for three adults & three children	120	0	0
Beer	10	0	0
	£258	10	0
Adding first estimate	112	7	4
Total	£370	7	4

[a]Presumably this is what he thinks an actual cost, the other being trimmed to Paterfamilias's estimate.

Actual expenses of *A Match-maker (Matrimonial, not Lucifer)*

Housekeeping (less rent, taxes, & coals, but including servants' wages, & washerwoman once in three weeks)	£84	0
Coals & coke, 5 tons a year, at 23s	5	15
Rent (£35) & taxes (£8)	43	0
Dress for both	25	0
Expenses to & from office, sundries about house	15	0
Wines, spirits, & medicines	10	0
Garden (man occasionally, & seeds & tools)	4	0
Total	£186	15

Reductions could be made:

Entertain fewer friends more economically	−£15	0
Smaller house (£24, taxes £6)	− 13	0
Cut down on dress, & walk to office	− 10	0
Wine, &c., but seldom	− 7	0
Do own gardening	− 3	0
Total	48	0
From	186	15
Leaves	£138	15

Vieux Moustache's calculations for *R.P.C.*

Rent & taxes	£18	0	0
Insurance of furniture, say £80		3	6
Insurance of life, say £100	1	18	4
'bus, 3d a day for six days a week	3	18	0
Coals, wood, gas, or candles	6	10	0
Washing materials, & charwoman once a month for large articles	5	0	0
Dress, self £16, wife, £13	28	0	0
Postage, papers, library	2	0	0
Dinners in City, 1s a day	15	12	0
Breakfast & supper for self	9	2	0
Meals for wife & three children, @3s per day	54	15	0
Medical attendance & medicine	3	0	0
Breakage, table, bed linen, & furniture, material for cleaning house, soap for family, sweep, & bin-clearing	6	0	0
Beer, @ 4d a day	10	1	8
Total	£164	0	6

One Who Would Be a Good Deal Happier If He Had It, married four years

House rent & taxes, including water rate & income tax	£40	0
Housekeeping, including husband's lunch in City, 30s per week	78	0
Coals, five tons (& little enough, too)	5	10
Gas	4	0
Clothes	20	0
Servant's wages (cannot do without one)	8	0
Life insurance, say on £200	5	0

Doctor, say	5	0
Chapel or church, charities, &c.	5	0
Sundries (no myth)	10	0
Total	£180	10

He has omitted confinements, and holidays and amusements, all "very expensive items."

Plain Fact

Rent of house	£35	0	0
Taxes	8	0	0
Coals & gas	8	5	0
To & from office	10	0	0
Clothes	25	0	0
Wages	10	0	0
Insurance	10	0	0
Doctor, say	5	0	0
Butcher, 14s per week	36	10	0
Fish, 1s per week	2	12	0
Baker, 5 1/2 quarters per week	4	17	6
Flour, 9d per week	1	12	0
Tea, 1/2 lb., at 2s 6d	3	4	6
Coffee, 1/2 lb., at 1s 4d	1	14	8
Butter, 1 lb., at 1s 4d	3	10	0
Lard, &c.	1	6	0
Sugar, 1 lb. lump, 6d; 1 lb. moist ditto, 6d	2	3	4
Milk, 1s per week	2	12	0
Vegetables, 1s per week	2	12	0
Bacon & eggs, 1s 4d per week	3	9	3
Washerwoman	1	14	0
Food for ditto	1	5	6
Soap, soda, &c.	1	0	0
Newspaper	1	6	0
Sundries about house	3	10	0
Beer, 3s 6d per week	9	2	0
Spirits, 2s 6d per week	6	10	0
Wine, say	10	0	0
Total	£232	2	9

This account leaves nothing to meet those "great bugbears," petty cash disbursements.

An Anxious Father

House rent & taxes	£37	0
'bus fares to office, 3d per day	3	18
Coals & gas	10	0
Servant's wages	10	0
Life insurance premium & income tax	10	0
Clothing for wife, self, & three children	30	0
Correspondence with relatives & friends	2	0
Wear & tear to household furniture	10	0
Dinners in the City, @ 1s per day	15	12
Housekeeping for three adults & three children, @ £7 per month, all inclusive	84	0
Doctor, average	5	0
Place of worship, three sittings	4	0
The *Daily Telegraph* £1 6, library 21s	2	7
Total	£223	17

Vieux Moustache

1. Rent, taxes, garden, pew rents, &c.	£47	19	9
2. Food & drink	136	18	2
3. Coals, wood, gas, & candles	20	10	
4. Wages & occasional assistance	22	14	8
5. Washing, soap, soda, &c.	15	19	2
6. Stamps, books, stationery, & papers	9	18	11
7. Breakage, repairing furniture, & renewing table & bed linen, & sweep, brooms, & materials for cleaning house	17	4	3
8. Medicine & medical attendance	8	15	10
9. Charity, gratuities, & amusements	11	7	7
10. Cabs & travelling	6	11	2
11. Insurance (fire)	1	7	
12. Dress for self & wife	37	10	
Total	£336	16	6

He admits to leaving out the income tax, and explains the omission of life insurance. If they were in the suburbs of London rather than a provincial town an additional £50 per year would go on rent, cab or 'bus hire, and wages and washing.

An Old Married Man, estimating for a clerk

Rent, rates & taxes, water, & gas	£38	0
Servant	10	0
Coals, 7 tons at 20s, wood 10s	7	10
Meat, 14s per week, say	36	0
Bread & flour	24	0
Tea, sugar, & milk	10	0
Butter & cheese	10	0
Beer, 6d per day	7	10
Travelling to office & home, @ 6d	7	10
Refreshments in town, @ 6d	7	10
Clothes, self & wife, including boots	30	0
Vegetables & fruit for pastry	5	0
Replacing furniture, &c.	5	0
Total	£198	0

A Draper

Rent & taxes	£25
Provisions for two	40
Clothing	30
Washing, coals, candles, &c.	5
Servant, half of every day	7
Pew rental at chapel, occasional trips, & petty expenses	10
Total	£117
Balance to put by or meet unforeseen expenses	33
Total	£150

Comparison of the Expenditures in "Marriage or Celibacy?" and Other Sources

Other Sources

The following table extracts the percentages of various types of expenditure given in accounts other than those in the *Daily Telegraph*.[1] The sources (in chronological order) are as follows—Married: no. 1: Anon., *Economy for the Single and Married* [1845?]; no. 2: Anon., *Domestic Economy* (1856); no. 3: Walsh, *Manual* (1857); no. 4: Warren, £200 (1865); no. 5: *Another Happy Man* (*The Times*, 1858); no. 6: Mrs. S. (1871); no. 7: Walsh, *Manual* (1873). Single: no. 1: Anon., *Economy for the Single and Married* [1845?]; no. 2: "Espoir" (1874). Different income levels in the same source are signalled by the non-superscript a, b, c, etc. The following lists are in order of total expenditure, rounded to the nearest pound.

A: MARRIED:

	Total	Food	Rent/ taxes	Clothes	Washing	Heat/ light	Church/ charity	Wages
1a	£100	55	5	15	5	8	3	4
3a	100	56	13	13	–	7	–	5
1b	150	35	20	15	4	6	7	5
7a	150	53	12	12	2	9	–	7
2	167	35	20	–[a]	5	4	–	6
1c	200	40	18	17	5	7	3	5
4	200	35	13	20	5	–	–	5
6	220	38	18	17	3	5	–[b]	4
5	230	30	13	17	1	7	9	5
1d	250	34	19	20	(4)[c]	7	(2)	2
3b	250	46	13	13	–	8	–	5
1e	300	37	22	18	(3)	7	(2)	6
7b	350	46	13	13	9	8	–	6

B: SINGLE:[d]

	Total	Food	Rent/ taxes	Clothes	Washing	Heat/ light	Church/ charity	Wages
1a	£100	40	35	12	7	–[e]	7	0
2	100	39	14	8	1	11	2	8
1b	150	40	25	8	8	–	17[f]	0

[a] A dash indicates that this category is not included, but does not imply that no expenditure is involved; usually one can infer that "extras" or some similar category includes the missing items.

[b] Included with clothes!

[c] Numbers in parentheses are inferred from the account, but are dubious.

[d] The first two are for a male; the third for a female. The differences also reflect a different kind of accommodation and consequent need for fuel and service.

[e] These would be covered in the rent.

[f] "Extras" are included.

"Marriage or Celibacy?"

Here two categories, travel [T] and meals in town [MinT], are added as constant concerns, often mentioned. The sources are as follows—Married: no. 1: *Paterfamilias*; no. 2: *A Draper*; no. 3: *Vieux Moustache* for R.P.C.; no. 4: *T.Z.*; no. 5: *One Who Would Be a Good Deal Happier If He Had It*; no. 6 (a, b, c, d, e): *A Clergyman, Aetat 47*; no. 7: *A Match-maker (Matrimonial, not Lucifer)*; no. 8: *An Old Married Man* for a younger person; no. 9: *C.S.C.*; no. 10: *R.F.H.*; no. 11: *E.F.H.'s* friend's young lady; no. 12: *An Anxious Father*; no. 13: *Plain Fact*; no. 14: *Vieux Moustache*; no. 15: *An English Wife*; no. 16: *Vieux Moustache* for *Paterfamilias*. Single: no. 1: *A Bachelor*. Once again the lists are in order of total expenditure, rounded to the nearest pound.

A: MARRIED:

	Total	Food	Rent/ taxes	Clothes	Washing	Heat/ light	Church/ charity	Wages	T	MinT
1	£112[a]	–	40	–	–	–	3	16	–[b]	–
2	£150[c]	27	17	20	3	–[d]	7[e]	5	–	–
3	£164	45	11	17	3	4	–	–	2	9
4	£169	47[f]	15	7	–[g]	6[h]	6	6	–	–
5	£181	43[i]	22[j]	11	–	5	3	4	–	–[g]
6a	£186	61[k]	–	8	2	–[g]	6	–	–	–

7	£187	50[l]	23	13	–[g]	3	–	–[g]	8[m]	–[n]
8	£198	47	19°	15	–	4[p]	–	5	4	4
9	£200	49[q]	19[j]	15	–[r]	5	–	4	–	–[g]
10	£200	–	13[s]	–	–	–	–	–	–	--
6b	£204	58[k]	–	10	4	–[g]	5	–	–	
11	£218	33	16	14	7	5	–	5	5	11
12	£224	38[t]	17	13	–[g]	4	2	4	2	7
13	£232	40	18	11	2	4	–	4	4	–
6c	£257	62[k]	–	7	2	–[g]	3	–	–	–
6d	£262	37[k]	–	14	3	–[g]	5	–	–	–
14	£337	41	14	11	5	6	3[u]	7	2	–
15	£350	–	10	–	–	–	–	7	–	–
16	£370	35	15[v]	12	3	3	(1)[w]	9[x]	–	–
6e	£388	46[k]	–	10	1	–[g]	5	–	–	–

B. SINGLE:

1	£100	27	30	20	–[g]	–[g]	–	–	8	16

[a] That the calculations are absurdly inadequate is shown by *Vieux Moustache* (see below, no. 16).

[b] He mentions "a trip every second year" at £10 10 (5 per cent), but not daily travel.

[c] With £33 for contingencies.

[d] Included with washing.

[e] And "extras."

[f] The entry is for "House (including beer, porter, washing, part done at home)," to which I have added, as usual, wine and liquor.

[g] With food.

[h] Entry includes also newspapers!

[i] Identified as "housekeeping" plus city meals, and so probably includes washing, which does not appear elsewhere.

[j] Includes water rate and income tax.

[k] "Household and living expenses."

[l] "Housekeeping . . . including servants' wages, and washerwoman."

[m] Includes "sundries about house."

[n] The economies he suggests had he only £150 a year would result in reduced percentages as well as absolute reductions in all the categories he covers: 41 per cent for food, etc., 20 per cent for rent and taxes, 20 per cent for clothes and travel (down from 21 per cent combined)—and he would have more than £11 over.

[o] Includes water and gas.

^p Gas is included in rent and taxes.

^q Housekeeping and "husband's luncheon in the City."

^r Presumably in "housekeeping."

^s Initially £40 rent and £8 taxes, but "the parlour floor furnished" is sublet for £22, leaving a total of £26. No other figures are given.

^t Housekeeping, "all inclusive."

^u Includes "amusements," but "pew rent" is in with rent and taxes.

^v Here taxes (plus water and poor rates) are added to the rent given in the lower calculation, which was 40 per cent of the £112 total.

^w Assuming the lower estimate holds.

^x Adding "wages for servant" to the earlier "daily governess," whose cost had come to 16 per cent of £112.

Notes

Introduction

1 Carlo Ginzburg's "Preface to the English Edition" of his *The Cheese and The Worms*, trans. John and Anne Tedeschi (Harmondsworth: Penguin, 1982), p. xii. Ginzburg here complains about being misinterpreted as an advocate of "the concept of the absolute autonomy and continuity of peasant culture"; see the fuller discussion in his "Preface to the Italian Edition," *ibid.*, pp. xiv–xvii and 154–5.

2 Studies of modern dailies as well as commonsense observation indicate that nothing much has changed, but the evidence is now less questionable.

3 For reasons more fully explored in chapter 6 below, I think the later letters are much more surely written by readers, without solicitation or faking.

4 For an unsettling account of the phenomenon, see Mike Hoyt, "Talk Radio, Turning up the Volume," Columbia Journalism Review, Nov./Dec. 1992, pp. 44–50.

5 I prefer that term to "discourse," which is currently in favour, because it has for me more precision and is attuned to the period.

6 The passage comes at the opening of the narrative part of his *Redgauntlet* (London: Oxford University Press, 1911), p. 175; the first part of the novel is totally epistolary.

7 *The Life and Work of Thomas Hardy*, ed. Michael Millgate (London: Macmillan, 1989), p. 52.

Chapter 1 The Great Social Evil

1 *Morning Star*, 15 June 1868, p. 2. It would appear that the leading article in the *Daily Telegraph* of the 16th used this account in the *Morning Star* or a similar account not located, because it includes information not in its own police report on the 15th.

2 The Post Office Directory for 1868 lists Madame Durant—of no stated occu-

pation—at 22 Somerset St., Portman Sq.; the house was on the corner of
Somerset and Orchard Streets. The Directory is not easy to interpret socio-
logically. Most of the occupants are given English designations, but
"Madame" Durant, as well as some doctors, dentists, and dressmakers, also
had as neighbours on Somerset Street Madame Waché at no. 17 and
Madame Edouard at no. 29 (no occupation is given for either). And at no.
41 was Madame Elise Delepine, milliner, and at no. 42 Horatio Mahomet,
"shampng. bath."—"shampoo" being then another term for massage, perhaps "massage parlour" would be a proper translation.

3 The other, signed *Mr. Nicholas*, offered, like *Harriet Barnett*'s, money for
prosecution of the brothel owner.

4 For Dr Miller, this was not an affair specially for the *Daily Telegraph*. On 23
June a letter of his appeared in the *Daily News* (again under the heading
"The Procuress") calling for a society to seek emendation of the law con-
cerning procuring, check "the sale of obscene publications," and close "the
Haymarket night houses."

5 *The Times*, 21 June 1854, p. 11.

6 *The Times*, 6 May 1857, p. 7.

7 *The Times*, 9 May 1857, p. 8.

8 In addition to the two from *I.R.B.* and that from *Theophrastus*, there was a
clerical correspondent, *St. Dunstans-in-the-West*.

9 This exchange also has found an historical niche through its brief citation by
J.A. Banks, *Prosperity and Parenthood: A Study of Family Planning among the
Victorian Middle Classes* (London: Routledge and Kegan Paul, 1954), pp. 41–4.

10 *The Times*, 7 Jan. 1858, p. 10. The main resolution, seeking wider support for
the aims of the Society, was moved by William Acton.

11 *Ibid.*, p. 12. The law in question was 2 & 3 Victoria, c. 47.

12 This is the first letter in this series signed by an actual name; Kempe was
the Rector of St James's.

13 Marylebone was anxious to join the campaign, its eastern division, the rector reported, having been "inundated by the evil, until whole streets were
now abandoned to the reign of profligacy. Portland-place, which for many
years was regarded as an aristocratic place of residence, was now notorious
as the favoured walk of the harlot."

14 The Rev. J.E. Kempe returned to the fray in a letter of the 19th in response to
comments in this vein on his having expansively asked that the necessary
legislation be applied to "the whole empire." This was, he explained, but
"rhetorical exaggeration," prompted by the comment that his efforts had
merely resulted in the moving of places of low resort; he was intending, he
said, only to deny the allegation that St James's was seeking an exclusive
benefit.

15 One cannot reliably estimate how many were actually elicited, but there is no reason to suspect that the proportion between received and published letters was different from that in the *Daily Telegraph* a decade later, so the comparison holds.

16 For contemporary accounts, see Bracebridge Hemyng, "Prostitution in London," in Henry Mayhew, *London Labour and the London Poor*, vol. 4, *Those That Will Not Work. Comprising Prostitutes. Thieves. Swindlers. Beggars* (London: Griffin, Bohn, 1862); "Medical Annotations," *Lancet*, 30 May 1857; William Logan, *The Great Social Evil: Its Causes, Extent, Results, and Remedies* (London: Hodder and Stoughton, 1871); James Miller (Professor of Surgery at Edinburgh), *Prostitution Considered in Relation to Its Cause and Cure* (Edinburgh: Sutherland and Knox; London: Simpkin, Marshall, 1859); Francis W. Newman, *The Cure of the Great Social Evil, with Special Reference to Recent Laws Delusively Called Contagious Diseases' Acts* (London: Trübner; Bristol: Arrowsmith, 1869); "The Greatest Social Evil," *Tait's Edinburgh Magazine*, 24 and 25 (1857–8); Edwin Utley, "The Social Evil in the City," *City Sketches* (London: The Author; printed Everett, 1863); Ralph Wardlaw, *Lectures on Female Prostitution: Its Nature, Extent, Effects, Guilt, Causes, and Remedy* (1842), 3rd ed. (Glasgow: Maclehose, 1843).

   Some modern assessments will be found in Fernando Henriques, *Modern Sexuality* (London: MacGibbon and Kee, 1968; Vol. III of *Prostitution and Society*); Judith R. Walkowitz, *Prostitution and Victorian Society: Women, Class, and the State* (Cambridge: Cambridge University Press, 1980).

17 See "The Greatest Social Evil," *Tait's Edinburgh Magazine*, 24 (Dec. 1857), 748, with references to other sources, including the *Lancet*, which estimated in the 1850s that one house in sixty in London was a brothel, and one in sixteen females a prostitute.

18 Walkowitz cites sources asserting that the number of reported brothels in London declined from 933 in 1841 to 410 in 1857, and that in 1868 there were only two "explicit brothels" (p. 24 and n68).

19 There are difficulties in assessing the accuracy of the figures or even comparing them fairly, for their bases are not compatible, some being impressionistic, some based on police reports that include only street-walkers and omit the City of London, some derived from reports on brothels and assumptions about the average number of inmates, and some on extrapolations from the numbers of women in various homes for reformed prostitutes.

20 One of the most celebrated in the 1820s and 1830s was that in Seymour Place, Bryanstone Square, run by Marie Aubrey (a French woman) and her lover, John Williams; they were reported to specialize in young French and Italian girls. (Henriques, p. 70.)

21 See Walkowitz, pp. 29 and 247; at the latter place she comments on the reverse trade, saying that "the women enticed into licensed brothels in Antwerp and Brussels were by no means the young innocents depicted in the sensational stories." See also Logan, pp. 82–4, where he quotes *The Times* (22 June 1854) on importing girls from France or Belgium.

22 "Medical Annotations," *Lancet*, 560.

23 See Newman, p. 12, and Henriques, pp. 125 and 259.

24 Logan, p. 108.

25 See Walkowitz, p. 23, and Henriques, p. 148.

26 At this time there was no public outcry against male prostitutes or homosexual brothels; all references may be assumed to be to men hiring women.

27 The Owenite view of marriage as prostitution without pay was not commonly held.

Chapter 2 Marriage or Celibacy? The *Daily Telegraph* Series

1 *The Times*, 9 Jan. 1858, p. 6.

2 *The Times*, 13 Jan. 1858, p. 12.

3 *Zuleika Dobson* (1911) (Harmondsworth: Penguin, 1988), p. 131.

4 See chapter 1, pp. 18–19 above.

5 *The Times*, 22 Jan. 1858, p. 6.

6 Celsus is accusing Coelebs, an Oxford Fellow (and hence celibate), of avarice in refusing a living worth £500 a year. Coelebs later responds: "the fact is, no man but a Cockney can marry, as the *Times* says, on three hundred a-year. I have been always used to ride, and shoot, and fish, and go about the world." G.C. Swayne, "Colleges and Celibacy: A Dialogue," *Blackwood's Magazine*, 83 (May 1858), 559 and 567.

7 *The Times*, 27 June 1861, p. 6. J.A. Banks calls attention also to this exchange, in *Prosperity and Parenthood: A Study of Family Planning among the Victorian Middle Classes* (London: Routledge and Kegan Paul, 1954), p. 45, though without reference to all the letters.

8 *The Times*, 28 June 1861, p. 12.

9 *Ibid.*

10 *The Times*, 29 June 1861, p. 12.

11 As a contrast with the space and syntax allowed modern newspaper correspondents, a single tremendous sentence may be quoted: "If high life or genteel society did not sanction and encourage, as it undoubtedly does, the perpetuation of the social evil,—if the high-born maiden, conscious and proud of her own unsullied virtue, were not so often to think so lightly of maiden honour frittered away by the accomplished wiles of her own lover,—if the 'maids of merry England' had more respect for themselves

than to scrupulously study and follow the example in the 'loudness of
dress' and the 'fast conversation' adopted by those whose smiles know full
well the talismanic power of gold,—if less adulation were paid to mere
wealth and less homage to some empty title,—if fewer parents looked up to
a higher level than their own for suitors for their daughters, and more to
noble-minded and ambitious youths lower down than themselves in the
social scale, but struggling in such a bold and heroic manner as to make it a
matter of certainty to ultimately reach the pinnacle of fame—if woman
were true to woman, and if every daughter of Eve were, in the hour of
temptation, to find in man a protector and a friend—if society adopted the
sensible plan of allowing daughters to marry when they feel inclined 'people of limited means and no position,' and if mothers thought more of their
daughters' happiness than to sacrifice them to heirs, 'in order to replenish
an exhausted treasury,' at a time when 'husbands become irritable,' 'milli-
ners press,' and 'jewellers are more pressing than becomes them,' perhaps
now seven very respectable mammas would not have to deplore the
unmatrimonially blessed condition of some four-and-twenty daughters, of
whom, we are informed, 'the majority are really amiable and can fairly be
considered attractive.'" (*Ibid.*)

12 He himself supplied the heading of his letter, "Hetaerae," because it "will
not be understood by ladies—whom [he does] not address—or by mere
'swells,' whose intellect and conscience appear equally dull." (*Ibid.*)

13 *Ibid.*

14 *Ibid.*

15 A related issue resulted in three letters to the editor at this time. On the
same day as *A Mother* and *Grandmamma*, yet another family member, *A
Brother*, appeared in outraged tones, under the heading "Decency in the
Pulpit," as one shamed by his inability to perform his familial duties in
supposedly protected premises. He is not concerned directly with either
mercenary marriages or the social evil, but with the pollution coming from
what should be a centre of purity. His concluding comment strangely
adumbrates modern advocacy of film classification, as he complains about
a sermon in St James's that must have outraged the feelings of every
"father, mother, or brother in that church" by open references "to that vice
which, though so prominent elsewhere, is veiled in the house of God," and
recommends "if the clergy in their earnest endeavours to support reformatories, consider it necessary to enter into the fullest details of 'the social
evil,' notice should be given to parents, in order that they may guard their
children from hearing such a sermon as the one to which I allude." (*The
Times*, 1 July 1861, p. 11.) A reply came from the Rev. John Edward Kempe, a
participatant in the exchange in 1858, who, though vicar of St James's, had

been absent on other duties and so had not delivered or even heard the sermon, but was well informed about it, and defended the "delicacy and discretion, . . . feeling and power," expressed in the sermon, delivered in fact by the Dean of Westminster. (*The Times*, 2 July 1861, p. 12.) *A Brother* was not contrite, and replied the next day with spirit: "I still think that a man should pause before he exposes, to girls of tender age, with 'great power and feeling,' those vices from which their homes have screened them, and I would entreat preachers, while endeavouring 'to stem the tide of profligacy,' and remove 'false delicacy,' not to forget the claims of innocence." (*The Times*, 3 July 1861, p. 10.)

While related to one of the themes of the other letters in this series, these three obviously make a detour, and so are not included in the main discussion.

16 *Ibid.*, p. 12.
17 *Ibid.*
18 *The Times*, 2 July 1861, p. 8 (3rd leader).
19 Thirteen, if the three concerning the propriety of preaching about prostitution in St James's church are included.
20 In a typical 16-page issue of *The Times*, for instance, advertisements appeared on pp. 1–5, 13–16, and parts of other pages.
21 One contemporary instance will support what was said above about the series in *The Times*: during the period when "Marriage or Celibacy?" was running in the *Daily Telegraph*, the *Daily News* (then an 8-page paper) published almost *no* letters to the editor. For example there were but five in the week of 13 to 22 June, 1868, all on "The Shilling Shakespeare"; on the 23rd, quite exceptionally, there were seven (including that from Dr Miller cited in chapter 1), but they were on scattered topics.
22 I am not denying the biases in news reporting, as evident then as now, but dwelling on the role of the editorial writers.
23 "On History Again," *Critical and Miscellaneous Essays*, 7 vols (London: Chapman and Hall, 1872), vol. 4, p. 215.
24 In these respects, he adds, "a kind of daily *Household Words*" (like the very popular weekly founded and run by Charles Dickens). *The Life and Adventures of George Augustus Sala, Written by Himself* (1895) (London: Cassell, 1896), p. 323.
25 *Ibid.*, 328.
26 See S.M.B. Coulling, "Matthew Arnold and the *Daily Telegraph*," *RES*, n.s. 12 (1961), 173–9. Sala assumes (p. 453) that Matthew Arnold would include in his "band of 'young lions,'" Edward Dicey, who also was a prolific leader writer for the *Telegraph*. Arnold's main target and his ironic habit of litotes are indicated in his "The Literary Influence of Academies": "Mr. James Gor-

don Bennett, of the *New York Herald*, says, I believe, that the highest achievement of the human intellect is what he calls 'a good editorial.' This is not quite so." *Lectures and Essays in Criticism*, ed. R.H. Super (Ann Arbor: University of Michigan Press, 1962), p. 255.

27 "English Comforts. (From the German of Dr. Francis Kottenkamp)," *Bentley's Miscellany*, 3 (1838), 171.

28 In *The Christmas Books*, 2 vols., ed. Michael Slater (Harmondsworth: Penguin, 1971), vol. 1, p. 157. That this is not a chance observation is indicated later when Toby's daughter, Meg, responds to his saying "they're always a bringing up some new law or other," by observing, "And according to what I was reading you in the paper the other day, father; what the Judge said, you know; we poor people are supposed to know them all" (p. 160). And again (p. 195), when Toby "took his newspaper from his pocket, and began to read. Carelessly at first, and skimming up and down the columns; but with an earnest and a sad attention, very soon. For this same dreaded paper re-directed Trotty's thoughts into the channel they had taken all that day, and which the day's events had so marked out and shaped. His interest in the two wanderers had set him on another course of thinking, and a happier one, for the time; but being alone again, and reading of the crimes and violences of the people, he relapsed into his former train."

29 *The Haunted Man* (1848), *ibid.*, vol. 2, pp. 332–3.

30 (1858) (London: John Long, 1903), p. 217.

31 The famed *Morning Chronicle*'s series on "London Labour" by Henry Mayhew and his collaborators comes to mind, but while there are similarities, the differences are much more obvious: the series was planned in advance, and most of the material came from paid contributors, with the only participation by readers being letters subscribing to ameliorative charitable causes.

32 Charley Pooter of George and Weedon Grossmith's *The Diary of a Nobody* (1892) supplies apt evidence. When Pooter is unable to pay his fare, a London cabman called him, he says, "every name he could lay his tongue to, and positively seized me by the beard. . . . We had to walk home in the pouring rain, nearly two miles, and when I got in I put down the conversation I had with the cabman, word for word, as I intend writing to the Telegraph for the purpose of proposing that cabs should be driven only by men under Government control, to prevent civilians being subjected to the disgraceful insult and outrage that I had had to endure." (Bristol: Arrowsmith; London: Simpkin, et al., 1919, p. 193.)

33 In their opening sentences they frequently laud the *Telegraph* for opening its "valuable" paper for such a "useful" discussion. The assumptions are that the space is costly (and could be used for purposes more profitable to the

propietors) and also that somehow the *Daily Telegraph* is itself responsible
for the discussion. This willing complicity enabled the *Telegraph* to reinforce
and broaden its desired image.

34 Though the law term began in October.

35 (London: Cassell, 1955), p. 88.

36 A rapid check of the summer months in the years before and after 1868,
from 1860 to 1890, reveals none previous. After "Marriage or Celibacy?"
there were brief flurries, lasting usually about a week, on such subjects as
"Servants at the Zoo" (July 1875), "Public Opinion on the [Russo-Turkish]
War" (Aug. 1877, with an unusual feature, some summary of letters), "Popular Ways and Words" (i.e., bad language) and "Bungling Executions"
(both late Aug. to early Sept. 1879), and "Fashion and Trade" (late Aug. to
mid-Sept. 1881). The earliest rival in size and range (though inferior in
both) to "Marriage or Celibacy?" was "Our Boys" (Sept. 1883), with usually
about one column of letters per day. Finally, in 1888, "Marriage or Celibacy?" was properly rivalled by "Is Marriage a Failure?" Series after it mentioned by Burnham include several that were "slight and short," such as
"The Age of Love," "Are Appearances Worth Keeping Up?," "The Slavery
of Drink," and "The Art of Losing Fat," and one that was a greater success
than any other, "Do We Believe?" (Burnham, *Peterborough Court*, pp. 146–7.)
Both "Marriage or Celibacy?" and "Is Marriage a Failure?" figure in a valuable article by Judith Knelman, "She Loves Me, She Loves Me Not: Trends
in the Victorian Marriage Market," *Journal of Communication Inquiry*, 18
(Winter 1994), 80–94.

37 A selection was edited by Harry Quilter, *Is Marriage a Failure? A Modern
Symposium* (London: Sonnenschein, 1888; Chicago: Rand, McNally, 1889).

38 1919 ed., p. 96.

39 Burnham's account is little help. Thornton Hunt could be considered editor,
but Edward Lawson (the son of J.M. Levy, the first proprietor), later 1st
Lord Burnham, was generally responsible. (He changed his name after his
uncle Lionel Lawson Levy changed his "for business purposes.") Le Sage
was not yet (on this evidence) in a position to be responsible, though he
was hired in 1863 as personal assistant to Lawson (p. 3). Sala is more informative: he describes himself as, among other things, the "social leader-
writer, with strong Liberal tendencies" (p. 323)—a rare type, in his view; he
seldom wrote on politics, but rather on subjects "literary, artistic, social, or
biographical." The political leaders were written, he says, by James Augustus St John (who, in spite of his blindness, wrote two or three leaders a
week), and St John's son Horace, who would "dash off a leader in an hour's
time" every day (pp. 326–7). He indicates that during 1868 his own "hard
but pleasant work" encompassed "so many hundreds of leaders written; so

many public functions described, so many picture exhibitions criticised and books reviewed" (p. 503).

40 It seems not improbable that in this case the writer was the one Sala says he became aware of in 1862, whose style was "replete . . . with refined scholarship, with eloquent diction, and with an Oriental exuberance of epithets." Edward Lawson told him that "the gentleman . . . who wrote so felicitiously about the Nilotic Butterfly and the sacred rivers and temples of burning Ind" was Edwin Arnold (later Sir Edwin, KCIE, CSI), "newly arrived from India" (p. 375). Indeed, given that Arnold wrote many leaders in the period, he might have authored all those in the series—but then Sala's hand may also have been active.

Chapter 3 Marriage and Mores

1 The sequence may be suggested thus—day 1: letters A, B, C. . . ; day 2: letters D, E, F. . . ; day 3, letters anti-A, pro-B, G, H. . . ; day 4, letters pro-A, anti-C, pro-D, I, J . . . and so on.

2 Initially the character Benedick, engaged in lively vituperative debate with Beatrice, jests that if he ever makes the error of marrying, the sign should appear over him, like that saying "Here is a good horse to hire," "Here you may see Benedick the married man" (I. i; cf. V. i). Finally, however, when taunted with the phrase after betrothal to Beatrice, he cares not for "a satire or an epigram" (V. iv), and so becomes the type of the husband.

3 Such arguments were becoming very popular and powerful in the period, with the growth of social sciences and the increasing use of comparison as an expository and argumentative tool.

4 In an aside *Benedick* raises the ante considerably by suggesting that £1000 is a better figure.

5 This last is my term; *Benedick* assumes the basis of judgment.

6 Perhaps his wife would sign herself *Beatrice* (a pseudonym sadly not used in the series).

7 To see irony is possible but not mandatory.

8 *Solon*, who is able to put Mill's *Principles* in his pocket, undoubtedly has bought a copy of the "People's Edition," a low-priced small-format version that sold well for decades.

9 For a full account, see Bruce Kinzer, Ann P. Robson, and John M. Robson, *A Moralist in Parliament: John Stuart Mill, the Westminster Years* (Toronto: University of Toronto Press, 1992).

10 Bk. II, chap. xiii, sect. 1; *in Collected Works*, ed. John M. Robson (Toronto: University of Toronto Press, 1967), vol. 2, p. 368n. Smiff has in mind not only this passage, but others such as these: "Every one has a right to live.

We will suppose this granted. But no one has a right to bring creatures into life, to be supported by other people. . . . If a man cannot support even himself unless others help him, those others are entitled to say that they do not also undertake the support of any offspring which it is physically possible for him to summon into the world." (*Ibid.*, bk. II, chap. xii, sect. 2; p. 358.) "[The] conduct of human creatures is more or less influenced by foresight of consequences, and by impulses superior to mere animal instincts: and they do not, therefore, propagate like swine, but are capable, though in very unequal degrees, of being withheld by prudence, or by the social affections, from giving existence to beings born only to misery and premature death. In proportion as mankind rise above the condition of the beasts, population is restrained by the fear of want rather than by want itself. Even where there is no question of starvation, many are similarly acted upon by the apprehension of losing what have come to be regarded as the decencies of their situation in life." (*Ibid.*, bk. I, chap. x, sect. 3; vol. 2, pp. 156–7.)

11 Just two years later, Anthony Trollope portrayed a close parallel in describing the passion of Ontario Moggs, who, stricken with love for Polly Neefit, on a Sunday "was at Hendon from ten till three, hanging about in the lanes, sitting on gates, whiling away the time with a treatise on political economy which he had brought down in his pocket, thinking of Polly while he strove to confine his thoughts to the great subject of man's productive industry." *Ralph the Heir* (1870–71) (Oxford: Oxford University Press, 1990), p. 243.

12 In its concluding editorial, the *Telegraph* identified *Erastes* as the champion of the love-at-any-cost troops, in opposition to *Benedick*'s hard-hearted army.

13 Cf. the instances cited from *The Times*, pp. 30 and 31 above, and Anthony Trollope's fun with the Eglinton Tournament in *Barchester Towers*.

14 Cf. *Macbeth*, I. vii. 42–6: "Wouldst thou . . . live a coward in thine own esteem, / Letting 'I dare not' wait upon 'I would,' Like the poor cat i' the adage?" (I have not identified "pale fears and half-nerved manhood.")

15 More accurately, "What costs . . . donor? / Merely an . . . part." (Part II, lines 264–5.)

16 West End areas standing in fashion just below Belgravia.

17 The echo here is more of Edmund Burke's assault on the French Revolutionaries than of William Blake.

18 That image, if nothing more, serves to date the comment.

19 *Erastes* is here probably not showing the geographic ignorance of some others in the series by implying that the Red River flows through Toronto, for both settlements were prominent targets at the time.

20 He ignores here the lines following: "Love in a hut, with water and a crust, / Is—Love, forgive us!—cinders, ashes, dust; / Love in a palace is perhaps

at least / More grievous torment than a hermit's fast." (*Lamia*, pt. 2, lines 1–4.)

21 "Fool, again the dream, the fancy! but I *know* my words are wild, / But I count the gray barbarian lower than the Christian child." ("Locksley Hall," lines 173–4.)

22 The *lex Caducaria* of AD 9 provided, among other things, that unmarried people under certain conditions forfeited everything given by testament.

23 In this people seem to accord with literary authority: "from one learn all" (*ab uno disce omnes*, Virgil, *Aeneid*). The general acceptance of the tactic seems not diminished by its logical weakness and legal failure: "one witness is no witness" (*testis unus, testis nullus*).

24 Perhaps, though *An English Girl* does not make the point explicitly, she wished to indicate that all women should not be thought to agree; there can, of course, be at least two typical female positions, for typicality is not universality. However, the issue here is not (though it is later in other letters) a difference attributed to the marital status of the two women, for *An English Girl* displays herself as, like *Materfamilias*, a housekeeper, the crucial point.

25 She reveals in her concluding sentence that she is a teacher, though of what and at what level she does not say.

26 Modern sensibilities will also be jarred by her willingness merely to "study him" as a guide, but in the series there is no complaint against such submissive attitudes, though more assertive ones are aired simply as examples from life.

27 The more learned allusions, like other consciously artful devices, are concentrated in the earlier letters. Later, as the discussion makes more use of facts and direct comment, there is less place and space for such allusions as those in *Benedick*'s first letter—Shakespeare, Pope, Macaulay, Artemus Ward, *All the Year Round*, the man who deliberates is lost, and (that rare punning joke) descending into the streets.

28 Using this term rather than "napkins" would signal to later sensitive observers a middle-class, "non-U" vocabulary.

29 More expansively, she says: "the work itself, making and mending, sewing, cooking, nursing, even doing the work of housemaids if necessary, is not degrading but ennobling."

30 She gives a side-blow to another male despondent correspondent, recalling that the Irish were likened by *Benedick* to Red Indians and adding: "par parenthèse, I have been subject to no squaw-like treatment yet." (An unlikely subjection, one may think, for anyone who says "par parenthèse.")

31 The costs are given in chapter 4 below, pp. 122–3.

32 Much like those of *An English Girl*, and, in the absence of other evidence, probably not uncommon.

33 Fearing that some correspondents may not understand this assertion, *Paterfamilias* recommends "Mr. Froude's 'Cat's Pilgrimage,'" where "they will see from so great an authority that to do one's duty is one of the greatest sources of pleasure." James Anthony Froude's "A Cat's Pilgrimage" (1850), republished in his *Short Studies on Great Subjects*, first series (reissued, London: Longmans, Green, 1901), vol. 1, pp. 630–50, is a beast fable whose moral is learning one's duty.

34 *A Plain Girl*, who had arraigned the billiard-playing young men of the period.

35 The reference is clearly to the lay figure, not to the correspondent so signing himself.

36 *Jane's* question still waits on an answer from me.

37 Polly is the fond version of Mary especially in labouring families, and Edith (not Edie) indicates some aspiration.

38 Probably hence the signature (Italian for lily), which has historically the specific denotation of fleur-de-lys.

39 Later she admits that when her husband proposed, he had an annual income of £200—but he unfortunately lost it soon after.

40 While there was much information about contraception by the mid-1860s, widespread knowledge came only late in the 1870s, following the Besant/Bradlaugh trial. In any case, the correspondence in the *Daily Telegraph* is not reticent on the subject of birth control; it merely affirms the certainty (with the single qualification about fertility cited below, p. 186) that children will arrive with a regularity as inexorable as the resultant costs.

41 I say "English Christian" to cover both Church of England and Dissenting congregations, though little specific to the latter shows. It is not puzzling, but emblematic, that though the proprietor of the *Telegraph* was a Jew, no trace of his faith is seen in the leading articles.

42 *Fraser's Magazine*, 65 (Feb. 1862), 234.

43 As indeed the phrase "man and wife" suggests.

44 *Pride and Prejudice* (1813) (New York: Norton, 1966), p. 86 (bk. I, chap. 22). The general acceptance is signalled in a telling passage in Shirley Foster's "Female Januses: Ambiguity and Ambivalence towards Marriage in Mid-Victorian Women's Fiction," *International Journal of Women's Studies*, 6 (1983), 224: "Curiously, the single woman who, for whatever reason, remains outside the bonds of matrimony, gets little direct treatment in the work of mid-century female novelists and does not often play a central role in the narrative. This in itself demonstrates the authors' ambivalence, since even though many of them were self-supporting spinsters and although the

working single woman is the most obvious illustration of female self-asser-
tion, they clearly appeared to devote most of their attention to the more traditional areas of women's courtship and betrothal, instead of arguing for
specific alternatives to female dependency."

45 George Eliot, *Daniel Deronda* (Harmondsworth: Penguin, 1967), epigraph,
chap. 10, p. 132.

46 *Cranford* (1851–3), in *Cranford/Cousin Phillis* (Harmondsworth: Penguin,
1986), p. 157. Cf. *Not Wisely, but too Well*: "that passion which forms the
main plot of a woman's life, and is only a small secondary byplay in a
man's," and "A woman in love thinks of nothing but her love; a man in
love thinks of his love parenthetically, episodically; it shares his thoughts
with his horses, his books, his dinner." (Pp. 49, 50.)

47 Harmondsworth: Penguin, 1983, p. 126; chap. 15.

48 Cited from chap. 67 in R.H. Super, *The Chronicler of Barsetshire: A Life of
Anthony Trollope* (Ann Arbor: University of Michigan Press, 1988). On this
theme, see also the quotations from John Stuart Mill and Harriet Taylor
Mill in Gail Tulloch, *Mill on Sexual Equality* (Hemel Hempstead: Harvester
Wheatsheaf, 1989), pp. 82, 86.

49 (London: Houlston and Wright), p. vi.

50 Joseph Verey, *Martyrs to Fashion* (1868), vol. 1, p. 120. Quoted from Myron
F. Brightfield, *Victorian England in Its Novels (1840–1870)*, 4 vols. (Los Angeles: University of California Library, 1968). As will be evident, I am much
indebted to that rich compendium.

51 Catherine Crowe, *The Adventures of a Beauty* (1852), vol. 2, pp. 278–9, quoted
from Brightfield.

52 Compare this sentiment from a fictional thrifty wife of a clergyman: "I
could not endure to degrade my children, but common sense daily argues
in favour of the middle-classes holding in respect all the practical knowledge necessary for family comfort. A girl at eighteen should be able to
direct how bread is made, meat prepared, stores hoarded, pickles and preserves put away. She may marry a man with three hundred pounds a-
year—quite sufficient in my day for everything; nothing now—only what
may be termed genteel beggary." (Elizabeth Jenings, *My Good for Nothing
Brother* [1863], pp. 34–5, quoted from Brightfield.

53 Charles Dickens, *The Personal History of David Copperfield* (1849–50) (Harmondsworth: Penguin, 1988), pp. 16–17; chap. 1.

54 *Ibid.*, p. 605; chap. 37.

55 Mrs Julia McNair Wright, *The Complete Home: An Encylopaedia of Domestic
Life and Affairs. The Household in Its Foundation, Order, Economy, Beauty,
Healthfulness, Emergencies, Methods, Children, Literature, Amusements, Reli-
gion, Friendships, Manners, Hospitality, Servants, Industry, Money, and History.*

A volume of Practical Experiences Popularly Illustrated (Philadelphia and Brantford, Ont.: Bradley, Garretson & Co.; Columbus, Chicago, Nashville, St Louis, San Francisco: William Garretson & Co., 1883). The passage comes from chap. 16, "The Use and Abuse of Money in the Home. Aunt Sophronia Tells How to Conduct Domestic Expenditures," p. 396.

56 Quoted by Duncan Crow, *The Victorian Woman* (London: Allen and Unwin, 1971), p. 82.

57 (Harmondsworth: Penguin, 1985), p. 39; chap. 1.

58 (Harmondsworth: Penguin, 1986), p. 138; chap. 10.

59 Frances Browne, *The Hidden Sin* (1866), vol. 2, pp. 22–3, quoted from Brightfield.

60 Wright, *The Complete Home*, p. 389.

61 Charles Darwin, *Descent of Man and Selection in Relation to Sex* (London, 1871), p. 893.

62 *Our Mutual Friend* (1864–5) (Harmondsworth: Penguin, 1971), pp. 174–5; bk. I, chap. 11.

63 Frederick Locker-Lampson, "The Jester's Plea," lines 13–16, in *A Selection from the Works of Frederick Locker* (London: Moxon, 1865), p. 67.

64 *Pygmalion* (1914) (Harmondsworth: Penguin, 1941), act V, pp. 120–9.

65 After quoting Franklin's explanation of Chastity, "Rarely use venery but for health and offspring, never to dulness, weakness, or the injury of your own or another's peace or reputation," Lawrence proposes a substitute creed: "Never 'use' venery at all. Follow your passional impulse, if it be answered in the other being; but never have any motive in mind, neither off-spring nor health nor even pleasure, nor even service. Only know that 'venery' is of the great gods. An offering-up of yourself to the very great gods, the dark ones, and nothing else." *Studies in Classic American Literature* (New York: Seltzer, 1923), pp. 18, 26.

66 Here is disguised no naivety about their private behaviour, which, as has been so gleefully disclosed in recent decades, included much that has been condemned in most ages and cultures but seems to be welcomed in the late twentieth century on condition that it become public.

67 Of course within marriage, justice operates in situations of "perfect" obligations; but the kinds of decisions pressing on those seeking marriage that would make such "justice" practicable involved "imperfect" obligations, in which there is no reciprocal duty until contracts are made.

68 That the poorest were unable to do so was the greatest engine of the "new Liberalism" that grew to dominate early twentieth-century politics and left as its legacy the Welfare State, with its attempt to ensure the free lunch and the happy hour.

69 Wright, *The Complete Home*, p. 393. When such fear is lacking, there are

reasons. For instance, the financial crisis that brings sad disaster in life and art through life-threatening sickness is not part of the anxiety in Thackeray's *Pendennis*, chaps. 52–3, in which the hero nearly dies and then has a ten-day, all-demanding convalescence. The issue can be avoided because Pen's mother Laura and his uncle have compétences, and the doctor refuses payment.

70 Banks uses this as the title of chapter 7 of his *Prosperity and Parenthood: A Study of Family Planning among the Victorian Middle Classes* (London: Routledge and Kegan Paul, 1954).

71 M.E. Braddon, *Lady Audley's Secret* (London: Simpkin, Marshall, Hamilton, Kent, n.d.), p. 22; chap. 3.

72 In W.S. Gilbert and Arthur Sullivan's *The Pirates of Penzance* (1879), the Pirate King never failed (nor does he now fail) to get a laugh when he says: "I don't think much of our profession, but, contrasted with respectability, it is comparatively honest." Ian Bradley, ed., *The Annotated Gilbert and Sullivan*, vol. 1 (Harmondsworth: Penguin, 1982), p. 95. The original version (licence copy) contains an exchange between Frederic and the Pirate King in which Frederic says of a *pilot*, "A highly respectable line of life though certainly not a high lot"; and the King offers in response, "You said 'a respectable line of life' we thought you meant a pirate" (p. 94). This mistake remains a joke in the final version, but without the reference to respectability.

73 P. 198–9; chap. 10. In an earlier passage, though the word does not appear, the dangerous nature of the desire is adumbrated:

"If I [Emily] was ever to be a lady, I'd give him [Dan'l Peggoty] a sky-blue coat with diamond buttons, nankeen trousers, a red velvet waistcoat, a cocked hat, a large gold watch, a silver pipe, and a box of money." ...
"You would like to be a lady?" I said.
Emily looked at me, and laughed, and nodded "yes."
"I should like it very much. We would all be gentlefolks together, then." (P. 85; chap. 3.)

74 *The Life and Adventures of Martin Chuzzlewit* (1843–4) (Harmondsworth: Penguin, 1968), p. 501; chap. 27.

75 Pp. 356–7; chap. 21. In a nice turn, he is in fact finally sentenced to transportation for theft. In another place, "we left him [Littimer] standing on the pavement, as respectable a mystery as any pyramid in Egypt." (P. 402; chap. 23.)

76 Pp. 450, 460; bk. II, chap. 15.

77 Indeed in the *Daily Telegraph* this danger is recognized as part of the disease of emulation: "No doubt the middle and lower-middle class of people in London suffer from country families having their thousands, all spending part of each year in London, and thus raising people's ideas of what is respectable and proper" (Z.Y.X.).

78 In addition to the uses cited, the term (or its cognates) appears in 34 other letters or leaders in the series, showing just how dominant a notion it was.

79 He goes on to complain, not unreasonably, that the term "respectable appearance" has been "a good deal sneered at, and the ladies seem inclined to attribute to selfishness what in reality arises from a desire on the part of the man to avoid bringing himself, and it may be a loveable girl, to a position of obscurity and wretchedness." A rare example in the series of such sneering appeared later: "As regards myself, I am at present employed behind a counter, but . . . have determined to throw off the conventional black coat, and buy some tools, and go off to Canada or elsewhere, and there be thoroughly prepared to rough it; taking to anything that turns up, be it carpentering, clerkship, employment in a store or in the backwoods— anything where perseverance, honest industry, and being able to avoid in a new country so many of the shoals of so-called respectability—dress, and keeping up an appearance one's means will not warrant" (J.A.B.).

80 *Our Mutual Friend*, p. 266; bk. II, chap. 1. For repeated attaching of the tag to Headstone's clothes, see pp. 268, 618, and 867. As to its inaptness, see the passage where he dresses as Rogue Riderhood: "And whereas, in his own schoolmaster clothes, he usually looked as if they were the clothes of some other man, he now looked, in the clothes of some other man or men, as if they were his own" (p. 697).

81 Two of these are singular, but worth noting: young men who live at home can afford "a decent cigar" (W.E.W.W.), and the son of an army officer is "decently connected" (J.A.V.C.).

82 The only exception comes not in reference to dress but to crowded housing, when it is asserted that a poor family in "decent" accommodation consisting of one room may "strive to obtain two rooms, for decency sake" (M.B.).

83 *A Mind to Murder* (1963) (London: Sphere Books, 1985), p. 130. A friend of mine in a London hospital with a broken pelvis was forced by the nursing staff to struggle into underwear for the visit of the consultant "Professor."

84 I am not denying either the existence of a valuable working-class "culture" or the growing sense of working-class separation; the point is only that many of the working class, especially its "elite," were in the 1860s objecting less to middle-class standards than to their inability to attain them. One illustration of the shared view—dare one call it commonsensical and not bourgeois?—of the need for good housekeeping at the manual labourer's income level is seen in John A. Leatherland's 'The Household Economy of the Workman," in his *Essays and Poems, with a Brief Autobiographical Memoir* (London: Tweedie, 1862), pp. 43–64.

85 George Grossmith and Weedon Grossmith, *The Diary of a Nobody* (1892) (Bristol: Arrowsmith; London: Simpkin, et al., 1919), p. 122.

86 See his "The Function of Criticism at the Present Time" (1865), *passim*.
87 The excoriation now engaged in by the educated middle class in the United States is comparable—and just as intelligible.

Chapter 4 "The Equation of Income and Expenditure"

1 George Eliot, "Amos Barton," *Scenes of Clerical Life* (1858) (Harmondsworth: Penguin, 1985): "the equation of income and expenditure was offering new and constantly accumulating difficulties to Mr and Mrs Barton" (p. 82; chap. 5).
2 *Ibid.*, p. 44; chap. 1.
3 For "respectability," see chapter 3. In this discussion I generally omit consideration of inflation in using materials that are roughly contemporary, because costs remained remarkably level throughout the period, though the levels of middle-class expenditure—and income—were slowly rising. A detailed comparison of artisans' family budgets—similar in most respects to those of the lower middle class—shows that, based on the price in 1900 of the items purchased in 1860, money had increased in purchasing power by 20 per cent, while based on the price in 1860 of the items purchased in 1900, its purchasing power had increased by 10 per cent. A.L. Bowley, "Wages," *Encyclopaedia Britannica*, 10th ed., 1902, vol. 33, p. 720.
4 London: Houlston and Wright, 1864. The tale appeared as a serial in *The Ladies' Treasury*, which Mrs Warren edited. Some of her sample budgets are given below. The table of contents of this fictional work runs *inter alia* from Ill-Management through Punctuality, Difference between Being Niggardly and Economising, How to Wash Small Things in a Bowl, to the conclusion: Work for Each Day in the Week, and Some Simple Directions for a Few Dainty Dishes of Food.
5 When David suggests prior to their marriage that it would be helpful if Dora learned something about housekeeping and accounts, she replies "with something that was half a sob and half a scream," and at his mention that she might read "a little Cookery Book," she goes into a complete fright. Charles Dickens, *The Personal History of David Copperfield* (1849–50) (Harmondsworth: Penguin, 1988), p. 605; chap. 37. See also pp. 606–7 (chap. 37), pp. 670–1 (chap. 41), pp. 701–16 (chap. 44, "Our Housekeeping"), and pp. 758–69 (chap. 48, "Domestic").
6 Knightly William Horlock, *Lord Fitzwarine* (1860), vol. 1, p. 188, quoted from Myron F. Brightfield, *Victorian England in Its Novels (1840–1870)*, 4 vols. (Los Angeles: University of California Library, 1968). Brightfield's extracts contain other large fictional estimates of matrimonial adequacy, ranging from a low of £550 through £600, £700–800, and £1000 to £1500–2000. I like

the fine precision of Mr Templeton in Edward Bulwer Lytton's *Ernest Mal-travers* (1837) (Chicago: Donohue, n.d.): "'As to being rich enough,' observed Mr Templeton [to the penniless Maltravers], with a calculating air, 'seven hundred and ninety-five pounds ten shillings a year will allow a man to keep *two* servants, if he pleases; but I am glad to find you economical, at all events'" (P. 266).

7 (1861) Harmondsworth: Penguin, 1986, p. 217.

8 (1865), p. 106, quoted from Brightfield.

9 William Makepeace Thackeray, *The History of Pendennis* (1848–50) (Harmondsworth: Penguin, 1972), p. 46; chap. 2.

10 Robert Bell, *The Ladder of Gold* (1850), vol. 2, p. 22, quoted from Brightfield.

11 Cf. Jo McMurtry, *Victorian Life and Victorian Fiction: A Companion for the American Reader* (Hamden: Archon Books, 1979), p. 55.

12 *The Three Clerks* (1857) (London: Long, 1903), p. 165; chap. 17.

13 Brightfield, vol. 2, pp. 84–5.

14 P. 138; chap. 11. The household he is imagining consists of himself and his daughter, married to Pen, who he mistakenly thinks has £500 a year.

15 *The Adventures of Philip* (1862) (London: Nelson, 1903), p. 474.

16 Lawrence Lockhart, *Doubles and Quits* (1869), vol. 2, p. 71, quoted from Brightfield.

17 (London: Routledge and Kegan Paul, 1954), pp. 36–7.

18 P. 343. For a surprising assertion that the French arrange these matters better—or perhaps worse—see *ibid.*, pp. 370–1.

19 Think, for example, in *The Warden* and *Barchester Towers*, of the rector of Puddingdale, Mr Quiverful, "a very poor man" who with his wife struggles with minimal success to raise twelve children on £400 per annum. The doubling of his income when he replaces Mr Harding as Warden of Hiram's Hospital secures his worldly happiness.

20 P. 532. For other passages bearing on the amount they had and needed, see pp. 544, 545, 548, 568 (Mrs Mugford's wisdom is typical of the dominant moral school: "Me and Mugford married on two pound a week; and on two pound a week my dear eldest children were born. It was a hard struggle sometimes, but we were all the happier for it; and I'm sure if a man won't risk a little he don't deserve much"), and p. 576.

21 Mary Elizabeth Braddon, *The Doctor's Wife* (1864), vol. 2, p. 40, quoted from Brightfield.

22 Dinah Maria Craik, *A Life for a Life* (1859), p. 200, quoted from Brightfield. Lady Blessington is in near agreement: "A single man in London can get a cheap lodging, live at his club for a mere trifle, and dine out when he is asked. I could manage the whole thing for seven pounds a week." *Country Quarters* (1850), vol. 1, p. 192, quoted from Brightfield.

23 1882; ed. R.H. Super (Ann Arbor: University of Michigan Press, 1982), pp. 272 and ff.

24 See chapter 3, pp. 78–92.

25 Charles Dickens, *Our Mutual Friend* (1864–5) (Harmondsworth: Penguin, 1971), p. 682.

26 Anthony Trollope, *The Way We Live Now*, bk. I, chap. 26, quoted from Brightfield.

27 McMurtry, p. 55.

28 *The Claverings* (1866–7) (Oxford: Oxford University Press, 1986), p. 37; chap. 4. Harry is a Fellow of his College, but has turned to engineering.

29 Private note, 27 July 1874, quoted in Phyllis Grosskurth, *Havelock Ellis: A Biography* (1980) (London: Quartet Books, 1981), p. 18.

30 (London: Ward, Lock, and Tyler, 1874), pp. viii–xi. The budgetary details are given below, pp. 291–2.

31 P. 22. At the end of her brief story, as though to emphasize its fictional character, we are told that in a little while her income will be £1000 per year— but how and why we are not told, nor is any reason assigned for her now having but £100.

32 Emily Charlotte Ponsonby, *Mary Lyndsay* (1863), vol. 1, p. 168, quoted from Brightfield.

33 (London: Mitchell, n.d. [BL copy stamped 1845]). The budgetary details are given below, p. 288.

34 (2nd ed., London and New York: Routledge, 1857). A "New Ed." in which the sums were altered to *£150 to £1500* appeared in 1879, also published in London and New York by Routledge. The budgetary details are on pp. 289–90 below.

35 *Vieux Moustache*, who seems to have it, and *Bunny*, who is sure it is not too much.

36 Cf. the earlier discussion in *The Times*. For more evidence see Banks, p. 48; Duncan Crow, *The Victorian Woman*, esp. p. 138n, where he mentions "Can We Live on £300 a Year?," *Englishwoman's Domestic Magazine* (Apr. 1859), in which "live" is defined as "in the fashion which our [middle-class] status demands"; and Brightfield's apt quotation from Alicia Helen Little, *One Foot on Shore* (1869), p. 206.

37 A survey of the purchasing power of the pound, setting its value in 1914 as 100p, gives 105.00 in 1850, dropping to 88.33 in 1859, and varying in the 1860s between a low of 80.08 in 1864 and a high of 86.25 in 1869, with a value of 85.08 in 1868. Angela Lambert, *Unquiet Souls* (New York: Harper, 1984), app. I. A more cheerful judgment is found in François Crouzet, *The Victorian Economy*, trans. Anthony Forster (London: Methuen, 1982), p.47.
    As to the crucial group, S.G. Checkland comments, "The commercial

clerk, if he was well connected, could hope to become a partner, but the host of ledger keepers and correspondence copiers, the sons of working-class families aspiring to respectability, had little chance to dazzle their employers." *The Rise of Industrial Society in England, 1815–85* (London: Longman, 1964), p. 220. For accounts of working-class incomes, see *ibid.*, p. 232, and for the composition of the lower middle class, p. 301.

38 The percentages are only suggestive, because the writers often mention more than one figure, and offer various qualifications.

39 However, in a passage from the *Spectator* quoted on 6 July by the *Telegraph*, the debate is said to focus on the £80–200 range.

40 *A Welsh Bachelor Pro-Tem* points out that married men cannot even afford a seaside holiday, such as he is enjoying.

41 *A Wife and Mother* and *C.A.J.*, for instance, both think about £150 will suffice in the country, though not in London. The latter is controverted by *M.B.E.*, who asserts that it is not enough even in the country.

42 *Ring* is blunt: "What intellectual intercourse with his fellow-men can a middle-class man have who has a wife and six children to support on £150 a year?" Perhaps the strongest statement about the evil result for men of marrying on £150 comes from *S.R.H.*: "By far the greater portion of those who marry on this sum will be found among clerks, who rarely consider that their marriage increases their dependence on their employers. Thus, unless one in this position be endowed with an exceptional spirit of energy and determination, he will be rendered incapable of ever striking out for himself, and acquiring a competence for his old age; but remain till the end of his life in the same station as that in which he entered it."

43 *Comfortably Single* asserts that it is "little short of cruelty to take a girl from her comfortable home to be harassed and pinched on £150 a year, and a gross injustice to any family which is born that they cannot be properly clothed, fed, and educated." *A Widow* speaks forthrightly and for many women in saying "marriage on £150 a year means slavery."

44 See chapter 2, pp. 42–3, for the source of this image.

45 Similar are *T.C.C.*, who says "it is mainly a matter of tact," which is very rare "among our lower middle class," and *T.T.*, who knows that there are hundreds who can manage on £100 to £300 (a very considerable difference, one might comment), while there are thousands on similar incomes "to whom life is one wretched struggle for existence"—and for him those odds suggest caution. *Giglio* reports that French couples commonly marry and live comfortably on £100, employing one servant, usually only for a part of each day.

46 *Self-Help* agrees, as do *A Prudent Bachelor* and *C.K.*, the last correspondent in

the series, who says that "to link oneself with a companion on such a paltry sum [as £100 to £200] would only be to jump into a sea of trouble, and rob life of all future happiness." Compare *Pegging at It*: "A respectable young man who gets married on £130 a year and hope, makes a mistake which may last him a lifetime to forget."

47 *One Who Can't Help It* and *F.M.*, clerks with, respectively, £100 and £90 per annum, are among those who agree that it is barely enough for a single man.

48 He wrote after the letter of *An Eldest Daughter*, but before that of *Three "Girls of the Period."*

49 For example *A Young Man*, who admits that £130 would be tight in London, but says it is adequate in the suburbs and country.

50 Of course the letter may have been written by a staff member, but if so (ruling out the wide speculation that they all were) he—there were no she's—closely echoes the views and voices of other correspondents.

51 "The National Income of the U.K. – Wages, Profits, Rents," *Contemporary Review*, 8 (May 1868), 93 (table C), based on figures from Dudley Baxter. In the category of "Large Incomes" he places 8500 at £5000 and above, and 48,800 at between £1000 and £5000. The "Middle Income" group (£300 to £1000) encompasses 178,300 people.

52 Evidence of Thomas Beggs (26 April 1866), "Second Report of the Select Committee on Metropolitan Local Government," *Parliamentary Papers*, 1866, vol. 13, p. 368.

53 R.H. Super, *The Chronicler of Barsetshire: A Life of Anthony Trollope* (Ann Arbor: University of Michigan Press, 1988), pp. 26, 36.

54 *The Three Clerks*, p. 16. Compare W.S. Gilbert, who at twenty-one passed a competitive civil service examination and obtained a post as assistant clerk in the education department of the Privy Council at £120 a year.

55 (1882), ed. R.H. Super (Ann Arbor: University of Michigan Press, 1982).

56 His status in the eyes of Lord Hampstead's servants is such that, even before his advancement, they seem "to forget that he was no more than a clerk and that he went off by railway into town every morning that he might earn ten shillings by sitting for six hours at his desk" (p. 8).

57 (1852–3) (Harmondsworth: Penguin, 1971), p. 175; chap. 9.

58 George Grossmith and Weedon Grossmith, *The Diary of a Nobody* (1892) (Bristol: Arrowsmith; London: Simpkin et al., 1919), pp. 157–61. One of the poignant details marking the account is that Pooter is kept waiting for days by the head of the firm, Mr Perkupp, for full details of his salary.

59 (London: Remington, 1878).

60 *Parliamentary Papers*, 1835, pp. 22, 41–4.

61 *Not Wisely But Too Well, by the Author of "Cometh Up as a Flower*, new ed. (London: Tinsley, 1868), p. 257.

62 P. 192; chap. 16.

63 His work included "translating comedies and farces from the French; copying out the parts; drawing up the advertisements for the newspapers; taking stock in the wardrobe, occasionally holding the prompt-book in the wing, and helping the treasurer to make out this accounts." *The Life and Adventures of George Augustus Sala, Written by Himself* (1895) (London: Cassell, 1896), p. 147.

64 *Ibid.*, pp. 175, 258.

65 Pp. 359, 381; chaps. 33, 36.

66 *The Adventures of Philip*, p. 544.

67 *The Three Clerks*, p. 269.

68 Stefan Collini, *Public Moralists: Political Thought and Intellectual Life in Britain 1850–1930* (Oxford: Clarendon Press, 1991), p. 35. He cites several more exalted figures, mainly for married men, perhaps the wildest that of Leslie Stephen, who determined in 1875 not to be like his brother Fitzjames, "slaving to death to keep up an expensive house," but to make do on £1000–£1200 a year, "for millions of people do it" (p. 36).

69 For an indication of the problems associated with fellowships of such an amount that depended on celibacy, see Trollope's *Mr. Scarborough's Family* (1882–3) (London: Oxford University Press, 1973), esp. p. 226.

70 Among those cited by Collini in this context are J.S. Mill and his father, Matthew Arnold, Thackeray, Trollope, Walter Bagehot, and John Morley, all of whom were far more successful than the average.

71 In the discussion of emigration the issue is closest to the surface, and a few correspondents believe the government should contribute to the cost of fares and possibly make easily repayable loans to help establish families in the colonies. But even then the main emphasis is on self-reliance or voluntary group cooperation. See chapter 7 for details.

72 Cf. with the following account that in Banks, *Prosperity and Parenthood*, pp. 55–62.

73 Dickens, *David Copperfield*, p. 231; chap. 12. Cf. *ibid.* p. 221; chap. 11.

74 Anon., *Domestic Economy* (London: Longman, Brown, Green, Longmans, and Roberts, 1856), p. 33. It appeared in the *School Series*, edited by the Rev. G.R. Gleig, MA, Inspector-General of Military Schools.

75 At £100 the "supper" allowance permits an occasional excursion, presumably down the river to Greenwich for a fish treat.

76 For all the detailed budgets in this chapter, see app. B.

77 "How I Manage on £200 a Year," *Girl of the Period Miscellany*, 1:7 (Sept. 1869), 236.

78 "The Englishwoman's Conversazione," *Englishwoman's Domestic Magazine*, 11 (Oct. 1871), 254. A full summary is given by Banks in appendix 2 to *Prosperity and Parenthood*, pp. 211–16.

79 In December also *Housekeeper* gave thanks for the advice, and others contributed to the issue, including *Aurora*, who thinks *Housekeeper*'s allowance more than adequate; £3 a week would do, leaving £1 10s for "company and extras." *Madd^{le}* agrees with *Aurora*, but remarks: "It is not pleasant for a lady to go to a butcher's shop generally," but she can go to all others.

80 Another rather odd conjunction.

81 Pp. 27, 51. On about the same, or an even lower level of expenditure, the anonymous *A Woman's Secret; or, How to Make Home Happy. With an Appendix Containing Recipes for Preparing Economical and Nutritious Food* (London: Griffith and Farran, 1860) offers, in a third-person narrative, recipes (not very appetizing) that are costed in an appendix, providing meals for five or six people at under a shilling (and usually under 6d).

82 See pp. 20–2 above. Banks glances at this exchange in *Prosperity and Parenthood*, pp. 41–3.

83 See chap. 3 for a fuller account.

84 Presumably what is now called "hire-purchase" in the UK.

85 This number and the wages bill suggest three servants.

86 This item will form, he says, a much heavier charge than the young imagine. Though he and his wife have no children at home and excellent servants, last year it amounted to 4 per cent of their expenditure, and in the last six months 6 per cent. (Of course it will be more when there are children.)

87 An index not merely of "respectability" but of the dirty environment and the limited bathing facilities.

88 This third use of the pseudonym may cover a second correspondent, but certainly the first two letters are from the same hand.

89 They have no children at home, though they assist two sons "residing in distant lands."

90 The following discussion includes details about servants' wages from several correspondents who do not supply comprehensive budgets, and so are not included in app. B.

91 *Victorian Life and Victorian Fiction*, pp. 168–9.

92 Duncan Crow, in *The Victorian Woman*, p. 49, notes that in a more economical household there would be a nursemaid rather than a parlourmaid, the single general servant would get £9–£10 a year, a housemaid or nursemaid £10–£11, and the cook £15–£19.

Banks, *Prosperity and Parenthood*, argues that a "complete middle-class household" would require three servants, and therefore would have to have £400–£600 a year (p. 77). For his comments on the situation for those with less, see his p. 70.

93 She is the only one in this series to make the complaint so common in the household management guidebooks about those who wrongly leave the management of household affairs in the hands of servants. She later in the series again makes assumptions about there being servants in a household. An illuminating account of the problems is given by Anne Gilchrist, "A Neglected Art (Cooking by Ladies to Save the Expense of a Cook)," *Macmillan's Magazine*, 12 (Oct. 1865), 494–500.

94 *Another English Girl*, arguing that £130 a year is not nearly enough, makes allusion to a home with several servants, as contrasted with one where a single one is sufficient. In *Cassio*'s letter also the danger of high-flying is illustrated by the case of a relatively low-paid man marrying one of his class who is probably used to living comfortably in a house with "two or three" servants. And quite cautious is *A Woman But Not a Slave*, who, coming from a wealthy home with "a full complement of servants," advises marriage on a minimum of £300, on which one should keep one servant, and "perhaps a girl."

95 There are four other comparable cases: *A British Matron* with five children on under £200 makes do with one servant; *A London Girl*, the only unmarried daughter of a professional man earning £150–200, mentions that they keep only one servant; *R.F.H.* has one servant on £200; and *An Old Married Man*, outlining a married clerk's expenditure of £198, includes one servant at £10 per annum.

96 *A Matchmaker* (£186 15s), *One Who Would Be a Good Deal Happier If He Had It* (he has expenditures of £180, including a servant at £8), *T.Z.* (£168; servant's wages £10), *Materfamilias* (£150), *One Who Speaks from Experience* (£150), *Nil Desperandum* (£150), *A Widow* (£150), and *An Active Wife and Mother* (£150).

97 In Belgium, on the evidence of Charlotte Brontë, who had experience there, much the same was true. In *The Professor* (1856) her protagonist, William Crimsworth, remarks: "In Belgium, provided you can make money, you may save it; this is scarcely possible in England; ostentation there lavishes in a month what industry has earned in a year." He knows he could not prudently marry in Brussels on his salary of the equivalent of £60, but would be able if to it were added the £50 that his beloved, also a teacher, earns annually. Luck aided by virtue gives him a much more remunerative post, and they marry—she continuing to teach. Chap. 21 (London: Collins, n.d.), pp. 363ff.

98 Expenditure on beer is probably related directly to the employment of servants, by whom it was a demanded perquisite.

99 £30 is the most common figure, though two who give it suggest that it is for

young couples (one specifically includes boots in the account, but since others do not mention footwear, presumably it is always intended).

100 That otherwise valuable source, *A Clergyman, Aetat 47*, does not mention rent or taxes, presumably because they are supplied with his living. The only other person to mention gardening expense explicity is *A Matchmaker*, who spends £4 annually.

101 Typically, in *Our Mutual Friend*, Mrs Wilfer, who tries also to use their home as a school for young ladies, rents off a room to John Harmon (in disguise) as a way of making ends meet.

102 Such items may be omitted from accounts that take a narrow view of "housekeeping" expenses, especially those that record expenditures from the wife's viewpoint.

103 *Vieux Moustache* in recapitulating *Paterfamilias*'s figures gives the amount as £12.

104 Banks, *Prosperity and Parenthood*, p. 95 (his comments come in his well-entitled chap. 7, "The Paraphernalia of Gentility"). Some working-class families managed a week's holiday through savings clubs.

105 The practice was neither habitual nor universal, Zachary Fay representing many: "[My father] never begrudges me anything," says Marion. "We did go down to Cowes for a fortnight in April, though I am quite sure that papa himself would have preferred remaining at home all the time. He does not believe in the new-fangled idea of changing the air." (Trollope, *Marion Fay*, p. 123.)

106 This was the great period for the building of those monumental insurance offices, many taking on the neo-Gothic form appropriate for other central cultural institutions such as parliament, churches, and municipal government offices.

107 The question is worded simply to hide another weakness: because they represent inadequately a considerable range, one cannot strike a statistically reliable average.

Chapter 5 Celibates and Celibacy

1 Margaret Oliphant, *Madonna Mary* (1867), vol. 1, p. 230. Quoted from Myron F. Brightfield, *Victorian England in Its Novels (1840–1870)*, 4 vols. (Los Angeles: University of California Library, 1968).

2 Harriet Grove Cradock, *Hulse House* (1860), vol. 1, p. 163, quoted from Brightfield. And such caution might have disastrous effects on another: "His worldly wisdom had blighted that fair young life. Because he had been prudent; because he had taken counsel with his long-headed friends of the world, and had believed them when they said that the horrors of

Pandemonium were less horrid than the dismal, muddling torments of a pinched household—because of these things Emily Jerningham's mind had been embittered and her fair name sullied." Mary Elizabeth Braddon, *Aurora Floyd* (1863), vol. 3, p. 56, quoted from Brightfield.

3 "A Neglected Art (Cooking by Ladies to Save the Expense of a Cook)," *Macmillan's Magazine*, 12 (Oct. 1865), 494.

4 The lack of parallelism in the terms "girls" and "young men" is obvious enough to modern eyes; they are, however, the ones used by the correspondents without apology. That the oddity was noticed by Anthony Trollope should not surprise: "Laying aside for the sake of clearness that indefinite term girl—for girls are girls from the age of three up to forty-three, if not previously married." *Framley Parsonage* (1861) (Harmondsworth: Penguin, 1986), p. 138; chap. 10.

5 Like several others, she incorporates her signature syntactically and semantically in the text.

6 A quantity that assures through easy conceptualization while disconcerting through vagueness. A colleague of mine, asked how many students there were on the then burgeoning University of Toronto campus, replied, "Oh, dozens and dozens."

7 There is only one other letter from a governess, signed *The Best of Things*, a claim not implying disconsolation. *A Young English Governess* infers that the earlier correspondent, *An English Girl*, is a governess, but she had identified herself as housekeeper for her father.

8 The immediately preceding letter, from *L.C.J.*, which of course *A Country Girl* could not yet have read, includes a satiric attack on another correspondent's saying that "respectable and proper" wives are to be found only in the country. "Poor town-bred girls, our chances are over," says *L.C.J.* "Strephon is going into the country, and he is right, if Phillis, in the City, habitually goes to the opera, and leaves the children's socks undarned." More from *L.C.J.* on the single man will be found below.

9 This ethical appeal, traditionally attached to country folk and women, is shrewdly inserted: "Now, remember, Mr. Editor, I only speak from short experience, and would not condemn all for the sake of a few."

10 *My Share of the World* (1861), vol. 2, p. 143, quoted from Brightfield.

11 Mary Elizabeth Braddon, *The Lady's Mile* (1866), p. 7, quoted from Brightfield. The follies and vices were not merely circumstantial for some critics. Women, said Louisa De la Ramée ("Ouida"), were "for the most part as cold, clear, hard, and practical as their adorers believe them the contrary." *Under Two Flags* (1867), p. 54, quoted from Brightfield. And that some were cunningly willing to take advantage of their image as properly weak and helpless is illustrated in Charlotte Elizabeth Riddell, *The Race for Wealth*

(1866), vol. 3, p. 333, quoted in Brightfield, and Julia Cecilia De Winton, *Lords and Ladies* (1866), p. 7, quoted in Brightfield.

12 Blanchard Jerrold, *Up and Down in the World* (1863), vol. 1, p. 269, quoted from Brightfield. Once more the fiction is portraying a level above that of the *Daily Telegraph*'s main readers. Almost all the fictional attacks on young women relating to the difficulty of marriage assume something like the expenditure given in Blessington's *Country Quarters* (1850), where the claim is that a "woman in the present day must have three or four hundred a-year for pin-money, . . . must ride a three-hundred guinea hack," and must have "a box at one of the opera-houses" and "go in for dogs and china—not vulgar modern Dresden abominations in the way of simpering shepherdesses, and creatures in hoops drinking chocolate or playing chess; but old Vienna, or Chelsea, with the gold anchor, or deliciously ugly Wedgwood, or soft paste," if she wants "not to be a disgrace to her sex." "In short, . . . a woman nowadays is a very expensive creature, and love in a cottage is an impossibility." (*Ibid.*, vol. 1, p. 62, quoted from Brightfield.) In Horlock's *Lord Fitzwarine* (1860) it is opined that a girl "has the right to expect" about £1000 to be settled on her "as pin-money" (vol. 1, p. 188, quoted from Brightfield).

13 *The Three Clerks* (1857) (London: Long, 1903), p. 220.

14 Perhaps another echo of Dickens, whose Eugene Wrayburn in *Our Mutual Friend* refers to "My Respectable father" as "M.R.F." (bk. IV, chap. 6).

15 Claude Melnotte has escaped me; if only the ostentatious Augustus Melmotte of Trollope's *The Way We Live Now* had had a slightly different name, and appeared in 1868 rather than 1874.

16 For the details, see app. B.

17 I.e., government bonds. (I have not located the quotation, which has a Gilbertian ring before its time.)

18 W.E.W.W. makes the parenthetic comment, "and wisely," thus adumbrating a rational cause-and-effect examination.

19 W.E.W.W. interrupts his logical analysis to unleash an intrusive attack on the young women of the day: "One often marries for company as much as for love, and the impression is widely prevalent among men of the present day that another mode of life is, perhaps, preferable on the score of economy to sharing it with wives who can do nothing, who know nothing, and who love nothing—but themselves."

20 In fact W.E.W.W., a travelled man, has another bleak comment prompted by *Colonista*'s effusions about "that sweet colony," British Columbia, in which he has seen houses that "were but pigstyes, and wives . . . but drudges." In a note perhaps echoing *Benedick*'s early comparison of civilized folk with savages and the Irish, W.E.W.W. concludes: "In England men will not live in

a house of boards on fish and potatoes; but till they do, I see no chance of people being able to marry on £150 a year."

21 In the course of his argument, he excludes from discussion "the very poor, and even . . . that lower middle class to which the advocates of marriage on £200 a year clearly belong," because "the case is so different that the two afford but little parallel; for wives in those classes, not coming from the section of society I am referring to, can and do undertake the domestic management—and often something more—of their own households."

22 This perhaps strains the sense of Exodus 32:20, in which Moses took the golden calf made by Aaron that was worshipped by the people as the god that brought them out of Egypt, "and burnt it in the fire, and ground it to powder, and strewed it upon the water, and made the children of Israel drink of it."

23 "A Neglected Art," p. 496. She, like many others as we shall see, attributes the conflict mainly to women's having quite lost the secret of the "indispensable art" of prudent housekeeping. But she is talking of the unmarried.

24 Much better, he says, as a guide to "those who show such a desire to put down early marriages . . . and to those maidens who are anxious to be married" is that "little darling 'Dot,'" in Dickens's "Christian work," *The Chimes*, "with the very description of whom we have all fallen in love." An apt enough reference, though he is undoubtedly thinking of Toby Veck's daughter, whose name is Meg, not Dot. See, e.g., "First Quarter" and "Fourth Quarter" of *The Chimes* (1844), in *The Christmas Books*, ed. Michael Slater (Harmondsworth: Penguin, 1971), pp. 158, 241–2.

25 *The Girl of the Period* (Bristol: Bingham; London, Berger, 1868), reprinted from *Saturday Review*, 25 (14 Mar. 1868), 339–40. The following quotations are from the original article; because it occupies only two pages, specific references are not given.

26 Merle Mowbray Bevington, *The Saturday Review 1855–1868* (New York: Cambridge University Press, 1941), discusses the furor on pp. 339–40. The latest version of the pamphlet (still 1868) in the British Library claims to be of the "Sixteenth Thousand" impression (priced at 2d).

27 Bevington, p. 110. A good competitor would be Linton's "Modern Mothers," *Saturday Review*, 25 (29 Feb. 1868), 265–9, which is almost as harsh, presenting mothers as selfish, vain, and anti-children.

28 James Albery, *Two Roses: An Original Comedy in Three Acts* (1870), act III, in George Rowell, ed., *Nineteenth-Century Plays* (London: Oxford University Press, 1968), p. 452.

29 This apparent oddity reflects an interest arising from the successful expedition under Robert Cornelius Napier in 1867 to release the British hostages held by the Emperor Theodore of Abyssinia.

30 The cartoons feature fast women, often smoking cigars; when men appear, they are performing "women's" roles. In the first number of the *Miscellany*, "In the Editorial Sanctum" comments significantly: "Let us get it recognized, say some people, with Mr. Mill at their head, that marriage is not the sole, or even the chief end of women. . . . She [modern woman] may become a powerful man of business; she may be like Julia Paetrana, or Hercules, or Mr. Mill himself, and be no more fit for a wife or mother than he is." (P. 6) The article then quotes from Mill's *Principles of Political Economy*, bk. IV, chap. vii, sect. 3, on "wife and mother" (*Collected Works*, vol. 3, pp. 765–6).

31 (St Leonards: Burg and Daniel; London: Snow, and Berger, 1868) (15 pp., 2d). In the British Library the pamphlet is attributed to Eliza Lynn Linton, but surely by mistake.

Also partly motivated by the same controversy is another twopenny pamphlet, the anonymous *Woman: Her Friends and Her Enemies: A Vindication by a Lady* (Bristol: Bingham; London: Berger, 1868). The author makes no jokes in echoing J.S. Mill's views, agreeing with him "that 'the passion of love plays far too prominent a part in human existence,' that is, if vain silly flirtations, and the thoughtless ill-judged marriages which still are constantly contracted, are to be attributed to the agency of love" (p. 5).

32 *Punch*, 4 July 1868, 2. Not that *Punch* was willing to miss such an opportunity for fun: see the issues for 4, 11, 25 July, and 1 August, 1868, pp. 7–8, 12–13, 44, 46.

33 Almost certainly the repressed names were those of Jane Lyon and Mary Tucker Borradaile, both of whom had cut a sorry figure in the public eye. The former's successful case for fraud against Daniel Dunglass Home, the original of Robert Browning's "Mr. Sludge, the Medium," had caused much public amusement through tags such as "Daniel in the Lyon's Den." (See for part of the fun, *The Times*, 22 Apr. to 2 May 1868.) The latter's also successful case for fraud against Sarah Rachel Leverson, better known as Madame Rachel, caused even more amusement as details were revealed of Rachel's expensive methods of making Borradaile "Beautiful for Ever" so that she could marry an Irish "noble" adventurer. (See *The Times*, 10, 17, and 27 June 1868, and for even better details, the reports in *The Times* that appeared in September after "Marriage or Celibacy?" had ended.)

34 Who these philosophers might be is not clear; certainly Mill would not reject his argument. But probably, as the context for the word "sages" below suggests, he means moralists who dwell on self-sacrifice.

35 An ironic inversion of the condition of the wedding guest in Coleridge's *Rime of the Ancient Mariner*, who "A sadder and a wiser man . . . rose the morrow morn"?

36 They mistakenly judge the author to be male; Linton's authorship was not yet public knowledge.

37 Their adieu is nicely phrased: "We *remain*, Sir, yours, &c., *Three "Girls of the Period."* (Emphasis added.)

38 For his typicality as a fledgling journalist, see p. 37 above.

39 *The Three Clerks*, p. 29.

40 Other authors depicted the same pattern. An innocent youth falls into the habits of his fellow-clerks—"they drink, they smoke, they swear, they idle about and play billiards"—with the near-certain consequences of vice, debt, and disgrace. Dinah Maria Craik, *A Brave Lady* (1870), p. 89, quoted from Brightfield.

41 *Danesbury House* (1860), p. 119, quoted from Brightfield.

42 Such matters were of course in common debate. The proliferation of government offices, in which patronage played a major role, produced such non-fictional comments as this: "Then there is our civil service, where little men with large families do all the work; while young men of title look on, play cards, yawn exceedingly, and pocket the pay, which, by the bye, is generally proportioned to their capabilities for spending it." George Fordham, *The Age We Live in; or, a Glimpse at Men and Manners* (London: Kent, 1855), p. 17.

43 It is, however, worth some citation: "And this personage [George Roden, who was to marry into a family connected closely with the Secretary of State for Foreign Affairs—his wife is the sister of the Marquis's second wife] was a clerk in the Post Office! There had no doubt been a feeling in the Foreign Office, if not of actual disgrace at any rate of mingled shame and regret, that a niece of their Secretary of State should have engaged herself to one so low. Had he been in the Foreign Office himself something might have been made of him;—but a clerk in the Post Office!" *Marion Fay* (1882), ed. R.H. Super (Ann Arbor: University of Michigan Press, 1982), p. 318. Lady Persiflage writes to Lady Kingsbury (the Marchioness), her sister: "It will be better to have a Duca di Crinola [Roden has been revealed to be entitled to the Italian rank] among us, even though he should not have a shilling, than a Post Office clerk with two or three hundred a year" (p. 321).

44 P. 407. Corroborating passages are to be found on pp. 33 and 211. It may be noted that though Trollope himself is obviously sympathetic to the public office claim, he emphasizes that the head of the office, "Sir Boreas," cannot bring himself to fire Crocker, a wretchedly lazy and incompetent clerk, even when, to cover his inattention to duty, he destroys official papers.

45 Among its recommendations for those new to London was "a very admirable little work" (and, at 1s 6d, good value), *The Guide to Employment in London; or, How to Arrive at Independence; with Information and Advice, &c.,*

together with the Grand Secret of Success in Life, which happened to have the same publisher, C. Mitchell of Red Lion Court. Following its guidance should keep young men clear of the "selfishness, dissipation, and vice, in every form in the 'great Metropolis'" (pp. 13n–14n; cf. p. 32n).

46 These are the Pantheon (Oxford St.), the Bazaar (Soho Sq.), the Lowther Bazaar (35 Strand), the Pantechnicon (Pimlico), the Western Exchange (Old Bond St.), the Lowther Arcade (West Strand), the Burlington Arcade (Piccadilly), and the Raker St. Bazaar (Portman Sq.). Some of these areas, as chapter 1 above shows, were rather less morally desirable later in the day.

47 Which he mistakenly describes as fought "between the advocates of early matrimony (almost entirely ladies) and the apologists for celibacy (chiefly of the other sex)." He is echoed in the leading article of 30 July; see p. 166.

48 "In some cases perhaps a slight increase of salary may accompany close and assiduous attention in the discharge of official duty, but to the vast majority no such prospect is afforded."

49 Like *A Plain Girl* earlier, and many others later, he integrates a characterizing signature into the justifying peroration.

50 He allows for different "grades of society," saying that a "mechanic, or small tradesman's daughter"—of whom he speaks "with respect"—could live happily ("as far as means is concerned") on £150 per annum, but not those in a grade where "gentility" (he "can can use no other word") "is aimed at."

51 He mentions generally his wife's help, and specifically his daughters' "doing such fancy work as they could obtain," and his abstinence from smoking and kid gloves, company and wine, and his rare indulgence in riding.

Chapter 6 Problems and Solutions

1 She cites "Racine's beautiful words, 'Aux petits des oiseaux Dieu donne leur pature et sa bonte s'etend sur toute la nature,'" and insists "that there are many girls with a good education, able to manage a household satisfactorily, and adepts at making a pudding, like Dickens's Ruth." For discussion and display of Ruth Pinch's unrivalled talents in pudding-making, see Dickens's *Martin Chuzzlewit*, (1843–4) (Harmondsworth: Penguin, 1986), chaps. 39 and 45.

2 A favourite text from Longfellow's *A Psalm of Life*.

3 Cf. *Prudens*, who notes that the letters' conflicting advice will confuse rather than help "Coelebs in search of a wife" (the title of a novel [1809] by Hannah More, which dwells on the qualities of the ideal wife), and argues that a man must provide a social position for his wife equal to his own and

to what she was accustomed to before marriage; any other course would be "unmanly in him and humiliating to her."

4 The "facetious contemporary" is *Punch*, who was then in the habit of offering advice on all manner of subjects in the form: "Advice to those who . . . Don't!" The same gag is used by the *Telegraph* in its leader of 16 July.

5 Here of course "natural" (if uncomprehended) causes were known to be at work, but still the onus was on coping with them, not helplessly blaming them.

6 There is no question that some segments, especially the agricultural labourers and the submerged slum dwellers in London, were not obvious beneficiaries of the increased wealth. There is equally little question, however, that their relative deprivation was becoming more visible and more subject to amelioration.

7 Myron F. Brightfield, *Victorian England in Its Novels (1840–1870)*, 4 vols. (Los Angeles: University of California Library, 1968), vol. 4, p. 92.

8 N.s. 1 (Mar. 1865), 89.

9 "A Neglected Art (Cooking by Ladies to Save the Expense of a Cook)," *Macmillan's Magazine*, 12 (Oct. 1865), 495.

10 (London: Kent, 1855), pp. 19–20.

11 *Tom Brown's School Days* (1857) (London and Glasgow: Blackie and Son, n.d.), p. 35.

12 *Political and Social Economy: Its Practical Application* (Edinburgh: Chambers, 1849), p. 129. J.A. Banks asserts that it seems "fairly well established that the period up to the 1870s was one in which the middle-class standard of living was rapidly changing. Something in the order of a 50 per cent increase in outlay was expected over the 1850 level on food, drink, and household requirements generally, although retail prices rose by only 5 per cent. . . . [A]lthough it did cost the middle classes much more money now [in the 1870s] to live than it had in the 1850s, the greater part of that added outlay was the result of a richer standard of life." *Prosperity and Parenthood: A Study of Family Planning among the Victorian Middle Classes* (London: Routledge and Kegan Paul, 1954), p. 101.

13 Julia McNair Wright, *The Complete Home*, p. 406.

14 Mrs Warren, *How I Managed My House on £200 a year* (London: Houlston and Wright, 1864), p. v.

15 Though the prospect of resolution is surely bleak, he ends his letter with a bow to the *Daily Telegraph* that embeds a supposition more hopeful than reason might suggest: "I am sure the ventilation of this subject will do great good, and if it has the effect of making young ladies of the class to which I belong lower their standard, it will be a blessing to many, and

perhaps alter the condition of some who are, like myself, *Comfortably Single.*"

16 Surely not intended as a variant on the carol "As Joseph was a-walking," which contains the stanza: "He neither shall be clothed / In purple nor in pall, / But all in fair linen, / As were babies all."

17 Brightfield, vol. 2, p. 84.

18 Mrs Warren, £200, p. v.

19 The full title is *Modern Domestic Cookery: Founded on the Principles of Economy and Practical Knowledge, and Adapted for Private Families. By a Lady. A New Edition, based on the work of Mrs. Rundell, including All the Recent Improvements in the Culinary Art. With Illustrative Woodcuts.* 245th Thousand (London: Murray, 1865), identified also as *Murray's Modern Cookery Book.* The work on which it was based is Maria Eliza Rundell's *A New System of Domestic Cookery,* first published in 1808, when the problems were somewhat different.

20 The signature reveals rhetorical intent, not least in "Another," which shows a devotion to the series while insisting on discrimination within a category, for as the text makes clear, she disagrees with *An English Girl* and is not merely "Another" instance of a stereotype.

21 Here she is supported by Margaret Hale, in Elizabeth Gaskell's *North and South,* who responds to her mother's regret at her performing such menial tasks: "I don't mind ironing, or any kind of work, for you and papa. I am myself a born and bred lady through it all, even though it comes to scouring a floor, or washing dishes." (P. 116.)

22 "Getting Our Daughters off Our Hands," n.s. 1 (July 1865), 216.

23 *Macmillan's Magazine,* 12 (Oct. 1865), 497–8.

24 If, he says, "an average were taken of the whole of the clerks' salaries through the country—i.e., of those who are now over twenty years of age, and consequently really useful and worth money to an employer," it would probably be found that "their salaries per man would be much less than £130, or even £100 per annum."

25 "God help," he says, "those poor slaves of the desk, married or single, who are forced to be applicants for some such position as I saw advertised a few days ago, for 'a young man as clerk, who can be honest on a small salary, and who is not afraid of long hours, &c.,' and to whose weary fingers and throbbing brain might well be inscribed a new 'Song of the Pen.'" (I.e., he is transferring to the clerks the sempstresses' plaint in Thomas Hood's famed "Song of the Shirt" (1843).

26 *T.T.* deals summarily with emigration: it will not serve the clerkly class with whom he is concerned, for colonial openings are only for men who are "tillers of the soil" and women who are "domestic servants, or ready to be a working man's wife."

27 See, e.g., anon., "The Statistics of Marriage," in Mrs Warren's *The Ladies Treasury: An Illustrated Magazine of Entertaining Literature, Education, Fine Art, Domestic Economy, Needlework, and Fashion*, 4 (Jan. 1860), 55–6. The author, not blaming illegitimacy, which she says is lower "than in any other land," remarks on the disproportionate number of spinsters as resulting from "an unaccountable diversity in the liabilities or disposition to celibacy in the two sexes" (p. 55). Celibacy is enforced on women from other than moral considerations; though deaths from pregnancy and childbirth decrease the numbers, widowers tend to marry widows. As to advice: "Seeing . . . how rapidly the chances of celibacy increase after 20, and how quickly the unwise habit becomes confirmed, let those who are discreet 'gather their roses while they may!'" (p. 56) Another comment is also relevant to the topic: "It is well known . . . that imprudent and early marriages are much more common among the labouring classes than elsewhere, because their sexual instincts are less under the control of moral or prudential motives" (p. 50).

28 "Of Miracles" (part II, para. 6), section X in *Enquiry Concerning Human Understanding*, ed. D.C. Yalden-Thomson (Edinburgh: Nelson, 1961), p. 123.

29 As usual, Mrs Warren's facts do not match her ideals; that is, her protagonists are given less money than the readers of the *Daily Telegraph* judged necessary for "decent" life. In this case, the husband has less than £200 a year, and while the wife has a legacy of £100, they eventually have eight children. Another unlikely element is the authoring by their daughter Janet of the "Book of Home Comforts for Small Incomes," the first instalment appearing in the *Ladies' Treasury*, June 1865.

30 The magazine ran a companion piece on sons, quoted in chapter 7 below.

31 *A Plain Man* employs a rare biblical example: "although such excellence as that exhibited in the marriage of Tobias and Sarah can hardly be expected, it would be well that some such example should direct the choice of those having marriage in view." The example is not wholly sound as a guide, however, for *A Plain Man* notes that "in those [biblical] days," money was not "so much considered," while (he is sorry to say) "it cannot be forgotten now . . . in considering the intended husband's position." The parallel fails in another respect, for in the apocryphal Book of Tobit Sarah had been plagued by a demon lover who had killed her seven previous grooms on their wedding nights before she met Tobias, who, with the angel Raphael's aid, killed the demon.

32 His epistemology of love is visual: "It is through the eye that the attention of a man is first attracted to a woman. He is pleased with her beauty and general appearance; her more sterling qualities come afterwards to complete the charm."

33 He has words of reassurance also for *A London Girl*; while there are some men who object to "girls who are in business," they certainly are not numerous.

34 This weak form of words occurs throughout the series, especially in letters from the pens of young women, probably reflecting their cautious first approaches to public debate.

Chapter 7 Emigration or Starvation

1 See, for much relevant information, Terry Coleman, *Passage to America* (Newton Abbot: Victorian [and Modern History] Book Club, 1973): among other popular works he cites *Proverbial Philosophy* by Martin F. Tupper, English versifier and philosopher, which sold more than a million copies, the pamphlet *Work and Wages; or, the Penny Emigrant's Guide to the United States and Canada, for Female Servants, Laborers, Mechanics, Farmers, etc.* (1855), by the philantropist Vere Foster, who gave away 250,000 copies, and the monthly *Sidney's Emigrant's Journal* published in London, which included letters. He emphasizes that home letters were more significant in stimulating family emigration than were the government, charitable ladies relieving distressed needlewomen, shovelling landlords, groups of mechanics and others, or the Mormons; in 1854 emigrants sent back to the UK at least £1,730,000 to help and encourage families and friends to join them (p. 203).

2 Julia Pardoe, *Reginald Lyle* (1854), p. 166. Quoted from Myron F. Brightfield, *Victorian England in Its Novels (1840–1870)*, 4 vols. (Los Angeles: University of California Library, 1968).

3 *Englishwoman's Domestic Magazine*, n.s. 1 (Mar. 1865), 74–6. In background and expectations of far lands, these youths are more typical of the emigrants of the 1880s than the 1860s.

4 He mentions specifically Thomas Mayne Reid (1818–83), who based his novels of adventure on his experience in the Red River area, Missouri, etc. None of his works deals with the "prairies of Toronto," wherever they might be. It is indicative that no one called into question the misapplication of the term.

5 Retired to England, he may return to Canada—perhaps because, in this case, things certainly have changed.

6 His acquaintance with the world as a naval surgeon is unrivalled: in addition to his beloved U.S.A. (Kansas as well as Kentucky), he knows enough to rule out India, Mauritius, Natal, the Cape Colonies and Free State, Brazil, River Plate (Carientes, Cordova, and the Banda Oriental), Chile, and Bolivia.

7 Perhaps a *hewer* of wood? He is of the mechanic class, and married; he also keeps a shop with his wife of twelve years. (Of their eight children, five died young.)

8 New South Wales and Victoria four times, South Australia thrice, and Western Australia and Queensland twice.

9 In the late nineteenth century, government clerks in Victoria and New South Wales began at about £140 a year, and rose gradually to about £300. (I am indebted to Allan Martin of the Australian National University for the Blue Book figures.)

10 The wealth gained by the convict Magwitch in *Great Expectations* is slightly less probable.

11 He has "been engaged in carrying out many emigrants to the colonies of Australia," with "opportunities of noticing the various successes—and very miserable failures they often meet with," and gives Canada the nod over Australia, "in distance, climate, and soil."

12 See the evidence of *T.H.M.*, a former clerk who had emigrated to rural Ontario some twelve years earlier, and was home to seek a wife: "I know that an advertisement for a clerk [in Canada] would almost at any time have one or two hundred answers within twenty-four hours; and it is the same in New York, or, indeed, any large city abroad, whether in Canada, Australia, or the Eastern or Western States of America."

13 Compare *N.Z.*: "for the city clerk, the man who has been brought up to the desk, unaccustomed to, and perhaps physically incapable of, severe manual labour, to emigrate is simply an absurdity. The colonies swarm with such men now; and I can assure you that, when any vacancy suitable for them occurs in Melbourne, Sydney, or even in the large towns of New Zealand, there are, relatively, as many applicants as there would be in London: the thing is overdone there as much as here."

14 One correspondent (*W.M.P.Y.*) had worries about *T.W.*'s scheme: "what would the poor emigrants do who had subscribed their only £100 till they benefited by the land they bought? and would the one or two thousand acres support so large a community as 250 persons? and whether land entirely cleared of heavy timber can be had in Australia for £1 per acre?"

15 It would be wrong to omit his self-advertisement in the latter respect: "I once, in my boyhood, as an experiment, designed and constructed a four-roomed wooden house, which was so much admired that it was forwarded to one of our colonies, and formed the pioneer of many others. It was so constructed that, in a day, the whole house-front, back, sides, roof, flooring, windows, doors, framework, &c., were unbolted and unscrewed, packed in a surprisingly small compass, and shipped."

16 My assumption, as indicated above, is that those who had family and

friends in the colonies did not feel the need for instruction from fellow readers of the *Daily Telegraph*.

17 Precise counting is difficult because there are overlapping references, then as now, to "America." Two correspondents whose remarks derive from *Erastes'* letter seem to assume that he meant the U.S.A., whereas he intended British North America, and another in his remarks about the U.S.A. mistakes *Delta's* reference to South America. A large number, of course, include general references to any and all parts of the world, including "America." Furthermore, three of the most enthusiastic boosters, *Professional, Traveller,* and *George Francis Train,* each contributed two letters.

18 He was the first to do so since the series began with non-pseudonymous signatures on prostitution.

19 A U.S. merchant, promoter, author, and self-styled "Champion Crank" (1829–1904), who was in the U.K. to work on behalf of imprisoned Fenians. His Irish sympathies appear in his second letter when he reports on the success in the U.S. of those who fled their desperate famine condition and are now able collectively to send home "a million sterling annually." He comments: "The Irish do it [without initial capital], and succeed. Cannot the English?"

20 These conflicting accounts must have puzzled *Viator,* who had written: "Among your numerous correspondents I do not see any who have given any information respecting California, San Francisco, Oregon, and the Pacific generally. I believe these States offer greater facilities and inducements for emigration than any other district in America."

21 He reports what has already been told above of other places: "A short time ago a merchant in New York advertised for a clerk, and, although the salary stated was small, and the advantages few, he received four hundred applications."

22 Compare *H.C.,* an Upper Canadian trapper, who in answer to *B.P.* admits that an intending emigrant can purchase land before going out, "but, *cave canem,* he would find his land a cedar swamp, or a dismal hole unfit for the rattle-snake."

23 One who did not remain silent was *T.C.W.,* who suggested that those who agreed with him that emigration was "the only immediately practicable solution of the 'Marriage and Celibacy' question" should meet to discuss their schemes "face to face," because "concerted action in this as in everything else is best."

24 He complains at the British government's discouraging emigration to the United States while encouraging "the tide to its own colonies."

25 *S.R.C.* is a little different in being further advanced in plan: "The Union Pacific Railway Company have extensive grants of land through the most

fertile portion of the United States, from whom land can be purchased on the most easy terms of payment. One or two others and myself have already matured the project so earnestly sought for by your numerous correspondents, viz., for assisted passages to this section of the country, with easy means for settling and purchasing land, and we shall have great pleasure in being joined by other gentlemen in promoting the cause advocated." Was "gentlemen" the best word rhetorically and semantically?

26 Even this was not enough, and *Traveller* contributed a second letter, including more authoritative yea-saying.

27 Cf. *A.B.* (who favours the U.S.A.): "The idea of South America has also been brought forward, but who wants to go to a half-civilised, bigoted, and lawless place?"

28 Neither notices that this might be taken as an example of *adianoeta*, that is, ambiguous praise.

29 This is the only mention of Peru.

30 For example, the sceptical *Scotch Civil Engineer* "earnestly caution[s]" against acceptance of the "numerous glowing descriptions . . . by interested parties" of such places as Queensland, the Cape of Good Hope, and South America, lest they come to repent their "credulity" as "bitterly" as he.

31 There is here a consonance if not an ideational echo of Dickens's *Bleak House*, in which Conversation Kenge, referring to Mrs Jellyby's philanthropic ventures, mentions "the happy settlement, on the banks of the African rivers, of our superabundant home population." Later in the novel the narrator reports that Mrs. Jellyby now has "one hundred and seventy families, . . . averaging five persons in each, either gone or going to the left bank of the Niger" (Harmondsworth: Penguin, 1971, pp. 82 and 385; chaps. 4 and 23). But these are mere dreams—or nightmares.

Chapter 8 Conclusions

1 For example, in the 1861 series in *The Times* there is only one budget, and the circumstantial considerations mentioned by correspondents do not include the terms of employment (the college tutor stands out as a special case).

2 This device is not absent in *The Times*, as is witnessed by the accounts of *A Friend of Jones* and *Jenny's Sister*, for example.

3 Duncan Crow, *The Victorian Woman* (London: Allen and Unwin, 1971), p. 271.

4 Cf. J.A. Banks, *Prosperity and Parenthood: A Study of Family Planning among the Victorian Middle Classes* (London: Routledge and Kegan Paul, 1954), p. 65: there "can be little doubt that members of the middle classes in the early

seventies *felt* that the cost of living had been rising considerably over the period."

5 "Life at High Pressure," *Contemporary Review* (Mar. 1875), 633.

6 Banks, p. 85.

7 Crow, p. 138; he here renders Banks's findings in more elegant terms.

8 In the *Telegraph*, as noted on p. 310 above, these were written in this period by James Augustus St John and his son, Horace (*The Life and Adventures of George Augustus Sala, Written by Himself* [London: Cassell, 1896], pp. 326–7).

9 *Ibid.*, p. 326. "To describe my life during 1868 would be only to chronicle so many days, weeks, and months of hard but pleasant work; so many hundreds of leaders written" (*ibid.*, p. 503).

10 It is no part of my purpose to compare the late twentieth-century editorial with those under study here, but many of the differences are consequences of the great change in length. Those of the mid-Victorian period (before the invention of the tabloid, it should be emphasized) were better able both to describe a problem and argue for a particular solution or set of solutions. They were also more given to recommending reasoned action than to mere jolting—though they certainly did the latter.

11 Sala (p. 375) comments that he spoke only to the owner, J.M. Levy, or Levy's son Edward.

12 Nothing specific is known about their keeping the gate for correspondence —except that they (or one designated editor) did so. Certainly there is no strong criticism of the newspaper in any of the published letters, but it is likely that the most effective censorship was exercised by the readers them-selves, anticipating reactions and also learning the rules of the game by reading others' published epistles.

13 A sub-type of the "social" leader, like those of 26 June and 16 July, adopts a friendly often chaffing tone in calling attention to manners and mores, not excluding eccentricities and foibles, while not abandoning condemnation.

14 A classical tag is apt: *haud ignota loquor*—"I speak of things by no means unknown," which might be interpreted as "you know as well as I that."

15 And also the seven specific references to leading articles, all of which are to the first three leaders, and the half dozen references in leading articles to specific letters.

16 It is not usually possible to identify which specific correspondent is intended when, as in the case of *An English Girl*, more than one writer used the same pseudonym; for convenience, here each pseudonym is treated as covering one correspondent.

17 Ten are cited by at least 5 correspondents. Of these, *Benedick* is well in front of the pack, with 23 citations, 14 of them favourable and 9 critical. His theme was matrimonial, and so was that of six of the other top ten: *Mater-*

familias with 11 citations (2 neutral, 8 con, and 1 pro), *Solon Smiff* with 10 (2 neutral, 6 con, and 2 pro), *An English Girl* with 9 (4 neutral, 2 con, and 3 pro). *Erastes*, chosen by the *Daily Telegraph* as the main protagonist for the romantic side of things, was cited by 7 correspondents, all of them con; *Paterfamilias* rated 6 mentions (3 neutral and 3 con), while *Therese Picot* had 5 (3 con and 2 pro).

Of 3 in the top 10 who dealt with emigration, the clear favourite was *Ring*, with 15 citations (1 con and 14 pro); *Clericus* was mentioned by 7 (2 neutral, 4 con, and 1 pro), and *Roamer Returned* by 6 (2 in each category).

Those meriting 4 mentions are *A London Girl*, *J.P.M.*, *Two Plain English Girls*, *W. Frank Lynn*, *W.M.P.Y.*, and *A Welsh Bachelor Pro Tem*. Mentioned 3 times are *H.H.F.*, *D.B.*, *T.H.M.*, *Colonista*, *A Pilgrim of Love*, *W.E.W.W.*, and *A Plain Girl*. Twenty appear twice, and 50 once.

18 A denigrating comparison would be with the supermarket tabloids of the late twentieth century.

19 Cf. *A Colonial Clergyman*, "I have by the mail arrived this week obtained information as to wages now current in one Australian colony"; and *S.C.H.*, "I quote . . . an extract from a letter received to-day from an intelligent friend of mine, who has been some years in Natal, at Durban, and Pieter-maritzburg."

20 I anticipated more reports of evidence drawn from newspapers, but the only specific allusion, and it not precise, is that of *Returned Emigrant*, cited above, to the heavy response in New York to an advertisement for a clerk.

21 Almost unseen in the series is a kind of reference found widely in other kinds of discourse then and now, mention of the opinion of a lesser and unnamed contemporary: one instance is seen in *Benedick*'s comment that the "other day a defender of the Irish Church asserted that we should con-tinue to support the Protestant clergy, because they were not only obliged to get married but 'expected to have large families.'"

22 See *Solon Smiff* for the earliest instance of the former; the latter is the view of *E.F.H.* Others who cite him are *J.W.J.*, *A Happy Nine Years' Wife*, *A Few True Girls of the Period*, *Humanus*, *Enemoplem*, *A Plain Man*, and *Another Mechanic*.

23 For instance, *Humanus*'s praise for Lord Eldon, Crabbe ("nature's sternest painter, yet the best"), and Flaxman.

24 For example, *Benedick*'s allusions to "the French revolutionists . . . 'descend-ing into the streets,'" and to the respect of Frederick the Great and Napoleon I for "women who bred fast"; and *A Woman*'s reminder of heroic behaviour during the Crimean War.

25 The epithet appears in two letters, those from *Solon Smiff* and *J.W.J.*, but the latter is merely repeating the former.

26 Here may be included the French ones, to Racine by *Lucy*, and to contem-

rary works by *Therese Picot* and her adversary, *Un Francais qui n'a plus 20 ans, et qui a fini ses etudes.*

27 *Benedick* is the star here, with his allusions to Pope's curate and to Porson's "Damn the nature of things," which must have puzzled even the most learned of the clerks of the time.

28 *Humanus* for Sterne's *A Sentimental Journey*, *Enemoplem* for Goldsmith's *Vicar of Wakefield*, and *Enemoplem* again with *A Widower* for Milton's *Lycidas*.

29 There are many, many more, most of them suggesting a contemporary source probably better known to readers then than to scholars now: "sweet simplicity of the Three per Cents" (*Erastes, E.F.H., and Enemoplem*), "Love in a hut, with water and a crust" (*Erastes*), "leave their country for their country's good" (*Never Say Die*), these young men "allow their hearts to beat" (*J.P.M.*), the "unco' good" girls (*Colonista*), painted and chignoned simpletons, who "gig and amble and nickname Heaven's creatures" (*Paterfamilias*), "How do they do it, 'I want to know, you know'" (*A Bachelor*), "clothed in purple and fine linen, and go somewhere" every day (*Spes*), a "ministering angel" (*Another Benedick*), "no green leaf springing in life's wintry way, no sunbeam flinging light on the darkened day" (*A Lover of Home*), "look the whole world in the face, not owing any man" (*A Dutchman*), thought "trouble" a name or a "tale that is told" (*An Active Wife and Mother*), the stern reality "which gives us serious pause, and makes the bachelors a numerous race" (*Pro Bono Publico*), "reap and mow, and plough and sow" (*Antipodes*), "in lands beside there's room enough for all" (*Kangaroo*), "Eternal summer reigns" in California (*Returned Emigrant*).

30 Tennyson also is brought in more vaguely when *M.B.E.* alludes to "the Laureate's last new poem."

31 "A man's riches consist not in the extent of his possessions, but in the fewness of his wants" (*C.L.W.*), and "a world where Canadian forests stand unfelled, boundless plains and prairies unbroken with the plough. On the west and on the east green desert places never yet made white with corn, and to the overcrowded little western nook of Europe, our terrestrial planet, nine-tenths of it yet vacant or tenanted by nomades, is still crying, 'Come and till me, come and reap me'" (*L——S*).

32 Preceded in this case by an enhancing lead-in: "Here is a bit from Ruskin. I wish you would print it in large type, or italics. 'They would be married quite as soon (and probably to wiser and better husbands) by dressing quietly as by dressing brilliantly, and I believe it would only be needed to lay fairly and largely before them the real good which might be effected by the sums which they spent in toilettes, to make them trust at once only to their bright eyes and braided hair for all the mischief they have a mind to.'"

33 *George* uses the same passage with the sublime attribution merely

assumed. Other examples of implied maxims include: "for better or for worse" (*Pegging at It, Hannah*), "beasts of the field" (*Benedick, Nil Desperandum*), housekeeping is "the one thing needful" [*porro unum est necessarium*] (*G.L.M.*), "the whole duty of man" (*W.H.S., One Who Can't Help It*), "the heavenly precept, 'Goodwill towards men'" (*Nil Desperandum*), "'Who is sufficient for these things?'" (*Nil Desperandum*), "in the state of life in which it has pleased God to call me" (*Bunny*), "Quite right, ye fathers, to 'forbid the banns!'" (*Bunny*), and—rare examples from emigrationists—"unstable as water, thou shalt not excel" (*Kangaroo*), and a "promised land" (*A.J.S.*).

34 There are, interestingly, wisps of evidence of growing secularization, in such gently ironic citations as that by *A Welsh Bachelor Pro Tem*, who exclaims, "Thank God, I am not as other men are," and has at least a portion of tongue in cheek when he modifies St Paul's judgment into "he who marries may do well, but he who does not marry most certainly doeth better." This same passage is placed in context so that its application can be seen as not universal by *J.W.H.*, who points out that St Paul was advising a struggling and persecuted Church, at a time "when love for their wives and children might induce many [men] to abjure their new-found faith and return to idolatry." This kind of subtlety is not common in the religious citations.

35 A Freudian might do better than I with *W.H.S.*'s unauthorized version: "forsaking mother and clinging to their wife."

36 Another standard text is also used on both sides. *Erastes* had alluded to God's care for the lowly sparrows as earnest of providential intervention for poor humans; *Benedick* was not impressed, scornfully saying that *Erastes*' message to him who worries about caring for his children is merely, "No; let him trust in God, and as He feeds the sparrows He will feed the young Joneses."

37 Though teachers (being one I know) enjoin students not to place clichés in quotation marks, the practice endures seemingly because they are what "everyone says," and so must be quotations not needing attribution.

38 Such as noting "how the shoe pinches" (*Jane*), remembering that "Birds of a feather flock together" (*Home-Made Bread*), trying to be "as happy as a sandboy" (*A Match-Maker*) and to make "both ends meet" (*A Clerk*).

39 *Before Novels: The Cultural Context of Eighteenth-Century English Fiction* (New York: W.W. Norton, 1990), pp. 12–13.

40 The best known are Thomas Carlyle, who responded to the debate over the Reform Bill of 1867 with a pamphlet called *Shooting Niagara—and After*, and Lord Derby, who called the Bill a "leap in the dark."

41 In 1881 there were 5989; in 1891, 17,859.

42 *Crotchet Castle* (1831), in *Nightmare Abbey/Crotchet Castle* (Harmondsworth: Penguin, 1986), p. 15; chap. 3.

43 James Bonar, *Malthus and His Work*, 2nd ed. (London: Allen and Unwin, 1924), pp. 1–2.

44 Thomas Robert Malthus, *An Essay on the Principle of Population* (1798), in Antony Flew, ed., *An Essay on the Principle of Population and A Summary view of the Principle of Population* (Harmondsworth: Penguin, 1985), p. 133; chap. 10.

45 *Ibid.*, p. 175; chap. 15.

46 *Ibid.*, p. 141; chap. 10.

47 *Ibid.*, p. 73; chap. 2.

48 *Ibid.*, p. 90; chap. 4.

49 The prevalence of this view is emphasized by Crow (p. 289), who points out that people worried in 1888 because "the marriage rate was the lowest on record and the age at which people married was still rising. But postponement of marriage made the other horn of the dilemma. It meant that prostitution would continue to be rife."

50 Malthus, pp. 91–2; chap. 4. In his revision for the second version, Malthus included in the preventive check "the restraint from marriage which is not followed by irregular gratifications" (quoted by Flew, *ibid.*, Introduction, p. 24). And cf. "Moral restraint . . . may be defined to be, abstinence from marriage, either for a time or permanently, from prudential considerations, with a strictly moral conduct towards the sex in the interval. And this is the only mode of keeping population on a level with the means of subsistence which is perfectly consistent with virtue and happiness. All other checks, whether of the preventive or the positive kind, though they may greatly vary in degree, resolve themselves into some form of vice or misery." *A Summary view of the Principle of Population* (1830), in *ibid.*, p. 250.

51 See, for comment on and analysis of the differences between relative and absolute poverty, and explanation of the crippling effect on policy of confusing the two, Christopher A. Sarlo, *Poverty in Canada* (Vancouver: Fraser Institute, 1992), *passim*. In discussing changed views of acceptable minimums, he incidentally (and in quotation marks) uses the term "decent" as the Victorians did (p. 50).

52 For summaries from different sources, see app. C.

53 It is not specially perceptive for those in a society where comforts are more easily attained than in any other in human history to think comical the Victorians' passionate espousal of, for example, cleanliness. (Cf. Banks, p. 63.)

54 *Collected Works* (Toronto: University of Toronto Press, 1977), vol. 18, p. 279.

55 Such attitudes are not, of course, tightly culture-bound, although commentators often wish they were. An Inuit woman's remarks are reported and

interpreted by David F. Pelly: "'We used to say, if you cannot build an igloo, you are not ready to get married,' said Ootoova, gazing thoughtfully out of the window at the range of mountains that embrace Pond Inlet [at the north end of Baffin Island]. She was speaking, in the subtle language of Inuktitut, of a level of comfort with one's environment that makes for a life beyond mere survival. A young Inuk may no longer need the skills to survive in the Arctic, but, in Ootoova's opinion, learning the traditional ways of this land is crucial to their sense of belonging here." Pelly, "Pond Inlet: An Inuit community caught between two worlds," *Canadian Geographic* (Feb./Mar. 1991), 49. Many lessons could be based on that text, including the transcultural appeal of the old days, but what is striking is the ideological reading by the modern "liberal" of her "subtle" meaning, whereas the surface meaning is patently the main one.

56 "Marriage," *Englishwoman's Domestic Magazine*, n.s. 1 (Mar. 1865), 91–2. In addition to passages quoted above in chap. 3, the following are particularly apt to the discussion in the *Daily Telegraph*: "As to what constitutes an adequate income, each one will form his own opinion and make his own calculation"; while there is increasing concern "about what we may call 'personalities'" (i.e., worldly possessions), there is "great carelessness" about "'persons'" (i.e., character), such as "qualifications of disposition, principle, ability, or constitution . . . to meet the wear and tear of life" (p. 91). Not that all delays are warranted: the author cites two literary examples of the dangers of improper caution in Crabbe's "Procrastination" and Austen's *Persuasion* (p. 92).

57 George Eliot, *Felix Holt, The Radical* (1866) (Harmondsworth: Penguin, 1972), p. 156.

58 Cf. Bernard Bergonzi, Introduction to George Gissing, *New Grub Street* (1891) (Harmondsworth: Penguin, 1985), p. 18.

59 The term would have seemed odd then because the comparative ethnological and historical studies that led to the definition were only beginning.

60 The urban poor had other practical solutions, but generally these incorporated traditional notions of family without the formality of marriage or a search for moral and financial responsibility.

61 Ellen Hall in May 1860, quoted by Crow, p. 66.

Appendix A

1 Apt comment on this matter—and also on the editors as "gate-keepers"—is seen in chapter 2 of Anthony Trollope's *Barchester Towers*. After Mr Harding had left the Wardenship, the *Jupiter*—Trollope's fictional name for *The Times*—developed a plan to fix all the problems: "The wisdom of this

scheme was testified by the number of letters which 'Common Sense,' 'Veritas,' and 'One that loves fair play' sent to the Jupiter, all expressing admiration, and amplifying on the details given. It is singular enough that no adverse letter appeared at all, and, therefore, none of course was written."

2 Throughout the series, the formula "One Who. . ." is favoured above all others, being seen in *One Who Has Tried It, One Who Married on £120 a Year, One Who Looks Before He Leaps, One Who Speaks from Experience* (used by two different correspondents), *One Who Would Be a Good Deal Happier If He Had It, One Who Is Content to Wait, One Who Waits and Hopes, One Who Can't Help It,* and *One Who Is Waiting Patiently.* The intended effect presumably is to claim a personal qualification among a relevant group.

3 Noteworthy to me as the not entirely appropriate motto of my secondary school.

4 Including the tri-epistled *Vieux Moustache,* who is (or, are) implying extensive military experience.

5 Oddly, *Salome* spelled backwards seems to be used by a male correspondent.

6 He presents a fine example of the fact/fiction puzzle. Of him another correspondent says, "if he be a real person." This query demands others: Is he a genuine correspondent writing under a pseudonym to describe (in elevated language) "real" experience? Or is the account (even deflated) also a fiction, perhaps concocted by the newspaper's staff? The chances that nothing is fictional are too meagre for me to suspend belief even willingly.

7 Some of the inferences are of course shakier than others. It seems reasonable, however, to include "probables"—admitting that a few of the probables are more like possibles—because the wrong inferences on both sides are likely roughly to cancel one another.

8 There are eight of these "unsexed" letters, but I have so labelled one of them only for ease: that signed *Paigntonians* is by clear inference from three women (a mother and two of her daughters) and a single man (probably engaged to one of the daughters).

9 A few of single men and women mention that they are engaged to be married, and two or three of the married indicate that they are newly wed.

10 Two of the correspondents who write in French are likely in London. It might be significant to look at the difference between the dates when the letters were written and published, but given the rapidity of the post then, and the lack of other information, any pretended inference would be but a wishful guess.

11 There is no indication that any letters, apart from *Precaution*'s from Brussels, were posted from overseas, all the colonists being either returned or

visiting—and of course no one further abroad than the Continent could have received the paper and responded within a month.

12 The others are from Ramsgate (the other French correspondent, obviously visiting), Brighton, Birkenhead, Burton-on-Trent, Derby, Hertfordshire, Penshurst, Norwood, Torquay, Norwich, Hemel Hempstead, seaside Wales, Newbury (Berks.), Hull, Lincoln, and Sheffield. Some of these are holiday sites, and may well hide further London habitation.

13 Here is an example of the danger of judging from signatures alone, for without internal evidence I would have identified the writer as male.

Appendix B

1 On about the same, or an even lower level of expenditure, the anonymous *A Woman's Secret; or, How to Make Home Happy. With an Appendix Containing Recipes for Preparing Economical and Nutritious Food* (London: Griffith and Farran, 1860), offers, in a third-person narrative, recipes (not very appetizing) that are costed in an appendix, offering meals for 5 or 6 people at under a shilling (and usually under 6d).

Appendix C

1 The figures were slightly rounded up before the percentages were calculated, and those for incomes below £100 are omitted. The totals are below 100 per cent because only the items that are almost always present are listed; as indicated elsewhere in this account, any conclusions based on the figures are far from certain: categories are mixed; obviously necessary expenses are missing from some; some silent rounding has undoubtedly occurred; there are repetitions in some calculations that suggest either easy or mistaken counting; in a few cases it appears likely that the author worked back from an attractive percentage to a figure; and some of the authors may well have borrowed figures from others.

General Index

To signal a quotation "q" appears after the page number.

Index of Correspondents

For consistency of treatment, all entries are alphabetized from the first letter of the signature. Consequently, e.g., entries for *A Barrister* are found under A rather than B, and for *Harriet Barnett* are found under H rather than B: however, actual names such as hers are also cross-referenced from the normal mode. Signatures that are numbers or symbols are placed at the beginning. No entries are necessary for appendix A, because all the correspondents are listed there in order of appearance in the *Daily Telegraph*. To signal a quotation "q" appears after the page number. To give some sense of the debate and interplay, indications are given of responses among the correspondents.